Human Rights in Africa

Human Rights in Africa

Cross-Cultural Perspectives

Abdullahi Ahmed An-Na'im
Francis M. Deng
editors

The Brookings Institution
Washington, D.C.

Library of Congress Cataloging-in-publication data:

Human rights in Africa: cross-cultural perspectives / Abdullahi
Ahmed An-Na'im and Francis Deng, editors.
   p.   cm.
Includes index.
   ISBN 0-8157-1796-2 (alk. paper). ISBN 0-8157-1795-4 (pbk.: alk.
paper)
   1. Human rights—Africa. 2. Human rights—Cross-cultural studies.
I. Na'īm, Abd Allāh Aḥmad, 1946–.   II. Deng, Francis Mading,
1938–.
JC599.A36H86 1990
323'.096—dc20   90-37742
                                              CIP

9 8 7 6 5 4 3 2 1

Set in Linotronic Meridien
Composition by Graphic Composition, Inc.
  Athens, Georgia
Printing by R. R. Donnelley and Sons Co.
  Harrisonburg, Virginia
Book design by Ken Sabol

Foreword

IN THE VIEW of many observers, a sharp discrepancy exists between the fundamental values of human dignity avowed by peoples and cultures throughout the world and the gross violation of human rights by many individual governments. The underlying assumption of the cross-cultural approach adopted in this book is that such a discrepancy cannot be justified. Building on the evidence from different cultural traditions, Islamic and Christian as well as specifically African, the thirteen authors make a strong case for the universality of the fundamental principles that underlie international standards of human rights. For the most part, their essays were originally presented at a workshop organized by the editors under the auspices of the Woodrow Wilson International Center for Scholars in June 1988.

The editors are both nationals of the Sudan. Abdullahi Ahmed An-Na'im was associate professor of law at Khartoum University and is now visiting professor of law at the University of Saskatchewan. Francis M. Deng, formerly Sudan's minister of state for foreign affairs and ambassador to the United States, is a senior fellow at Brookings responsible for African Studies. The editors wish to express their gratitude to the Woodrow Wilson Center for sponsoring the workshop on human rights and especially to Prosser Gifford, former deputy director and acting director of the Center, for his personal support and guidance, and to the succeeding director, Charles Blitzer, and the deputy director, Samuel F. Wells, Jr., for continuing the support for the project. Janice Tuten, then an associate of the Wilson Center, helped to organize the workshop; and the cooperation and support of Ann Sheffield and her staff were crucial to its success.

The editorial work was done under the auspices of the Ariel F. Sallows Chair in Human Rights of the College of Law, University of Saskatchewan, and the Brookings Foreign Policy Studies program. The editors would like to thank John D. Steinbruner, director of the Brookings program, for his helpful comments on the manuscript. They would also like to thank Kate Southerland for preparing the original manuscript and Beth Elzinga-Marshall for typing and preparing the later versions for publication. Annette D. Proctor, Louise F. Skillings, Yvonne S. Sabban, and Ann M. Ziegler also assisted in the preparation of the manuscript. Caroline Lalire, James McEuen, Venka Macintyre, and Robert Pini edited the manuscript; Yuko Iida Frost, Wendy J. Glassmire, Vernon L. Kelley, Susanne E. Lane, Myles Nienstadt, and Amy R. Waychoff verified its factual content; and Fred L. Kepler prepared the index.

Financial support for the workshop was provided to the Wilson Center by the Ford Foundation. African Studies at Brookings are sponsored by the Carnegie Corporation of New York, the Rockefeller Brothers Fund, and the Rockefeller Foundation. The Wilson Center and Brookings are grateful for that support.

The views expressed in this book are those of the authors and should not be ascribed to the people whose assistance is acknowledged above, to the organizations that supported the project, or to the trustees, officers, or other staff members of the Brookings Institution.

BRUCE K. MACLAURY
President

July 1990
Washington, D.C.

Contents

Editors' Preface   xi

1. Introduction   1
   Abdullahi Ahmed An-Naᶜim and Francis M. Deng

   Part 1: Western Cultural Origins

2. The Effect of Western Perspectives on International   15
   Human Rights
   Virginia A.Leary

3. Human Rights and Western Liberalism   31
   Jack Donnelly

   Part 2: Religious Perspectives

4. A Christian Perspective on Human Rights   59
   David Little

5. The European Tradition of Human Rights and   104
   the Culture of Islam
   Bassam Tibi

6. Current Muslim Thinking on Human Rights   133
   Ann Elizabeth Mayer

   Part 3: The Context of the Nation-State

7. Group versus Individual Identity in the African   159
   Debate on Human Rights
   Rhoda E. Howard

8. Human Rights in Francophone West Africa   184
   Claude E. Welch, Jr.

9. Participatory Approaches to Human Rights in   213
   Sub-Saharan Africa
   James C. N. Paul

Part 4: African Cultural Perspectives

10. An Akan Perspective on Human Rights   243
    Kwasi Wiredu

11. A Cultural Approach to Human Rights among the Dinka   261
    Francis M. Deng

12. Traditional Culture and the Prospect for Human Rights   290
    in Africa
    James Silk

Part 5: Prospects for a Cross-Cultural Approach

13. Problems of Universal Cultural Legitimacy for   331
    Human Rights
    Abdullahi Ahmed An-Na'im

14. Human Rights in an Evolving World Culture   368
    Richard D. Schwartz

    Contributors   383

    Subject Index   385

    Name Index   393

Editors' Preface

MOST of the essays in this volume were presented at a workshop on cross-cultural perspectives on human rights in Africa which we organized at the Woodrow Wilson International Center for Scholars, Washington, D.C., on June 23–24, 1988. Participants included sociologists, philosophers, historians, political scientists, human rights lawyers, and other informed observers, who engaged in two days of intensive discussions on the bases of prepared papers. Authors were then invited to revise their papers in light of those discussions.

Our primary objective in conceiving and organizing the workshop was to reinforce and promote universal respect for and protection of human rights. We sought to do so by countervailing the conventional view that the concept of human rights is peculiar to the West and therefore inherently alien to the non-Western traditions of third world countries to which it is now being extended. Our policy concern was that this conventional approach to human rights not only denies universality to the concept but also deprives it of the substantive enrichment from the variety of cultural values underlying the diverse notions of human rights around the world. Furthermore, the conventional view is likely to have the adverse effect of justifying the rejection of international human rights standards on the ground of cultural relativism.

Even though the philosophical characterization of human rights as Western is questionable on both empirical and normative grounds, the cultural justification this idea gives the rejectionists must be a matter of grave concern to human rights advocates. Some governments and elites from developing countries maintain that the current international human rights standards are not binding on them not only because the standards were conceived and formulated largely by Westerners, but also because they reflect cultural values and mores that are foreign to non-Western traditions and therefore antithetic to third world priorities.

At worst, the rejectionists allege that the concept of human rights does not exist in non-Western societies or cultures; at best, they contend that non-Western notions of human rights are inherently different from the Western concept and that a blanket application of Western principles to non-Western conditions is unjustifiable. These arguments have been used, explicitly or implicitly, to justify even the most blatant human rights violations that could not be defended on any moral grounds. Similar arguments could be used to explain the apparent lack of public support for human rights and the absence of pressure groups and nongovernmental organizations monitoring and protecting human rights violations in many third world countries.

That analysis may seem a negative way of making a positive argument for a cross-culturally sensitive and enriching approach to the conceptualization and promotion of human rights. Put in more positive terms, we believe every society or culture recognizes certain values, mores, norms, and operational principles by which it seeks to approximate the ideals of human dignity as contextually defined or understood. These may differ from one society or culture to another, and the degree of success in advancing the cause of human dignity may also vary greatly. So does the extent to which the system benefits all members of the community or of the human race, including those who fall outside the membership of that particular community. Our position is that the promotion of international standards of human rights not only should be done with due respect to meritorious cultural values and traditions of the wide variety of world communities, but would indeed be reinforced and strengthened by these diverse standards.

The interplay between local and global standards of human rights is a dynamic process of give and take, ideally through persuasion and cooperation rather than through coercion. Insofar as universal standards reflect the collective conscience and political will of the international community, they represent a higher order of human aspirations, with a more effective mechanism for promotion and enforcement. But it is important to stress that whatever the apparent differences between local and international standards in this regard, the idea if not the content of human rights—as claims to which every person is entitled by virtue of being human—is founded on fundamental values that we believe are shared by all cultural traditions.

The misconception that the idea of human rights is alien to some cultural traditions may arise because those cultures do not conceptualize or articulate the values underlying these rights and apply them to all human beings on an equal basis. Some cultural traditions tend to accord certain persons, such as women, minors, and outsiders, a lower status, thereby denying them the full range of claims to which the more privileged members of the society are entitled. To establish the legitimacy and universality of human rights within those cultures, the elements that justify such discrimination or deprivation need to be exposed and redressed either through an internal reinterpretation of cultural sources to support the international standards of human rights or by upholding international standards as offering a transcendent code of desirable behavior that is universally valid.

By definition, cultural arguments have to rely on the norms and institutions of the particular culture involved. If meaningful and lasting changes in attitudes and practice are to be achieved, the proposed reinterpretation has to be undertaken from within the culture by those who, while promoting universal values, are sensitive to the integrity and authenticity of the local culture. Their arguments need to be consistent with the internal logic of the culture, yet guided by the growing international consensus on the scope and implications of human rights.

In addition to the internal legitimization of human rights within indigenous cultural traditions, corresponding legitimization at the national and international levels must be achieved. To enable individuals and groups to assert their human rights against dominant cultures as well as against the state, international recognition is vital. The critical issue then is whether cross-cultural analysis can be used to demonstrate the legitimacy of notions of human dignity within the various cultural traditions, and to transform those notions into human rights principles on which there is global consensus. Besides its utility in strictly legal enforcement, the notion of "rights" thus becomes a useful political and sociological instrument for promoting human dignity at the different levels of the nation-state and the international community.

This book examines the field of human rights from the perspective of several cultural traditions and international standards to make a case for cross-fertilization and mutual reinforcement. We hope it will contribute to the process of using the creative tension between the demands of cultural relativism, on the one hand, and those of universalism, on the other, in favor of greater recognition and implementation of human rights. The first aspect of this tension requires respect for the right of people within a given community or society to live in accordance with the precepts of their own culture and to promote human rights within the logic of that culture. People are likely to be more motivated to observe the precepts of their own culture than those that they perceive as imposed from outside. The second aspect of the tension relates to the need to have universal standards of human rights by which all cultural traditions can be judged. Otherwise, serious human rights violations may be condoned because they happen to be tolerated or sanctioned by the cultural tradition of the society or the community in question.

While recognizing the genuine tension between the relativist and universalist perspectives on human rights, we believe it is desirable and possible to achieve universal validity for human rights through an appropriate degree of interplay between the two. The values underlying international standards of human rights, in our view, should and can be shown to be universal through the processes of internal cultural reinterpretation and cross-cultural analysis and formulation.

We have organized the contributions to this volume into an introduction and five parts. In the introduction we argue the case for the cross-cultural approach in the light of the arguments for and against presented by the contributors to this volume. The first part, which follows, consists of two chapters. In the first, Virginia A. Leary assesses the nature and implications of the role of Western cultural perspectives in formulating the current international human rights instruments. Rather than finding a one-way influence from the West, she shows that non-Western cultures have influenced the contemporary international human rights standards of Western origin and made them universal. The argument that these standards are alien to the non-Western world has therefore become unjustified. In the other chapter, Jack Donnelly argues that the "conventional, minimalist" liberal conception of human rights as (only) property rights and "negative civil and political rights" does not exhaust the liberal tradition. He demonstrates the existence of a radical social democratic strand even in the earliest theoretical formulations of liberalism. In his view, the inclusion of this radical strand renders liberalism a more coherent political doctrine. Donnelly also argues that the broader social democratic conception of liberalism is morally preferable to the conventional minimalist conception. This approach is particularly significant for a cultural reinterpretation in support of a wide range of social and economic rights that may not be supportable from the conventional liberal standpoint.

Although the main religions of the world have had their positive or negative effects on secular thought, religious traditions are better addressed separately. This task is undertaken in the three chapters constituting the second part of the book. We confined ourselves to the two world religions of particular relevance to Africa: Christianity and Islam. Whereas David Little and Bassam Tibi apply the reinterpretative approach to the Christian and Islamic traditions, Ann Elizabeth Mayer offers a critique of current Muslim thinking on human rights. The interplay between the moral and ethical values of these traditions and the international standards of human rights is a pervasive theme in all three chapters.

Aspects of the creative tension between relativism and universalism in relation to human rights in Africa are addressed in the three chapters of part three. Rhoda E. Howard discusses the similarities and differences between human rights and African conceptions of human dignity and explains the conditions favoring the evolution from the second to the first in the context of the modern nation-state. Assessing recent experiences in four West African states, Claude E. Welch, Jr., underscores the need to legitimize human rights and assert them more effectively against governments, without allowing indigenous cultural norms to be manipulated to justify human rights violations. Finally, James C. N. Paul makes the case for greater accessibility to legal resources and participation by the rural poor in sub-Saharan Africa. He emphasizes the need for the people to set the standards affecting their lives and to articulate internal cultural norms in terms of human rights that they can assert against the state.

The three chapters of part four, by Kwasi Wiredu, Francis M. Deng, and James Silk, are efforts to evaluate indigenous African cultural traditions in light of international human rights standards. Whereas Wiredu and Deng focus on specific cultural traditions, Silk evaluates the relationship between traditional norms and international standards of human rights in a broader cross-cultural framework.

In the last part, Abdullahi Ahmed An-Na'im expounds the case for the cultural approach, identifies its major problems, and assesses its prospects. In its general orientation and major themes, this chapter presents a positive approach to cultural diversity, seeing it as an asset rather than an obstacle in promoting a universal validity for human rights. In conclusion, Richard D. Schwartz cites historical and contemporary evidence to emphasize the importance of the cross-cultural approach and sees the evolution of a universal culture, enriched rather than impoverished by diversity, that can be a basis for the promotion of a universalist agenda on human rights.

A. A. A.-N.
F. M. D.

CHAPTER ONE

Introduction

Abdullahi Ahmed An-Na'im
and Francis M. Deng

THE ESSAYS in this volume reveal a far more complex picture of divergent and even conflicting views than expected when the theme of cross-cultural perspectives on human rights was first conceived. To make matters worse, it has been almost impossible to avoid normative ambiguity on the issues involved because of the enormous cultural diversity and mixed motivations the authors have had to contend with. Such ambiguity leads to the inevitable fusion of the "is" and the "ought" in our perception of human rights. In the final analysis, however, most of us seem to agree that the contextual cultural approach is the appropriate means by which to promote universal recognition of the concept of human rights.

Some people, however, think that this approach actually retards the evolution of international standards. They argue that the cultural approach fosters a relativism that is opposed to universalism, whether it is because of a sincere commitment to local cultures and traditions or a purposeful manipulative effort to justify violations of human rights at the local or national level. Whatever the case, it is nearly always the elite who interpret the culture and use it or abuse it for their own political ends. Those who fall victim to such abuse can hardly be expected to reject international human rights standards by invoking local cultures. We believe, however, that local cultural values can indeed be invoked to check the leaders who violate human rights and seek shelter behind cultural relativism.

The contributors to this volume all say they would like to see the countries of the world adopt international standards for the protection of human rights. The problem is that most of them have mixed feelings about the proper role of the various cultural traditions in this regard, largely because they feel that the assertiveness of these traditions acts as a force that casts doubt on the universal validity of international standards. Oftentimes, as Virginia Leary observes, the objection is not so much to universalism as it is to the Western character of the international standards, which has led some people to question "the universality of those norms and their suitability for application in non-Western cultures." Another important point has been raised by Ann Mayer, who finds that even though many Muslim countries are signatories to the international human rights conventions (which means they formally acknowledge the international human rights standards), other Muslim countries reject them on religious grounds: "Here, the latent tensions between Islamic and international law become, at least ostensibly, the cause of conflict." Rhoda Howard makes the same point: "In objection to the liberal concept that one has human rights simply by virtue of being human, and that human rights entail claims that the individual can make against the state and against society as a whole, some scholars have posited a relativist approach, suggesting that each continent or religious tradition has generated its own concept of human rights." Thus some African authors have argued for an "African" concept of human rights on the grounds that "Africans are community or group oriented, rather than individualistic, and hence the rights of the individual are not relevant to them." Both Mayer and Howard note, however, that the Muslim and African scholarly communities have not been able to agree on what the relative tradition entails or the extent to which their traditions contradict the international standards of human rights.

Bassam Tibi and Ann Mayer see dynamic tensions in the Muslim world between Islamic tradition and the international human rights standards, which they say have influenced both sets of standards. According to Mayer, many Muslims seem eager to find ways to reconcile the competing claims of Islamic and international law and thus will argue that "international law is itself a product of Islamic influences, even though neutral historical scholarship has not so far established this proposition." Mayer believes that this desire to maintain allegiance to both Islam and international law "can serve as a foundation for crafting schemes of human rights that fit both international and Islamic criteria, provided a genuine effort is made to eliminate potential conflicts by offering new interpretations of the Islamic sources that accommodate a modern rights philosophy." At the same time, Tibi finds many people from third world countries, particularly Muslims, ready to "dispute the claim that the human rights tradition originated in modern Europe." Some will go so far as to say that "Islam was the very first culture on earth to which God imparted a complete set of human rights values."

Many Western scholars concede that the broadly defined human values underlying the concept of human rights may be universally shared, but they insist that a distinction must be made between the moral standards of human dignity, which all cultures share, and the specific human rights that are enforceable against the state, which are believed to be a modern European creation. As Bassam Tibi notes, "Non-Westerners tend to confuse *human rights* . . . with *human dignity*. If one is talking about the latter, there is no doubt that fully developed notions of human dignity exist in many non-Western cultures." (He also points out that "medieval Europe itself had no inkling of human rights in the modern sense.") Similarly, Rhoda Howard finds that "the African concept of human rights is actually a concept of human dignity, of what defines 'the inner (moral) nature and worth of the human person and his or her proper (political) relations with society.' . . . [D]ignity can be protected in a society that is not based on rights."

Although it may be useful to distinguish between the abstract ideals of human dignity and the more precise legal principles of human rights, we must not overlook the close connection between these two sets of concepts and the way they reinforce each other. Only if the ideals embodied in the concept of human dignity were used to dilute or distract from the content of human rights would there be any purpose in focusing on the differences between the two. If anything, there would seem to be obvious merit in correlating them and seeing them as mutually reinforcing.

However, the argument that human rights are enforceable whereas the rights derived from principles of human dignity are not also raises substantive jurisprudential and procedural issues of a cross-cultural nature that must be addressed. In traditional African society, for example, there is no clear-cut line between religious values, moral precepts, and laws. On the contrary, they are interrelated. And if it is conceded that African societies have their own institutions and enforcement procedures that might differ from those of the West but are nonetheless effective within their context, then it goes without saying that the rights and obligations derived from religious, moral, and cultural values associated with human dignity in traditional society are enforceable and, indeed, enforced against and for the benefit of both the community and the individual. Furthermore, the significance of the community should not be exaggerated and allowed to overshadow the vital place of the individual in it, for the relationship between the two is as mutually augmenting as it is constraining.

Nor can we fall back on the argument that in traditional society rights accrue to the individual by virtue of membership in the community rather than by the mere fact of being human, which may be valid to a degree, but is no basis on which to insist that the African situation is drastically different from that of any other tradition or modern practice. Every society accords its members certain rights by virtue of the fact that they are human beings. Traditional African society is no exception to this principle of universal humanity. At the same time, membership in a community or a state in any society entitles one to certain advantages or privileges that are denied to outsiders. The dichotomy between the security of being an insider and the deprivations of being an outsider, a stranger, a foreigner, or an "alien" is by no means peculiar to any tradition, African or otherwise; indeed, it is a characteristic even of the states that follow more modern cultural practices.

The challenge for all societies today is to recognize not only where they have fallen short in promoting human rights but also what the prospects are for realizing human rights ideals. They must be willing to admit that no culture, society, or country has achieved the ideal, while pushing ever harder toward it, building on local cultural resources combined with ideas and practices received from the outside, including the principles developed, formulated, and postulated by the international community as universal standards for human rights.

Although some Western scholars distinguish between the concept of human rights and the culturally oriented values of human dignity, others tend to see the two as converging toward the international human rights standards acknowledged as being Western in origin and advocated as universally valid imperatives. Bassam Tibi, for example, argues that, historically, the concept of human rights—meaning individual rights of autonomy and equality that can be individually claimed against the state and are to be institutionally protected by the society— is "a modern cultural achievement of Europe," and that "it is . . . imperative to recognize the universal applicability of human rights, even though these rights have not yet been realized in the majority of non-Western states." Tibi sees a future human rights agenda based on the convergence of universal and local values. As he puts it, "The fact that the cultural values of non-Western cultures are compatible with the modern human rights ideals should smooth the way for their eventual realization."

Claude Welch agrees that historically international standards of human rights and the machinery designed to promote them originated in the West, but he adds that "considerable 'domestication' of international norms . . . has occurred since the end of World War II." Through their adherence to international agreements on human rights, the four African countries he covers in his essay have, in varying degrees, accepted these global standards.

The increasing tendency to contextualize human rights—whether as part of the indigenous ideals or as concepts received from the West but internationally defined and universally accepted—has led some observers to suggest that it is no longer necessary to establish local cultural justification for these rights. Ann Mayer makes this point with reference to the Islamic countries: "There seems to be a growing tendency in the Muslim world to assume that public international law is part of the heritage of humankind, so that no special Islamic justification is required for adhering to it."

This line of thought has a compelling moral and practical force to it, especially as it reinforces the global consensus on human rights; however, it overlooks several issues that are important to developing countries. Both in principle and in fact, Africans reject any suggestion that the moral ideals at the core of the human rights concept are alien to African culture or tradition. To deny African culture a share in that human heritage would be to reduce its standing in the world of comparative moral philosophy. Besides, if there is indeed fertile soil in which to plant and nourish the internationally defined standards of human rights in the African context, why would anyone object to doing so? It looks as though more were involved than merely a question of justifying the acceptance of international standards

Virginia Leary shows us in her essay that in fact non-Western countries have greatly influenced modern international standards. "Concepts of human dignity can be expressed by many terms: social justice, dharma, human rights. The particular form in which the international community, under Western influence, has chosen to express human dignity, however, is the concept of human rights." But even then, "despite its Western origin, the concept of human rights must now be recognized as a universal term accepted throughout the world," not merely because the West has exported it, but also because "the concept is a dynamic and evolutionary one that has recently been extended to cover many aspects of human dignity not contemplated under the traditional Western rubric of human rights." According to Leary, "Western influence, dominant in the origin of the development of international human rights norms, is now only one of a number of cultural influences on the development of international human rights standards. Its contribution to the development of human rights has been great, but it has not been unique, and other cultures have made and are making significant contributions to our collective conception of human dignity."

Even within the Western framework, the interplay between moral principles and the more legalistic approach to human rights has been and continues to be a dynamic process. This is the theme of Jack Donnelly's critique of the narrow interpretation of the liberal tradition in the West. He says it needs to be seen in a broader light that would widen the scope of the concept and the content of human rights.

Christianity is widely thought to be the birthplace of modern human rights standards, but as David Little observes, there is no consensus on the extent to which the concept is related to Christianity. "Some Christians do not believe in universal human rights at all," whereas "other Christians, with a less radical attitude, regard existing human rights norms with ambivalence." Little concludes:

> It is assumed that there are many possible ways in which Christians, along with members of other religious traditions, might relate to a belief in human rights. [Still,] for better or worse, there does exist an unmistakable, if complex, historical link between one strand of the Christian tradition and the emergence of the Lockean theory of natural rights, a theory that appears to have constituted an indispensable source of modern ideas of human rights. In short, Locke's theory is incomprehensible if it is divorced from its Calvinist context.

David Little also shows that Judeo-Christian values and the international human rights standards have been mutually reinforcing, even though the cultural values and the precise human rights standards involved have not been considered inseparable. Little cautions, however, that "none of this means, of course, that thinking about human rights by Christians (or by anyone else, for that matter) is constrained by this historical legacy." All it means is that "anyone wishing hereafter to argue a case about Christianity and human rights must take full account of the character and complexity of the Calvinist context of natural rights philosophy."

Of course, there is a difference between a cultural tradition that has allegedly contributed directly to the evolution of human rights standards as they are now defined and a tradition that may not have influenced the definition of human rights standards but nonetheless provides fertile soil for its legitimization and acceptance within that cultural context and may perhaps contribute to the further development of those standards in the future. It can be said that both these patterns typify the Judeo-Christian tradition. If the Judeo-Christian tradition has developed such a positive relationship with universal human rights standards, why can't we expect traditional African cultural values—which often embody similar ethical, moral, spiritual, and religious norms—to serve the same overriding goals of legitimizing and promoting universal human rights ideals?

The issue in the final analysis, as James Paul argues, is one of empowering the people to appreciate their rights and to see the legitimacy of these rights both in the law and in the value systems of their indigenous cultures. Consider the case of the Dinka of Sudan, whose cultural traditions and tragic contemporary situation are discussed in this book. Both Francis Deng and Rhoda Howard indicate that the Northern Sudanese Arab tribesmen have reintroduced slavery to this area and that the Dinka are its principal victims. Is it not significant to the realization of human rights in the Sudan that the Dinka condemn the practice as being incompatible with the universal belief in the dignity of the individual, whatever his or her race or country of origin? Is it not a moral and legal challenge to the Arab-Muslim leaders and people of the North when a traditional Dinka elder says, as Deng quotes in his essay: "A human being created by God was never made a slave by the black man [meaning the Dinka]; it was the Arabs who made them slaves. . . . Slavery is not known to us. . . . To capture people to become slaves among us is unknown." In response to the allegation that in the past the Dinka likewise captured Arabs in tribal warfare, the elders have argued that although this may have happened on occasion, it was a retaliatory act and its purpose was not to enslave; rather, a person thus captured was adopted and became "a member of the family." According to another elder, "What the Arabs have written down [about the Dinka participating in slavery] is a lie. . . . People kill themselves in war, face to face, but we do not go and capture people. . . . We have something God gave us from the ancient past, from the time our ancestors came leading the people. . . . [We] have war ethics that came with us from the ancient past. We never ambush . . . we kill face to face. It is the Arabs who treat us as slaves and capture us in secrecy." Why would one insist that this traditional Dinka perspective pertains only to human dignity and not to human rights? The fact that the ancestors are described as "leading the people" is an obvious reference to political authority for upholding and enforcing these principles. Is not a Dinka with these cultural traditions more likely to accept universal standards than his or her Northern Sudanese compatriot who believes that the practice is condoned and sanctioned by the customs and the religious traditions of the Muslim community?

The eclectic, cross-cultural approach to universal human rights that we are proposing tends to stir up controversy because some people mistakenly believe it reflects a relativist definition of human rights. Consequently, they construe it as a rejection of the international standards and an endorsement of African violations of human rights on the basis of local cultural standards. James Silk sums up the standard rejectionist argument as follows: "Traditional African culture was or is compatible with human rights, but with an African conception of human rights—consistent with the African context—not with the inevitably Western norms embodied in the International Bill of Human Rights." In Silk's view,

> the proposition—that international human rights are not universal but Western and that there is an African notion of human rights that is not ultimately consistent with international norms—is troublesome. First, it can be and is used as an apology or an excuse for Africa's poor human rights record: Africa cannot be held to standards that are culturally inappropriate and that Africans had no part in establishing. Also, denying the universality of human rights may effectively destroy the meaning and value of the entire concept of human rights: there can be no basis for international protection if each society can determine its own list of human rights. The very significance of international human rights is in their universality.

This is precisely the point we wish to make in advocating a cross-cultural approach to human rights. However, it is easy to see how this approach can be confused with the standard "African" position. That can be the only explanation for Rhoda Howard's reaction to the essays on the Akan and the Dinka concepts of human rights: the contributions by Deng and Wiredu to this volume "could be taken to support the viewpoint of those who argue for an African concept of rights based on the differences between 'traditional' African and 'modern' Western culture and values." Whatever our failure to communicate the message, the purpose of those chapters was certainly not to make a case for a separatist approach to African human rights. On the contrary, as we have indicated by means of the Dinka example, the current international human rights standards are by no means alien to African traditions, and could even be defended on the basis of traditional African value systems and institutional practices. Our objective, then, has been twofold: first, we wanted to emphasize that human rights, whether locally or globally defined, are not without roots in African traditional societies, and are actually well grounded in African cultural values; and second, we hoped to show that the conceptualization, formulation, and promotion of international or universal human rights standards can be positively reinforced and enriched by the moral values and normative behavior of traditional African societies. Far from representing a rejection of international standards and an argument for a unique African version of human rights, our position, we believe, discourages African leaders from justifying human rights violations by invoking African tradition.

Whatever the reason for the controversy surrounding cross-cultural perspectives on human rights, the essays in this volume clearly demonstrate that the debate has just begun and that its parameters are still to be defined and its course is still to be charted. The central issue in this debate is whether looking at human rights from the various cultural perspectives that now coexist and interact in the world community promotes or undermines international standards. In James Silk's view, the way to resolve this question is first to recognize

> differences in culture and in levels of development. But [that approach] does not seek, within African traditional culture, broadly defined, the presence or absence of specific rights. Instead, it assumes that underlying the International Bill of Human Rights . . . is some fundamental metaphysical idea (an idea that may well be "Western" *as articulated*). It calls then for a close look at a specific traditional culture to see if a substantially similar idea is present. The identification of such an idea in a given culture would suggest that international human rights norms are not fundamentally inconsistent with that culture's values. The inability to locate such an idea would provide more compelling evidence for the conclusion that international human rights are not universal and are not likely to take root in the particular non-Western society in question.

Silk suggests that the Dinka view of all human beings as God's children, and the dignity it accords every individual as God's child, is the basis for the universality of human rights among the Dinka. According to the Dinka moral code, every human being, regardless of race or religion, has a moral or spiritual value that should be respected. To wrong him or her is to wrong God himself and therefore to invite a curse. As one Dinka elder has pointed out, it is only by caring for the interest of other human beings as individuals that every individual can best secure his or her interests: "If you push [a person] onto the ground and do not give him what he needs, things will spoil [for you] and even your big share, which you guard with care, will be destroyed." The example of slavery given earlier shows how this basic value can be interpreted and applied to a specific human rights situation.

Although Silk's approach puts us on a more productive course of investigation, it tends to focus on the microcultural aspects of a given culture, whereas the scale of analysis actually needs to be enlarged. We are really talking not about this or that level of particularity or generality, but about the complementarity between the "specifics" and the "overalls" of a given cultural context and its compatibility or mutual reinforcement with the universal concept and content of human rights.

As a result, we have tended to concentrate on the contextual legitimacy of the concept or the idea of human rights, rather than on the substantive content of those rights from a cross-cultural point of view. But it is not enough to advocate the universal application of international human rights standards with the backing of local cultural arguments. We must also conceptualize the process of mutual reinforcement and enrichment involved in interpreting and implementing these standards if we hope to maintain a pluralistic world order. As Richard Schwartz says in the conclusion of his essay: "Every culture will have its distinctive ways of formulating and supporting human rights. Every society can learn from other societies more effective ways to implement human rights. While honoring the diversity of cultures, we can also build toward common principles that all can support."

Is this a fanciful ideal or an achievable objective? Are we being romantic and are we unnecessarily complicating the process of universalizing the cause of human rights, or are we presenting a cultural challenge for all members of the human family and their respective cultures that can help shape the lofty ideals of universal human rights? And could such worldwide involvement in itself lead to a realization of the universality of human dignity, which is the cornerstone of international human rights? Or would it be more practical to assume that some cultures are just not blessed with these human ideals, and that the sooner they recognize this and try to adjust and live up to the challenge presented by the pioneering leadership of those more endowed with these lofty values, the better for their own good and for the good of humanity?

These questions are by no means rhetorical or cynical, although they may be provocatively phrased. The wide variety of perspectives presented in this volume tells us that we have no definitive answers to the questions surrounding human rights. Even if our proposed cross-cultural approach is correct and holds great potential for expanding human rights, we still do not know how to implement it. We need to move into the realm of methodological conceptualization, analysis, and examination of policy implications. Much needs to be done to improve our understanding of individual societies and cultures, particularly their interpretation of human dignity, and to find ways in which their precepts can be applied creatively to legitimize and reinforce international human rights standards within the context of given cultures.

We hope that this book will help to promote dignity for all human beings—as individuals or as members of communities or nations. We trust that all societies and cultures, in their wide variety of ways and means, are dedicated to protecting and promoting human rights, which we believe are owed to all human beings by virtue of their very existence. But we also recognize that no society or system of government is anywhere near the ideal. The next step that we must take if we are to make any headway in this direction is to determine how the situation can be improved, especially for the people of the developing countries, where the record on human rights is particularly dismal.

Part One
Western Cultural Origins

CHAPTER TWO

The Effect of Western Perspectives on International Human Rights

Virginia A. Leary

WESTERN CULTURE dominated the formulation of early international standards of human rights. Although this cultural influence has been mitigated considerably since the newly independent developing countries began participating in the drafting of international standards in the 1960s, the undeniable effect of Western perspectives on the development of international human rights norms has led some to cast doubt on the universality of those norms and their suitability for application in non-Western cultures.

"Western" is an ambiguous term that is used in this essay to refer to Western Europe and the Americas. It is not used here to refer solely to economically developed countries. The countries of Latin America, usually placed in the category of third world or developing countries, are included here among Western nations because their culture is primarily European in origin. It is their state of economic development that links them with the third world, and thus in the early development of human rights standards they often emphasized economic and social rights. The Soviet Union and the Eastern European countries are culturally of European origin and can also be considered Western, but their contribution to the development of international human rights law and policy has been distinct from that of other Western countries.

In assessing the influence of the West on the development of international human rights standards, it should not be forgotten that the horrifying atrocities committed by Nazi Germany were the primary impulsion for the development of an international system for the protection of universal human rights. Thus, ironically, although Western philosophical thought influenced the development of international human rights norms, it was Western violations of those same elementary standards of humanity that focused world attention on the need for international promotion and protection of human rights. The Western phil-

15

osophical roots of the concept of human rights did not prevent the most serious violations of human dignity by Western nations. Indeed, the historical development of concepts of human rights coincided with the development of powerful modern states in the West that were capable of more serious violations of individual dignity than were possible under earlier forms of social organization.

Awareness of the historical influence of Western concepts on international human rights standards has led to ideological conflict in international forums and to considerable discussion in the current literature on human rights.[1] The lack of influence of major non-Western cultures in the early drafting of international human rights standards has been cited as a serious deficiency in the development of a universally acceptable concept of human rights. The rich cultures of Asia and Africa express matters of human dignity in terms other than "rights."[2] Many of these cultures, in contrast, value a sense of community and stress duties to family and community more than they emphasize individualism and rights.

Although the Western concept of human rights was introduced into the legal systems of many non-Western cultures through colonialism and the cultural influence of the West, it has not always been an easy transposition. To many in the third world, human rights remain an alien concept and an example of cultural imperialism. In addition, the supposed protection of human rights has often been seen as a pretext for continued intervention by former colonial Western powers in the internal affairs of sovereign states. Freedom from particular forms of oppression experienced in ex-colonial and developing countries has not been included in the traditional enumeration of Western rights. Efforts by these countries to actively promote self-determination, the right to economic development, and economic and social rights have met with resistance from the West—sometimes because these efforts supposedly dilute Western conceptualizations of individual human rights and

1. See Adamantia Pollis and Peter Schwab, eds., *Human Rights: Cultural and Ideological Perspectives* (Praeger, 1979); Rhoda Howard, "Evaluating Human Rights in Africa: Some Problems of Implicit Comparisons," *Human Rights Quarterly,* vol. 6 (May 1984), p. 160; Yougindra Khushalani, "Human Rights in Asia and Africa," *Human Rights Law Journal,* vol. 4, no. 4 (1983), p. 403; Cornelius F. Murphy, Jr., "Objections to Western Conceptions of Human Rights," *Hofstra Law Review,* vol. 9 (Winter 1981), p. 433; Jack Donnelly,"Human Rights and Human Dignity: An Analytic Critique of Non-Western Conceptions of Human Rights," *American Political Science Review,* vol. 76 (June 1982), p. 303.

2. R. Panikkar, "Is the Notion of Human Rights a Western Concept," *Diogenes,* vol. 120 (Winter 1982), p. 75.

sometimes because of political resistance to their ideological implications. But opposition to the Western origin of the human rights concept has also been used on occasion to mask or excuse serious violations of human dignity.

In this chapter I examine Western conceptualizations of human rights and the influence of these constructs on the development of international human rights standards, particularly through the role played by people of Western culture in the drafting of those standards. The main part of the essay is devoted to a discussion of Western influence on the drafting of the Universal Declaration of Human Rights, since it is in that instrument that Western influence is most prominent. I also propose to examine the evolution in Western thinking about international human rights as it has developed, at least in part, through non-Western political and cultural influences. In this argument I suggest that cultural influence is not a one-way street and that, despite the conceptualization of human dignity in terms of human rights (originally a Western concept), the present concept of international human rights has become a universal one that is not inimical to non-Western cultures.

Ideological Underpinnings of Western Concepts of Human Rights

Participation of former colonies, newly independent in the 1960s, in the drafting of the two international covenants—on civil and political rights and on economic, social, and cultural rights—diminished the dominance of the West in developing human rights standards. But the conceptualization of human rights incorporated in international instruments has, with some few but important exceptions, represented traditional Western philosophical influences.

Elsewhere in this book, the roots of Western concepts of human rights are treated in detail. Reference is made here only to those philosophic tenets that are essential to understanding the effect of Western perspectives on the formulation of international human rights standards. An emphasis on individualism and on property rights is at the basis of Western perspectives on human rights. Although it is often stated, particularly by Western European scholars, that the concept of human rights dates back to Stoic conceptions in Greece and Rome, as well as to medieval traditions of "natural right," the present Western notion of human rights has its roots in eighteenth-century Western European philosophical theory. That tradition emphasized the individual's rights against the state and the protection of private property as an essential aspect of individual autonomy. Little attention was paid to social inequalities, and the tradition often neglected the rights of entire social groups, such as slaves and women.

Given the primacy of the individual in the traditional Western conception of rights, there is little room for a concept of group or communal rights. Restrictions on individual liberty are limited and permissible normally only when another's rights are endangered. Rights, therefore, are negative, a protection against state action. Positive rights, which imply action by the state to implement rights, are not part of the tradition.

Western perspectives on the development of international human rights standards have reflected these philosophical notions. But among the Western nations they have been emphasized to varying degrees. There are substantial differences, rooted in history, between the stress that the United States has placed on certain aspects of the Western tradition of rights and the emphases of other Western nations with social democratic traditions. For example, Canada and the United States, culturally similar and economically integrated in many ways, view rights from slightly different perspectives as a result of their different historical pasts. The Western tradition is thus not monolithic, but it does exhibit sufficient commonality to permit generalizations in relation to other traditions.

Western Influence in the Drafting of the Universal Declaration

The effort to protect human rights at the international level began in nineteenth-century Europe. The slave trade was outlawed among Western powers, and the foundations of humanitarian law were laid. The International Labour Organization was founded in 1919 to protect workers' rights. Minority rights in some European countries were protected by provisions of treaties after World War I.

An attempt to include a provision on human rights in the Covenant of the League of Nations, however, proved fruitless. President Woodrow Wilson had proposed that all members of the future league be required to pledge that they would make no law interfering with freedom of religion.[3] His proposal, supported by the United Kingdom, was eventually

3. Louis B. Sohn and Thomas Buergenthal, *International Protection of Human Rights* (Bobbs-Merrill, 1973), p. 217.

dropped, allegedly because Baron Makino of Japan suggested that the pledge should also include a commitment to the equal treatment of all races and nondiscrimination in the treatment of aliens.[4] Discrimination against Japanese in the United States had long been a source of controversy between the two governments.

A qualitative advance in the international protection of human rights occurred when the original members of the United Nations included the promotion of human rights among the purposes of the organization.[5] At the San Francisco Conference, where the UN Charter was drafted, U.S. Secretary of State Edward R. Stettinius urged that the promotion of human rights be so emphasized, stating that the "Four Freedoms" enunciated by President Franklin D. Roosevelt encompassed all other rights and freedoms.[6] In his Four Freedoms speech to Congress in 1941, Roosevelt had said,

In the future days, which we seek to make secure, we look forward to a world founded upon four essential human freedoms. The first is freedom of speech and expression everywhere in the world. The second is freedom of every person to worship God in his own way everywhere in the world. The third is freedom from want, which, translated into world terms, means economic understandings which will secure to every nation a healthy peacetime life for its inhabitants— everywhere in the world. The fourth is freedom from fear, which, translated into world terms, means a world-wide reduction of armaments to such a point and in such a thorough fashion that no nation will be in a position to commit an act of physical aggression against any neighbor—anywhere in the world.[7]

The San Francisco Conference did not have time to draft a lengthy catalog of human rights, and it was decided to leave to the future General Assembly the responsibility of developing more detailed provisions

4. Albert Verdoodt, *Naissance et Signification de la Déclaration Universelle des Droits de l'Homme* (Louvain-Paris: Editions Nauwelaerts, 1963), p. 36.

5. Article 1 of the UN Charter (1945) cites the achievement of international cooperation "in promoting and encouraging respect for human rights and for fundamental freedoms for all without distinction as to race, sex, language, or religion." See also articles 55 and 56 of the charter.

6. Sohn and Buergenthal, *International Protection of Human Rights*, p. 509.

7. "Address of the President of the United States," January 6, 1941, *Congressional Record*, vol. 87, part 1 (Government Printing Office, 1941), pp. 46–47.

on human rights. In 1948 the UN General Assembly adopted the Universal Declaration of Human Rights (by forty-eight votes in favor, no votes against, and eight abstentions—by Saudi Arabia, South Africa, and the Soviet Union and its Eastern European allies). Most of the present Asian and African member states of the United Nations were still colonies in 1948 and thus did not participate in the drafting of this "common standard of achievement for all peoples and nations."

The General Assembly had assigned the task of drafting the declaration to the Human Rights Commission. The persons who carried the most responsibility for the drafting of the declaration were from Western Europe or the Americas or were non-Europeans educated in the West. Although many people participated in the UN Commission on Human Rights or the Third Committee of the General Assembly, a small number can be said to have been the primary drafters of the declaration. Verdoodt lists René Cassin of France, John P. Humphrey of Canada, Eleanor Roosevelt of the United States, Hernán Santa Cruz of Chile, Charles Malik of Lebanon, P. C. Chang of China, and Fernand Dehousse of Belgium as playing the most important roles in the drafting.[8] Humphrey was the director of the Division on Human Rights of the UN Secretariat; the others were members of the Human Rights Commission. Verdoodt considers this group to be representative, since three of the principal drafters came from the Americas, two from Europe, and two from Asia. All, however, had received their education mainly in Western universities. Chang and Malik, the only non-Westerners in the group, were educated at Clark College and Columbia University in the United States and at the American University of Beirut and Harvard University, respectively. Malik had taught at Harvard. Both made clear their Western philosophical orientation at various points in the drafting of the declaration. At one point Malik urged inclusion in one of the articles of the declaration of the phrase, inspired by the U.S. Declaration of Independence, that each person is "endowed by the Creator with unalienable rights." The proposal was rejected.[9] Chang referred on various occasions, with approval, to eighteenth-century Western philosophical theories as the source of the declaration.

The initial draft of the declaration prepared by John Humphrey drew from proposed declarations submitted by a number of Western organi-

8. Verdoodt, *Naissance et Signification de la Déclaration Universelle*, pp. 332–34.
9. Verdoodt, *Naissance et Signification de la Déclaration Universelle*, pp. 275–81.

zations and individuals, particularly from the Western hemisphere.[10] Most of these declarations followed closely the French Declaration of the Rights of Man and of the Citizen or the U.S. Bill of Rights, although the Latin American declarations included references to economic and social rights. Humphrey was asked what doctrine formed the basis of his draft. He stated that it was not based on any particular doctrine, but the influence of the Latin American submissions was noticeable in his draft.[11] René Cassin of France is frequently cited as the author of the declaration. Cassin was the leading member of the Drafting Committee of the Human Rights Commission. He made substantial changes in Humphrey's draft and edited the version that was close to the one finally adopted. According to Verdoodt, it was at the first session of the Drafting Committee, led by Cassin, that the declaration received its Western character.[12]

The influence of Western perspectives is evident in the language of many of the declaration's provisions and their content. Article 17 states, "Everyone has the right to own property alone as well as in association with others. No one shall be arbitrarily deprived of his property." This article is a clear reflection of the emphasis on property in the traditional Western perspective on human rights. But the right to property was not included in either of the two later international covenants on human rights drafted with the participation of the newly independent nations. The declaration contains phrases that would be familiar to U.S. citizens, for their source was the U.S. Constitution. For example, article 7 refers to "equal protection of the law," and article 5 refers to "cruel, inhuman or degrading . . . punishment."

Although the declaration, in general, bears an unmistakable Western stamp, it does include references to economic and social rights that are not included in the well-known Western documents on human rights. Articles 22 through 27 refer to rights to social security, to work, to rest and leisure, to an adequate standard of living, to education, and to participation in the cultural life of the community. Article 28 states that

10. Verdoodt states that drafts of model declarations were submitted by, among others, Latin American legal organizations, the American Bar Association, the American Federation of Labor, the Committee for the Study of the Organization of Peace (U.S.), American Jewish organizations, and several Western individuals. Verdoodt, *Naissance et Signification de la Déclaration Universelle*, pp. 41–43.

11. Verdoodt, *Naissance et Signification de la Déclaration Universelle*, p. 57–58.

12. Verdoodt, *Naissance et Signification de la Déclaration Universelle*, p. 61.

"everyone is entitled to a social and international order in which the rights and freedoms set forth in this Declaration can be fully realized." The latter article was introduced by Malik of Lebanon. Although it might be thought that these articles were added at the behest of the Soviet Union and the Eastern European socialist bloc, it appears that their inclusion was due as much to the Latin American countries, some of which had such provisions in their own constitutions.[13] The American Declaration of the Rights and Duties of Man, adopted at the Ninth International Conference of American States at Bogotá, Colombia, in 1948, included most of the same economic and social rights, and the Latin American delegates in the Human Rights Commission and Third Committee referred frequently to it.

A provision that was not included in the declaration is significant because it related to a concern of Asian countries. Mrs. Mehta of India, a member of the Human Rights Commission, proposed an article on minorities, stressing the prevention of discrimination against them and the encouragement of their cultural development rather than assimilation. The proposed article was rejected, mainly because of opposition from Latin American countries and the United States. The proposed article led to considerable controversy in the Human Rights Commission and Third Committee. It was clear from the discussion that most of the New World representatives were in favor of the assimilation of minorities and against any encouragement of their separate development.[14]

Given this preponderant Western influence on the philosophy and language of the declaration, must we renounce its pretensions to universality? Some have so contended. It has been stated that the declaration reflects a "moral chauvinism and ethnocentric bias" that renders it irrelevant in non-Western societies and that it is "based on the notion of atomized individuals . . . and predicated on the assumption that Western values are paramount and ought to be extended to the non-

13. The initial draft of article 22 concerning social security, prepared by the Secretariat, closely resembled a draft presented by Panama. Verdoodt, *Naissance et Signification de la Déclaration Universelle*, p. 210.

14. Verdoodt, *Naissance et Signification de la Déclaration Universelle*, pp. 287–99. The question of assimilation of minorities and indigenous peoples is an issue of current controversy in international human rights law. Convention no. 107 of the International Labor Organization, relating to indigenous populations, is being revised because of objections to its emphasis on assimilation. The Working Group on Indigenous Peoples of the UN Sub-Commission on Prevention of Discrimination and Protection of Minorities is currently developing standards relating to the treatment of indigenous peoples. Assimilation efforts have been widely criticized within the Working Group by indigenous groups.

Western world."[15] Yet despite its Western inspiration, since it was adopted in 1948 the declaration has achieved a truly universal status. Its provisions have been included almost verbatim in the post–World War II constitutions of many non-European countries. Although the Soviet Union and the Eastern European countries abstained in the vote on the declaration, they have since evidenced their acceptance of it on many occasions. The African Charter on Human and Peoples' Rights and the 1960 Declaration on the Granting of Independence to Colonial Countries and Peoples also cited the declaration. Most important, the declaration has not inhibited development of concepts of human rights in subsequent instruments that reflect more fully the views of non-Western cultures.

In a thoughtful article written on its thirty-fifth anniversary, Philip Alston examined non-Western critiques of the declaration:

> It is sometimes suggested that the doctrines of human rights as embodied in the Universal Declaration of Human Rights may not be relevant to societies with a non-Western cultural tradition or a socialist ideology. In its extreme form such an approach would thoroughly undermine the existing system for the international protection of human rights and create a "free for all" situation in which each dictator and each military junta, as well as each democratically elected but embattled government, could design its own bill of rights to suit not only local traditions but also its own self-interest.[16]

Alston points out that criticizing the declaration as not suited to non-Western cultures entails an analysis of which rights might be dispensed with from a different cultural perspective. There are provisions of the declaration that do not meet with universal approval. As pointed out earlier, the right to property that is contained in the declaration was not included in later human rights covenants. The reason for its omission is due less to controversy about the individual right to property than to disagreement about compensation for the nationalization or expropriation of such property. But the Western emphasis on private property as a fundamental human right and the interpretations that the West has traditionally made regarding this right are unacceptable in many parts

15. Pollis and Schwab, eds., *Human Rights*, p. 14 and p. 8, n. 1, cited in Philip Alston, "The Universal Declaration at 35: Western and Passé or Alive and Universal?" *Review of the International Commission of Jurists*, no. 31 (December 1983).

16. Alston, "The Universal Declaration at 35," p. 65.

of the world today, as the failure to include it in the later human rights covenants attests.

Saudi Arabia abstained in the vote on the declaration because of opposition to two provisions in the covenant, and Islamic opposition to these provisions presumably continues.[17] Article 18 provides that everyone has the right to freedom of thought, conscience, and religion and that "this right includes freedom to change his religion." Islam does not accept the right of Moslems to change their religion. Article 16 provides that men and women "are entitled to equal rights as to marriage, during marriage, and at its dissolution." The representative of Saudi Arabia in the Third Committee abstained during the vote on this provision. Some commentators, particularly Western ones, have ridiculed the declaration by citing article 24, which provides that "Everyone has the right to rest and leisure, including reasonable limitation of working hours and *periodic holidays with pay*" (emphasis mine). They refer to the absurdity of this detail, given the severe economic underdevelopment of many parts of the world. The objection to this article from Western writers is often made in the context of a denial that economic and social "claims" are human rights.

The Soviet Union had several objections to the declaration that accounted for its abstention during the final vote. It criticized the failure to cite Nazism and Fascism as egregious violations of human rights, as well as the failure to give economic and social rights equal billing with civil and political rights.[18] Only five of thirty articles relate to economic, social, and cultural rights. Finally, the USSR contended that the declaration lacked a clearly defined political character.

The declaration has also been criticized as incorporating an individualistic concept of rights, ignoring group and community rights. It does not include a provision on self-determination, nor one on minority rights (as does the later Covenant on Civil and Political Rights).

Within the total context of the thirty articles of the declaration, these are minor objections. The overwhelming majority of the articles relate to matters of fundamental importance such as the right to life and freedom from torture, slavery, and arbitrary arrest and detention. Alston suggests that "most of the concerns dealt with in the Declaration had long been recognized within the varying conceptions of human dignity which are an integral part of the world's major religious and cultural

17. Verdoodt, *Naissance et Signification de la Déclaration Universelle,* p. 77.
18. Verdoodt, *Naissance et Signification de la Déclaration Universelle,* pp. 69–71, 77.

traditions." He concludes that "the Declaration's philosophical under-pinnings are sufficiently eclectic, its text sufficiently flexible, and recent developments sufficiently responsive, to ensure its continuing relevance as a 'living' instrument of incomparable importance in the field of human rights." [19]

Subsequent Developments in Setting Standards of Human Rights

In the forty years since the Universal Declaration of Human Rights was adopted, the United Nations and regional intergovernmental organizations have adopted a large number of human rights instruments. The two most important UN instruments are the International Covenant on Civil and Political Rights and the International Covenant on Economic, Social and Cultural Rights. Two trends are noticeable as regards Western influence in the years after adoption of the declaration. Western dominance in the formulation of human rights standards has ebbed, and the West no longer appears homogeneous in its perspective on human rights. I mention in this section the effect of Western perspectives on the formulation of the two covenants adopted since the declaration and on the recent evolution of the concept of the right to development.

Elaboration of the Universal Declaration of Human Rights required only a few years. The drafting of the two international covenants that followed it took twenty years. The difference in time illustrates the difficulties involved in the two exercises. By and large, the underlying views of the drafters of the declaration were relatively homogeneous; the states represented were primarily Western states reflecting traditional Western perspectives on rights. Despite some controversies, particularly between the Western democracies and the Eastern European socialist states, the adoption of the declaration was relatively uncontentious. In the 1960s, in contrast, many new countries of Africa and Asia had become members of the United Nations, and their outlook on international problems and human rights differed from those of the West. In addition, political and ideological confrontations from the cold war divided the West and the Eastern European countries more profoundly than during the period the declaration was drafted.

At the time of the adoption of the UN Charter, it was assumed that the charter's brief references to human rights could be supplemented by

19. Alston, "The Universal Declaration at 35," pp. 62, 61.

a future declaration, treaty, or covenant on human rights and by a subsequent instrument relating to the implementation of these rights. The concept of a single covenant including both civil and political rights and economic, social, and cultural rights (as had the declaration) died during the period from 1948 to 1968. Opposition from the West led to the adoption of two separate covenants—an unfortunate occurrence that continues to hinder the development of human rights. Despite President Roosevelt's Four Freedoms and his invocation of "freedom from want," traditional Western views of human rights extend to the economic, social, and cultural spheres of human activity only with difficulty. Instead of being regarded as entitlements, rights in these areas are often seen as demands or claims. It is contended that there is an intrinsic difference between the two sets of rights, particularly in the means of implementing them. Economic and social rights, it is claimed, require positive state action and are not justiciable. Civil and political rights, however, require only that the state refrain from action, are negative and can be enforced more easily, and do not depend on the economic development of a nation. All these contentions can be disputed, but they represent traditional Western thinking on rights.

A substantial body of Western scholarship continues to refer to the fundamental difference between these set of rights.[20] In the period from 1948 to 1968 the Western states urged that, in view of the allegedly different methods of implementing the two sets of rights, there should be two covenants rather than one. The West won the day, and two separate covenants were drafted. An Optional Protocol was attached to the Covenant on Civil and Political Rights that, if accepted by a state, provided for the possibility of complaints of violations of human rights by a state to be filed by organizations and individuals. No such system was provided under the Covenant on Economic, Social and Cultural Rights. The civil and political covenant also provided for a committee of independent experts to be created for the monitoring of the covenant. The economic covenant simply provided for reports to be sent to the UN Economic and Social Council. Although ECOSOC has now established a committee of independent experts to monitor the economic covenant, such a committee was not provided for in the covenant itself. The necessary conclusion arising from the difference between the two covenants

20. The best-known Western proponent of the view that the two sets of rights are fundamentally different is Maurice Cranston. See Cranston, "What Are Human Rights?" reprinted in Walter Laqueur and Barry Rubin, eds., *The Human Rights Reader* (Philadelphia: Temple University Press, 1979), pp. 17–25.

is that economic and social rights are held to be less important. The separation of the two sets of rights into independent covenants has also served to perpetuate an ideological and sterile controversy between the Western countries and the Eastern European and developing countries about the relative value of the two sets of rights.

It has already been mentioned that the right to property was not included in either of the two covenants. Some of the provisions of the covenant on economic rights do, however, relate to property questions and have continued to elicit objections from Western states. In its letter submitting the International Covenant on Economic, Social and Cultural Rights to President Jimmy Carter for transmission to the U.S. Senate for advice and consent to ratification, the State Department suggested that a declaration be attached to article 2 (relating to developing countries' determination of the degree to which they will guarantee to noncitizens economic rights recognized in the covenant) and article 25 (which states that nothing in the covenant shall be interpreted as impairing the inherent right of all peoples to enjoy and use fully and freely their natural wealth and resources). The proposed declaration read as follows:

> The United States declares that nothing in the Covenant derogates from the equal obligation of all States to fulfill their responsibilities under international law. The United States understands that under the Covenant everyone has the right to own property alone as well as in association with others, and that no one shall be arbitrarily deprived of his property.[21]

As the State Department letter commented:

> This declaration and understanding will make clear the United States position regarding property rights, and expresses the view of the United States that discrimination by developing countries against nonnationals or actions affecting their property or contractual rights may only be carried out in accordance with the governing rules of international law. Under international law, any taking of private property must be nondiscriminatory and for a public purpose, and

21. Department of State, "Letter of Submittal," in *Four Treaties Pertaining to Human Rights: Message from the President of the United States Transmitting . . . the International Covenant on Economic, Social and Cultural Rights . . .* , U.S. Senate, 95 Cong., 2d sess. (GPO, 1978), p. ix.

must be accompanied by prompt, adequate, and effective compensation [p. ix].

The Western emphasis on property rights as an essential element of human rights—or at least the concern that new concepts of human rights may interfere with the rights of property—is illustrated by this suggested declaration. In this same State Department letter the U.S. position that economic rights are goals to be accomplished, rather than immediately enforceable rights, is made clear, thus distinguishing them from civil and political rights. The letter stated:

Articles 6 through 9 of the Covenant list certain economic rights, including the right to work (Article 6), to favorable working conditions (Article 7), to organize unions (Article 8), and to social security (Article 9). Some of the standards established under these articles may not readily be translated into legally enforceable rights, while others are in accord with United States policy, but have not yet been fully achieved. It is accordingly important to make clear that these provisions are understood to be goals whose realization will be sought rather than obligations requiring immediate implementation [p. x].

The influence of the developing countries in the drafting of the two covenants is exemplified by the inclusion in both of a provision on self-determination. No similar article appears in the Universal Declaration of Human Rights, which was adopted under strong Western influence.

On December 4, 1986, the UN General Assembly adopted the Declaration on the Right to Development.[22] The United States cast the only negative vote, and has since withdrawn from the Working Group of Governmental Experts on the Right to Development. In the U.S. view, "the right to development is little more than a rhetorical exercise designed to enable the Eastern European countries to score points on disarmament and collective rights and to permit the Third World to 'distort' the issue of human rights by affirming the equal importance of economic, social and cultural rights with civil and political rights and

22. United Nations, General Assembly, *Declaration on the Right to Development*, A/41/153 (December 4, 1986).

by linking human rights in general to its 'utopian' aspiration for a new international economic order."[23]

The antipathy of the Reagan administration to the right to development was not shared by other Western European countries, which participated actively in the drafting of the declaration and continue to participate in the working group. The homogeneous attitude toward human rights that appeared to exist among Western powers in the early days of the development of international standards on human rights no longer exists. In recent times the United States' exceptional emphasis on property rights and its skepticism about economic and social rights have not always been shared by other Western powers.

It is clear, then, that non-Western perspectives on human rights have begun to influence Western thinking on the subject. Internal developments in Western countries, many of which have adopted social democratic principles at home, have also influenced Western conceptions of human rights. An increasing number of Western scholars are reevaluating conceptions of human rights and becoming sympathetic to formulations that include economic, social, and cultural rights, the right to self-determination, and the right to development. Henry Shue, Fried von Hoof, and Philip Alston have been leaders in the international human rights field in rethinking Western conceptions. An evolution in Western thinking has taken place, and it is no longer possible to discern with ease a common Western approach to human rights which distinguishes that approach from those of other cultures. Western human rights activists and scholars have become sensitive to the cultural bias affecting their conceptions.

Conclusion

Concepts of human dignity can be expressed by many terms: social justice, dharma, human rights. The particular form in which the international community, under Western influence, has chosen to express human dignity, however, is the concept of human rights. Despite its Western origin, the concept of human rights must now be recognized as

23. Philip Alston, "Making Space for New Human Rights: The Case of the Right to Development," in *Harvard Human Rights Yearbook*, vol. 1 (Spring 1988), p. 22. An extensive discussion of the right to development is contained in Lois Gully, "The Significance of International Human Rights Law to Developing Countries: An Examination of the Right to Development," paper prepared for the Seminar on International Protection of Human Rights, University of Saskatchewan, College of Law, Saskatoon, 1987.

a universal term accepted throughout the world. But the concept is a dynamic and evolutionary one that has recently been extended to cover many aspects of human dignity not contemplated under the traditional Western rubric of human rights. Western influence, dominant in the origin of the development of international human rights norms, is now only one of a number of cultural influences on the development of international human rights standards. Its contribution to the development of human rights has been great, but it has not been unique, and other cultures have made and are making significant contributions to our collective conception of human dignity.

CHAPTER THREE

Human Rights and Western Liberalism

Jack Donnelly

THE "WESTERN" or "liberal" conception of human rights is conventionally characterized as resting on a social vision of largely isolated individuals holding (only) property rights and "negative" civil and political liberties. This view is almost universal among critics of liberalism, from C. B. Macpherson on the left to Leo Strauss on the right.[1] For example, Adamantia Pollis has argued that the liberal conception of human rights rests on a definition of a person as "an isolated, autonomous individual . . . with inherent rights in the domain of the civil and the political," and that in the liberal tradition "individual self-aggrandizement, defined as power through ownership of material things, [is] the essence of man [and] private property . . . a fundamental inalienable human right."[2] As Ian Shapiro has recently put it, "the negative libertarian view of the substance of rights has been an integral part of the liberal

I wish to thank Steve Leonard and Rhoda Howard for their helpful comments on, and criticism of, early versions of this chapter.

1. C. B. Macpherson, *The Political Theory of Possessive Individualism: Hobbes to Locke* (Oxford: Clarendon Press, 1962); and Leo Strauss, *Natural Right and History* (University of Chicago Press, 1953).

2. Adamantia Pollis, "Liberal, Socialist, and Third World Perspectives of Human Rights," in Peter Schwab and Adamantia Pollis, eds., *Toward a Human Rights Framework* (Praeger, 1982), pp. 7, 5. For further statements of such a view in the human rights literature, see John Somerville, "Comparison of Soviet and Western Democratic Principles, with Special Reference to Human Rights," in UNESCO, ed., *Human Rights: Comments and Interpretations* (Allan Wingate, 1949), p. 152; Tom J. Farer, "Human Rights and Human Wrongs: Is the Liberal Model Sufficient?" *Human Rights Quarterly,* vol. 7 (November 1985), pp. 189–204; Josiah A. M. Cobbah, "African Values and the Human Rights Debate: An African Perspective," *Human Rights Quarterly,* vol. 9 (August 1987), pp. 309–31. See also Hiroko Yamane, "Approaches to Human Rights in Asia," in Rudolf Bernhardt and John Anthony Jolowicz, eds., *International Enforcement of Human Rights,* Reports submitted to the colloquium of the International Association of Legal Science, Heidelberg, August 28–30, 1985 (Springer-Verlag, 1987), p. 99.

conception of individual rights since its inception."[3] Many self-professed liberals share this understanding.[4]

There is, of course, a substantial element of truth in these characterizations, which reflect what I will call the conventional, or minimalist, conception of liberalism. But this is only one strand of the liberal tradition of political theory and practice. There is an alternative strand that rests on a broader, more subtle—and, I will argue, more coherent and defensible—social vision. This radical, or social democratic, conception of liberalism will be the focus of this paper.

The liberal tradition can be distinguished from other traditions by a threefold commitment to autonomy, equality, and the protection of these values through natural or human rights.[5] Individualism, private

3. Ian Shapiro, *The Evolution of Rights in Liberal Theory* (Cambridge University Press, 1986), p. 276. Compare Christian Bay, *Strategies of Political Emancipation* (University of Notre Dame Press, 1981), pp. 7–26; Anthony Arblaster, *The Rise and Decline of Western Liberalism* (Basil Blackwell, 1984), pt. 1, especially pp. 55–91; and, in two rather different veins, Sheldon S. Wolin, *Politics and Vision: Continuity and Innovation in Western Political Thought* (Little, Brown, 1960), pp. 286–351; and Alasdair MacIntyre, *After Virtue: A Study in Moral Theory* (University of Notre Dame Press, 1981).

4. Isaiah Berlin's "Two Concepts of Liberty," in *Four Essays On Liberty* (Oxford University Press, 1969), pp. 118–72, gives a classic contemporary exposition of the emphasis on negative rights and liberties. In the literature on human rights, this view is associated especially with the work of Maurice Cranston, *What Are Human Rights?* (London: Bodley Head, 1973), although A. I. Melden, *Rights and Persons* (University of California Press, 1977), pp. 166–226, provides a far more subtle and nuanced defense of this view of human rights. The libertarian variant is represented by such writers as Ludwig von Mises, *Liberalism in the Classical Tradition*, 3d ed., trans. Ralph Raico (Irvington-on-Hudson, N.Y.: Foundation for Economic Education; San Francisco: Cobden Press, 1985); F. A. Hayek, *The Constitution of Liberty* (University of Chicago Press, 1960); and Robert Nozick, *Anarchy, State, and Utopia* (Basic Books, 1974). See also Ramon M. Lemos, *Rights, Goods, and Democracy* (University of Delaware Press, 1986); and Loren E. Lomasky, *Persons, Rights, and the Moral Community* (Oxford University Press, 1987). For a Straussian variant, see Harvey C. Mansfield, Jr., *The Spirit of Liberalism* (Harvard University Press, 1978), for example, p. 10: "There are two principal rights in a liberal democracy. . . . The first is the right of acquiring private property. . . . The other right is the right of free speech."

5. See Ronald Dworkin, *A Matter of Principle* (Harvard University Press, 1985), pp. 181–204. John Rawls, *A Theory of Justice* (Cambridge: Belknap Press, 1971), is the best known contemporary theoretical defense of liberalism thus understood. With special reference to human rights, see Alan Gewirth, *Human Rights: Essays on Justification and Applications* (University of Chicago Press, 1982); and Henry Shue, *Basic Rights: Subsistence, Affluence, and U.S. Foreign Policy* (Princeton University Press, 1980), although both works are cast in self-consciously universal, rather than Western, or liberal, terms. For the purposes of this chapter, which is on the liberal Western theory of human rights, I stipulate that liberalism is a rights-based, rather than a utility-based, theory. A more complete account of liberalism, however, would need to take account of utilitarian liberal theories.

property rights, and civil and political rights—the three elements singled out in the conventional conception—do indeed have a special place in the Western liberal human rights tradition. But they do not exhaust that tradition. More precisely, in the radical liberal tradition individualism is moderated by social values, private property rights are limited rather than absolute, and civil and political rights are coupled with economic and social rights.

My argument proceeds on three levels. First, and most important, I try to demonstrate the existence of this radical strand in even the earliest (seventeenth-century) theoretical formulations of liberalism. This descriptive or historical argument seeks to show that the conventional or minimalist conception is inaccurate; at best, it takes a part for the whole. Second, I try to show that the conventional conception is analytically inadequate: liberalism is a more coherent political doctrine when viewed through the radical, rather than the minimalist, conception. Third, I suggest—although I do not argue in much detail—that the broader social democratic conception is morally preferable.

Locke and the Roots of Liberalism

The roots of the liberal Western approach to human rights are conventionally, and correctly, found in the seventeenth century, particularly in seventeenth-century England. It is generally agreed that by the time Locke's *Two Treatises of Government* was published in 1689, a fully developed, liberal conception of politics based on natural rights had become well established in the mainstream of English political debate. To simplify and focus the argument, I devote this essay to a careful reading of Locke's "Second Treatise," which is not only a seminal—almost canonical—work in the liberal tradition, but also one of the standard sources of the conventional, Western conception of human rights.[6] If one can identify the elements of the radical conception even in Locke, one will have done so in a place that most critics consider particularly unpromising.

After the brief introductory comments in chapter 1, Locke begins his analysis in the "Second Treatise" by arguing that men naturally are in

6. John Locke, "The Second Treatise of Government," in *Two Treatises of Government*, ed. Peter Laslett, 2d ed. (Cambridge University Press, 1967). All otherwise unidentified references are to Locke's "Second Treatise" in Laslett's edition, by section and line number. For example, the reference in the next paragraph is s. 4, 1–8—that is, section 4, lines 1 through 8.

"a *State of perfect Freedom*" and "a *State* also *of Equality*" (s. 4, 1–8). This state of nature, however, albeit a state of "perfect Freedom," is not a state of license: "The *State of Nature* has a Law of Nature to govern it, which obliges every one: And Reason, which is that Law, teaches all Mankind . . . that being all equal and independent, no one ought to harm another in his Life, Health, Liberty, or Possessions" (s. 6, 6–10). Locke argues, in other words, that each person not only is naturally free and equal but also has natural *rights* to freedom and equality.[7]

In addition, all men in the state of nature hold a natural right to execute the natural law (ss. 7–11)—in effect, a right to protect one's natural rights through individual or collective self-help. Partiality, "Ill Nature, Passion and Revenge," however, will lead to abuses in executing the natural law. Such abuses will produce "Confusion and Disorder" and engender a desire to form civil society and government as a "Remedy for the Inconveniences of the State of Nature" (s. 13, 2–11).

To escape these "inconveniences," each, in conjunction with his fellows, contractually transfers to a public authority his individual right to execute the law of nature, thus creating a common judge on earth to settle disputes (ss. 87–89). This transfer, however, is conditional; it is limited by the ends for which it is made: to protect individual rights and freedoms from invasion and to secure their more effective guarantee. A government that systematically invades its subjects' rights is, according to Locke, due no obedience.

To use twentieth-century vocabulary, all human beings are born with natural or human rights to freedom and equality.[8] In the state of nature, however, the enjoyment of these rights is insecure. Society and the state are devices to guarantee a more secure enjoyment of human rights, and a government is legitimate (only) to the extent that it protects human rights through positive law and practice. This threefold commitment to equality, autonomy, and natural rights—rather than the conventional conception's emphasis on radical individualism, private property, and negative civil and political rights—is, I will argue, the essence of the liberal approach to human rights, from Locke to our own day.

7. See also ss. 7, 1–2; 54, 10–12; 87, 1–7; 95, 1–6; 123, 1–8.
8. I use the terms *natural rights* and *human rights* interchangeably. By using the term natural rights I do not, however, want to imply that natural or human rights are necessarily either absolute or transhistorical. For an attempt to construct a historically specific account of natural or human rights, based on an understanding of human nature as *both* naturally given and socially determined, see Jack Donnelly, *The Concept of Human Rights* (St. Martin's Press, 1985), pp. 27–44.

The Individual and Society

The very idea of human rights does entail a certain individualism. Human rights are those rights that one has simply as a human being, irrespective of one's membership or place in society. One's rights and duties cannot be fully, or even fundamentally, defined by one's place in society, whether that place is defined by birth, age, occupation, achievement, or class; each person, regardless of status or past actions, has certain fundamental human rights that ordinarily take priority over other moral and political claims and obligations. The idea of *human* rights, in other words, implies that there is a certain irreducible moral value in each individual human being.

The practice of *rights* implies a further type of individualism. A right provides a *title* to an "object" (condition, good, activity, or goal). A right also grounds *claims* with respect to the enjoyment of that object, claims that have a special force: in ordinary circumstances, rights claims take priority over ("trump") other justifications for action. Furthermore—and hence the essential individualism—rights and the claims they ground are largely under the control of the rights holder who, through the exercise of his or her rights, controls the relationships and obligations established by those rights.[9]

Thus human rights establish special and particularly strong obligations owed specifically and directly to each individual by every other person or group and, in particular, by the state.[10] Each person, simply as a human being, is specifically entitled to the treatment demanded by human rights.

Besides being an individual, one is of course a member of a family, a society, and other communities and associations, as well as a citizen of a state (at least in the contemporary world). For many people the particularities of such communal memberships are at least as important to the shape and meaning of their lives as the individuality protected by human rights. A standard charge against the conventional Western liberal conception of human rights, however, is that it cannot adequately encompass the communal aspect of human existence; liberalism's indi-

9. This analysis is developed in some detail in Donnelly, *Concept of Human Rights*, pp. 3–15.

10. This is in sharp contrast to the diffuse and impersonal demands of, for example, natural law, divine law, or the categorical imperative. See Jack Donnelly, "Natural Law and Right in Aquinas' Political Thought," *Western Political Quarterly*, vol. 33 (December 1980), pp. 520–35.

vidualism, it is argued, is a radical, competitive, atomizing individualism that is both phenomenologically inaccurate and morally indefensible:

The only reality liberalism perceives is the reality of the individual.[11]

The difficulties of modern liberal-democratic theory lie deeper than had been thought. . . . The original seventeenth-century individualism contained the central difficulty, which lay in its . . . conception of the individual as essentially the proprietor of his own person or capacities, owing nothing to society for them. The individual was seen neither as a moral whole, nor as part of a larger social whole, but as an owner of himself.[12]

The extreme version of this charge is that liberal rights theory is largely a crude device to guarantee individual self-preservation. "The individual is consumed by a desire for self-preservation in a state of nature."[13] As Strauss puts it, for Locke "the individual, the ego, [has] become the center and origin of the moral world," and "the most fundamental of all rights is therefore the right of self-preservation."[14]

Locke does indeed argue that "Men, being once born, have a right to their Preservation" (s. 25, 2), and he does speak of the "Fundamental, Sacred, and unalterable Law of *Self-Preservation*, for which they enter'd into Society" (s. 149, 24–25). But individual self-preservation is hardly

11. Asher Horowitz and Gad Horowitz, *"Everywhere They Are in Chains": Political Theory from Rousseau to Marx* (Scarborough, Ontario: Nelson Canada, 1988), p. 151.
12. Macpherson, *Political Theory of Possessive Individualism*, p. 3. See also Karl Marx and Frederick Engels, *Collected Works*, vol. 3: *Marx and Engels, 1843–44* (New York: International Publishers; Moscow: Progress Publishers, 1975), p. 162: "The so-called *rights of man* . . . are nothing but . . . the rights of egoistic man, of man separated from other men and from the community"; Ahmad Zaki Yamani, *Islamic Law and Contemporary Issues* (Jidda: The Saudi Publishing House, 1968), p. 15: "[The West] is so over-zealous in its defense of the individual's freedom, rights, and dignity, that it overlooks the acts of some individuals in exercising such rights in a way that jeopardizes the community"; and Asmarom Legesse, "Human Rights in African Political Culture," in Kenneth W. Thompson, ed., *The Moral Imperatives of Human Rights: A World Survey* (Washington, D.C.: University Press of America, 1980), p. 124: "There is a perpetual, and in our view obsessive, concern with the dignity of the individual, his worth, personal autonomy, and property." For a good selection of some of the major arguments in the liberalism-communitarian debate in contemporary American political theory, see Michael J. Sandel, ed., *Liberalism and Its Critics* (New York University Press, 1984).
13. Cobbah, "African Values and the Human Rights Debate," p. 314.
14. Strauss, *Natural Right and History*, pp. 248, 227.

the central element of Locke's theory. *Self*-preservation typically appears not alone but in conjunction with the right and duty to preserve all *mankind*; there are at least as many references in the "Second Treatise" to the preservation of *all* mankind as to individual self-preservation.[15] Locke argues that the preservation of all mankind (or society) is *the* fundamental law of nature:

> For *by the Fundamental Law of Nature, Man being to be preserved,* as much as possible, when all cannot be preserv'd, the safety of the Innocent is to be preferred [s. 16, 9–11].

> The *first and fundamental natural Law,* which is to govern even the Legislative it self, is *the preservation of the Society,* and (as far as will consist with the publick good) of every person in it [s. 134, 5–8].

> The *fundamental Law of Nature* being *the preservation of Mankind,* no Humane Sanction can be good, or valid against it [s. 135, 30–32].

> The Fundamental Law of Nature being, that all, as much as may be, should be preserved, it follows, that if there be not enough fully to *satisfy* both, *viz.* for the *Conqueror's Losses,* and Childrens Maintenance, he that hath, and to spare, must remit something of his full Satisfaction, and give way to the pressing and preferable Title of those, who are in danger to perish without it [s. 183, 22–28].[16]

Notice further that, in the first and last of these passages, the preservation of all takes priority over egoistic claims. Egoistic self-preservation is at best one strand in Locke's argument.

In the "Second Treatise" there is also a recurrent, if secondary, theme of natural sociability, of "the love, and want of Society" (s. 101, 4). Locke speaks of men "sharing all in one Community of Nature" (s. 6, 15–16), and in his account of the ends of political society he argues that "he and all the rest of *Mankind are one Community*" (s. 128, 5–6). In fact, the chapter entitled "Of Political or Civil Society" begins as follows:

15. See Locke, "Second Treatise," ss. 6, 19–22; 11, 11–16; 128, 3–4; 129, 1–4; 135, 10–12, 16–17; 143, 1–3; 171, 12–17. Locke treated self-preservation as both a right and duty. See, for example, ss. 6, 19; 168, 28–29. For the right and duty to preserve all mankind, without parallel references to self-preservation, see ss. 7, 2–4; 8, 17–18; 16, 9–11; 134, 5–8; 135, 30–32; 159, 17–19; 182, 6–7; 220, 5–6.

16. Compare with s. 171, 19–23. On special duties to preserve children, see also ss. 56, 10–11; 60, 16–19.

"God having made Man such a Creature, that, in his own Judgement, it was not good for him to be alone, put him under strong Obligations of Necessity, Convenience, and Inclination to drive him into *Society,* as well as fitted him with Understanding and Language to continue and enjoy it" (s. 77, 1–5).

Certainly self-preservation is an important part of Locke's account of both human nature and the ends of society. Avoiding the state of war, which threatens the preservation of both self and others, "is one great *reason of Mens putting themselves into Society"* (s. 21, 4). But it is (only) *one* reason; the preservation of all is given at least equal prominence. Furthermore, as discussed below, what is to be preserved is not merely life but also liberty and property.

Locke does see the individual as having interests separate from those of society, and, in the areas protected by human rights, he does give individual interests prima facie priority over those of society. But even for Locke the individual is *also* part of the natural community of mankind and, except in the state of nature, a member of society, a citizen of a state, and a member of other social groups—especially the family— as well.

Whether Locke strikes the proper balance between individual and society is arguable, but it is obvious that he does not simply sacrifice society to the individual. The very practice of rights implies—makes no sense unless it is embedded in—a cooperative social context.[17] Rights claims are, to be sure, adversarial, but even the most competitive of rights, if they are to have any chance of being regularly enjoyed, must be exercised in the context of cooperative social practices.

Private Property and the State

Human rights do provide individuals with inalienable entitlements that hold even against state and society. So long as the rights in question are not extravagant, there need be nothing socially corrosive about such individual rights. This, however, brings one to the second element in the conventional conception: the claim that liberalism not merely recognizes but privileges a right to largely unlimited individual accumulation of private property. Liberalism, so this argument runs, is committed

17. See R. E. Ewin, *Liberty, Community, and Justice* (Totowa, N.J.: Rowman and Littlefield, 1987).

to a radical, property-based individualism that Macpherson aptly calls "possessive individualism."[18] Because most other contemporary critics of possessive individualism draw heavily from Macpherson's account, it will be considered in some detail in what follows.

As Macpherson asserts, "Locke's case for the limited constitutional state is largely designed to support his argument for an individual natural right to unlimited private property. Defenders of the modern liberal state see, or sense, that that right is at the heart of their state."[19] Liberals, Macpherson argues, view human freedom simply as independence from the will of others, as freedom even from social relations with others except insofar as those relations rest on mutual, voluntary consent.[20] Individuals are viewed as proprietors of their persons and capacities with respect to which they owe nothing to society. Social relations are thus conceptualized as a series of voluntary market relations between individual proprietors and political society merely as a device to protect individual property and maintain the minimal order required for successfully engaging in market relations.

Macpherson is correct that the principal aim—or at least the principal conclusion—of the property chapter of the "Second Treatise" is to justify largely unlimited individual accumulation. Furthermore, Locke does, at many points, argue that the end of civil society is the preservation of property.[21] But possessive individualism is only one side of his theory, and the possessive individualist defenses of property, as will be seen, succeed only in particular contingent historical circumstances—circumstances that no longer exist in most of the world.

Property Accumulation

Locke begins chapter 5, "Of Property," by asking how private property can be justified if God has given the earth to man in common (s. 25). His answer is that the earth has been given to man to use for his comfort and support, and that use clearly requires appropriation (ss. 26; 35). Although the earth is given in common, moreover, one's person is one's own, to use as one sees fit (within the limits set by the law of

---

18. Macpherson, *Political Theory of Possessive Individualism.*

19. C. B. Macpherson, "Introduction," in John Locke, *Second Treatise of Government,* ed. C. B. Macpherson (Indianapolis: Hackett Publishing, 1980), pp. vii–viii.

20. Macpherson, *Political Theory of Possessive Individualism,* especially pp. 263–64.

21. See, for example, Locke, "Second Treatise," ss. 3, 1–3; 85, 15–16; 94, 22–23; 124, 1–3; 173, 6–8.

nature): "Every Man has a *Property* in his own *Person*. This no Body has any Right to but himself" (s. 27, 2–3). By laboring, one mixes the property one has in one's person with the common stock of nature, thus fixing a property in, and excluding others from, the resulting product (ss. 27–30). Because labor gives nearly all the value to any product (ss. 40–43), individual appropriation actually increases the stock effectively available to mankind (ss. 37; 44).

Natural law, Locke argues, sanctions such appropriation and is the basis for all positive property law (s. 30). But natural law also limits appropriation. One has a duty to labor productively (s. 32), to use the common stock of nature for human betterment, and a parallel right to appropriate whatever one can put to use,[22] but no more. "*God has given us all things richly,* I Tim. vi. 17. is the Voice of Reason confirmed by Inspiration. But how far has he given it to us? *To enjoy.* As much as any one can make use of to any advantage of life before it spoils; so much he may by his labour fix a Property in" (s. 31, 5–9).

The right to take only as much as one can use I will call the use limit on appropriation. The "spoilage" limit is simply a corollary of the use limit: if something spoils, it cannot be used. Locke's third limit on accumulation is introduced in the initial discussion of labor fixing a property: "*Labour* being the unquestionable Property of the Labourer, no Man but he can have a right to what that is once joyned to, *at least where there is enough, and as good left in common for others* [emphasis added]" (s. 27, 10–13). This "sufficiency" limit—that "enough, and as good" remain for others—recurs in at least five additional sections of the property chapter (ss. 33–37) and ensures that no one can complain of injury as a result of another's appropriation (ss 31; 33; 36), and that the use of some does not deny minimum equality for others.

Take (only) what you can use, and leave enough and as good for others. With such limits, it is difficult to see how one can object to Lockean property rights. But "Locke's astonishing achievement was to base the property right on natural right and natural law, and then to remove all the natural law limits from the property right."[23]

This transformation, which occurs in section 46 of the "Second Treatise," is brought about by the introduction of money: "Every one had a

---

22. Compare, for example, Locke, "Second Treatise," ss. 37, 39–41; 38, 3–5; 46, 7–9 with ss. 32, 10–19; 35, 18–19.

23. Macpherson, *Political Theory of Possessive Individualism,* p. 199.

Right (as hath been said) to as much as he could use" (s. 46, 8–9). Barter, however, can be no injury. And if one person will take a piece of gold in exchange for a useful item, no one is injured. That piece of gold, however, as opposed to, say, a measure of grain, will not spoil. Because it will not spoil, Locke argues, it can be accumulated without limit, "the *exceeding of the bounds of his* just *Property* not lying in the largeness of his Possession, but the perishing of any thing uselesly in it" (s. 46, 28–30). The tacit consent to the use of money implied by accepting it in exchange thus effectively circumvents the limits placed by natural law on individual accumulation.

Notice, however, that here Locke speaks only of the spoilage limit; the use and sufficiency limits are not taken into account. If there is an abundance of land (and other essential resources), such as existed in "the first Ages of the World" (s. 36, 11), each may take all that he can use while leaving enough and as good for others. This follows simply from the definition of abundance. Locke's frequent references to the abundance of America (for example, ss. 36, 18; 41, 1–6) and his argument that "there are still *great Tracts of Ground* to be found, which . . . *lie waste*" (s. 45, 19–22) suggest that he believed that abundance still prevailed,[24] at least on a global scale,[25] providing a contextual, empirical justification for his exclusive focus on the spoilage limit.

In our current world of scarcity, however, *we* must explicitly consider all three limits that natural law places on accumulation. *In conditions of material scarcity,* moreover, the defense of unlimited accumulation developed in the "Second Treatise" fails.

Consider once more the crucial conclusion: "the *exceeding of the bounds of his* just *Property* not lying in the largeness of his Possession,

---

24. I take Locke's apparent belief in abundance at face value. His occasional use of the past tense, however, when talking about abundance (for example, ss. 31, 12–13; 36, 33–39; 49, 1–3) might suggest that he was beginning to see the specter of scarcity on the horizon, in which case the assumption of abundance in the property chapter might be a bit more problematic, even blameworthy, than my account suggests.

25. Locke did, however, recognize the existence of local scarcity, most clearly in his explicit argument against enclosing the English commons, because "the remainder, after such inclosure, would not be as good to the rest" (s. 35, 8–9). One might also ask whether a defense of property that requires others to make a wrenching, even dangerous, move to America in order to acquire their share of the "enough and as good" that is left really is as unproblematic as Locke seems to believe. Again, I have given Locke the benefit of the doubt because my principal argument does not require a less sympathetic reading. I am grateful to Steve Leonard for several long discussions about this matter.

but the perishing of any thing uselesly in it" (s. 46, 28–30). Mere size, it is true, is not evidence of unjust accumulation. But, *on Locke's own argument*, the absence of spoilage alone is not sufficient evidence of just accumulation. We must also ask whether the accumulated property is being put to use and whether "enough and as good" has been left for others.

Although *use* is a slippery notion—adopting a broad and elastic definition, such as one that counts the pure pleasure of possession as use, may make the use limit largely a formality. It is clear that once a certain stage of scarcity has been reached, private appropriation simply will not leave either as much or as good for others. If justice in accumulation is to be secured in *all* circumstances, one must focus on the sufficiency limit, for it alone guarantees minimum equality and ensures that others are not injured by private appropriation.

The use and spoilage limits focus attention on the process of accumulation and on the person of the accumulator; sufficiency shifts attention to the resulting distributional pattern and the consequences of individual accumulation *for others*. Sufficiency thus requires one to ask not whether the accumulator acquired his or her wealth "fair and square," but whether his or her holding such wealth is just or fair to others.

When unlimited private accumulation threatens the very life of others—as it did in early industrial England, as it would do again today, even in the wealthy West, without state intervention, and as it certainly did for the very poorest in seventeenth-century England—Locke seems committed to not merely allowing but actually *requiring*, remedial political action (that is, limits on accumulation), even if that accumulation has satisfied the use and spoilage limits. Such arguments, as I suggest later, point toward a Lockean defense of economic and social human rights.

But what of the "tacit and voluntary consent" (s. 50, 6) to money? Locke is quite insistent that "the *Invention of Money*, and the tacit Agreement of Men to put a value on it, introduced (by Consent) larger Possessions, and a Right to them (s. 36, 37–39). However, as already noted, consent cannot cancel limits of natural law: "The *fundamental Law of Nature* being *the preservation of Mankind*, no Humane Sanction can be good, or valid against it." [26] In conditions of scarcity, unlimited accumulation simply will not leave "enough and as good" for others, as natural law requires. Therefore, to the extent that positive law allows

26. Locke, "Second Treatise," s. 135, 30–32. See also ss. 12, 16–19; 135, 23–27.

such accumulation in circumstances of scarcity, it is unjust and not to be obeyed.

This leaves an interpretative problem: must liberals, to the extent that they are Lockean, defend a right to unlimited accumulation? Critics such as Macpherson clearly believe that they must, and many self-professed liberals, over not merely generations but centuries, have indeed defended a largely unlimited right to property. But the use of "Lockean" arguments by Locke and some other defenders of private property is no more decisive than, for example, an attack on socialism based on Soviet practice that is backed by selective quotations from Marx.

The extent to which a theory has been put to use cannot be ignored, especially when that use can be plausibly traced to (at least part of) the original theoretical source. Locke did argue for unlimited accumulation, and contemporary libertarians can situate themselves within a tradition of thought and practice that goes back at least to Locke. But, as mentioned, there is also a very different strand in Locke's argument. Furthermore, this radical strand informs another quite different "Lockean" tradition, which runs through Thomas Paine to contemporary theorists such as Rawls and Dworkin and has been embodied in the welfare state.

If one's interests were purely historical or hermeneutical, one might stop here, with the demonstration of two competing strands in the liberal tradition that flow from Locke's "Second Treatise." But because Locke is cited as a representative, and a source, of the liberal tradition, one must move beyond descriptive or historical questions to deeper analytical or interpretative, and perhaps even moral, issues and ask whether there are grounds for choosing one of these strands over the other.

I would suggest that if one strand of a theory can be shown to be substantially more compatible with its central theoretical premises, then that strand deserves interpretative priority. By such a test, the "best" interpretation of Locke (and liberalism) will give priority to the limits on accumulation.

Recall the starting point of Locke's theory: the natural freedom and equality of all men, within the limits of the law of nature (which enjoins respect for that freedom and equality). Recall also Locke's conception of a legitimate society: one that secures enjoyment of the rights and privileges of nature (which cannot be securely enjoyed in the state of nature). Restrictions on the right of individual accumulation clearly are required by these fundamental theoretical presuppositions: in many cases unlimited accumulation would violate Locke's natural law and threaten not merely the freedom and equality of the propertyless but their very existence.

The argument for unlimited accumulation is valid, on Locke's own terms, only in conditions of abundance. Even accepting that there was global abundance in Locke's time, as he seemed to believe, scarcity is the rule today. Locke's defense of unlimited accumulation is, thus, at best an argument applicable only to a bygone era. The property chapter of the "Second Treatise" simply does not justify a universal right to unlimited accumulation. Liberals today, therefore, are—on Lockean grounds—under no obligation to defend such a right.

Lockean liberals may, as I suggested earlier, actually be obligated to deny claims of right to unlimited accumulation in conditions of scarcity. Liberals are simply not necessarily committed to privileging a right to unlimited individual accumulation of private property. Quite the contrary: Locke's "Second Treatise" provides the resources for—even demands—an attack on unlimited accumulation in the conditions of scarcity that prevail today.

Property and the Ends of Government

Although Locke does not privilege a right to *unlimited* accumulation, he does repeatedly claim that the purpose of society and government is to preserve property. Such passages do suggest that he privileges a more limited right to property; thus Locke may be a "possessive individualist" in a somewhat more limited sense of that term.

But Locke repeatedly states that by "property" in such contexts he means men's lives, liberties, and estates, not merely their possessions:

> He seeks out, and is willing to joyn in Society with others who are already united, or have a mind to unite for the mutual *Preservation* of their Lives, Liberties and Estates, which I call by the general Name, *Property* [s. 123, 14–17].

> to preserve his Property, that is, his Life, Liberty and Estate [s. 87, 5].

> (By *Property* I must be understood here, as in other places, to mean that Property which Men have in their Persons as well as Goods) [s. 173, 4–6].[27]

27. See also Locke, "Second Treatise," ss. 85, 12–15; 171, 15–17; 221, 4–8; 222, 16–21.

It is true that Locke often uses "property" in the sense of estates only, including in one discussion of the ends of government (ss. 138, 139). But Macpherson is simply wrong in his claim that "in his crucial argument on the limitation of the power of governments he [Locke] is clearly using property in the more usual sense of lands and goods."[28] Locke begins chapter 11, his principal discussion of the limits on state power, by arguing that the great end of entering society is the peaceful and secure enjoyment of property. The great means and instrument of achieving that end is government through settled laws. Therefore, establishing the legislative power is "the *first and fundamental positive Law* of all Commonwealths . . . as the *first and fundamental natural Law*, which is to govern even the Legislative it self, is *the preservation of the Society*, and (as far as will consist with the publick good) of every person in it" (s. 134, 4–8). We have already seen above how this line of argument undercuts the charge of atomistic individualism.

Locke then begins to list the limits of the legislative power implied by this end of preserving property.

> *First*, It is *not*, nor can possibly be absolutely *Arbitrary* over the Lives and Fortunes of the People. . . . [The legislative] Power in the utmost Bounds of it, is *limited to the publick good* of the Society. It is a Power, that hath no other end but preservation, and therefore can never have a right to destroy, enslave, or designedly to impoverish the Subjects [s. 135, 4–5, 19–23].

Notice the clear presence here of the triple definition of lives (destroy), liberties (enslave), and estates (impoverish). And in this section as well, the fundamental natural law of the preservation of all mankind is prominently featured.

Locke's second limit requires the legislature to rule "*by promulgated standing Laws, and known Authoris'd Judges*" (s. 136, 4) to ensure that it will fulfill its charge "to determine the Rights, and fence the Properties of those that live under it" (s. 136, 9–10). Otherwise, "their Peace, Quiet, and Property will still be at the same uncertainty, as it was in the state of Nature" (s. 136, 23–24). Property here includes estates only, but it is explicitly linked, through the reference to peace and quiet, to the other elements of the broader definition.

Locke here also explicitly states that the purpose of government is to

28. Macpherson, *Political Theory of Possessive Individualism*, p. 198.

determine (*all*) the rights of the citizens, not just to fence their properties (estates). In the following section as well, he repeats the central claim that the reason men enter society is "to preserve their Lives, Liberties and Fortunes; and by *stated Rules* of Right and Property to secure their Peace and Quiet" (s. 137, 4–6).[29] Without such protections, "their Persons and Estates" would be subject to arbitrary power (s. 136, 4–6, 9).

Only after all of this, as a third limit on the legislature, does one come to the passages (ss. 138–39) that Macpherson emphasized almost exclusively:[30] "*Thirdly,* The *Supream Power cannot take* from any Man any part of his *Property* without his own consent" (s. 138, 1–2). Locke is indeed speaking here about the preservation of estates only, but Macpherson is simply wrong in his claim that these are the chief passages on the ends of government. They are quite explicitly subsidiary. In all the crucial passages, and even in most of the minor passages as well, lives, liberties and estates constitute the full meaning Locke clearly attaches to "property" when he specifies it to be the end of government.[31]

Furthermore, because property in the sense of estates alone is part of the broader definition, it seems most appropriate to read those rare passages that reflect the estates-only sense as simply partial accounts of the ends of government. Occasionally Locke does refer to estates only. But, as seen, he also sometimes talks of lives only (for example, s. 149, 24–25). At times he even talks about lives and liberties together, without reference to estates (for example, s. 66, 23). Even though Locke at points talks about the parts separately, these are, quite explicitly, only

29. Notice, again, that Locke says rules of right *and property*. Here, as in most other places where Locke uses "property" in the narrow sense of estates when discussing the ends of government, he speaks of rights (or right) generally *and* property, not of property alone.

30. Macpherson, *Political Theory of Possessive Individualism*, p. 198, note 6.

31. See also Locke, "Second Treatise," ss. 123, 13–17; 173, 1–8. Note also that the lives, liberties, and estates occur at several points throughout the work (for example, ss. 57, 25; 59, 29–30; 65, 30–32; 69, 14; 209, 5–6), along with such similar or equivalent formulations as "Peace, Liberties, and Fortunes" (s. 75, 16–17); "Life, Liberty or Possession" (s. 135, 15), "Life, Health, Liberty, or Possessions" (s. 6, 9–10); "the Life, the Liberty, Health, Limb or Goods" (s. 6, 24–25). See also ss. 95, 7; 120, 15; 123, 2; 171, 18–19; 74,10. Furthermore, there are passages (for example, ss. 3, 1–3; 87, 10–11; 94, 22–23; 127, 5–9; 199) linking society and the preservation of property in which property is not defined. In almost all these passages, the broad definition of property makes at least as much sense as the narrow definition. See also the discussion of the slave as one incapable of having property (ss. 173–74), which makes little sense except under the broad definition of property.

parts of the broader whole; that is, estates are only one part of the "property" that government is created, and obliged, to protect.

Locke also offers several alternative formulations of the ends of politics that make sense only within a broad interpretation of property as roughly equivalent to *all* natural rights. The very last words of the chapter on the ends of political society are, "And all this to be directed to no other *end*, but the *Peace, Safety,* and *publick good* of the People" (s. 131, 20–21). As seen, there are several passages in which Locke argues that "the *end of Government* [is] the *preservation of all*" (s. 159, 26–27). In the discussion of the dissolution of government, moreover, he argues that "where there is no longer the administration of Justice, for the securing of Mens Rights . . . there certainly is *no Government left*" (s. 219, 10–14).

I would thus suggest that a reading of Locke in line with the radical conception of liberation is to be preferred to Macpherson's minimalist reading. But before leaving the topic of property, let me to try make clear precisely what I have—and more important, have not—argued.

I have not denied that John Locke attempts to justify an unlimited right to individual accumulation. I have not denied that many self-professed liberals do privilege a right to property. And I have not denied that the historical record of the liberal democratic West—especially before the twentieth century and, until quite recently, in its relations with the third world in particular—has given inordinate emphasis to individual property rights. Rather, I have argued that even in the "Second Treatise," one of the two central texts (along with Thomas Hobbes's *Leviathan*) to which the theory of possessive individualism is traced, there is another strand to the argument that is *at least* as important. The liberal tradition, even in its seventeenth-century roots, possesses theoretical resources that allow—and I would argue require—a broader, more truly human approach to human rights.[32]

Positive Rights

The third element in the conventional conception of liberalism is the argument that the liberal tradition recognizes only "negative" (especially civil and political) rights. Henry Shue has shown that the nega-

---

32. To be absolutely clear, let me also note that I have not tried, and in the remainder of the discussion of Locke will not try, to present a completely "balanced" picture. Rather, I have emphasized those parts of Locke's theory that reveal theoretical resources, and thus a richness and plausibility, that are denied the liberal tradition by the conventional conception—without, I hope, having distorted the whole in any significant way.

tive-positive rights distinction is artificial and incorrect;[33] virtually all rights have both positive and negative correlative duties.[34] Let us grant, however, that in many ordinary circumstances many rights entail *primarily* positive or *primarily* negative correlative duties.

The liberal tradition has indeed given considerable—often preponderant—emphasis to primarily negative rights. Even today, it is mainly defenders of liberal democratic rule who emphasize "negative" civil and political rights; most other theoretical perspectives and social systems devote the bulk of their attention to duties and to "positive" rights and protections. Locke in particular does emphasize that protecting the lives, liberties, and estates of citizens requires restraint—negative action—on the part of the government: the government may not destroy, enslave, or impoverish its citizens (s. 135, 22–23); it must not *interfere* with their lives, liberties, or estates except in very limited circumstances. In many cases Locke even defines liberty as the absence of dependence on the will of others (for example, s. 4, 3–6).

But Locke also has a much more positive conception of liberty:

> *Freedom* then is not what Sir R[obert] F[ilmer] tells us. . . . *A Liberty for every one to do what he lists, to live as he pleases, and not to be tyed by any Laws*: But *Freedom of Men under Government*, is, to have a standing Rule to live by, common to every one of that Society, and made by the Legislative Power erected in it. . . . As *Freedom of Nature* is to be under no other restraint but the Law of Nature [s. 22, 8–16].

> *Law*, in its true Notion, is not so much the Limitation as *the direction of a free and intelligent Agent* to his proper Interest. . . . *The end of Law* is not to abolish or restrain, but *to preserve and enlarge Freedom* [s. 57, 10–12, 17–18].

Unlike Hobbes, who in *Leviathan* defines liberty in almost entirely negative terms (as absence of constraint), Locke's accounts include the limits of natural and civil law as *part* of, not a restriction on, liberty (see s. 6, 1–10).

33. Henry Shue, "Rights in the Light of Duties," in Peter G. Brown and Douglas MacLean, eds., *Human Rights and U.S. Foreign Policy* (Lexington, Mass.: Lexington Books, 1979), pp. 65–81; and Shue, *Basic Rights*, pp. 41–46.

34. See Charles Taylor, "What's Wrong with Negative Liberty," in Alan Ryan, ed., *The Idea of Freedom: Essays in Honour of Isaiah Berlin* (Oxford University Press, 1979), pp. 175–93; and Gerald C. MacCallum, Jr., "Negative and Positive Freedom," in Richard E. Flatham, ed., *Concepts in Social and Political Philosophy* (Macmillan, 1973), pp. 294–308.

The liberal commitment to personal autonomy does imply a considerable degree of freedom from external determination. The practice of rights does put considerable power in the hand of the individual rights holder, power that is often used to prevent external interference with individual choices. But to the extent that the core values of equality and autonomy require positive rights for their realization—for example, to protect the basic moral equality of despised and long-oppressed minorities—liberalism is not only free but also *committed* to embrace them.

Both liberty and equality can be plausibly interpreted in (primarily) negative, (primarily) positive, and mixed terms. The fundamental ideas of natural rights to freedom and equality simply do not demand a negative interpretation. Recall, also, that even Locke gave a prominent place to the principally positive, not negative, rights to political participation and private property.

Economic and Social Rights

Even if the positive-negative distinction is fully accepted, it does not match up with the distinction between civil and political rights and economic and social rights. For example, protection from torture in many states requires major positive initiatives by the government, and the right to political participation certainly is far more a positive than a negative right.[35] The argument that liberalism does—let alone can—only recognize civil and political rights is, therefore, clearly without basis. In fact, Locke's own defense of private property (estates) makes this abundantly clear: the right to private property is manifestly an economic or social, not a civil or political, right.

One might respond, however, that the point of the argument made by the conventional conception is that liberalism recognizes *only one* economic and social right, the right to property. This is at least an accurate description of Locke's "Second Treatise," and of most liberals until at least well into the nineteenth century. But I think it is clear that this is a conditional historical fact rather than an essential tenet of liberalism.

The fundamental natural law of the preservation of *all* mankind clearly allows the recognition of additional economic and social rights. Rights to food and health care would obviously serve this end better

---

35. See Shue, *Basic Rights*, pp. 41–46, and "Rights in the Light of Duties," pp. 69–71; and Donnelly, *Concept of Human Rights*, pp. 94–95.

than a right to private property (especially a right to unlimited accumulation). Furthermore, if it is recognized that liberty has a significant positive component—that is, that liberty is not merely the absence of restraint, but the genuine opportunity to choose a way of life—then economic and social rights are likely to be essential for establishing the material prerequisites for true freedom, especially for the propertyless. Likewise, if equality is interpreted as having a substantial positive component, economic and social rights are likely to follow as well.

More generally, there simply is no theoretical reason that liberals ought to—let alone must—restrict their understanding of either liberty or equality to civil and political relations, to the exclusion of the economic and social dimensions that are so important to both individual and social life. Not even Locke did that, as the triad of life, liberty, and estates indicates. It is impossible, moreover, to (consistently) exclude other economic and social rights.[36]

The commitment to private property, which has indeed been an important part of the liberal tradition, probably does rest in large part on a Lockean argument of entitlement: one is the proprietor of one's labor and thus the rightful owner of its products (insofar as natural law allows). It also reflects a recognition of the important sphere of autonomy that property can provide. The related preference for market mechanisms rests on the minimal (direct) interference with personal liberty entailed by market systems of production and distribution, along with considerations of efficiency (which became a central part of the tradition beginning with Adam Smith).

These liberal preferences, however, are just that: prima facie preferences that must give way to the basic rights and values of liberty and equality. Unless property is balanced by other human rights, and unless the market gives way when it infringes on human rights, one has not a liberal theory of human rights but a partisan, and quite crude, defense of class privilege.[37]

If government is to preserve the "property" of all, it should do precisely that: it must guarantee the life and liberty, as well as the justly held estates, of all individuals. Locke emphasizes the achievement of

36. Rhoda E. Howard and Jack Donnelly, "Human Dignity, Human Rights, and Political Regimes," *American Political Science Review,* vol. 80 (September 1986), pp. 806–07.

37. In many ways, this is the broader theoretical point, and the essential insight, of the theory of possessive individualism: to privilege a right to private property *is* to reduce human relations to market relations and to erode social bonds in favor of a clutching, competitive individualism.

this imperative through the protection of citizens against arbitrary political power. But there is no theoretical reason to preclude requiring the government to protect life and liberty from other threats, including the threats of economic scarcity and deprivation.

In human rights terms, this implies recognizing at least the rights to food and health care. I would argue, further, that life and liberty can probably be best protected from economic threats by a right to work. The right to work also has the special advantage, from a liberal perspective, of guaranteeing life and providing the material bases for liberty in a way that ensures at least some minimum of economic autonomy and equality.

I am, of course, well aware that I am taking liberal principles not only beyond where Locke took them, but well beyond where he would have been comfortable in going. My point simply is that John Locke's failure to pursue this particular development of his principles no more binds liberals to repeat his secondary theoretical choices (or even errors) than, for example, contemporary Aristotelians are bound to believe that some men are naturally slaves and that all women are rationally deficient, or contemporary utilitarians must accept Jeremy Bentham's particular catalog of pleasures and pains or John Stuart Mill's low opinion of "barbarian" races.

Liberalism is not a matter of a fixed set of canonical details set out in Locke or anywhere else; there is no set scripture or canon law in this tradition. Its essence is found instead in its fundamental principles—that is, in its commitments to equality and autonomy, and to protecting these values through human rights.

Theoretical traditions do have founders and seminal figures, but so long as a tradition is alive and not merely a ritual formality or a matter of antiquarian interest, it will evolve in response to the challenges and opportunities of new circumstances, criticism from within and from without, past errors, the unintended consequences of previous actions, and so forth. The only traditions that are static are dead, dying, or dogmatic. To insist on restricting liberalism to what Locke wrote and nothing more (or less) would be not to conduct an exercise in defense, fidelity, or even rational thinking, but to write the epitaph for that tradition or to participate in an unreflective, ritual affirmation of dogmatic faith.

The core values and fundamental principles of a tradition are, of course, contestable; their precise meaning, content, and implications are matters over which reasonable and thoughtful people not only may, but are likely to, disagree.[38] Political debate within a tradition is largely a matter of controversy over the proper understanding of the core values: in the case of liberalism, the values of equality, autonomy and human rights. As a living political tradition, liberalism—like all other traditions—is characterized by an evolving self-understanding of the meaning and implications of its central theoretical commitments.

Locke, Liberalism, and the Bourgeois Political Revolution

In discussing Locke and liberalism, only glancing attention has thus far been given to the revolutionary character of liberal ideas of natural rights. The "Second Treatise" was for the most part written before 1688, but it was in an important sense "produced"—in the way that a play is produced; that is, brought before the public—by the Glorious Revolution, and it concludes with a defense of the right to revolution.

That defense may not be all that rousing: Locke's right to revolution turns out to be restricted to a right of "society," which in effect means the majority of those qualified to vote. The Glorious Revolution may not have been all that "revolutionary," at least by today's standards, but it was a crucial step in the consolidation of the bourgeois political revolution in England, which was indeed a radical change from the Elizabethan political system of the beginning of the century. Locke's "Second Treatise," however sedate and "moderate" it may seem today, was a revolutionary document when it appeared in 1689.

Like most revolutionary tracts, however, it is strongest in its *negative* arguments—arguments against arbitrary rule, against absolute power, against unlimited royal prerogative, an unconditional duty to obey, the right of conquest, tyranny, usurpation, and so forth. Natural rights are used by Locke principally for criticizing inequality, privilege, and oppression under Stuart rule. They provide him with only a very vague and general model of what society ought to look like; the "Second Treatise" is much more about how society and government should *not* act than about how they should.

The specific revolutionary character of the "Second Treatise," however, also points to the particular historical limits of Locke's project, limits that arise to great extent from the limited aims of the bourgeois political revolution. For all the shortcomings of the conventional con-

38. See W. B. Gallie, *Philosophy and the Historical Understanding*, 2d ed. (Schocken Books, 1968), pp. 157–91.

ception as a general theory of liberalism, it does at least accurately highlight the fact that in the seventeenth and eighteenth centuries liberalism was principally about overthrowing traditional aristocratic rule and replacing it with bourgeois rule.

The bourgeoisie, who provided the principal support for early liberalism, demanded equality, simply as human beings, against the traditional inequalities of birth. Whatever the philosophical merits or shortcomings of this claim, it was undeniably in their interest to make it. The bourgeoisie demanded both political and economic liberty against royal prerogative, aristocratic privilege, and (both traditional and mercantilist) economic regulations. This too was in their interest. They emphasized their rights, in contrast to the traditional emphasis on duty; their individuality, based on an allegedly universal human nature, in contrast to traditional ascriptive and communitarian definitions of persons; and labor, accumulation, and property rather than leisure, display, consumption, and status. They also emphasized the limits on the state and the civil and political rights of the citizenry. And Locke gave one of the richest and most compelling defenses of these arguments in the entire liberal corpus.

It is therefore not merely fair, but informative, to say that *in the beginning* liberalism was the bourgeois revolution of the seventeenth and eighteenth centuries. It is also fair and informative to say that in the eighteenth and nineteenth centuries the *mainstream* of liberalism, both in theory and in practice, tended to lose its initially revolutionary character and to solidify into a new form of privilege, inequality, and oppression that was based on property rather than on birth.

But liberalism is not *merely* the bourgeois revolution or its fossilized remains. One must avoid the genetic fallacy in interpreting a theoretical tradition: its origins simply do not necessarily define—however much they may condition, constrain, or limit—its ultimate development. The original underlying principles of equality, autonomy, and natural rights could be, and indeed were, used by more radical liberal theorists, activists, and politicians to attack precisely this new form of class rule and inequality.

I would suggest that this implies that liberalism—or at least the radical strand of liberalism that I have stressed here—is essentially and inherently "revolutionary." Locke was only one of many liberals, for more than three centuries now, who have used, and continue to use, human rights arguments to rebel against injustice and oppression. It is not coincidental, therefore, that liberals are today contrasted with conservatives; liberals, from Locke to now, have been champions of rights-based political change. Human rights for liberals thus are primarily "negative" rights in a very different sense of that term: their principal use is to demand that old ways, however convenient or time honored, give way to the legitimate demands of the equal and inalienable rights of all human beings.

This "negative" character of human rights is, I would argue, not accidental but essential to their character as rights. As I have argued elsewhere, although we *have* human rights simply as human beings, human rights, like other rights, are *claimed*—put to use, actively advanced against duty bearers—principally when they are violated or at risk.[39] The principal use of human rights is to bring about political change. Thus the very idea of human rights commits their defenders to a politics of change, change for which human rights provide the model.

Postscript: From Locke to the Welfare State

I have focused my attention on Locke both because he is a seminal source of the liberal tradition and because the standard reading of Locke sees him (and thus Western liberalism) as fundamentally incompatible with international human rights standards (as embodied in such authoritative documents as the Universal Declaration of Human Rights and the two International Human Rights Covenants). Having demonstrated the existence, perhaps the primacy, of the radical conception of liberalism even in Locke, I think there can be little quarrel with my broader claims that Western liberalism is the source of the contemporary idea of human rights and that a (radical or social democratic) liberal regime is demanded by international human rights standards.[40]

Let me add, however, that this radical or social democratic strand of liberalism is not merely a theoretical ideal. It has been embodied in practice in most Western liberal democratic states. Whether the concern is with economic and social rights or civil and political rights—and especially if the concern is with both sets of interdependent and indivisible human rights—it is in the liberal democratic regimes of Western Europe that human rights have been most fully realized in practice.

39. Donnelly, *Concept of Human Rights*, pp. 11–26.
40. For a somewhat detailed defense of these arguments, see Jack Donnelly, "Human Rights and Human Dignity: An Analytic Critique of Non-Western Conceptions of Human Rights," *American Political Science Review*, vol. 76 (June 1982), pp. 303–16; and Howard and Donnelly, "Human Dignity, Human Rights, and Political Regimes," pp. 801–17.

Furthermore, the social democratic strand of liberalism was fairly well developed in the theoretical tradition backing the emerging working class struggle against capitalism at least half a century before Karl Marx. For example, Thomas Paine in *The Rights of Man* (part 2), advocated a state-funded system of social security, and in *Agrarian Justice* developed a strong argument for a variety of economic and social rights.[41] It would be another century or more until positive economic and social rights became firmly established within the mainstream of liberal practice, but the struggle for these rights was part of the radical strand of liberalism well before the emergence of revolutionary socialist parties in the mid-nineteenth century.

I do not want to deny the horrors that have been committed in the name of liberalism (understood as the political complement to an economic system of unlimited capitalist accumulation), both in the West and in the third world. But all doctrines have been abused by dictators and tyrants; consider, for example, the fate of socialism in the hands of Joseph Stalin, or of traditional African values in the hands of Francisco Macias Nguema (in Equatorial Guinea). In the case of liberalism, however, there is a long tradition of theory *and practice*, culminating in the social democratic welfare state of today, that suggests that liberalism is the source not only of contemporary human rights ideas but of the type of political system that is best able to realize those rights in practice.

41. For an excellent discussion of the crucial role of Paine in the emergence of the English working class movement at the end of the eighteenth century, see E. P. Thompson, *The Making of the English Working Class* (Pantheon Books, 1964), pp. 86–113.

Part Two
Religious Perspectives

CHAPTER FOUR

A Christian Perspective on Human Rights

David Little

JUST AS Christians have many ways of expressing their beliefs, their attitudes toward human rights vary widely. Some Christians do not believe in universal human rights at all. Stanley Hauerwas, the contemporary theologian, represents a tradition of long-standing skepticism, especially in Protestant circles, concerning the existence of a common "natural" morality that transcends cultural and religious diversity. Beliefs in universal human rights ignore the fact that "there is no actual universal morality," but rather "a fragmented world of many moralities."[1] Basic religious and moral commitments are the product of particular historical circumstances and convictions, and typically are incommensurable with one another.

Other Christians, with a less radical attitude, regard existing human rights norms with ambivalence. Without challenging the relevance and accessibility of universal standards, some contend that prevalent beliefs in human rights are encumbered by certain fallacies produced by the Enlightenment, and by the excesses of Anglo-Saxon liberalism. For example, Latin American "liberation theologians," both Protestant and Catholic, have argued that the third world needs to create an alternative language concerning human rights.

Such a language would replace the bourgeois liberal emphasis on individual liberty and private property—frequently emphasized by North Americans and West Europeans with a primary concern for economic rights. These would be conceived of as "the fundamental rights to life and the means of life," which are considered a necessary condition for the satisfaction of all other rights.[2] Toward that end, liberation

---

1. Stanley Hauerwas, *The Peaceable Kingdom: A Primer in Christian Ethics* (University of Notre Dame Press, 1983), p. 63.

2. See Hugo Assmann, "El Tercer Mundo Comienza a Crear un Lenguaje Alternativo Sobre los Derechos Humanos," in Hugo Assmann, ed., *Carter y la Lógica del Imperialismo,*

theology frequently draws on collectivist themes represented by Marxist philosophy, contending that such an emphasis corresponds more consistently with the central message of the New Testament than does the concern for self-interest believed to be associated with the liberal individualism of John Locke.

Sharing the same antipathy toward "an almost unqualified individualist bias" purportedly typical of current Western secular interpretations of human rights, other Christians, including the Protestant theologian Max Stackhouse, offer still different perspectives. Stackhouse holds that collectivism, Marxist or otherwise, is no real corrective to the excesses of liberalism. The solution is to place the discussion of human rights in the context of "biblical and theological materials," organized specifically around the idea of a religious covenant between God and human beings. Only then, Stackhouse asserts, will the proper basis of human rights become clear: "the *bonding of persons* to others *under God's law, for God's Kingdom, empowered by God's love.*"[3]

Contemporary North American Catholic theologians such as Lisa Cahill and David Hollenbach affirm the need to place the discussion of human rights in "the transcendent framework of Christian theology," as Cahill puts it, to counteract the alleged liabilities of the liberal tradition.[4] Rather than emphasize the idea of covenant, these thinkers highlight the notion of a common good, theologically conceived. In such a view, "rights are not spoken of primarily as individual claims against other individuals or society. They are woven into a concept of community which envisions the person as a part, a sacred part, of the whole. Rights exist within and are relative to a historical and social context and are intelligible only in terms of the obligations of individuals to other persons."[5]

Father Hollenbach comes to similar conclusions:

---

vol. 2 (San José, Costa Rica: Editorial Universitaria Centroamericana, 1978), pp 451–56; quotation is on p. 455.

3. Max Stackhouse, "A Protestant Perspective on the Woodstock Human Rights Project," in Alfred Hennelly, S.J., and John Langan, S.J., eds., *Human Rights in the Americas: The Struggle for Consensus* (Georgetown University Press, 1982), pp. 144–46.

4. Lisa Sowle Cahill, "Toward a Christian Theory of Human Rights," *Journal of Religious Ethics*, vol. 8 (1980), p. 285. See also David Hollenbach, S.J., *Claims in Conflict: Retrieving and Renewing the Catholic Human Rights Tradition* (New York: Paulist Press, 1979), especially pp. 107–37.

5. Cahill, "Toward a Christian Theory of Human Rights," p. 284.

All the doctrines and symbols of the Christian faith—creation of all persons by the one God, the universal graciousness of God toward all, the redemption of all by Christ, and the call of all persons to share in the mystery of Christ's death and resurrection—all these are the foundation of a conception of mutual love and human solidarity that is richer than any philosophical or empirical discussion of the mutual obligations of human beings toward each other, whether liberal or Marxist. It is deeper precisely because it is based on a claim about the ultimate meaning of human community. This religious perspective is leading the Catholic rights theory to an intensified emphasis on human solidarity as the precondition for any adequate theory of human rights. It is moving social rights to the center of recent Catholic discussions of human rights. Those rights which guarantee access of all to participation in the political, economic and cultural life of society have a priority in the most recent phase to the Catholic tradition.[6]

In short, Christians are clearly not of one mind about whether there are such things as human rights, and, if so, about their nature, basis, and scope. In one sense, therefore, it is impossible to speak univocally of the relation between Christianity and human rights. Different views of Christianity go together with different conceptions of human rights.

In another, strictly historical sense, however, the connection is more determinate. So far as existing human rights formulations derive from the philosophy of "natural rights" associated with John Locke, it is possible to trace connections to one particular strand of Christian belief: the tradition of radical Calvinism embodied in European and British religious movements that culminated in certain seventeenth-century Puritan sects. Their thought directly anticipated Locke's theory of fundamental moral rights and duties.

For several reasons, there is special virtue in exploring this historical linkage. First, as the survey above reveals, Christian theologians, in commenting on human rights, often react to what they take to be natural rights liberalism. However negative the reaction, they thereby acknowledge the centrality of that point of view. The problem is, they usually react without investigating in much depth what Locke and his associates and forerunners actually believed. Thanks to an abundance of new, illuminating scholarship concerning Locke and the background from which he wrote, it is now possible to demonstrate both how in-

6. Hollenbach, *Claims in Conflict*, p. 132.

compatible Locke's ideas are with the stereotypes applied to him, and how far familiar "liberal" interpretations of human rights deviate from Locke's original ideas. Obviously, if Locke's views are to be corrected, a fair reading of those views is a necessary first step.

Second, many—especially contemporary secular interpreters—do not sufficiently appreciate the deep interconnections of Locke's ideas and certain explicitly Christian beliefs, nor how those beliefs shaped his particular arguments about political obligations and natural rights. If Locke does create some room for a nonreligious foundation of rights, as modern observers tend to emphasize,[7] his assumptions nevertheless derive from well-established lines of thinking within the Christian tradition. They are not a rejection of that tradition. Accordingly, any serious discussion of Christianity and human rights must devote careful attention to Locke's ideas and to the sources of those ideas in Calvinism and earlier—even if, of course, it need not end with them.

The Natural Rights Philosophy of John Locke

Locke's understanding of natural rights and duties only makes sense as an application and elaboration of certain traditional Christian ideas. As such, it is neither as detached from religious belief nor as committed to self-interested bourgeois individualism as is conventionally believed.

The Role of Religion

There can be no doubt that, whatever the complexities of Locke's theory, religious conviction is at the center of his reflection:

There is indeed one science . . . incomparably above all the rest . . . I mean theology, which, containing the knowledge of God and his creatures, our duty to him and our fellow creatures and a view of our

7. Jack Donnelly, "Human Rights and Human Dignity: An Analytic Critique of Non-Western Conceptions of Human Rights," *American Political Science Review,* vol. 76 (June 1982), p. 305 (especially note 7), appears to associate nontheistic theories of rights with the Lockean tradition, which is, as will be seen, partially correct. Still, this familiar claim is misleading in two respects. It entirely ignores the explicitly religious appeals as a basis for rights that are prominent in Locke's writings; and it fails to recognize that the "secular" emphasis, such as it is, represents an application of certain traditional Christian teachings rather than a disavowal of the Christian tradition. The classical examples of the thesis of Locke as secularist are found in George H. Sabine, *A History of Political Theory,* 3d ed. (Holt, Rinehart and Winston, 1961), pp. 518–19; and Franklin L. Baumer, *Religion and the Rise of Scepticism* (Harcourt, Brace, 1960), pp. 57–58, 94–95.

present and future state, is the comprehension of all other knowledge directed to its true end, i.e, the honour and veneration of the Creator and the happiness of mankind. This is that noble study which is every man's duty and everyone that can be called a rational creature is capable of.[8]

Locke frequently restates the proposition laid down in his *Essay Concerning Human Understanding* that "the true ground of morality . . . can only be the will and law of a God,"[9] because "ultimately, all obligation leads back to God, and we are bound to show ourselves obedient to the authority of His will because both our being and our work depend on His will, since we have received these from Him, and so we are bound to observe the limits He prescribes."[10]

In particular, the idea of the law of nature, the idea that underlies Locke's theory of natural rights, itself has a religious grounding. The law of nature, which is "discernible by the light of nature and indicat[es] what is and what is not in conformity with rational nature," "can be described as being the decree of the divine will."[11] He goes on:

[The law of nature] appears to me less correctly termed by some people the dictate of reason, since reason does not so much establish and pronounce [it] as search for it and discover it as a law enacted by a superior power and implanted in our hearts. Neither is reason so much the maker of that law as its interpreter, unless, violating the dignity of the supreme legislator, we wish to make reason responsible for that received law which it merely investigates; nor indeed can reason give us laws, since it is only a faculty of our mind and part of us. Hence it is pretty clear that all the requisites of a law are found in natural law. For, in the first place, it is the decree of a superior will, wherein the formal cause of a law appears to consist. . . . Secondly, it lays down what is and what is not to be done, which is the proper function of a law. Thirdly, it binds men, for it contains in itself all that is requisite to create an obligation. Though, no doubt, it is not made

8. *John Locke's "Of the Conduct of the Understanding,"* ed. Francis W. Garforth (Teachers College Press, Columbia University, 1966), para. 23, p. 77.

9. John Locke, *An Essay Concerning Human Understanding,* ed. Alexander Campbell Fraser, 2 vols. (New York: Dover, 1959), book 1, chap. 2, para. 6. See also book 1, chap. 2, para. 18.

10. John Locke, *Essays on the Law of Nature,* ed. W. von Leyden (Oxford: Clarendon, 1954), p. 183.

11. Locke, *Essays on the Law of Nature,* p. 111.

known in the same way as positive laws, it is sufficiently known to men . . . because it can be perceived by the light of nature alone [pp. 111, 113].

There can be no serious doubt that religion plays a central role in Locke's thought, but scholarly dispute exists about *how* it functions. The issue is the status of reason in regard to knowing the grounds and content of the moral law. On the one hand, Locke argues that reason, working in conjunction with sense-experience, "lead[s] us to the knowledge of natural law" simply by reflecting on what it means to be governed by law. To recognize that one is bound by law is, Locke says, to "know beforehand that there is a law-maker, i.e. some superior power to which [one] is rightly subject":[12]

The originall & foundation of all Law is dependency. A dependent intelligent being is under the power & direction & dominion of him on whom he dependes & must be for the ends appointed him by [the] superior being. If man were independent he could have noe law but his own will [,] noe end but himself. He would be a god to himself, & [the] satisfaction of his own will the sole measure & end of all his actions.[13]

Moreover, on this line of thinking, reason, informed by sense-experience, is both required and capable of concluding that God's authority "derive[s] partly from the divine wisdom of the law-maker, and partly from the right which the Creator has over His creation."[14] In other words, God's sovereignty is based not on divine caprice or arbitrary power, but on the fact, first, that the deity himself (as Locke would say) conforms to the canons of moral reason. "God is an holy, just, and righteous God," who is, like all humankind, bound by "eternal obligation."[15] Consequently, "*Grants, promises* and *Oaths* are *Bonds* that *hold*

12. Locke, *Essays on the Law of Nature*, p. 151.
13. John Locke, "Ethica B," cited in John Colman, *John Locke's Moral Philosophy* (Edinburgh University Press, 1983), p. 46.
14. Locke, *Essays on the Law of Nature*, p. 183.
15. John Locke, *The Reasonableness of Christianity*, with a *Discourse of Miracles* and part of *A Third Letter Concerning Toleration*, ed. I. T. Ramsey (Stanford University Press, 1958), p. 46.

the Almighty." [16] Second, God has authority by means of proprietary entitlement. Because acts of creation establish legitimate control over the created product, God rightly "owns" the world and therefore possesses dominion over it by reason of calling it into existence.

Although Locke frequently iterates that human reason is sufficient for apprehending the grounds and character of natural law, he is not altogether consistent.[17] One line of argument stresses the sufficiency of reason for recognizing the proper grounds and content of morality, by means of working back reflectively to the divine foundations of morality. A second line of argument, however, introduces the idea that reason is in and of itself seriously deficient when it comes to discovering the basis and content of morality. In this second line, Locke's view of reason is considerably more "disjointed" than in the first:

> Though the works of nature, in every part of them, sufficiently evidence a Deity; yet the world made so little use of their reason, that they saw him not, where, even by the impressions of himself, he was easy to be found. *Sense and lust blinded their minds in some, and a careless inadvertency in others, and fearful apprehensions in most.* . . . In this state of darkness and ignorance of the true God, vice and superstition held the world; nor could any help be had or hoped for from reason, which could not be heard, and was judged to have nothing to do in the case. . . . Experience shews that the knowledge of morality, by mere natural light (how agreeable soever it be to it), makes but a slow progress, and little advance in the world. *And the reason of*

16. John Locke, "The Second Treatise of Government," in *Two Treatises of Government,* ed. Peter Laslett, 2d ed. (Cambridge University Press, 1967), section 195 (hereafter s.). See also "Promises and Oaths . . . tye the infinite Deity" (Locke, "The First Treatise of Government," in *Two Treatises of Government,* s. 6); and Locke, *Reasonableness of Christianity,* p. 53.

17. I dissent here from Colman's conclusion that Locke's theory of moral obligation is consistently theological legalist; see Colman, *John Locke's Moral Philosophy,* chap. 2, especially p. 46. That is not to say that I entirely agree with Colman's chief antagonist, W. von Leyden, who argues that alongside a "voluntarist notion of law" there is "an *alternative* explanation," that is, "a purely rational foundation of ethics" (Von Leyden, "Introduction" to Locke's *Essays on the Law of Nature,* p. 52); Colman rejects von Leyden's thesis in *John Locke's Moral Philosophy,* pp. 32–42. Von Leyden correctly points to another line of reasoning in Locke's writings concerning the connection of reason and religious belief, a line that Colman does not sufficiently follow, but von Leyden goes too far when he characterizes Locke as being committed to a purely rational foundation of ethics, as though one part of Locke's thought could be cleanly divorced from another. As I read him, Locke's thinking on these subjects is less tidy than either author makes out, and, however divergent his patterns of thinking may have been, he never intended for them to be dissociated.

it is not hard to be found in men's necessities, passions, vices, and mistaken interests, which turn their thoughts another way. . . . ['*T*]*is plain in fact, that human reason unassisted, failed men in its great and proper business of morality.* It never, from unquestionable principles, by clear deductions, made out an entire body of the law of Nature. . . . '*Tis true, there is a law of nature*: but who is there that ever did, or undertook to give it us all entire, as a law; no more nor no less, than what was contained in, and had the obligation of that law? Who, ever made out all the parts of it, put them together, and shewed the world their obligation? Where was there any such code, that mankind might have recourse to, as their unerring rule, before Our Saviour's time? *If there was not, 'tis plain, there was need of one to give us such a morality.* . . . *Such a law of morality, Jesus Christ hath given us in the New Testament.*[18]

Locke develops this second line especially in *The Reasonableness of Christianity,* although strong echoes can also be found in "The Second Treatise of Government" as well.

The notion of reason described here is disjointed in the sense of having only partial and segmented capability as the result of the "fallen condition" of human beings. Reason can still grasp that there is a natural law—in other words, that there exist certain natural obligations and duties in a general sense. However, because of "vice and superstition" and "passions" and "mistaken interests," reason simultaneously discovers that it is incapable of deciphering of its own accord either the full reality of divine authority or the "entire body of the law of Nature." (Reason's appreciation of its own limitations is suggested by the statement excerpted above, that "'tis plain in fact, that human reason unassisted, failed men in its great and proper business of morality.") Finally, reason is deficient in empowering human beings to live up adequately even to those portions of the moral law that can be apprehended. ("The knowledge of morality, by mere natural light, . . . makes but a slow progress, and little advance in the world," p. 61.)

In all three of these respects, if reason is to fulfill its prescribed function in guiding practice, it will need to be assisted by religion. Thus, for Locke, the law of morality revealed in the life, death, and teachings of Jesus Christ supplements the various deficiencies characteristic of fallen

18. Locke, *Reasonableness of Christianity.* Selections are taken in sequence from pp. 57, 61, 63 (emphasis added).

humanity. In particular, Christ's coming provides the basis for the "new covenant," as Locke says. This new covenant between God and human beings promises a "gracious allowance" for the "defective righteousness" of all those who undertake to recommit themselves to the duties that were originally inscribed on human nature but that have subsequently been disobeyed or disregarded.[19]

In his *Essays on the Law of Nature*, Locke adopts the same disjointed understanding of reason. By means of the residual knowledge of the law of nature that human beings continue to possess, they know that "all men alike are friends of one another and are bound together by common interests."[20]

More precisely, they have knowledge of certain natural rights and duties that follow from one fundamental and unmistakable principle: "being all equal and independent, no one ought to harm another in his Life, Health, Liberty, or Possessions."[21] This nonharm principle implies that everyone has a right and a duty to protect himself against arbitrary threats to personal life, health, liberty, or possessions, as well as a right and a duty "to preserve Mankind in general," when the individual's "own Preservation comes not in competition." Moreover, these basic rights and duties of self-defense and limited beneficence, which are the consequence of membership in a natural moral community, entail that originally "the *Execution* of the Law of Nature is . . . put into every Mans hands, whereby every one has a right to punish the transgressors of that Law to such a Degree, as may hinder its Violation." In other words, to have a natural right is to possess inalienably an enforceable title or warrant to constrain the behavior of others in certain ways. Correlatively, to have a natural duty is to be bound inescapably to enforce, when necessary, one's rights, to refrain from "invading others Rights, and from doing hurt to one another," and "as much as [one] can," to advance "the Peace and *Preservation of all Mankind*."

But it is, of course, this prior and ineradicable moral knowledge, which may be said to constitute human nature, that becomes enfeebled in various ways as human beings attempt to put moral knowledge into practice. What human beings naturally ought to do, they naturally do not do. Locke describes the original state as follows:

---

19. Locke, *Reasonableness of Christianity*, p. 49.
20. See Locke, *Essays on the Law of Nature*, p. 163.
21. See Locke, "Second Treatise," ss. 6–8, for the citations contained in this paragraph.

Though the Law of Nature be plain and intelligible to all rational Creatures; yet Men being biassed by their Interest, as well as ignorant for want of study of it, are not apt to allow of it as a Law binding to them in the application of it to their particular Cases. . . . Secondly, In the State of Nature there wants *a known and indifferent Judge*, with Authority to determine all differences according to the established Law. For every one in that state being both Judge and Executioner of the Law of Nature, Men being partial to themselves, Passion and Revenge is very apt to carry them too far, and with too much heat, in their own Cases; as well as negligence, and unconcernedness, to make them too remiss, in other Mens.[22]

Just as human beings need religious assistance to overcome the moral and spiritual liabilities of their fallen state, so for a similar reason they need civil government. Being "biassed by their Interest" and "partial to themselves," through willful inattention to the law of nature, and carried away by "Passion and Revenge," they need to designate, and commit themselves to, governmental officials in order to compensate for these deficiencies. Such officials would be empowered to provide relatively impartial, disinterested service in regard to establishing, adjudicating, and executing "settled laws." They would thereby minimize the risks of the arbitrary exercise of power that invariably threatens the original condition in which human beings find themselves.[23]

Two things bear emphasizing. First, in this view, civil government serves a fundamentally moral purpose. It ought to be established and obeyed to compensate for inherent human deficiencies in perceiving and complying with the basic natural rights and duties that follow from the law of nature. The exercise of governmental power and authority is thus shaped inalterably by the moral requirements of the law of nature.[24] Accordingly, Locke's comments on the design of government, including the importance of division of powers, representative institutions, and majority rule, are intended to ensure the fidelity and accountability of government to basic moral standards.[25] Locke's posi-

---

22. Locke, "Second Treatise," ss. 124, 125.

23. See Locke, "Second Treatise," ss. 124, 125; see also ss. 13, 87–90.

24. "The *Municipal Laws* of Countries . . . are only so far right, as they are founded on the Law of Nature, by which they are to be regulated and interpreted." Locke, "Second Treatise," s. 12.

25. See Locke, "Second Treatise," ss. 13, 95–99, 154–59, for some of Locke's passing recommendations on the structure of government. His argument in favor of majority rule

tion is that individual citizens, having appreciated their need for government so as to compensate for the endemic moral deficiencies that plague them in the "state of nature," are rationally motivated to covenant together as a "people" for the purpose of committing themselves to civil institutions. Thus the primary "social contract" is among the citizens and is followed by a secondary, "fiduciary" arrangement with designated civil officials. These officials are understood to represent the people by undertaking to protect and advance the basic natural rights and duties of the citizens.[26]

Given that the people are the final sovereign in governmental affairs (s. 141), Locke infers a rather radical right of resistance against rulers who are perceived to violate the terms of the original trust conferred on them. In usual circumstances *"the People shall be Judge"* "whether the Prince or Legislative act contrary to their Trust":

> For who shall be Judge whether his Trustee or Deputy acts well, and according to the Trust reposed in him, but he who deputes him, and must, by having deputed him have still a Power to discard him, when he fails in his Trust? If this be reasonable in particular Cases of private Men, why should it be otherwise in that of the greatest moment; where the Welfare of Millions is concerned? [s. 240].

In extreme circumstances, however, Locke goes so far as to allow the right of individual rebellion "if any Men find themselves aggrieved, and think the Prince acts contrary to, or beyond that Trust." Where there is no possible appeal to "a Judge on Earth," then an individual has no recourse but to appeal "to Heaven." "In that State the *injured Party must judge* for himself, when he will think fit to make use of that Appeal, and put himself upon it" (s. 242).

Second, although the line of reasoning by which Locke establishes

---

(see s. 98) is in effect that, under real-world conditions, a majority is in general the most probable feasible approximation of unanimity that can be achieved. "Nothing but the consent of every individual can make any thing to be the act of the whole: But such a consent is next impossible ever to be had, if we consider the Infirmities of Health, and Avocations of Business, which in a number, though much less than that of a Commonwealth, will necessarily keep many away from the publick Assembly. To which . . . we [may] add the variety of Opinions, and contrariety of Interests, which unavoidably happen in all Collections of Men."

26. See Locke, "Second Treatise," ss. 95, 149, for Locke's discussion, respectively, of the primary "social contract" and the "delegated" status of civil authority. The next three citations are from this document, with section numbers given in the text.

the need for religious assistance with respect to the moral life is analogous to his reflections on the origins of government, he nevertheless differentiates between religious affairs and the affairs of civil government. In declaring that the "liberty of conscience is every man's natural right, equally belonging to dissenters as to [church members]; and that nobody ought to be compelled in matters of religion either by law or force," he sharply restricts the jurisdiction of civil authority.[27]

The idea is that civil government properly supervises and controls only "civil interest," that is, "life, liberty, health, . . . and the possession of outward things. . . . It is the duty of the civil magistrate, by the impartial execution of equal laws, to secure unto all the people in general, and to every one of his subjects in particular, the just possession of these things belonging to this life. . . . [T]herefore is the magistrate armed with the force and strength of all his subjects, in order to [effect] the punishment of those that violate any other man's rights" (p. 17). In supervising "outward things," the magistrate may employ outward means of enforcement—that is, physical "force and strength," including various forms of bodily coercion and confinement. Such authority follows from the prior agreement of citizens to ascribe to the civil magistrate the right to enforce the law, thereby avoiding the danger of arbitrary injury that exists when individuals enforce the law as they see fit.

By contrast, "the life and power of true religion consist in the inward and full persuasion of the mind; and faith is not faith without believing." In such matters, where the conscience alone has jurisdiction, the civil apparatus is entirely inappropriate: "Such is the nature of the understanding that it cannot be compelled to the belief of anything by outward force. Confiscation of estate, imprisonment, torments, nothing of that nature can have any such efficacy as to make men change the inward judgment that they have framed of things" (p. 18).

Locke's view seems to be that "inward" matters—matters of the "salvation of souls" and ultimate spiritual destiny—are by definition deeply personal, intimate matters. They involve questions of heartfelt commitment and conviction, and as such are subject to the diversity and variation of personal judgment in ways that "outward" matters—matters of civil interest—are not. Accordingly, because protection against arbitrary injury to "life, liberty, health, . . . and the possession of outward things"

---

27. John Locke, *A Letter Concerning Toleration*, 2d ed. (New York: Liberal Arts, 1955), p. 52. The citations from the rest of this section are from this book, with page numbers given in the text.

(p. 17) is a common interest, a "public good" (p. 36), shared by all human beings, general consensus and acquiescence is easier to achieve in the civil realm than it is in the realm of conscience.

Locke's assumptions about the civil realm as distinct from the realm of conscience also imply that there exists a range of natural or outward morality (as differentiated from religious morality or morality derived directly from revelation) that affords a common foundation on which to organize and conduct the affairs of civil government. So understood, the standard natural rights and duties Locke enunciates—protections against arbitrary taking of life, confinement, injury, and theft, as well as against violations of conscience—would all be grounded in a set of moral beliefs that take priority over and are relatively independent of any particular religious beliefs. In other words, individuals would be held accountable according to these basic rights and duties without regard to their religious views or lack of religious belief.

The phrase *relatively independent* demands stress when making statements like these about Locke's views. Although Locke clearly held that the basic natural rights and duties mentioned take priority over and are independent of specific religious beliefs—and would, therefore, be understood to constitute a common foundation for a religiously inclusive, pluralistic society—he nevertheless does declare Catholics, Muslims, and atheists to be unacceptable members of society. Locke excludes Catholics in part because they are unwilling to commit themselves to the sort of pluralistic system he advocates (p. 51). Although in one place he suggests that a "Mahometan" should not "be excluded from the civil rights of the commonwealth because of his religion" (p. 56), he does worry about the civil loyalty of Muslims insofar as they acknowledge themselves "bound to yield blind obedience to the Mufti of Constantinople, who himself is entirely obedient to the Ottoman Emperor" (pp. 51–52). Atheists are not to be trusted because the "taking away of God, *though but even in thought,* dissolves all" (p. 52, emphasis added). "Promises, covenants, and oaths, which are the bonds of human society, can have no hold upon an atheist" (p. 52).

The harsh judgments about Catholics and Muslims are understandable, in Locke's thinking, to the extent that either of these traditions claimed the right to total religious control over a society and would have required adherents to work to impose such control. There is, however, deeper ambiguity in Locke's thought in regard to atheism. If theological understanding is as open as Locke says to the diversity of individual judgment, both because of the fallibility of reason and the intimacy of religious matters, then it is not clear why atheism, among other beliefs, could not be experimented with so long as adherents did not outwardly violate the natural civil rights of others. Locke might still hold, as he clearly did, that reason, when it functions properly, requires a belief in God. It would seem, however, that judgments of that sort ought to be arrived at by the terms of the laws of reason—that is, freely—rather than by the terms of the law of the sword, given what Locke says about the workings of the inner realm of conscience. Accordingly, to deprive atheists of civil rights because of their beliefs would appear to disregard Locke's own warning against changing or violating any civil rights "upon account of religion." He specifically protects even idolaters so long as they do no injury to "neighbors and to the commonwealth" (p. 42). It is difficult to see, even on grounds of Locke's own thinking, why the same protection ought not apply to atheists.

Economic Rights

If the centrality and complexity of religiously oriented thinking must not be ignored in considering Locke's views, neither may Locke be described, as he so often is, as an unwavering advocate of rapacious bourgeois individualism.[28] It has already been seen that, contrary to certain popular impressions, Locke does not emphasize rights of self-preservation to the exclusion of the duties of beneficence. His list of natural rights and duties follows from membership in the human family, whose mutual responsibilities are indicated by one common law of nature according to which "[any individual] and all the rest of *Mankind are one Community*."[29]

It is true that Locke was committed to the new ideology of contract as it applied not only to political but also to economic, familial, and religious organizations. As regards economic life specifically, Locke's

28. Such an image of Locke was given special credence by C. B. Macpherson in his famous book *The Political Theory of Possessive Individualism: Hobbes to Locke* (Oxford: Clarendon, 1962), but Macpherson's views have been subjected to severe criticism by more recent Locke scholars. I have developed the arguments against Locke as bourgeois individualist with some care in my essay "Natural Rights and Human Rights: The International Imperative," in Robert P. Davidow, ed., *Natural Rights and Natural Law: The Legacy of George Mason* (George Mason University Press, 1986), especially pp. 80–89, and in an unpublished essay, "Common Good, the Protestant Ethic, and Economic Liberalism: The Foundations for a Reformed Theory of Taxation." A volume that provides an especially powerful case against the old stereotypes is James Tully, *A Discourse on Property: John Locke and His Adversaries* (Cambridge University Press, 1980).

29. Locke, "Second Treatise," s. 128.

writings stress the significance of occupational "calling," including the importance of hard, disciplined labor as a response to God's command. Indeed, in certain respects he is properly seen as a pioneer of the "spirit of capitalism."[30]

It is also true that Locke rather complacently justified substantial social and economic inequalities as maximizing general productivity. In the fifth chapter of the "Second Treatise," for example, he contends that an "overplus [of] Gold and Silver . . . may be hoarded up [by the well-to-do] without injury to any one" (s. 50). In some of his writings, Locke seems to have believed that maintaining workers at a subsistence level of wages would help to ensure the peace and stability necessary for increased productivity, a condition that would in turn, purportedly, maximize general benefit.[31]

But whatever one may think of these aspects of his economic thinking, Locke is emphatically not a philosophical egoist, nor does he minimize the importance of sustained regard to the public welfare. To the question "Is every man's own interest the basis of the law of nature?" he answers simply, "No."[32]

For if the source and origin of all this law is the care and preservation of oneself, virtue would seem to be not so much man's duty as his convenience, nor will anything be good except what is useful to him; and the observance of this law would be not so much our duty and obligation, to which we are bound by nature, as a privilege and an advantage, to which we are led by expediency. And thus, whenever it pleases us to claim our right and give way to our own inclinations, we can certainly disregard and transgress this law without blame, though perhaps not without disadvantage.[33]

This basic moral concern for more than just one's own advantage manifests itself in Locke's underlying ambivalence toward economic life.

30. John Dunn, *The Political Thought of John Locke: An Historical Account of the Argument of the "Two Treatises of Government"* (Cambridge University Press, 1969), p. 210. Tully's absolute claim that there is no basis in Locke's thought for "the capitalist" (*A Discourse on Property*, p. 137) is, I think, too extreme a view, although he is right to emphasize the modifications and qualifications of the doctrines of private property and free trade that do exist in Locke.

31. For a good discussion of the "dark side" of Locke's attitude toward day laborers, see Neal Wood, *John Locke and Agrarian Capitalism* (University of California Press, 1984), pp. 43–48.

32. See Locke, *Essays on the Law of Nature*, pp. 205–15.

33. Locke, *Essays on the Law of Nature*, p. 181.

With all the benefits of a money economy and of free enterprise, there were at the same time, he believed, enormous infirmities and temptations that he often depicted graphically. In the original state of nature, before the existence of money, there was "little matter for Covetousness or Ambition," little "Temptation to enlarge . . . Possessions of Land, or contest for wider extent of Ground."[34] But it is, he urges, precisely "Covetousness, and the Desire of having in our Possession, and under our Dominion, more than we have need of [that is] the Root of all Evil."[35] If not the cause, money "accentuate[s] many forms of human corruption"[36] and in that way undermines the common rights of access and enjoyment that are dictated by the law of nature. Thus, however complacent about "bourgeois inequities" Locke undoubtedly could be, these are not the sentiments of a consistently rapacious bourgeois individualist.

Nor do his comments about the natural common ownership of property, and the consequent claims that the poor may legitimately make against the affluent, mark such sentiments. "God . . . hath given the World . . . to Mankind in common," Locke writes, and therefore all human beings share exactly the same common rights in using the earth to preserve life. Each individual is entitled to use what is needful so long as everyone's equal need is respected: "The same Law of Nature, that does . . . give us Property, does also *bound* that *Property* too." Individuals may supply themselves with the necessities of survival, but because they must always observe the equal rights of others, they may not cause waste by taking more than they need, and they must leave "enough, and as good . . . in common for others."[37]

The idea here is that because property originally belongs to all in common, all individuals by birthright possess certain prior "inclusive rights" to it. In other words, everyone possesses an enforceable title, or what might be called a fair survival share, not to be excluded from access to the means of preservation and sustenance. Accordingly, all human beings have an inclusive natural right to use property for the sake of survival. "Exclusive rights" to property—that is, the authority to con-

34. Locke, "Second Treatise," ss. 107, 108; see also s. 111.

35. *The Educational Writings of John Locke*, ed. James L. Axtell (Cambridge University Press, 1968), p. 213.

36. Dunn, *Political Thought of John Locke*, p. 248. See also Tully, *Discourse on Property*, p. 150.

37. Locke, "Second Treatise," ss. 26, 31, 27.

trol or "have dominion" over the means of preservation and sustenance, and thereby to exclude others from one's "domain"—may be obtained, for example, by exerting "honest Industry" or by inheriting "the fair Acquisitions of [one's] Ancestors." Such control, however, rightfully exists only so long as everyone's inclusive rights are observed.[38]

Locke concedes that important changes in the distribution system occur with the advent of a money economy. Because money, unlike the fruits of nature, can be saved up without waste, a "disproportionate and unequal Possession of the Earth"[39] becomes permissible, particularly because such inequality allegedly stimulates general productivity, as noted above. At the same time, in the "First Treatise" Locke has only the harshest words for those who use their economic advantage to exploit and oppress fellow human beings:

> We know God hath not left one Man so to the Mercy of another, that he may starve him if he please: God the Lord and Father of of all, has given no one of his Children such a Property, in his peculiar Portion of the things of this World, but that he has given his needy Brother a Right to the Surplusage of his Goods; so that it cannot justly be denyed him, when his pressing Wants call for it. And therefore no Man could ever have a just Power over the Life of another, by Right of property in Land or Possessions; since 'twould always be a Sin in any Man of Estate, to let his Brother perish for want of affording him Relief out of his Plenty. As *Justice* gives every Man a Title to the product of his honest Industry, and the fair Acquisitions of his Ancestors descended to him; so *Charity* gives every Man a Title to so much out of another's Plenty, as will keep him from extream want, where he has no means to subsist otherwise; and a Man can no more justly make use of another's necessity, to force him to become his Vassal, by with-holding that Relief, God requires him to afford to the wants of his Brother, than he that has more strength can seize upon a weaker, master him to his Obedience, and with a Dagger at his Throat offer him Death or Slavery [s. 42].

38. Locke, "First Treatise," s. 42. See Tully, *Discourse on Property*, especially chaps. 3 and 5, for a generally excellent discussion of these matters. I am not entirely satisfied, however, with Tully's discussion of the "exclusive" or "private" rights to property that Locke understood to be acquired by performing "honest Industry." There is considerably more leeway here for the capitalist spirit than Tully concedes. See Locke, "Second Treatise," ss. 27, 28, 32.

39. Locke, "Second Treatise," s. 50.

In short, Locke's understanding is that the rights to private property, however unequally property may be distributed, are rigidly bounded by the initial conditions of the natural law, conditions requiring that the inclusive rights of *all* human beings be given priority.

The Calvinist Context of Locke's Thought

To describe Locke's *Two Treatises of Government* as "the classic text of radical Calvinist politics," as Quentin Skinner does, is properly to underscore the distinctive influence of northern European Calvinism on Locke's philosophy of natural rights.[40] Many of Locke's other writings which develop that philosophy—*Essays on the Law of Nature, The Reasonableness of Christianity*, and *A Letter Concerning Toleration*—ought to be interpreted similarly.

Locke's ideas are, to be sure, the direct product of radical seventeenth-century Calvinism, especially as manifest in Holland and England. That is not the same thing as the ideas and practices of John Calvin. Nor is it exactly equivalent to the thinking of the majority of Calvin's sixteenth-century followers in Geneva, France, Holland, England, and Scotland, nor of his more conservative seventeenth-century disciples in Europe and America.

Nevertheless, there are important lines of continuity between early Calvinism and its later forms that must not be overlooked. Whatever else it was, Calvin's Geneva of the sixteenth century was a powerful center of revolutionary politics. Both as a source of ideas and as an inspiration to action, its effects would long be felt in Europe, Great Britain, and America.

Calvin himself was deeply ambivalent about the consequences of political disturbance, and that spirit continued to be reflected in the Calvinist movement in various ways. Still, Calvin articulated the theological foundation and focus for a revolutionary impulse; what is more, he provided a gathering place in Geneva for exiled political activists, many of whom worked out their programs of agitation in collaboration with him, even if they sometimes exceeded his expressed wishes. All of this

---

40. Quentin Skinner, *The Foundations of Modern Political Thought*, vol. 2: *The Age of Reformation* (Cambridge University Press, 1978), p. 239. Despite this description, Skinner does not, in my view, apprehend the full influence of the Calvinist tradition on Locke, in part because of Skinner's improbable preoccupation with deflating the importance of Calvinism as a source of resistance theories and reducing its distinctive ideas and impulses to purely "secular" and pragmatic objectives.

was the intellectual basis for the radical politics of seventeenth-century England that so influenced Locke's theory of natural rights.

Background

It would, of course, be a mistake to imply that John Calvin was the sole originator of a theory of rights. Although Calvin played an important role in the development of that theory—particularly of the variety articulated by Locke—it is in medieval Western thought that the origins of a "modern rights theory" are to be discovered.[41] If "modern rights theory" means the belief in the existence of "subjective" rights, or rights that, above and independent of governmental authority, ascribe to individuals an enforceable title or warrant to constrain the behavior of others in the control of property, political participation, the exercise of conscience, and the like, then that belief apparently began to coalesce in medieval legal and theological thinking from the twelfth century onward.

Before that time, there did exist in legal and theological circles a developed idea of "objective right," synonymous with the concept of *ius naturale,* or natural right. That idea implied an invariant standard of righteousness, there to be discovered and applied to human conduct in general. Such natural law would, of course, prohibit various forms of doing harm, and would also require a variety of charitable acts.

Moreover, natural law was understood to constrain civil government, thereby providing the basis for an early form of constitutionalism. If the natural law was the norm of proper conduct for all human beings, then everyone's interest was necessarily promoted when that law was complied with, by rulers and everybody else. Indeed, it is a pervasive, if somewhat ambiguous, idea in medieval literature that a ruler exists to serve the common good of the people, as defined by natural law, and that political legitimacy therefore endures only as long as the people's good is achieved.[42]

41. See Richard Tuck, *Natural Rights Theories: Their Origin and Development* (Cambridge University Press, 1979), pp. 13–31. There is much of great value in this book, particularly regarding the medieval roots of the modern theory of rights. It is with Tuck's treatment of Calvinism that I have the most difficulty. Although I agree that [sixteenth-century] "Calvinists were not putting forward a theory of natural rights," I do not agree that they "were not particularly concerned with the notion of a right at all" (p. 43). As I will suggest, some of the important ingredients for a theory of rights existed in Calvinist thought as it developed in the sixteenth century.

42. See Sabine, *History of Political Theory,* especially pp. 198–263. See also Charles Howard McIlwain, *Constitutionalism: Ancient and Modern,* rev. ed. (Cornell University Press,

Nevertheless, the idea of objective right as such specified nothing in particular about the natural authority or "dominion" of individuals in regard to the possession of property, political participation, the exercise of conscience, or the permissibility of individual resistance to tyrannous rulers. There are hints of an idea of natural rights in the thought of the medieval theologian Thomas Aquinas, but he advanced no fully developed theory. Perhaps the strongest suggestion of a belief in individual rights can be found in his case for freedom of conscience. As Eric D'Arcy indicates, Thomas argues that because an individual's "act of faith is essentially a free act," it is "therefore not lawful to use compulsion in any way to force [nonbelievers] to accept the Christian faith."[43] He thereby implies a sharp restriction on the right of the state to exercise coercion against individuals in matters of inner conviction. If force may not legitimately be so applied, then, D'Arcy says, it follows that "the State is guilty of injustice if it interferes with a person's [obeying] conscience in matters of religious choice, profession and worship" (p. 185). Conversely, the state would appear to be acting justly by enforcing the free exercise of conscience. Such a consequence, in effect, ascribes a subjective right of conscience—that is, an enforceable title, individually claimable, to constrain the behavior of others against coercively interfering with conscience.[44] As we know, this line of thinking resonates in Locke's arguments about the right of free conscience.

There also may be the beginnings of an idea of natural rights in Thomas Aquinas's understanding of property, beginnings that appear directly to anticipate Locke's views.[45] For Thomas, following the church

---

1947), pp. 69–88. McIlwain points out the ambiguity in medieval theories of government found in the writings of Bracton, a thirteenth-century English thinker. On the one hand, "Bracton considered the oath taken by the kings of England at their coronation in some ways analogous to the *lex regia* by which the Roman emperors at their accession had received the *imperium* and *potestas* of the people" (p. 71); on the other hand, Bracton also seems to suggest that a ruler, once installed, approaches being a *solutus legibus*—a law unto himself. "The significant fact is that acts of government strictly defined are in the hands of the king alone. There he 'has no peer, much less a superior'" (p. 77).

43. Eric D'Arcy, *Conscience and Its Right to Freedom* (Sheed and Ward, 1961), pp. 153–54. D'Arcy makes a powerful case for believing that there exists in Thomas's thought the basis, at least, for a subjective right to freedom of conscience. See especially part 4, pp. 190–272.

44. This is but the bare bones of D'Arcy's subtle and elaborate argument. It ought also to be noted that Thomas harbors serious reservations about extending the right of conscience to apostates and heretics, since they have broken their promise to God and are thus liable for "breach of contract."

45. Tuck suggests that Thomas "must be reckoned to have had at least the basic concept of a right." *Natural Rights Theories,* p. 19.

fathers, nature was created for the common benefit of human beings, and its ownership ultimately resides with God. By divine sufferance, human beings naturally share a "common possession of things."[46] Thus it may be inferred that all individuals possess an "inclusive" claim to property in the sense that no one should be prohibited from gaining access to common property for preservation and sustenance.[47]

Even though there is no initial division of property according to natural law, individuals come to acquire "natural *dominium* over material things," as Thomas puts it, and thus obtain certain "exclusive rights" over them, by putting those things to use in the task of providing for preservation and sustenance.[48] If this is a correct reading, then the connections between Thomas Aquinas and Locke as regards the development of both inclusive and exclusive natural rights to property are important indeed.

The link between the two is further exemplified with respect to a natural right to assistance. Such a requirement follows from the idea of an inclusive right to property that prohibits exclusion of anyone from access to the basic means of sustenance. Tully points out that Locke's discussion is "strikingly similar" to Thomas's:

> Since a person has a property for the sake of preserving himself and others, once his own preservation is secured, any further use for enjoyment is conditional on the preservation of others. Locke, rather than undermining the traditional obligations associated with prop-

46. Thomas Aquinas, *Summa Theologica*, in *Aquinas: Selected Political Writings*, ed. A. P. D'Entrèves, trans. J. G. Dawson (Oxford: Basil Blackwell, 1959), pp. 169, 171.

47. Tully, *Discourse on Property*, p. 65.

48. Thomas Aquinas, *Summa Theologia*, 2a, 2ae, 66.1, quoted in Tuck, *Natural Rights Theories*, p. 19. Tuck suggests this reading. It is, in effect, denied by Tully (*Discourse on Property*, p. 120): "We have seen that [Thomas] begins with the same inclusive framework as Locke, although not expressed in terms of subjective rights, and also denies that individual ownership is natural to man as such." But one wonders at this conclusion in the light of what follows: "[Thomas] proceeds to say that there is a form of natural right (*ius naturale*) which applies to the individual agent (*ST*: ii.ii.57.2). Natural right is embodied in the logical relation between the reason of an agent and the non-contingent result of his application of reason, exemplified in the relation of cultivator and cultivated field: 'Take the ownership of property (*proprietas possessionum*) [writes Thomas]; considered in itself there is no reason why this field should belong to this man rather than to that man, *but when you take into account its being put under cultivation and farmed without strife; then . . . it tallies with it being owned by this, not that, individual*'" [emphasis added]. Tuck's plausible reading, together with evidence supplied by Tully himself, suggests that Thomas may not always have drawn quite as sharp a line between natural and private property as is sometimes inferred.

erty, gives them a particularly firm basis. Charity is a right on the part of the needy and a duty on the part of the wealthy.[49]

Thomas writes in confirmation:

> Whatever a man has in superabundance is owed, of natural right, to the poor for their sustenance. . . . If . . . there is such urgent and evident necessity [for] necessary sustenance [a person in need] may [in the last resort] take what is necessary from another person's goods, either openly or by stealth. Nor is this, strictly speaking, fraud or robbery.[50]

However important these suggestions in Thomas's writings are, they nevertheless do not constitute a thorough rights doctrine. Something much closer to that emerged in the fifteenth century with the work of Pierre d'Ailly and Jean Gerson, leaders of the Conciliar movement. Conciliarism came to advocate a radical doctrine of constitutionalism, according to which the official power of church and state might be restricted. One important feature of that campaign was the development of an explicit concept of natural right that could serve as a reference point for limiting ecclesiastical and political authority.

In building his theory, Jean Gerson linked the notions of "right" (*ius*) and "dominion" or "sovereignty" (*dominium*) with "liberty" and "right reason."[51] The idea was that, as the result of God's creation, individuals naturally possess a right of liberty. That means they are entitled to act, unobstructed, in accord with right reason and to exert control (*dominium*) over the means necessary to satisfy the requirements of right reason; that is, to pursue safety and sustenance for oneself and others:

> There is a natural *dominium* as a gift from God, by which every creature has a *ius* directly from God to take inferior things into its own use for its own preservation. Each has this *ius* as a result of a fair and irrevocable justice, maintained in its original purity, or a natural integrity. In this way Adam had *dominium* over the fowls of the air and the fish in the sea. . . . To this *dominium* the *dominium* of liberty can also be assimilated, which is an unrestrained *facultas* given by God.[52]

49. Tully, *Discourse on Property*, p. 132.
50. Thomas Aquinas, *Summa Theologica*, in *Aquinas: Selected Political Writings*, p. 171.
51. I am indebted to Tuck's discussion in *Natural Rights Theories*, pp. 25–29.
52. Jean Gerson, *Oeuvres*, vol. 3, p. 145, quoted in Tuck, *Natural Rights Theories*, p. 27.

As Gerson's doctrine was worked out by successors such as Conrad Summenhart and John Mair (Major), the interconnection between *ius* and *dominium* was emphasized. To have a right is at the same time to possess dominion or sovereignty over a designated sphere of activity. Furthermore, a "natural right" was distinguished from a "non-natural" or "conventional right." The former guarantees "inclusive" title to the necessary provisions for safety and sustenance, and it attaches to individuals by birth rather than by any particular action, undertaking, or distinctive characteristic. "Exclusive" rights to use would be permitted by nature so long as such use were governed by consideration for the equivalent inclusive rights of all other human beings. By contrast, a non-natural right occurs as the result of conventional acts, such as promises and contracts.[53]

The idea of natural right advocated by Gerson and his followers provided a pivotal part of Conciliar constitutionalism. In a thoroughly anti-Aristotelian way, natural rights are taken to exist before creation of the civil order. In their original, precivil state, human beings are governed by God-given reason and a knowledge of their common natural entitlements. There is no need for coercion because people are inclined to comply with natural law.

That state of affairs is, however, inherently unstable and leads to a "fall." Human beings find themselves to be incapable of living up to their natural obligations. They readily violate one another's legitimate liberty by arbitrary and biased actions, and they eventually conclude, in the interests of right reason and fulfilling their natural moral vocation, that they must agree to submit to civil power and to the coercive enforcement of the natural law.[54]

There are two decisive implications with respect to a doctrine of the sovereignty of the people. First, civil authority derives from the original covenanting community; second, civil rulers are but "delegates" of the people's interests, rather than absolute sovereigns. The central task of rulers is to protect and promote the natural rights of citizens; so long as they live up to that requirement, they exercise legitimate authority. If they do not, they forfeit their authority and may, if necessary, be deposed by the people. As to who, exactly, may exercise the right of re-

53. See Tuck, *Natural Rights Theories*, pp. 27–29.
54. There are parallel implications (with some differences) for the governance of the church. Conciliarism, strictly understood, emphasized the overriding authority of church councils, which were regarded as the repository of the "general consent" and therefore were considered the proper basis of ecclesiastical authority.

sistance, the Conciliarists fluctuated between the people themselves and a representative assembly of the Estates. There is, however, no indication that they believed that individuals were entitled to take things into their own hands.[55]

Calvin's Thought

Although many of the intellectual connections between Calvin and Locke are indirect and attenuated, the basic theological orientation of the two men was quite similar in several important respects.[56] Calvin affirmed, as did Locke, a modified form of "theological voluntarism." According to that position, the moral law was taken to be an expression of God's will.[57] God's sovereign authority over the world and human beings, moreover, derived from divine authorship: "Since you are [God's] handiwork, you have been made over and bound to his command by right of creation."[58] The version of theological voluntarism in

55. See Skinner, *Foundations of Modern Political Thought*, vol. 2, p. 117. Skinner points out that there was some development in Conciliar thought, though its general themes remained constant. So far as the confidence and radicalism of Conciliar doctrines goes, there seems to be some progression from Gerson, to Mair, to the later "Sorbonnists," such as Jacques Almain. See Skinner, pp. 114–23.

56. See von Leyden's "Introduction" to Locke's *Essays on the Law of Nature*, pp. 42–43, for a brief discussion of the theological connections between the two men. On the one hand, even though Locke had been brought up a Calvinist and owed a great debt to Calvinist Puritans such as John Owen, he was clearly no orthodox Calvinist; there are, for example, strong Arminian (or antipredestinarian) themes in his writing. Nor does he give the sort of attention Calvin does to the investigation of scripture or to the relatively systematic elaboration of theological doctrines. Still, von Leyden properly singles out the "'voluntarist' notion of law as the expression of God's will" (p. 43) as an important point of contact with Calvin's teaching. Such beliefs were, as von Leyden suggests, no doubt mediated through thinkers such as Culverwel, whose own "attachment to Calvinism was [also] not absolute" (p. 43). But that does not diminish the significance of the similarities. Richard Ashcraft, *Revolutionary Politics and Locke's "Two Treatises of Government"* (Princeton University Press, 1986), p. 260, n. 124, remarks that "Locke's relationship to Calvinist theology is extremely elusive, but with respect to the obligation the individual owes to God by 'the right of creation,'" there is an obvious connection.

57. "In the law of God a perfect rule (reigle) of all righteousness is presented to us which with good reason can be called the eternal will of God." "The precepts of the law ... comprehend the will of God." "God has revealed his will in the law." Citations from Calvin's writings in I. John Hesselink, "Calvin's Concept of the Law," Ph.D. dissertation, 1961, chap. 1, p. 19.

58. *Calvin: Institutes of the Christian Religion*, ed. John T. McNeill, trans. Ford Lewis Battles, 2 vols. (Philadelphia: Westminster Press, 1960), I, ii, 2 (book 1, chap. 2, section 2). See also Colman, *John Locke's Moral Philosophy*, p. 248, n. 29, for a brief discussion of the connections between Locke and Calvin in regard to God's authority by "right of creation." Colman makes two mistakes, however: he miscites the reference to a right of crea-

both men is "modified" because, unlike certain extreme medieval positions, God's will is not divorced from rational and moral standards: it is neither capricious nor arbitrary but invariably conforms to the requirements of justice, fidelity, and love.[59]

Whereas Locke may have placed more confidence than Calvin in human reason and in the capacity of reason to apprehend natural law, independent of religious revelation, the differences between them ought not to be exaggerated. Earlier, Locke's own ambivalent and, at times, pessimistic attitude toward the role of reason in the religious and moral life was pointed out. Calvin displays a similar attitude, with perhaps even greater emphasis on what was called previously in the chapter the "disjointed" quality of reason. Many of the same consequences that, for Locke, followed from such a view also followed for Calvin.

However suspicious Calvin was of the power of reason, he by no means disparaged it altogether. With regard to understanding "heavenly things," such as "the mysteries of the Heavenly Kingdom," or "the pure knowledge of God," Calvin did consider reason to be virtually worthless.[60] But when it comes to moral matters, the "human mind sometimes seems more acute . . . than in higher things" (*Institutes*, II, ii, 22; see also II, ii, 24).

We observe that there exist in all men's minds universal impressions of a certain civic fair dealing and order. Hence no man is to be found who does not understand that every sort of human organization must be regulated by laws, and who does not comprehend the principles of those laws. . . . While men dispute among themselves about

---

tion in Calvin's *Institutes*, and he wrongly claims that Locke is different from Calvin (and from a contemporary named John Wilkins) "in emphasising that human beings are dependent on God not only in the sense that He gave them being, but also in that He constantly preserves them." One has only to consult *Institutes*, I, ii, 2 (and many other passages) to see Calvin's similar concern: "Because [the pious mind] understands [God] to be the Author of every good, . . . immediately it betakes itself to his protection, waiting for help from him."

59. See Hesselink, "Calvin's Concept of the Law," chap. 1, pp. 23–26. For example, Calvin writes, "This invention which the Schoolmen have introduced about the absolute power of God is shocking blasphemy! It is the same as if they said that God is a tyrant who resolves to do what he pleases, not by justice, but through caprice (pro libidine)." Cited in Hesselink, chap. 1, p. 24.

60. Calvin, *Institutes*, II, ii, 12–13. Calvin does mention (I, iii, 1) that "there is within the human mind, and indeed by natural instinct, an awareness of divinity," but, after the fall, such awareness is not reliable. It is either smothered or profoundly corrupted by ignorance and malice. These deficiencies may be overcome only by divine revelation.

individual sections of the law, they agree on the general conception of equity. In this respect the frailty of the human mind is surely proved: even when it seems to follow the way, it limps and staggers. Yet the fact remains that some seed of political order has been implanted in all men. And this is ample proof that in the arrangement of this life no man is without the light of reason [II, ii, 13].

In short, "there is nothing more common than for a man to be sufficiently instructed in a right standard of conduct by natural law" (II, ii, 22). Calvin's notion of the selective capability of reason, as between "higher things" and the things of "this life," is already one way in which reason, for him as for Locke, is regarded as being disjointed.

An additional disjuncture can be found in Calvin's belief that the primary purpose of the unassisted knowledge of natural law is to prompt in human beings an awareness of the deficiencies of reason as a complete and reliable moral guide (II, ii, 22). In the first place, it is possible to know well enough the generalities of the moral law, but it is not so easy to know how such principles apply to particular cases. As the complexity of circumstance increases, so also does the opportunity for evasion, hypocrisy, and distortion (II, ii, 23).

In the second place, even in those instances in which what ought to be done is relatively clear, perversity frequently produces "a failure to endure." "In all our keeping of the law," says Calvin, "we quite fail to take our concupiscence into account" and refuse "to recognize the diseases of [our] lusts." Pagan philosophers describe these "immoderate incitements of the mind as 'vices,'" but they "take no account of the evil desires that gently tickle the mind" (II, ii, 24).

Calvin's description of original moral competency, which is associated with a "natural" human ability to recognize an inborn law of reason that then becomes seriously perverted, parallels Locke's account. The same two conclusions Locke draws are also found in Calvin. Because of the fundamental dilemma of knowing something of what ought to be done, but neither knowing fully nor being able satisfactorily to implement it, human beings, first, are prompted to seek God's gracious assistance. In Calvin's words, the primary purpose of the natural law is to give "sufficient reason for [the] just condemnation" of human beings, and thereby to render them "inexcusable" on their own account (II, ii, 22; see also II, ii, 11–12). Such awareness becomes the motivation for entering into a covenant with God in order to counteract the "depravity" of the human condition.

Second, Calvin picks up on the Conciliar tradition with regard to the origins of the state, contending—as does Locke—that "God established the order of earthly justice . . . because He considered the corruption that is within us" and the consequent need for a remedy to "our vices." Before human beings fell, they all carried the law in their own hearts, knowing and voluntarily performing it in a mutually harmonious order. But as they came, through their perversity, to seek their own interests above the interests of others, and to implement the law to their own advantage, that order broke down, and there was need for the coercive enforcement of the natural law by means of civil authority.[61]

Again, the covenantal image is applicable. In the civil realm, Calvin came to advocate representative government "by common consent" as the "best condition by far," since "when men become kings by hereditary right this does not seem consistent with liberty."[62] Incidentally, with respect to the organization of the church, Calvin espoused Conciliarist sentiments; he considered any system other than "election by the people's consent," to be "a violent imposition" (*Institutes*, IV, v, 2). He repeatedly recounts his objection to the Roman Catholics of his time for "taking away the right from the citizens" and forcing on the people "a bishop whom they have not desired or have not at least approved with free voice!"[63]

Although Calvin never systematically elaborates this idea of the right of the people to liberty, nor exactly what other rights people might have before entering into a political covenant, he frequently refers to a notion of natural rights, either directly or by implication, as constituting a fixed standard for designing and measuring the structure and conduct of civil

61. Calvin, quoted in David Little, *Religion, Order, and Law: A Study in Pre-Revolutionary England* (University of Chicago Press, 1984), pp. 41–47; quotation from p. 41.

62. John Calvin, quoted in *Collected Papers of Herbert D. Foster: Historical and Biographical Studies* (privately printed, 1929), p. 81.

63. Calvin, *Institutes*, IV, v, 3. Of course, Calvin was no thoroughgoing democrat. He favored a "polyarchic" system in both church and state. "Men's fault or failing causes it to be safer and more bearable for a number to exercise government. . . . This has both been proved by experience, and also the Lord confirmed it by his authority when he ordained among the Israelites an aristocracy bordering on democracy." "I will not deny that aristocracy, or a system compounded of aristocracy and democracy, far excels all others: not indeed of itself, but because it is very rare for kings so to control themselves that their will never disagrees with what is just and right" (IV, xx, 8).

government: "God has equipped government for the purpose of maintaining the rights of each individual (*les droits d'un chacun*), not allowing the person or property of anyone to be violated."[64] In short, Calvin seems to include as part of the rational structure of original human nature what Bohatec calls the idea of the "subjective rights of freedom."[65] These natural rights are essentially identified by the second table of the Decalogue, including guarantees against such things as arbitrary killing, libel, and sexual infidelity.[66] Of special interest is Calvin's discussion of the eighth and fifth commandments, prohibiting theft and the dishonoring of legitimate earthly authorities.

With respect to ownership, Calvin believed in inclusive property rights as part of God's original order of nature, in a way that was fully

64. "Dieu a voulu armer les magistrats pour maintenir les droits d'un chacun, pour ne point souffrir que nul soit outragé en sa personne, ou en ses biens." "Ioannis Calvini Opera quae supersunt omnia," *Corpus Reformatorum* (hereafter *CR*), ed. Guilielmus Baum, Eduardus Cunitz, and Eduardus Reuss (Brunsvigae: Apud C. A. Schwetschke et filium, 1863–1900), vol. 28, p. 214; cited in Josef Bohatec, *Calvins Lehre von Staat und Kirche: mit besonderer Berücksichtigung des Organismusgedankens* (Scientia Aalen, 1961), p. 94, n. 220. For Calvin's other references to the prior rights of individuals, see *CR*, vol. 26, p. 349, "que la iustice quelque fois sera comme une foire pour vendre le droit d'autruy, pour pervertir toute equité"; *CR*, vol. 26, p. 355, "mais qu'il veut que nous cheminions en telle integrité, qu'un chacun ait son droit, et que nul ne soit molesté, ni empesché en son bien, et en sa substance."

65. "Kurz, die subjektiven Freiheitsrechte haben keinen sicheren Bestand, wenn sie nicht durch die Obrigkeit und die Gesetzgebung geschützt." Bohatec, *Calvins Lehre von Staat und Kirche*, p. 95. Bohatec's comprehensive command of the sources is impressive. My discussion here is intended to counteract Tuck's thoroughly deficient treatment of "the Calvinist context" of natural rights thinking. I do not argue that Calvin had developed a systematic theory of rights, but as already noted, the proposition that he (and many of his followers) "were not particularly concerned with the notion of a right at all" is seriously in error. Tuck is generally correct that Renaissance humanism discarded any notion of natural rights and a precivil moral order in favor of elevating the role of positive rights based on the existence of civil authority (see Tuck, *Natural Rights Theories*, pp. 32–57; quotation is on p. 43). This is the basis for the strong connection between the humanist tradition and, for example, the thought of Thomas Hobbes. Calvin and Locke represent a different line of thinking, however much Calvin, in particular, may have been influenced by the Renaissance.

66. See *John Calvin's Sermons on the Ten Commandments*, ed. and trans. Benjamin W. Farley (Grand Rapids, Mich.: Baker Book House, 1980), especially pp. 133–253. "For if we want to protect each other's rights, then we must not harm or injure anyone." "We have seen with respect to explaining God's prohibition against killing that that [commandment] meant for us to abstain from all outrage and injury, and not only that, but that we should endeavor to live in peace with our fellowman and not allow anyone to be molested" (p. 168). See *Institutes*, IV, xx, 16, for mention of the connections between the "law of God" and the "natural law . . . engraved upon the minds of men." See also the lengthy discussion of the relevant commandments, *Institutes*, II, viii, 35–48.

consistent with the understanding of Thomas and Locke. In their spirit, Calvin emphasizes that the order of creation was designed so that "none of the conveniences and necessaries of life might be wanting" to human beings.[67] Indeed, God lavishes "upon us a more abundant supply of good things than our necessities require."[68] Accordingly, property is conceived of as common to all in the sense that individuals are intended to enjoy it so long as the similar opportunity for enjoyment applies universally.[69] Every individual has a right not to be excluded from fair access.

It is probable that Calvin further assumed that "exclusive property rights," based on use, also obtain in the original natural order. He states clearly that the destroyer of property violates the order of nature and sins against the general principle of equity that is built into creation.[70] Like Thomas and Locke, he emphasizes that human beings are required not simply to refrain from the arbitrary appropriation of what others need for their sustenance, but also to "share the necessity of those whom we see pressed by the difficulty of affairs, assisting them in their need with our abundance" (Institutes, II, viii, 46). When confronted with the duty to assist others in need, an individual ought to recall that "what God has given me is not mine. . . . For there is a community [among human beings]. God did not intend for as many people to live apart as he individually created. Rather, he united us all."[71]

In a remarkable passage from his Commentary on the Book of Psalms, Calvin underscores the basic role of government in guaranteeing the twin sets of natural rights to safety and sustenance that all individuals are born with:

We are here briefly taught that a just and well-regulated government will be distinguished for maintaining the rights of the poor and afflicted. . . . [F]or it cannot be doubted that rulers are bound to observe justice towards all men without distinction. But the prophet, with

67. John Calvin, cited in David Little, "Economic Justice and the Grounds for a Theory of Progressive Taxation in Calvin's Thought," in Robert L. Stivers, ed., Reformed Faith and Economics (University Press of America, 1989), p. 62.

68. John Calvin, Commentary on the Book of Psalms, trans. The Rev. James Anderson, vol. 4 (Edinburgh: Calvin Translation Society, 1847), psalm 104, verse 15 (p. 156).

69. See André Biéler, La Pensée Economique et Sociale de Calvin (Geneva: Librarie de L'Université, Georg and Co., 1959), pp. 306–90.

70. CR, vol. 27, p. 566; cited in Josef Bohatec, Calvin und das Recht (Feudingen: Buchdruckerei und Verlagsanstalt G. m. b. H., 1934), p. 11, n. 52.

71. John Calvin's Sermons on the Ten Commandments, pp. 164–65.

much propriety, represents them as appointed to be the defenders of the miserable and oppressed, both because such persons stand in need of the assistance of others, and because they *can only obtain this where rulers are free from avarice, ambition, and other vices. The end, therefore, for which judges bear the sword is to restrain the wicked, and thus to prevent violence from prevailing among men, who are so much disposed to become disorderly and outrageous. According as men increase in strength, they become proportionally audacious in oppressing the weak....* Were the truth deeply fixed in the minds of kings and other judges, that *they are appointed to be the guardians of the poor, and that a special part of this duty lies in resisting the wrongs which are done to them, and in repressing all unrighteous violence,* perfect righteousness would become triumphant through the whole world.[72]

The fifth commandment—the duty (as he interprets it) to honor legitimate authorities—is the basis for Calvin's remarkable and complex discussion of "a right of resistance," including his important thoughts on the rights of conscience and the separation of "spiritual" and "earthly" authority. After an extensive examination of the duty of children to honor their parents, Calvin makes this explosive remark: "If [parents] spur us to transgress the law, we have *a perfect right* to regard them not as parents, but as strangers who are trying to lead us away from obedience to our true Father. *So should we act toward princes, lords, and every kind of superiors.*"[73]

Two things bear emphasis here. First, Calvin assumes that the law—the will of God, including the moral or natural law—is the fundamental standard against which all forms of earthly legitimacy are to be measured. Because Calvin is usually remembered for advocating certain forms of resistance against religious oppression, or what he regarded as violations of the first table of the Decalogue, it is worth reiterating that violations of the second table—against the natural rights to safety and sustenance just mentioned—are also in opposition to the standard of legitimacy and equally might serve as a permissible cause of resistance. Calvin says as much when, for example, in the *Institutes* he discusses the "inborn feeling" human beings have "to hate and curse tyrants" who subvert "the common people of their money" or "exercise sheer robbery, plundering houses, raping virgins and matrons, and slaughter-

---

72. Calvin, *Commentary on the Book of Psalms,* vol. 3, psalm 82, verse 3, pp. 331–32 (emphasis added).
73. Calvin, *Institutes,* II, viii, 38 (emphasis added).

ing the innocent" (IV, xx, 24) and consequently "betray the freedom of the people" (IV, xx, 31).

Second, Calvin introduces a quite revolutionary idea, also hinted at by the Conciliarists: if rulers violate the law of God, the primary basis for a duty of political obligation is removed, suggesting a presumption in favor of resistance. Of course, Calvin was reluctant to take the consequences of this suggestion, and he therefore attached important conditions to implementing it. Unlike Locke, he consistently denied an individual right of resistance because he feared that anarchy and chaos would be the result. At the same time he countenanced forcible opposition against illegitimate rulers, waged if necessary by lesser magistrates who are "appointed to restrain the willfulness of kings" (*Institutes*, IV, xx, 31). This was an important concession in the direction of encouraging active enforcement of God's will, at least by certain authorized officials.

Whereas the standard of legitimacy clearly included moral requirements, Calvin's special concern in applying his resistance theory was the matter of religious violations. Because God's authority is absolutely sovereign, any attempt by earthly rulers to enforce idolatry by the power of the sword is an especially grievous affront. Such was the unmistakable mark of an illicit exercise of force. "For earthly princes lay aside their power when they rise up against God, and are unworthy to be reckoned among the number of mankind. We ought, rather, utterly to defy them (. . . 'to spit on their heads') than to obey them."[74] As Carlos Eire has recently shown, it was this campaign against religious idolatry, growing stronger toward the end of Calvin's career, that became "a prelude to sedition" on the part of European and British Calvinists in the sixteenth century and later.[75]

74. *CR*, vol. 41, p. 25; quoted in *Institutes*, IV, xx, 31, n. 54.

75. Carlos M. N. Eire, *War against the Idols: The Reformation of Worship from Erasmus to Calvin* (Cambridge University Press, 1986), especially chaps. 6, 7. Against Skinner (*Foundations of Modern Political Thought*), who belittles the importance of Calvinism in generating a distinctive resistance theory, and against Michael Walzer (*The Revolution of the Saints*), who reduces the Calvinist impulse to nonreligious social-psychological obsessions, Eire presents an altogether more convincing case for both the originality of the Calvinist position and its irreducibly religious center (whatever may have been the additional influence of other considerations). The main point is that Calvin, however unintentionally, laid out the ideas that were taken up and applied in a somewhat more radical way by his followers. The impulse for revolution nonetheless is clear in Calvin's thought. Perhaps more than Eire, I would tend to stress the importance of the whole structure of Calvin's ideas as lying behind the explicit campaign against idolatry, and as exerting their own continuing influence with the spread of Calvinism. The suggestions of a natural rights idea are, I believe,

When Calvin urges his followers to disregard completely laws that contradict the will of God, in effect he invokes his doctrine of the freedom of conscience, a doctrine that both draws on certain Thomist themes and anticipates Locke. In asserting the "right" to defy idolatrous magistrates, in the *Institutes* Calvin is simply seeking "to rescue consciences from the tyranny of men" (IV, x, 5).

The conscience, for Calvin as for Thomas, constitutes an inner "forum" of self-judgment in regard to basic belief and action. Questions of the relation to God, and obedience to divine law, are central. In an adversarial vein, there is a process of internal assessment of "arguments . . . we adopt . . . to defend a right course of action . . . we have taken, while on the other hand there are [other arguments] which accuse and convict us of our evil deeds."[76] For Calvin, human beings are *naturally* capable of recognizing the deliberations of conscience "to be higher than all human judgments." Consequently, "human laws, whether made by magistrate or by church . . . still do not of themselves bind the conscience."[77] The conscience is a special inborn province of freedom and sovereignty, and its cultivation and implementation is a central concern of Calvin's theology.

The "forum of conscience" or "spiritual" jurisdiction is distinguished, as in Thomas and Locke, from the "earthly forum" or "temporal" or political jurisdiction. The first has to do with the life and conduct of the soul, whereas the latter has to do with "outward behavior," with "the concerns of the present life—not only with food and clothing," but with creating laws of social commerce: "There are in man, so to speak, two worlds, over which different kings and different laws have authority" (*Institutes*, III, xix, 15). Accordingly, the proper sphere of coercion is the outward or political jurisdiction; "the right of the sword to punish or compel" must be excluded altogether from the sphere of conscience (IV, xi, 3).

In a way consistent with Thomas and Locke, the theoretical ingredients are present for the basis of a right of free conscience: a privileged

a signal part of that structure. Still, Eire is certainly right to dwell on the war against idolatry as central to the seditious activities of Calvinists.

76. *Calvin's Commentaries: The Epistles of Paul The Apostle to the Romans and to the Thessalonians,* ed. David W. Torrance and Thomas F. Torrance, trans. Ross Mackenzie (Grand Rapids, Mich.: Wm. B. Eerdmans, 1973), chap. 2, verse 15.

77. Calvin, *Institutes,* IV, x, 5. "While the whole world was shrouded in the densest darkness of ignorance, this tiny little spark of light remained, that men recognized man's conscience to be higher than all human judgments."

range of activity is set apart from the competency of civil authority and power and rendered "sovereign" over its own affairs. Any earthly intrusion is a violation of the right or entitlement of every individual to autonomy so long as exercise of that autonomy does not violate the other rights that the state is called on to protect.

As with Thomas and Locke, it would not seem amiss to include the right of conscience as one more of the natural rights taken to be guaranteed by God's law of creation, or the natural law. That individuals were prohibited, by Calvin's account, from taking things into their own hands in face of violations of that right did not mean that the right was not a requirement of political legitimacy. Indeed, as mentioned, violations of this right were to become, for Calvin and for many of his followers, the preeminent cause for resistance.

Like Thomas, Calvin was unwilling to draw the line between the inner and outer realms so liberally as did Locke, or many seventeenth-century radical Calvinists. As is well known, Calvin tolerated considerable civil interference in matters of religious belief and practice. Despite the sharp theoretical distinction between the inner and the outer forums, he nevertheless urged that the state had a role in cherishing and protecting "the outward worship of God" and in defending "sound doctrine of piety and the position of the church" (*Institutes*, IV, xx, 2). Without state support for "correct religion," Calvin feared that citizens could not be trusted to resist the relentless temptations of idolatry.

Still, this question was the subject of an internal debate among people who were similarly committed to a belief in the natural right of conscience. The different sides agreed that if citizens were compelled by a tyrannical state to worship against conscience, then counterforce (under the right conditions) might legitimately be used to restrain or replace the tyrant. The sides divided over whether it was legitimate, in addition to resisting illicit force, to endeavor to prevent the recurrence of compelled idolatry by enforcing certain "correct" religious beliefs and practices, or whether such action itself amounted to a new form of tyranny. Calvin and his conservative followers believed the former, whereas the more radical descendants of Calvin believed the latter.

Sixteenth-Century Calvinism after Calvin

Although John Calvin cannot be classified as an out-and-out natural rights theorist, the makings of a theory—at least of the kind Locke developed—clearly exist in his thought. Just as Calvin drew on and adopted certain crucial strands of thought in Thomas Aquinas and the Conciliarists, so his own ideas would have to be modified and adapted in order to make them useful to Locke.

The process of modification began before Calvin died in 1564 and accelerated throughout the remainder of the sixteenth century. During the 1550s a group of British exiles from Queen Mary's "Catholic tyranny" assembled in Geneva and began radicalizing Calvin's doctrines. People like John Knox, Christopher Goodman, and John Ponet, prompted by Calvin's uncompromising verbal assaults against magistrates who coerced citizens to commit idolatry, took what they thought were the consequences of those assaults. They published pamphlets intended to justify and mobilize political resistance, thereby undertaking, as Calvin put it, "to rescue consciences from the tyranny of men" (*Institutes*, IV, x, 5).[78]

To take one example, Christopher Goodman, in *How Superior Powers Ought to Be Obeyed of Their Subjects* (1558), places the natural right of conscience at the center of his case:[79]

"Verie nature doth teach all men, which be not destitute of their common sense and reason, that God ought rather to be obeyed than man. . . . Shall authority of man, or power of Princes blear our eyes any longer: seeing there is none so ignorant whose conscience does not bear him witness, that God is most worthy of all honor . . . ?

78. The following pamphlets give voice to this view: John Knox, *The First Blast of the Trumpet against the Monstrous Regiment of Women* (1558; New York: Da Capo Press, 1972); John Knox, *Appellation to the Nobility,* in *The Political Writings of John Knox*, ed. Marvin A. Breslow (1558; Washington: Folger Books, 1985); Christopher Goodman, *How Superior Powers Ought to Be Obeyed of Their Subjects* (1558; New York: Da Capo Press, 1972); and John Ponet, *A Short Treatise of Politic Power, 1556* (Yorkshire: A Scolar Press Facsimile, 1970).

79. If anything, John Ponet's *Short Treatise of Politic Power* is an even stronger example than Goodman's book of the defense of sovereignty of conscience in religious and political matters and of constitutional principles and natural rights against the crown. See Barbara Peardon, "The Politics of Polemic: John Ponet's *Short Treatise of Politic Power* and Contemporary Circumstance, 1553–1556," in *Journal of British Studies*, vol. 22 (Fall 1982), pp. 35–49. Peardon argues that, in fact, Ponet was unique in protesting against violations by Queen Mary of England of constitutional and inalienable rights, rather than concentrating primarily on religious persecution, as, for example, Goodman inclined to do. When Mary threatened to confiscate the lands and goods of the exiles, Ponet replied that the sovereign must ensure economic and political justice as well as recognize the right of private property. In the face of violations by the magistrate, citizens have a right to withdraw obedience and rebel. Obviously, Ponet is simply expanding on themes that are contained in the writings of Calvin and Goodman, as well as Philippe du Plessis Mornay, as will be seen.

Shall the threatenings of man or punishment of Princes move us to leave undone that which he commandeth, and our vocation requireth?[80]

"Natural reason compel[s] every man" to admit the legitimacy of armed resistance against rulers who use their sword to enforce idolatry (pp. 79–80). For it "maketh all men to wonder and be astonished" "when they both hear and see those that profess the Gospel, and would be counted Christ's sheep, turned for fear of displeasure, or losing of their office in to the nature of bloodthirsty wolves, to execute against God and their conscience, the ungodly commandments of the papists" (p. 37).

Goodman shared many of Calvin's assumptions. A conscience left free to submit itself directly to what were believed to be God's commandments was considered to be a fundamental part of the liberty of the people, a liberty guaranteed both by the natural law of reason as well as by God's revealed word. Because civil authority has its origin in the need to enforce the law of the people's liberty against arbitrariness and selfishness, and is based on a covenant consistent with this objective (pp. 164–65), the sole criterion of a government's legitimacy is whether it fulfills these primary obligations (pp. 106–13). If a government fails in this regard, it forfeits "all right from the people" and thereby surrenders its title to official authority. Members of the government then are reduced to "private persons," and may be "examined and punished" accordingly (pp. 187–88).[81]

In a way also similar to Calvin, Goodman occasionally interprets the idea of the "right of the people" in the idiom of subjective natural rights, which include not only the natural right of conscience but also the idea that individual human beings "may lawfully claim" their liberty "as their own possession": "If they suffer this right to be taken from them" by a despotic ruler, Goodman writes, they are being treated exactly as though the ruler were stealing their private property from them (pp. 160, 149).[82]

80. Goodman, *How Superior Powers Ought to Be Obeyed*, p. 85; see also p. 41.

81. In *Foundations of Modern Political Thought*, vol. 2, pp. 220–21, Skinner points out that Calvin also held this "private-law theory of resistance," according to which a tyrant forfeited authority and became "nothing more than an ordinary man."

82. I am indebted to Skinner, *Foundations of Modern Political Thought*, vol. 2, p. 320 and n. 1, for this important reference to a "'subjective' concept of rights." Needless to say, I do not agree with Skinner's thoroughly unsubstantiated conclusion that, concerning

Goodman also shared with Calvin the "conservative" attitude toward the need for curtailing conscience by publicly enforcing Reformed faith, once the tyrants were removed. Without any qualms regarding the establishment of religion, he expresses his deep appreciation for the haven Geneva afforded him and his associates against religious persecution. There, one might "with great freedom of conscience hear the word of God continually preached, and the Sacraments of our Saviour Christ purely and duly ministered, without all dregs of popery, or superstition of mans invention."[83] Apparently conscience might be compelled, as was the practice in Calvin's Geneva, so long as religious truth was considered as unmistakable as it was for the conservative Calvinists.

The point at which Goodman, like Knox and other Genevan exiles, "embarrassed and annoyed" Calvin was apparently their unrelenting and unqualified call for rebellion against illicit rulers.[84] Goodman does not go so far as to break explicitly with Calvin by advocating that private persons might themselves take up arms against illegimate rulers, but he does speak rather open-endedly about God having "giveth the sword in to the peoples hand, and he him self is become immediately their head," "when the Magistrates and other officers cease to do their duty."[85] Gone is Calvin's painstaking concern to restrict rebellion to duly authorized lesser magistrates. Just where the limits were on the kind of exercise Goodman allowed was anybody's guess.

An example of later sixteenth-century Calvinism that exhibits the

---

early Calvinist revolutionaries like Goodman, "such allusions to natural-law argume/nts had been little more than marginal asides, which remained unrelated to—and rather obviously inconsistent with—their basic appeal to the idea that all the powers that be are directly ordained by God" (pp. 320–21). Goodman's arguments are quite consistent with his emphasis on natural law and natural right throughout this treatise, as well as with his explicit legitimist interpretation of the passage in Romans 13 concerning God's ordination of the powers that be, to which Skinner calls attention (see *How Superior Powers Ought to Be Obeyed*, pp. 106–13). Also, and perhaps even more significant, Goodman's views are consistent with Calvin's own emphasis on, and application of, natural law doctrine to political affairs, as outlined earlier.

Interestingly enough, Tuck himself, in a passing footnote, admits that Goodman's "extensive" use of the language of rights may well run afoul of his thesis that Calvinism had nothing to add to the development of a natural rights theory. Tuck, *Natural Rights Theories*, p. 43, n. 27. Tuck would have been well advised to have used that admission as a basis for rethinking altogether the relation of Calvinism to natural rights theory.

83. Goodman, *How Superior Powers Ought to Be Obeyed*, p. 224.

84. See John T. McNeill, *The History and Character of Calvinism* (Oxford University Press, 1954), p. 312.

85. Goodman, *How Superior Powers Ought to Be Obeyed*, p. 185.

further development of the natural rights idea—an example that moves still closer to Locke—is *A Defence of Liberty against Tyrants* (1572) by the French Huguenot author Philippe du Plessis Mornay. This influential document expands and further sharpens the essential themes of Goodman's treatise. Like Goodman, Mornay gives prominent attention to what he regards as the threat to free conscience that is represented by rulers who enforce idolatry:

> The princes exceed their bounds, not contenting themselves with that authority which the almighty and all good God hath given them, but seek to usurp that sovereignty, which [God] hath reserved to himself over all men, being not content to command the bodies and goods of their subjects at their pleasure, but assume license to themselves to enforce the consciences, which appertains chiefly to Jesus Christ.[86]

Like Goodman and Calvin, Mornay assumes the natural right of conscience to honor the perceived commands of God above those of earthly rulers. Faced with a choice between God and king, Mornay asks, "is any man so void of reason" that such a person will not side with God, and resist what is contrary to God's law? (p. 80).

For Mornay, human beings know by natural reason that "if the prince commands to cut the throat of an innocent, to pillage and commit extortion, there is no man (provided he has some feeling of conscience) who would execute such a commandment." "Is there not yet more reason to disobey," he asks, a prince who commands citizens "to be idolaters, [to] crucify Christ Jesus, [and to] blaspheme and despise God?" (pp. 80–81).

There are two justifications for this disobedience. First, the conscience is, presumably, so constituted as naturally to defy the coercive intrusion of human authority in matters of deep spiritual commitment. Second, as a theological voluntarist like Calvin and Locke, Mornay claims that God possesses the ultimate authority to command conscience, since "God hath created of nothing both heaven and earth; wherefore by good right He is lord, and true proprietor, both of the one and the other" (p. 68).

Again, as with Calvin and Locke, the fundamental failure of human

---

86. Philippe du Plessis Mornay [Junius Brutus, pseud.], *A Defence of Liberty against Tyrants*, a translation of the *Vindiciae contra Tyrannos*, ed. Harold J. Laski (New York: Burt Franklin, 1924), p. 66.

beings, of their own accord, to live up to God's will generates the need for a religious and a civil covenant. The religious covenant is addressed by giving people an opportunity freely to submit their consciences to the honor and majesty of God. The need for the civil covenant follows from the inability of people in their natural state to prevent violations against the law of equal freedom in which everyone was conceived. Thus, Mornay says, governments are established "to maintain by justice, and to defend by force of arms, both the public state, and particular persons from all damages and outrages" (p. 140). It is, therefore, by the people and for the people's sake that magistrates reign, and for no other reason.

Mornay is quite clear that, whereas earthly rulers are legitimately chosen only by means of election or confirmation from the people, the terms according to which such confirmation takes place are necessarily defined by the prior law of nature. If, for instance, a ruler attempted to coerce citizens into submitting to arbitrary control, that sort of "agreement" would be disallowed: "Is it not an unquestionable maxim in law, that a promise exacted by violence cannot bind, especially if anything be promised against common reason, or the law of nature?" (p. 181). In short, Mornay is emphatic, as was Locke after him, that people are prohibited by the law of nature from enslaving themselves.[87]

Perhaps most striking of all is Mornay's explicit assumption of a subjective theory of natural rights when he undertakes to show why rulers do not own the property of their subjects. Given, he says, that "every one loves that which is his own, [and] that many covet that which belongs to other men," individuals would reasonably be expected to favor an impartial ruler whom they could rely on "for the administering of justice equally both to the poor and rich," a ruler "who would not assume all to himself, *but rather maintain every one in the fruition of his own goods.*" If, then, with the establishing of governments, individuals "gave not their own proper goods unto them, but only recommended them to their protection; by what other right then, but that of freebooters, can [governments] challenge the property of other men's goods to themselves?"[88]

Skinner's comment is to the point. Like Locke a hundred years later,[89]

---

87. See Locke, "Second Treatise," s. 23.

88. Mornay, *Defence of Liberty,* pp. 158–59 (emphasis added).

89. For an excellent discussion of the "obvious similarity" "of the principles of Locke and those of the author of the *Vindiciae,*" see Sir Ernest Barker, *Church, State, and Education* (University of Michigan Press, 1957), pp. 98–99, and note C, pp. 106–08.

the Huguenots assume that amongst the things we may be said to have the freedom and thus the right to dispose of within the bounds of the laws of nature are those properties—as we still punningly call them—which are intrinsic to our personalities, and in particular our lives and liberties. So when the Huguenots treat the people's welfare as the final cause of the commonwealth, and proceed to equate this with their right to enjoy their properties, they often make it clear that what they have in mind is the duty of the ruler to uphold the inalienable and natural rights of the people to their lives and liberties— these being the fundamental and natural properties which everyone may be said to possess in a pre-political state.[90]

In two respects, Mornay would appear to be closer to Calvin than to Locke. First, like Calvin and unlike Locke, Mornay absolutely disallows armed resistance to tyranny by private citizens.[91] Second, although here he may be somewhat more ambivalent, there is no evidence in the *Defence* of the more liberal interpretation of the right of conscience that is found in Locke. Rather, in the discussion of the fourth question— whether neighboring princes are bound "to aid the subjects of other princes" who are being religiously persecuted—Mornay appears, like Calvin, to assume that the sword may be used, not just to defend against the civil coercion of conscience, but also to "amplify and increase" "true religion" (pp. 215, 217). But he is not altogether consistent on this matter, appearing to be torn by the conflicting impulses within Calvinism concerning freedom of conscience: elsewhere he writes, "Idolatry [must be] overthrown by the word of God and not by the hammer-blows of men."[92]

Seventeenth-Century Radical Calvinism

Thanks to the recent work of Richard Ashcraft, a convincing case exists for closely associating Locke with the Levellers, a radical Puritan sect active in resisting the English crown during the Puritan Revolution

90. Skinner, *Foundations of Modern Political Thought*, vol. 2, p. 328. For reasons I have tried to make clear, I agree with Skinner that Mornay's arguments here can be traced in part to the Conciliarists, such as Gerson and Mair, although they flow more immediately, I think, from Calvinist sources. In any case, Mornay's position stands, as I hope I have shown, within a distinct lineage of ideas.

91. Mornay, *Defence of Liberty*, pp. 109–16.

92. Cited in *A Huguenot Family in the XVI Century: The Memoirs of Philippe de Mornay*, written by his wife; trans. Lucy Crump (New York: Dutton, [1926]), p. 172.

of the 1640s.[93] Like the Puritans in general, in their origins the Levellers were influenced in important respects by Calvinist thought and outlook, although they, perhaps more than others, extended and reinterpreted the tradition in ways that no doubt would have horrified Calvin himself.

The Levellers were an important part of Oliver Cromwell's New Model Army, which finally succeeded in defeating the royal forces and in temporarily overturning the monarchy. In extensive debates with other Puritans over the system of government that would obtain in England once the king had been removed, the Levellers made a series of remarkable constitutional proposals known, significantly, as "Agreements of the People." In 1649 John Lilburne, a leader of the movement, explained that such an agreement was necessary to clarify "the principles of a just government under which the glory of God may shine forth by an equal distribution unto all men; that the obtaining of this was the sole intended end of the war; and that the war cannot be justified upon any other account than the defence of the people's right unto that just government and their freedom under it."[94] In the same spirit, the preamble to "An Agreement of the People of England . . . for a Firm and Present Peace upon Grounds of Common Right and Freedom," declares that "we do now hold ourselves bound, in mutual duty to each other . . . to avoid both the danger of returning into a slavish condition and the chargeable remedy of another war. . . . [W]hen our common rights and liberties shall be cleared, their endeavours will be disappointed, that seek to make themselves our masters."[95]

The document goes on to propose a representative form of democracy based upon a system of extensive manhood suffrage.[96] Its articles enumerate electoral and legislative procedures, terms of elected office, and separation of powers. Several amendments guarantee freedom of conscience, due process of law, and freedom from excessive punishment, self-incrimination, and religious tests for public office.[97] These

---

93. Ashcraft, *Revolutionary Politics,* especially pp. 149–65. Because of limitations of space, I single out the Levellers. A fuller account would take up other groups in the Puritan movement and would look at Dutch Calvinists, such as Hugo Grotius, who were also important in the development of a natural rights theory. See Tuck's generally excellent chapter on Grotius in *Natural Rights Theories,* pp. 58–81.

94. A. S. P. Woodhouse, ed., *Puritanism and Liberty,* 2d ed. (University of Chicago Press, 1974), p. 342.

95. Woodhouse, ed., *Puritanism and Liberty,* p. 356.

96. See Ashcraft, *Revolutionary Politics,* pp. 149–66, for an excellent discussion of just how revolutionary the Leveller proposal was at the time.

97. Woodhouse, ed., *Puritanism and Liberty,* pp. 356–67.

proposals were considered far too revolutionary by the mainstream of Puritan leadership and were strongly resisted by Cromwell and his associates. By the 1650s the Levellers were severely defeated as a political force, and the movement faded from the scene. As Ashcraft makes clear, however, the Levellers' influence did not die out. Many of their ideas were enshrined in Locke's "Second Treatise."

In a pamphlet entitled "The Free-man's Freedom Vindicated" (1646), Lilburne makes clear some of the theological foundations of Leveller thinking. Although here he puts his theological voluntarism with rather less qualification than either Calvin or Locke were inclined to do, the political conclusions he draws from his doctrine of God are thoroughly consistent with them:

> God, the absolute sovereign Lord and King of all things in heaven and earth, the original fountain and cause of all causes, who is circumscribed, governed, and limited by no rules, but doth all things merely and only by his sovereign will and unlimited good pleasure, who made the world and all things therein for his own glory, by his own will and pleasure gave man, his mere creature, the sovereignty (under himself) over all the rest of his creatures . . . and endued him with a rational soul or understanding, and thereby created him after his own image. [Adam and Eve] are the earthly original fountain . . . of all and every particular and individual man and woman . . . in the world since, who are, and were, by nature all equal and alike in power, dignity, authority, and majesty, none of them having by nature any authority, dominion, or magisterial power one over or above another; neither have they, or can they exercise any, but merely by institution or donation, that is to say, by mutual agreement or consent, given, derived, or assumed by mutual consent and agreement, for the good benefit and comfort each of other, and not for the mischief, hurt, or damage of any; it being unnatural, irrational, . . . wicked, and unjust, for any man or men whatsoever to part with so much of their power as shall enable any of their Parliament-men, commissioners, trustees, deputies, . . . or servants, to destroy and undo them therewith.[98]

98. Woodhouse, ed., *Puritanism and Liberty*, p. 317. The theological positions of the Leveller leadership were varied and somewhat unstable. Lilburne himself was finally converted to Quakerism, and other leaders such as Richard Overton and William Walwyn were far from orthodox believers. Although Overton began as a member of a General Baptist congregation in Holland, his theological views (assuming he wrote *Mans Mortalli-*

Or, in John Wildman's words:

> Every person in England hath as clear a right to elect his representa-
> tive as the greatest person in England. . . . [A]ll government is in the
> free consent of the people. If [so], then upon that account there is no
> person that is under a just government, or hath justly his own, unless
> he by his own free consent be put under that government. This he
> cannot be unless he be consenting to it, and therefore, according to
> this maxim, there is never a person in England [but ought to have a
> voice in elections].[99]

The elaboration of Leveller ideas, especially because those ideas bear
on the subject of natural rights and anticipate Locke's views, is especially
well executed in Richard Overton's "An Appeal from the Commons to
the Free People" (1647).[100] In Overton, a subjective natural rights
theory achieves unmistakable expression.

Overton assumes the standard Conciliarist-Calvinist theory of the
origin of the state. Human beings, created according to the law of reason
as declared by God, are endowed with certain "natural human rights
and freedoms" "that all men may have a human subsistence and safety"
(pp. 332–33). Because in the state of nature human beings do not honor
the natural law but declare war against one another and incline to act
so as to subvert the equal freedoms of all humankind, it is necessary to
establish government, whose exclusive function is to uphold and ensure
the "common right and freedom." Just as the rule by which one would
agree to submit oneself to a government on these terms is preeminently
rational, so any act by which one undertakes justly to "deliver [oneself]
from all oppression, violence and cruelty whatsoever" is fully in accord
with "an undoubted principle of reason," or with what Overton also
calls the "natural radical principle of reason." Indeed, "to deny it is to
overturn the law of nature, yea and of religion too; for the contrary lets
in nothing but self-murder, violence, and cruelty" (p. 325).

The authority of civil magistrates is derived, then, from the "agreement of the people" in keeping with these basic standards. Overton's

---

tie) deviated substantially from standard Calvinism. See Joseph Frank, *The Levellers: A
History of the Writings of Three Seventeenth-Century Social Democrats: John Lilburne, Richard
Overton, William Walwyn* (Harvard University Press, 1955), pp. 39–44, 263–65. On occa-
sion Walwyn described himself in quite unorthodox terms (pp. 29–39).

99. Woodhouse, ed., *Puritanism and Liberty*, p. 66.

100. Woodhouse, ed., *Puritanism and Liberty*, pp. 323–34, contains the words of Overton cited in the following paragraphs.

emphasis on the twin pillars of legitimacy—subsistence as well as safety—recalls Calvin's teaching concerning "inclusive rights to property" (and those of Thomas Aquinas, upon whom he drew), and also, obviously, anticipates Locke. In that spirit, Overton stresses that it is "against the radical law of nature and reason that any man should be deprived of a human subsistence, that is not an enemy thereto" (p. 333). Here is the suggestion—as in Thomas, Calvin, and Locke—that natural rights include economic rights.

It is in the area of conscience and the range of its freedom that the radicalism of the Levellers, and some of their associates, comes out most strongly. Unlike Calvin and most of his sixteenth-century followers, the Levellers reject the idea that the civil authority has any role to play in the restriction of religious belief and practice, except, of course, to protect against outward injury. Overton, for example, simply applies more rigorously than did Calvin himself Calvin's own distinction between the "inner" and the "outer" realms:

For the limits of magistracy extend no further than humanity or human subsistence, not to spirituality or spiritual being. . . . The inward man is God's prerogative; the outward man is man's prerogative. God is the immediate Lord over the inward, and mediately over the outward; but man is only lord over the outward, and though immediate thereover, yet but by deputation or commission from him who is thus both over the one and the other. And God, who only knoweth the heart and searcheth the reins, hath reserved the gubernation thereof to himself as his own prerogative. And the only means which he useth in this kind of government, that by his ministers must be dispensed, is only by the Word, not by the sword. For the sword pierceth the flesh; it toucheth but the outward man; it cannot touch the inward. Therefore where by the Word . . . a conversion is not, or cannot be, obtained, there no human compulsive power or force is to be used [p. 332].

Here the natural right of conscience is interpreted in a thoroughly liberal way, providing the basis for the seemingly modern Leveller guarantee that government "shall not disable any person from bearing any office in the commonwealth for any opinion or practice in religion."[101]

This emphasis upon the freedom of individuals to pass judgment for

101. Woodhouse, ed., *Puritanism and Liberty*, p. 365.

themselves on religious questions, unencumbered by public coercion, also suggests another area in which the Levellers may represent a radical departure from Calvin's own teaching and that of his Huguenot followers like Mornay. That pertains to the question whether individuals might permissibly take up arms against an unjust ruler, as Locke (contrary to Calvin) thought they might. Whereas (to my knowledge) the Levellers do not openly advocate the right of individual resistance, they do open the door to such an interpretation. Their liberal doctrine of individual conscience—together with their emphasis on the rights of "every man in particular" (as Overton put it) "to save, defend, and deliver himself from all oppression, violence and cruelty whatsoever, and . . . to leave no just expedient unattempted for his delivery therefrom" (p. 325)—appears to provide warrant for Locke's individualistic interpretation of the right of resistance.

Conclusion

It is assumed that there are many possible ways in which Christians, along with members of other religious traditions, might relate to a belief in human rights. Nevertheless, I have endeavored to show that, for better or worse, there does exist an unmistakable, if complex, historical link between one strand of the Christian tradition and the emergence of the Lockean theory of natural rights, a theory that appears to have constituted an indispensable source of modern ideas of human rights. In short, Locke's theory is incomprehensible if it is divorced from its Calvinist context.

Calvinism is itself a complex phenomenon. Locke represents the radical part of that tradition, according to which human beings are accorded a comparatively wide range of individual rights with regard to property, conscience, political participation, and resistance to arbitrary authority. They are understood to possess these rights "naturally," which means that they hold them before and independent of any specific religious beliefs they may come to profess.

However radical Locke's application—and however deviant, in certain ways, from Calvin's original intention—Locke does no more than follow through with one set of implications that is present in the original structure of ideas that Calvin and his immediate followers enunciated in the sixteenth century. If Calvin had no "natural rights theory," he did provide the groundwork for one. By comparing that groundwork with Locke's thought, I have been able, it is hoped, to correct some common misconceptions of both Calvin and Locke.

None of this means, of course, that thinking about human rights by Christians (or by anyone else, for that matter) is constrained by this historical legacy. It only means that anyone wishing hereafter to argue a case about Christianity and human rights must take full account of the character and complexity of the Calvinist context of natural rights philosophy.

CHAPTER FIVE

The European Tradition of Human Rights and the Culture of Islam

Bassam Tibi

ISLAM is currently going through a period of repoliticization that appears to have substantial implications for human rights. A number of political and religious leaders are calling for the implementation of Islamic law (*shariʿa*) within the framework of an Islamic system of government (*niẓam islami*), but Islamic *shariʿa* and basic human rights are clearly in conflict in certain respects. Islam is a monotheistic religion that recognizes only two other religions, Judaism and Christianity, which are also monotheisms. Furthermore, *shariʿa* accords non-Islamic monotheists the status of *dhimmis* (protected minorities) and thus denies them equality with Muslims. Muslims themselves are not allowed to retreat from Islam. A Muslim who repudiates his or her faith in Islam can be prosecuted as a *murtadd* (apostate).[1] Are these precepts compatible with current standards of human rights?

It has been said that these standards can only be met through secularism, which "is the guarantee of human rights without regard to religion. Secularism rejects discrimination between people on the basis of race and color."[2] Therefore, human rights must be treated as a political,

The research for parts of this chapter was conducted at the Center for Near Eastern and North African Studies, University of Michigan, Ann Arbor, under a Rockefeller Research Fellowship. A draft of the paper was completed while I was at the Center for International Affairs at Harvard University. I am especially grateful to Ann Mayer and Rhoda Howard for their useful comments on an earlier version of this chapter.

1. See Adel Théodor Khoury, *Toleranz im Islam* (Munich: Kaiser Press, 1980), pp. 43ff. and 138ff. on the *dhimmis* (Christians and Jews), and pp. 110–15 on the *murtaddun*.

2. Joseph Mughaizel, *al-ʿuruba wa al-ʿalmaniyya* (*Arabism and Secularism*) (Beirut: dar al-nahar, 1980), p. 107. See also Mughaizel, "al-islam wa al-masiḥiyya al-ʿarabiyya wa al-qawmiyya al-ʿarabiyya wa al-ʿalmaniyya" (Islam, Arab Christianity, Arab Nationalism and Secularism), in Center for Arab Unity Studies, *al-qawmiyya al-ʿarabiyya wa al-islam*, 2d ed. (Beirut: markaz dirasat al-waḥda al-ʿarabiyya, 1982), p. 383. Mughaizel quotes article 18 of the Covenant on Civil and Political Rights: "Everyone shall have the right to

cultural, and institutional issue rather than a religious one. In the case of Islam, human rights should be analyzed in the framework of Islam as a cultural system—that is to say, as a model of the reality that determines the worldview of Muslims—and also as a political ideology.[3] The central question of this chapter is whether it is possible for Muslims to arrive at an understanding of human rights that is acceptable both at the local cultural (Muslim) level and at the pluricultural, universal level.

The point of departure of this inquiry is that "human rights" are a modern achievement. Indeed, as others have pointed out, "the term 'human rights' as such is not found in traditional religions."[4] Therefore, we should not expect to find it in Islam. The concept originated in Europe when "the modern secular theories of natural law . . . detached natural law from religion. . . . Natural law theory led to natural rights theory—the theory most closely associated with modern human rights."[5] This background is clearly reflected in the modern understanding of human rights as natural rights, as documented in the Universal Declaration of Human Rights.[6] The declaration has been supported by Islamic as well as non-Islamic states, although it is "not generally seen as a binding agreement."[7] Nevertheless, its very existence, together with the ensuing international covenants, marks the formal assent of the international community to the core of rights contained therein.

The problem for many countries is that the local cultural underpinnings for these universal pronouncements are missing. Human rights still lack cultural legitimacy in most third world societies, including Islamic societies. Thus the formal assent given to the Universal Declaration of Human Rights should not distract us from the fact that there is a

---

freedom of thought, conscience and religion. This right shall include to have or to adopt a religion or belief of his choice."

3. See Clifford Geertz, *The Interpretation of Cultures* (Basic Books, 1973), pp. 3–30, 87–125, 193–233. I have employed this Geertzian frame of reference in my study of Islam. See Bassam Tibi, *Islam and the Cultural Accommodation of Social Change* (Boulder, Colo.: Westview Press, 1990), especially chap. 1.

4. Jerome J. Shestack, "The Jurisprudence of Human Rights," in Theodor Meron, ed., *Human Rights in International Law: Legal and Policy Issues*, 2d ed. (Oxford: Clarendon Press, 1985), p. 75.

5. Shestack, "Jurisprudence of Human Rights," pp. 77–78.

6. See Jack Donnelly, "Human Rights as Natural Rights," in *Human Rights Quarterly*, vol. 4, no. 3 (1982), pp. 391–405.

7. L. Henkin, "The International Bill of Rights: The Universal Declaration and the Covenants," in Rudolf Bernhardt and John Anthony Jolowicz, eds., *International Enforcement of Human Rights*, Reports submitted to the colloquium of the International Association of Legal Science, Heidelberg, August 28–30, 1985 (Springer-Verlag, 1987), p. 5.

large discrepancy between the global view regarding the universalism of human rights and the perspectives reflected in the moral standards of particular cultures and ideologies. The discrepancy is greatest "when the particularism in question is religious in nature."[8] Religions are inherently exclusive in their claims unless they are enriched by a tradition of tolerance that accepts other religions as equals and provides "the others" with the right to be different in the sense of *le droit à la différence*. Tolerance in Islam extends only to other monotheists, namely, Christians and Jews, who, as indicated earlier, are considered to be merely protected minorities and not autonomous individuals.

Given the diverse cultural contexts in which human rights are interpreted in the world and the simultaneous need for a universal understanding of these rights, we must find a way to transcend the existing cultural distinctions.[9] At the same time, we cannot expect more than a limited intercultural consensus on human rights, as will become clear later in the chapter.

Secularism as a *Weltanschauung* endorsing the separation of religion and the state will undoubtedly help us move closer to such a consensus, but it alone will not bring us to a genuine global and interculturally shared understanding of human rights. We are in search of "something quite different from an intensified process of global secularization."[10] Perhaps it can best be compared to a language that is acquired by learning to speak one's own language in a new way. What this means is that significant cultural change must take place within religions, as cultural systems and as sources of values. Only in this way can religions be enriched and freed from charges of exclusiveness.[11]

In this chapter I seek to establish a contextual understanding of Islam's position on human rights. Since human rights are not simply val-

---

8. David Hollenbach, "Human Rights and Religious Faith in the Middle East: Reflections of a Christian Theologian," *Human Rights Quarterly*, vol. 4 (February 1982), p. 95.

9. See R. J. Vincent, *Human Rights and International Relations* (Cambridge University Press, 1986), p. 39. Vincent observes correctly: "the term is general but the rights are specific . . . if there are human rights, they are the rights of particular people." It follows that the universality of human rights is not consonant with the particularity of cultures, thus the need for a breakthrough becomes obvious and urgent. For an interpretation of the Universal Declaration of Human Rights, see Henkin, "International Bill of Rights," pp. 1–19, especially pp. 5–6; the documents appear on pp. 161–265.

10. Hollenbach, "Human Rights and Religious Faith," p. 109.

11. See Bassam Tibi, "The Interplay between Social and Cultural Change: The Case of Germany and the Arab Middle East," in George N. Atiyeh and Ibrahim M. Oweiss, eds., *Arab Civilization: Challenges and Responses*, Studies in Honor of Constantine K. Zurayk (Albany: State University of New York, 1988), pp. 166–82.

ues or norms that can be misused or betrayed, but rather rights in the sense of entitlements, they can only exist where they are backed by a legal institutional framework for their enforcement. Rhetoric alone cannot safeguard human rights; people need to develop "human rights techniques" to defend these rights.[12] They must be legally enforced. Islam is said to have a long-standing legal tradition.[13] Muslims claim that *shari'a* (Islamic law) provides the needed framework for the protection of human rights. The question is, does it really provide this kind of protection?

Throughout the chapter I focus on civil and political rights, although scholars have recently turned their attention to other rights, including the rights to peace and development.[14] One of the reasons for my "preference for the language of human rights over the language of social justice is precisely the added force of the claim of natural or human rights, the true rights of man."[15] Human rights are entitlements. The demand for social justice as well as for the right to development are normative commitments that do not carry this force.

Islam and the Universality of Human Rights

It is imperative to define at the outset what is meant by human rights. The concept of human rights is a modern cultural achievement of Europe whereby new values have been coupled with a system of legal enforcement.[16] This tradition has evolved along with modern civil society. The concept is based on the assumption that autonomy and equality should be accorded all human beings by virtue of their status as individuals. This view does not merely reflect a commitment to values, since equality and autonomy are considered to be natural human rights. It also reflects the belief that these rights must be protected from infringement by the state. The need to restrain the state and to place limitations

12. H. Yamane, "Approaches to Human Rights in Asia," in Bernhardt and Jolowics, eds., *International Enforcement of Human Rights*, p. 111.

13. N. J. Coulson, *A History of Islamic Law* (Edinburgh: University Press, 1978); and Joseph Schacht, *An Introduction to Islamic Law*, 5th ed. (Oxford: Clarendon Press, 1979).

14. David Trubek, "Economic, Social and Cultural Rights in the Third World," in Meron, ed., *Human Rights in International Law*, pp. 205–71. See also the comments of Shestack, "Jurisprudence of Human Rights," p. 99.

15. Jack Donnelly, "Human Rights as Natural Rights," p. 405.

16. See Vincent, *Human Rights and International Relations*, chaps. 1, 2; Jack Donnelly, *The Concept of Human Rights* (London: Croom Helm, 1985); and the chapter by Donnelly in this volume.

on its actions constitutes one of the primary concerns of the liberal theory of human rights. These human rights can be vindicated and are therefore legal entitlements. Under this theory, all humanity has the right to enjoy equality and autonomy, as well as to seek their protection; in other words, these rights are universal. Europeans, in the course of their conquests throughout the world over the past three hundred years, introduced to other societies certain processes taking place in European societies, which have come to be known collectively as "the civilizing process."[17]

To be sure, European colonial penetration was neither what the French claim to be a *mission civilatrice* nor what the Germans call a *Kulturbotschaft*. The colonization was aimed at exploiting non-Western regions economically and subjecting their peoples to colonial rule. The Europeans could not, however, prevent the export of their own revolutionary values to non-Western cultures, and even less could they impede the incorporation of these values, such as the sovereignty of the people, as legitimizing principles into the anticolonial drive of non-Western peoples.[18] The European colonialists unwittingly exported the genuinely Western cultural values of human rights into a foreign context where the native populations were denied these rights.[19] In this way, in the long run, the Europeans indirectly undermined their own colonization of other peoples. This is the historical phenomenon that Hegel referred to as *List der Vernunft* (the cunning of reason).

By proposing that this definition of human rights (that is, rights of autonomy and equality that individuals can demand from the state and that must be institutionally protected by society) be the basis for our universal standards of human rights, I am exposing myself to criticism from two different camps. A Marxist, or at least a social democrat, would complain that this definition smacks of classic liberalism, in that it rejects social and economic rights. A citizen of a third world country would no doubt charge that it smacks of Eurocentrism. Many people from third world countries dispute the claim that the human rights tradition originated in modern Europe. Muslims would go even further and say that Islam was the very first culture on earth to which God imparted a complete set of human rights values.

17. The classic by Norbert Elias, written in German, is now available in an English translation, *The Civilizing Process*, 2 vols. (Pantheon Books, 1978, 1982).
18. F. H. Hinsley, *Sovereignty* (Cambridge University Press, 1986), chap. 6, pp. 214ff.
19. See Peter Worsley, *The Third World*, 2d ed. (University of Chicago Press, 1972), pp. 21–49.

It is said that non-Westerners tend to confuse *human rights*, as explained and defined above, with *human dignity*.[20] If one is talking about the latter, there is no doubt that fully developed notions of human dignity exist in many non-Western cultures, in Islamic and African cultures, as well as in Buddhist and other nonmonotheistic cultures.[21] If one is talking about the former, medieval Europe itself had no inkling of human rights in the modern sense. The point is that many non-Western and Western cultures alike possess moral values in this regard. Thus one has to distinguish between the modern concept of human rights as being institutionally protected and the cultural concept of human dignity. Of course, it is also imperative to recognize the universal applicability of human rights, even though these rights have not yet been realized in the majority of non-Western states. However, the fact that the cultural values of non-Western cultures are compatible with the modern human rights ideals should smooth the way for their eventual realization. As Francis Deng has remarked elsewhere in this volume, "Human rights are . . . inherent in the very notion of humanity; to hold otherwise would . . . impede progress toward a universal consensus on human rights. To argue for the principle of universality is not to deny the significance of the cultural context for the definition."[22] To accept this statement is tantamount to conceding that in a pluricultural world each culture recognizes human rights in its own way. Being committed to cultural pluralism and opposed to cultural relativism, I share this view, provided that we can reach a universal consensus on the basic human rights shared by different cultures.

One should also be wary of falling into the trap of accepting human rights violations because they are said to emanate from "authentic non-Western cultural values." To avoid such a trap, one must specify the points on which local cultures conflict with the projected universal standards. It is not acceptable to claim cultural exclusiveness, as some societies do, particularly Islamic ones, for this is antithetical to the very thing we are striving to achieve—universal and pluricultural consensus on human rights. Moreover, the rights in question pertain to individuals

20. Jack Donnelly, "Human Rights and Human Dignity: An Analytic Critique of Non–Western Conceptions of Human Rights," *American Political Science Review,* vol. 76 (June 1982), pp. 303–16.

21. See the chapter by Rhoda Howard in this volume as well as her book, *Human Rights in Commonwealth Africa* (Totowa, N.J.: Rowman and Littlefield, 1986).

22. See chapter 11, p. 261. See also Francis Mading Deng, *Africans of Two Worlds: The Dinka in Afro-Arab Sudan* (Yale University Press, 1978).

and are not communal entitlements that can be passed off as religious duties in the name of human rights, as is the case in Islam.[23]

Another factor that is impeding progress toward a universal consensus on human rights is that some societies pay no heed to civil and political rights because they think these rights are opposed to their all-important social and economic rights. This attitude undermines the efforts to establish societal roots for the practice of legally protecting human rights. Civil and political rights, understood as a legal claim for a corresponding practice, are not in conflict with social and economic rights. To argue that they are is akin to saying that basic rights have no place in one's own cultural tradition. Although the concept of human rights originated in Europe, in the Western liberal tradition it is universally applicable. It can neither be restricted to the West nor be said to represent an exclusively liberal philosophy. If anything, human rights as individual rights of autonomy and equality, institutionally protected by society through the imposition of limits on state action, can be enriched by non-Western cultural notions of human dignity that may be lacking in the West, particularly in the sphere of economic and social rights. However, basic human rights, as natural rights, should not be confused with the concerns of social justice and economic development as normative commitments.

The foregoing remarks are based on a historical frame of reference, which I believe is the only one that will lead us to an understanding of, and consensus on, human rights. The question is, where does Islam fit into this picture, since the Islamic claim to exclusiveness seems to dash our hopes for a pluricultural consensus on human rights? According to prevailing interpretations, a fundamental precept of Islam is that Muslims are superior to non-Muslims. Islam divides humanity into (1) Muslims, (2) *dhimmis* (Jews and Christians), and (3) nonbelievers. As noted earlier, *dhimmis* can be tolerated, but only as a second-rank minority. The third group cannot be tolerated at all. Muslims who voice opposition to these views can be prosecuted as apostates. Is such a doctrine consonant with the smallest possible core of values that could constitute the basis for a transcultural understanding of human rights?

Let us say that resistance to the intolerable should be the basic principle behind a transcultural understanding of human rights on a global level.[24] This would mean rejecting any claims of superiority and all va-

23. See Vincent, *Human Rights and International Relations*, pp. 42–44, 48.
24. See Richard Falk, *Human Rights and State Sovereignty* (Holmes and Meier, 1981).

rieties of cultural exclusiveness. Can Islam be reformed to make it compatible with the needed core value wherein *le droit à la différence* is respected as a basic human right that can be claimed by all non-Muslims, be they Dinkas, Jews, Christians, Buddhists, Hindus, or simply nonbelievers? Can Muslims learn to speak unambiguously and fluently this universally necessary language of human rights?

I pose this question assuming that a tradition of human rights cannot be established without a cross-cultural consensus on these rights and an institutional framework to guarantee them. I also maintain that, historically, the necessary cultural and institutional groundwork for human rights was first laid in the modern societies of Western Europe, and not in Islamic scriptures, as suggested in the Universal Islamic Declaration of Human Rights of September 1981 (which was, incidentally, pronounced in Paris and not in an Islamic city).[25] Hence my task here is to determine whether this particular European tradition is compatible with Islam.

Islam can be approached either as a religion based on scripture or as a social phenomenon. Islam is indeed based on scripture: the Qur'an, which all Muslims accept as the final and complete revelation of God to all humankind, and the *ḥadith*, or *sunna*, the transmitted sayings and deeds of the Prophet Muhammad. The scriptural understanding of Islam, shared by Muslims and Western Orientalists alike, derives from the study of Islamic primary texts (the Qur'an and the *ḥadith*) as well as secondary texts (the writings of Muslim scholars). The goal of all such study is to properly understand the textually fixed revelation of God.

Social scientists study Islam—or any religion, for that matter—as a social fact. They focus on the way Muslims act and interpret their actions in the framework of existing social structures. Muslim scripturalists focus on the religious texts and interpret Muslim actions in the framework of Islamic precepts; they believe that the revealed text is ahistorical, that is, valid for all times and every place, and thus do not think its meaning is a problem for any given social context. In contrast, social scientists are concerned with the problem of meaning, as they realize that believers in different historical and social contexts ascribe

---

25. *al-bayan al-ʿalami ʿan huquq al-insan fi al-islam* (The Universal Islamic Declaration of Human Rights) has been published in several places. See, for example, Muhammad Salim al-ʿAwwa, *fi al-niẓam al-siyasi li al-dawla al-islamiyya* (On the Political System of the Islamic State), 6th ed. (Cairo: al-maktab al-misri al-ḥadith, 1983), pp. 303–33. For an English translation, see C. G. Weeramantry, *Islamic Jurisprudence: An International Perspective* (St. Martin's Press, 1988), pp. 176–83.

different meanings to the same symbols.[26] The Islamic Declaration of Human Rights is a cultural document that clearly reveals an effort to read the Western tradition of human rights into Islam—and to demonstrate that Islam has always encompassed the values embodied in the concept of human rights. Thus the declaration can be considered a typical example of the scriptural approach to Islam.

I have already mentioned that some type of institutional underpinning is required to safeguard human rights. Of the systems of rules that societies live by—the traditional, charismatic, and legal—only the last one provides an institutionalized body of law that can ensure basic human rights. This is a modern concept that Muslims do not acknowledge. Yet Muslim authors consider Islamic *shari'a* to be the institutional underpinning of political rule. They are, in effect, putting a modern interpretation on Islamic law. They also consider the concept of *shura* (consultation), which appears in two passages of the Qur'an, to be a legal precept calling for political participation in an Islamic system of government.

Viewed in this light, the current Muslim debate on *al-niẓam al-islami* (the Islamic system of government) appears to be contributing to the development of an Islamic tradition of human rights.[27] I believe this reflects a change in Muslim attitudes in the wake of Islam's exposure to and interaction with Western cultures. I have described this process of global cultural interaction as "the crisis of modern Islam."[28] Cultural interaction is nothing new. It has been going on for most of human history, although it did not reach a global scale until the modern age. However, certain cultures did spread far beyond their own boundaries. Islam is one of these.[29]

At the outset of the revelation of Islam, it was "an Arab religion for Arabs."[30] But even before it reached the end of its first century, this new religion was no longer an exclusively Arab one. Nonetheless, many

26. See generally Tibi, *Islam and the Cultural Accommodation of Social Change.*

27. For an Islamic view on this debate, see the book of al-ʿAwwa, *fi al-niẓam al-siyasi li al-dawla al-islamiyya;* and particularly Bassam Tibi, "The Iranian Revolution and the Arabs: The Quest for Islamic Identity and the Search for an Islamic System of Government," *Arab Studies Quarterly,* vol. 8, no. 1 (1986), pp. 29–44, especially pp. 36–37.

28. Bassam Tibi, *The Crisis of Modern Islam: A Preindustrial Culture in the Scientific-Technological Age* (Utah University Press, 1988), pp. 1–8.

29. See the authoritative survey of Marshall G. S. Hodgson, *The Venture of Islam: Conscience and History in a World Civilization,* 3 vols. (University of Chicago Press, 1974).

30. Maxime Rodinson, *Mohammed* (Luzern: C. J. Bucher Press, 1975), pp. 46ff.

people still associate Islam with "Arabness." Although Islam spread far and wide, it never became a universal frame of reference. If we define culture as the local setting underlying the social production of meaning,[31] a culture can become global in the sense that it may spread to other settings and there become locally restricted in its social production of meaning. This is what happened to Islam, as can be illustrated in Morocco and Indonesia, where we find two enormously different varieties of the same religion.[32] In other words, there is no universal Islam, but a variety of local Islamic cultures.

Using the concept of the "civilizing process" as a backdrop, I suggest that European culture since the French Revolution is the first in world history to have become both a global phenomenon and a universal frame of reference.[33] Our understanding of human rights is inexorably linked to the basic rights established within the framework of the French Revolution and earlier articulated by the European philosophers who first proposed the modern theory of natural law. Without doubt, the idea of human rights originated in this European tradition, but today it is considered a part of human heritage in general.

Some writers committed to the ideology of "tiers mondisme" associate human rights with liberalism and even cultural imperialism, which they often use as an excuse to deny these rights. What they fail to recognize is that these values can no longer be considered exclusively characteristic of the political tradition of liberalism. Moreover, some scholars have been reassessing liberal theory as it appears in our age and have begun to question its abstract individualism, its emphasis on political rights devoid of social justice, and its formal participatory politics.[34] In arguing that the modern understanding of human rights is

31. Geertz, *Interpretation of Cultures*, pp. 193–233.

32. Clifford Geertz, *Islam Observed: Religious Development in Morocco and Indonesia* (Yale University Press, 1971); see also my essay on Geertz, "Religio-kulturelle Entwicklung und sozialer Wandel: Gespräche mit Clifford Geertz in Princeton," in C. Geertz, ed., *Religiöse Entwicklungen im Islam Beobachtet in Marokko und Indonesien* (Frankfurt: Suhrkamp Press, 1988), pp. 185–200.

33. Elias, *The Civilizing Process*. See also Tibi, *Crisis of Modern Islam*, pt. 1; and Theodore H. von Laue, *The World Revolution of Westernization: The Twentieth Century in Global Perspective* (Oxford University Press, 1987), especially pts. 6 and 7.

34. For a discussion of the history of liberal theory, see Anthony Arblaster, *The Rise and Decline of Western Liberalism* (Oxford: Basil Blackwell, 1984). See also C. B. Macpherson, *Democratic Theory: Essays in Retrieval* (Oxford: Clarendon Press, 1973). For an analysis of the deficiencies of liberal thought, see, for example, Carole Pateman, *The Problem of Political Obligation: A Critique of Liberal Theory* (Polity Press, 1985).

based on the globalization of the European heritage of democracy and the liberal values of this tradition, I am not taking a liberal approach to the modern world, nor am I reading liberalism into non-Western history.

Indeed, some third world authors have criticized liberal theory in the extreme and thus have helped to distract their audience from the arbitrary acts of their political rulers. They reverse the liberal arguments and emphasize the social rather than the political dimension of human rights.[35] Some of them refuse to discuss political human rights on the grounds that these are the concern of bourgeois intellectuals, even though, as they themselves proceed to argue, human rights can be realized only by satisfying basic human needs for things such as food and shelter.

By focusing on political human rights I do not wish to downplay the importance of meeting material needs (that is, of ensuring social and economic rights), but rather I hope to draw attention to the difference between the two types of rights, which, though interrelated, should not be confused. Famine and food shortages due to economic problems are often used to justify the arbitrary policies of undemocratic regimes, but they cannot explain away the lack of basic human rights. The need for economic development cannot be used to legitimize dictatorship or to excuse acts that violate human rights.[36] The time has come to incorporate what was originally a European tradition of human rights into non-Western cultures. This cultural synthesis amounts to a fusion of such rights and local cultures in such a way that the freedom of the individual is preserved.

The problem is that the notion of *individual freedom* is new to Islamic as well as to many other non-Western cultures. Some might also question how we can expect to have a universal concept of human rights and maintain cultural pluralism at the same time. I believe that by working toward a basic interculturally shared understanding of human rights we can move toward this universality. If we agree that "there is no universal morality . . . there is a plurality of cultures in the world, and these cultures produce their own values," our task is to encourage

35. For an example, see Mohammed Bedjaoui, *Towards a New International Economic Order* (Holmes and Meier, 1979). See also International Institute for Labour Studies, *Islam and a New International Economic Order: The Social Dimension* (Geneva, 1980).

36. See Rhoda E. Howard and Jack Donnelly, "Human Dignity, Human Rights, and Political Regimes," *American Political Science Review*, vol. 80 (September 1986), pp. 812–13.

people of different cultures to speak the language of human rights in their own tongue.[37] In other words, these local values must be made compatible with the concept of human rights.

Before I move on to discuss the feasibility of aligning Islamic values with a pluricultural or universal understanding of human rights, I should clarify some of my terms. By "human rights" I do not simply mean the *normative commitment* to the freedom of individuals. Although I am fully aware of the need to establish cultural—that is, normative—grounds for an authentic tradition of human rights in non-Western cultures, it is equally important to have an institutional system to enforce these rights. Otherwise, any normative tradition of human rights will remain meaningless. The Universal Islamic Declaration of Human Rights of September 1981 strikes me as apologetic in this respect, since it is restricted to the normative assertion that Islam guarantees all norms of human rights without referring, even in passing, to the fact that these rights never existed in a material sense in Islamic history.

The distinction between a norm and its institutional embodiment can best be explained by looking at the European tradition from which human rights have emanated. Long before the French Revolution, the feudal societies of Europe had developed certain concepts that paved the way for democracy, which then gave rise to the institutions needed to safeguard human rights. The most important aspect of these was the idea

> of the immunity of certain groups and persons from the power of the ruler, along with the conception of the right of resistance to unjust authority. Together with the conception of contract as a mutual engagement freely undertaken by free persons . . . this complex of ideas and practices constitutes a crucial legacy from European medieval society to modern Western conceptions of a free society.[38]

In Islam, too, one can find the sectarian view that Muslims should resist unjust rulers, although here it is advanced by religio-political minorities (the Kharijites). The majority, in contrast, would argue that "sixty years of unjust rule is less harmful [to the Islamic community] than one night of disorder." Underlying this view is the precept *al sultan*

37. Vincent, *Human Rights and International Relations*, p. 38.
38. Barrington Moore, Jr., *Social Origins of Dictatorship and Democracy: Lord and Peasant in the Making of the Modern World* (Boston: Beacon Press, 1966), p. 415.

ẓill Allah fi al-ard (the ruler is the shadow of God on earth).[39] The normative justification of resistance against arbitrary rule never became an established and protected tradition in Islam. The fact that such a norm existed in some sources had little historical importance because the Islamic thinkers who approved of such opposition failed to develop the mechanisms and institutions that would have enabled Muslims to curb despotism. To reiterate, as long as a norm of resistance is not backed by institutional support, it has little meaning for society at large.

The history of Europe is marked by an evolving separation of *society* and *state*, which is a necessary prerequisite for establishment of a tradition of human rights. Such a separation never occurred in any of the stages of Islamic history.[40] Consequently, the cultural heritage of Islam consists not of individual rights "against" the state and safeguarded by civil society, but of religious duties.[41]

Despite the complaints about the European tradition—for example, that it has fostered Eurocentrism—the West "still constitutes an island in time and space, the end of which in the ocean of tyranny would also signify the end of culture."[42] Therefore, I believe it is essential to establish an Islamic, though not religiously exclusive, understanding of human rights that learns from Europe. To move forward with such an endeavor, we must recognize that laying the ground for human rights on a local cultural level cannot be isolated from the pluricultural efforts at establishing a universal concern for these rights, and that accepting cultural pluralism does not mean denying that human rights originated in Europe. We must also recognize that human rights cannot be realized without the necessary institutional support.

In November 1983 the Beirut-based Institute for Arab Unity Studies organized a pan-Arab conference on the theme, "Crisis of Democracy in the Arab Homeland." The participants, including myself, represented a good cross section of current political trends. One point on which all

39. Ibn Taimiyya, *al-siyasa al-sharʿiyya fi islah al-raʿi wa al-raʿiyya* (Legal Policy for the Betterment of the Shepherd and the Flock), ed. Muhammad Ibrahim al-Banna and Muhammad Ahmad ʿAshur (Cairo, 1971), p. 185. For a French translation of this maxim, see Henri Laoust, trans., *Le traité de droit public d'Ibn Taimiya* (Beirut, 1948), p. 173.

40. B. Tibi, "al-binaʾa al-iqtisadi al-ijtimaʿi li al-dimuqratiyya" (The Socio-Economic Underpinnings of Democracy), in *azmat al-dimuqratiyya fi al-watan al-ʿarabi* (The Crisis of Democracy in the Arab Homeland) (Beirut: Center for Arab Unity Studies, 1984), pp. 73–87.

41. See Vincent, *Human Rights and International Relations*, pp. 42–44.

42. Max Horkheimer, *Kritische Theorie*, 2 vols., 2d ed. (Frankfurt: S. Fischer Press, 1972), vol. 1, p. 13.

the participants agreed was that Arab regimes, regardless of their political orientation, deny their citizens (perhaps better described as subjects) all basic human rights. At the end of this conference the Arab
Organization of Human Rights was established, and it has since produced several reports to document the sad state of human rights in the
Arab world.[43]

The organization treats human rights as a social issue concerned with
freedom. In contrast, the Islamic Declaration of Human Rights treats
these rights as a religious issue. This document merits closer attention
since it is considered to be the authoritative Islamic statement on the
question of human rights.

The Islamic Declaration of Human Rights

Earlier in this discussion I argued that the concepts of cultural pluralism and the universality of human rights need to be integrated before
human rights can gain legitimacy in non-Western societies. That is to
say, it is essential to reconcile both diversity and universality. At the
same time, one must be careful to specify whose rights are at issue.
When dealing with human rights in Islam, for example, it has to be
made clear whether the objective is to secure the rights of Muslims and
those expected to convert to Islam or to secure the rights of all human
beings.

Put another way, what I am proposing is that an originally European
concept be integrated into non-Western cultures, which in the case of
Islam we can refer to as the Islamization of human rights. However,
some analysts might consider this stage of the Islamization of human
rights to be "only a temporary and transitional one, which will be succeeded by a more complete assimilation of the international human
rights principles in the future." Of course, it is possible that the reverse
may occur, "that Islamic criteria may be used to block a full understanding of the meaning of genuine human rights protections from penetrating into the local legal culture."[44]

43. See my report on the conference and the establishment of the Arab Human Rights
Organization in *Orient*, vol. 25, no. 4 (1984), pp. 473–83. See also the report of the
organization in *IFDA Dossier* 62 (November–December 1987), pp. 63–72 (IFDA is the
International Foundation for Development Alternatives). The latest report of the Arab
Human Rights Organization is *ḥuquq al-insan fi al-waṭan al-ʿarabi* (Human Rights in the
Arab Homeland) (Cairo, 1989); it includes a general introduction and country sections.

44. Ann Mayer, "Islam and Human Rights." I am grateful to Ann Mayer for allowing
me to quote from her manuscript. Quotations on pp. 312–13.

The Islamic Declaration of Human Rights seems to represent an effort toward the integration of the European concept into local culture, even though it fails to resolve the apparent conflict between the notion of Islamic centrality and human rights. At present, the only alternative to this Islamic understanding of human rights is the complete denial of these rights, as advocated by the late Ayatollah Ruhollah Khomeini: "What they call human rights is nothing but a collection of corrupt rules worked out by Zionists to destroy all true religions."[45] One has to keep in mind that the concept of *communal* religious duties is central to Islamic thought and tradition, and so the modern Western concept of *individual* human rights is difficult for the followers of Islam to accept.

The Islamocentric view also prevents Muslims from accepting non-Muslim communities as equals. Therefore, any concept of human rights adopted by Muslims seems likely to be concerned with the rights of Muslims. Yet the Universal Islamic Declaration of Human Rights claims that Islam addresses all humanity: "Fourteen centuries ago Islam rendered human rights legal in full depth and extent. Islam attached to these rights all necessary guarantees to protect them. Islam shaped society according to these rights and thus provided the basis for their realization."[46] The declaration states categorically that human rights are not a new addition to Islam, but have always been included in the Islamic precepts, and that this declaration is based on the Qur'an and the *sunna* of the Prophet, the assumption being that "human reason is incapable of finding the right path for a proper life without the guidance of God" (pp. 308–09). Its authors also state that "knowledge of the tribulations that the world is suffering currently as well as of the very existence of oppressive regimes" has led them to make this declaration.

A careful reading of this declaration indicates that its authors are not actually associating human rights with the history of Islam, but rather are constructing a model, tacitly based on the modern European tradition of human rights, which they are injecting into Islam while claiming that Islam was the first to pronounce these rights to humanity. Although the Qur'an and *sunna* (*hadith*) are cited extensively, the ideas concerning human rights are taken from international documents on human rights without acknowledging them. Strictly speaking, this model is not

45. As quoted by Mayer, "Islam and Human Rights." Mayer also quotes Khamenei as saying that the Universal Declaration of Human Rights is a "collection of mumbo-jumbo by disciples of Satan," p. 40.

46. "The Islamic Declaration," reprinted in al-ʿAwwa, *fi al-niẓam al-siyasi li al-dawla al-islamiyya*, p. 307.

based on scripture, and one need not be a Muslim to agree with the twenty-three principles embodied in this Islamic declaration. As most students of Islamic history and many Islamists will agree, the claim that the fairly sympathetic interpretation of Islamic texts presented in the twenty-three principles has always been the prevailing interpretation of Islam is historically inaccurate.

The fact is, these rights never existed in Islamic history. It seems to me useful to examine these so-called human rights principles of Islam, each of which is accompanied in the declaration by a quotation from the Qur'an or the *sunna* (*ḥadith*) of the Prophet.[47]

—The right to live in dignity.

—The right to freedom.

—The right to equality.

—The right to justice.

—The right to lawful and just treatment in courts. (It amazes me that the legal precept of the presumption of innocence, *al-bara'a hiya al-asl*, is considered Islamic legal doctrine, despite the completely modern character of this rule.)

—The right to protection from the arbitrariness of political rule. (Every student of Islamic history knows that the Islamic state, as well as other traditional states, had no restraints. This should not be understood as an indictment of Islam. It is only in modern times, with the unfolding of "civil" society, that the state has been perceived as a Leviathan whose powers must be limited in order to protect the freedom of the individual. Before the emergence of the modern state based on the principle of "legal rule," *legale Herrschaft*, in the Max Weberian sense, there were no institutions to protect citizens from arbitrary political rule. The Islamic state was no exception.)

—The right to protection from torture.

—The right of the individual to protect his honor and his reputation.

—The right to political asylum. (This right is listed in the declaration as an Islamic human right even though the Arabic term used to refer to it, *luju' siyasi*, clearly reflects a modern concept.)

—The rights of minorities. (The declaration refers here to verse 256 of *Surat al-Baqara*: "There is no compulsion in religion." In fact, Islam protects only the *dhimmis* [Christians and Jews] as minorities, but no others.)

47. The following list of twenty-three Islamic principles of human rights is included in al-ʿAwwa, *fi al-niẓam al-siyasi*, pp. 313–33.

—The right of participation. (The modern Arabic word for this idea is *al-musharaka,* which introduces a new cultural-political meaning. The declaration refers to the *shura* principle, which is discussed later in the chapter.)

—The freedom of thought, of conviction, and of speech. (The detailed description of these rights in the declaration conveys the same meaning as the principle of *le droit à la différence.* This right guarantees the individual complete freedom to subscribe to points of view other than those of the majority. This is a modern principle of human rights that clearly originated in the European tradition of the Enlightenment and has no roots in Islam. It is most tempting to think that there is an Islamic tradition in line with this basic human right, but the claim that this has always been an authentically Islamic norm is completely unfounded.)

—The right to freedom of religious thought. (The declaration states that every person is free to have his own conviction and to pursue it in line with the Qur'anic revelation, "You have your religion and I have mine" [*lakum dinakum wa liyya din*], Qur'an, *Surat al-Kafirun,* verse 6.)

—The right to campaign for and disseminate one's own beliefs.

—Economic rights. (The description of these rights in the declaration accords with the modern critiques of pure political liberalism that emphasize the economic dimension of freedom.)

—The right to private property.

—The right of labor.

—The right to satisfy basic human needs.

—The right to build a family.

—The rights of wives, which include the right of the wife to ask for a divorce, thus ending the monopoly of the husband in this matter.

—The right to education.

—The right to privacy.

—The right to travel (freedom of movement) and choice of residence.

If we agree that the origin of the tradition of human rights has little bearing on establishing these rights worldwide, we might consent to let Muslims believe that they were the first to pronounce these rights, as the declaration suggests, provided that they accepted the universality of these rights and did not reduce them to the "rights of Muslims." But here again the assertions would have no force without a well-established institutional framework to guarantee that these rights were protected and not violated by political rules. To ascribe human rights to the

Qur'an introduces a new cultural concept but does not provide evidence of the material existence of these rights or how they can be protected.

In the Islamic model of human rights we see modern cultural values being attributed to Islam. The normative concerns of human rights, defined as values, are said to be compatible with those of Islamic scripture, but restricted by the notion of Islamic centrality. If these ideas have been part of Islamic doctrine, as is claimed, we should see some evidence of how they are practiced and enforced. As mentioned earlier, the institutional framework required to enforce these rights must be a legal, as opposed to a traditional or charismatic, one.[48] In a political system that can be depicted as legal, political rule is embodied in an office with a restricted term and is defined by rational-legal norms controlled by institutions. To hold political office, a person must comply with the legal rules of that office. In a sophisticated institutional system, an independent and autonomous judiciary is the custodian of this setup. It is not enough to rely on the piety of the rulers or their religious sense of duty. Institutionally controlled subordination to the law is the backbone of any legal rule. The need for such a system is determined by human consensus and not by a divine edict issued through a ruler. In classical Islam, however, political rulers are accountable only to God.[49] But what about the present?

The Universal Islamic Declaration of Human Rights states that political office is rendered by God and that rulers and ruled are equal before God, who has ordained the Islamic law, shari'a, to regulate their relationship: "The ruler has the responsibility to act in accordance with the shari'a with regard to goals (ghayat) and method (minhaj)."[50] The authors of the Islamic declaration are clearly associating "legal rule" with Islam. To them, shari'a is not simply Islamic law, but law in general.

These authors have overlooked the fact that legal rule is based on modern legislative law, whereas shari'a is based on the interpretation of God's will as revealed in the Qur'an. Historically, Islamic jurists have merely been subjects of the ruler, who interpreted the law to justify his actions. To get around this problem, the Islamic declaration invokes another Islamic principle, the shura (counsel or consultation), which it

48. Max Weber, "Die drei reinen Typen der legitimen Herrschaft," in J. Winckelmann, ed., Max Weber: Soziologie. Weltgeschichtliche Analysen-Politik (selected writings) (Stuttgart: Alfred Kröner Verlag, 1968), pp. 151–66.

49. See Ibn Taimiyya, al-siyasa al-shar'iyya. Ibn Taimiyya lived from 1263 to 1328.

50. Islamic declaration as quoted in al-'Awwa, fi al-nizam al-siyasi, p. 311.

interprets as a precept of political participation. Thus, in Islamic society, "policies concerning the public affairs of the umma [Islamic community] as well as the conduct of the authorities who implement these policies are established in accordance with the system of *shura*."[51] This statement is followed by a quotation from the Qur'an: "and they conduct their affairs by mutual consent" (*Surat al-Shura*, verse 38).

References to the *shari'a* and *shura* can also be found in the political literature of Islamic revivalism. Before considering the precepts of Islamic law further and their possible contribution to the cause of human rights, it is important to touch on the Arab-Islamic predicament in our age, which is the close association between religion and the state, on the one hand, and the growing recognition that only a secular order can guarantee democracy and thus the enforcement of human rights, on the other. This predicament has led many Arabic scholars to look for ideas akin to democracy in the Arab-Islamic cultural heritage. Some of them believe that intellectual foundations of democracy are certainly present in Islamic history. But, as one scholar has noted, the institutions needed to enforce such democratic ideals have been lacking: "The great problem or gap remains that only the establishment of corresponding institutions and adequate orders can be the guarantee for the implementation of such ideas, as well as for their further evolution."[52]

Another leading scholar argues that Muslims will have difficulty getting out of the predicament because Islam is based on a long and uninterrupted tradition: "Our present is inexorably linked with the past we have inherited. . . . From this it follows that the problems of freedom and democracy are not simply restricted to the present, but are rather an expression of a cultural state of affairs which has continued for more than one thousand years."[53] Still others have argued that democracy is a modern issue.[54] Therefore, the Arab-Islamic predicament is that democratization is needed in societies that lack the cultural roots for this

51. al-'Awwa, *fi al-nizam al-siyasi*, p. 311.

52. Abdulaziz al-Duri "Democracy in the Islamic Political Philosophy" (in Arabic), in Institute for Arab Unity Studies, *al-dimuqratiyya wa huquq al-insan fi al-watan al-'arabi* (Democracy and Human Rights in the Arab Homeland) (Beirut: Center's Press 1983), p. 212.

53. Hasan Hanafi, "The Historical Roots of the Crisis of Freedom and Democracy in our Contemporary Conscience" (in Arabic), in Institute for Arab Unity Studies, *al-dimuqratiyya wa huquq al-insan*, pp. 175–76.

54. See generally, Center for Arab Unity Studies, *azmat al-dimuqratiyya fi al-watan al-'arabi*.

process. Arabic has no equivalent word for democracy. The Arabic term *al-dimuqraṭiyya* is simply a transliteration of the Western term. Others counter that Islam does provide a pattern of democracy named *shura*. The debate continues even now, and there seems to be no way out of the predicament.

The Reinterpretation of the *Shariʿa* and *Shura*

Recently, there has been a movement to revitalize the legal tradition of Islam embodied in the *shariʿa*. Paradoxically, the *shariʿa* has been invoked by oppressive regimes (like the ones in Sudan under Nimeiri and in Pakistan under Zia al-Haq) to suppress political opposition as well as by their opponents, who see the *shariʿa* as an ideological tool for chipping away at existing regimes. That is to say, "Islam . . . can be quite as effective in legitimizing an opposition movement as it has been historically in legitimizing incumbent regimes."[55] The ambiguity in the application of the *shariʿa* is a reflection of the modern Arab-Islamic predicament referred to earlier. In fact, there is no longer such a thing as pure *shariʿa*.

Islamic legal thought has been greatly influenced by Western law for well over a century. The first Arab-Muslim scholar to study in Europe was Rifaʿa Rafi al-Tahtawi, who in his Paris diary of the 1820s urged the "East" to adopt heavily from the "West" if it wished to see development occur, but only on the condition that this was "not in contradiction to our Islamic laws."[56] Rifaʿa subsequently helped transplant Western concepts to Islamic culture and was one of the first to describe the Arab-Islamic predicament.[57]

In view of "the great diversity in the Islamic legal tradition, rulers rarely tried to impose one version of Islamic law as the sole orthodox

55. Michael Hudson, "Islam and Political Development," in John L. Esposito, ed., *Islam and Development: Religion and Sociopolitical Change* (Syracuse University Press, 1980), p. 12.

56. Quoted in Bassam Tibi, *Arab Nationalism: A Critical Inquiry,* 2d ed. (St. Martin's Press, 1990), p. 86; see pp. 84–88 for a discussion of Tahtawi's work and the Arab-Islamic predicament.

57. The term *legal transplants* was coined by Alan Watson. Transplants come about "when a people voluntarily accepts a large part of the system of another people or peoples." Alan Watson, *Legal Transplants: An Approach to Comparative Law* (University Press of Virginia, 1974), p. 30. Modern Islamic law includes a great deal of such legal transplants.

one."[58] There is no single body of law that constitutes Islamic shari'a. Rather, shari'a refers to various interpretations of Islamic scripture. That is why shari'a can be used to serve modern as well as traditional ends, or to justify the actions of oppressive regimes as well as those of the opposition. There simply is no common understanding of Islamic shari'a, particularly with respect to human rights. That is why "Muslims are currently deeply divided on where Islam stands regarding human rights."[59]

The mainstream of political opposition in contemporary Middle Eastern societies consists of various Islamic groups pressing for the implementation of the shari'a. Even though most of them suffer repeated violations of human rights by the ruling undemocratic political regimes of the region, these groups make it clear that under their rule, should they ever be able to seize power, only the law of Islam will govern. Their main political goal is to see that the Islamic shari'a is implemented. In most cases, the totalitarian element in the various ideologies underlying Islamic revivalism is obvious. The reference to the principles of human rights is simply a tactical move and does not signify an honest commitment to securing these rights for others, including their rivals. Muslim neofundamentalists do not consent to the liberal principle of droit à la différence, be it on political, denominational, or cultural grounds. The harsh attitude of the Sudanese Muslim Brothers under the leadership of Turabi toward non-Muslim and non-Arab Southerners and toward nonfundamentalist Arab and Muslim Northerners is typical, and it provides strong evidence in support of this argument.

One should avoid sweeping generalizations in this regard, however, since Islamic shari'a may serve to promote human rights. Not all of its proponents have totalitarian ends in mind. Although Islamic revivalism is concerned with pursuing an Islamic system of government (nizam siyasi islami) and applying shari'a, not everyone agrees on how this should be done. Furthermore, the term nizam is a literal translation of "system" that does not even appear in the Qur'an.[60] Al-nizam al-islami is a recent concept that has not yet been clearly defined. Consequently,

58. Ann Elizabeth Mayer, "Law and Religion in the Muslim Middle East," in *American Journal of Comparative Law*, vol. 35, no. 1 (1987), p. 133. See also Schacht, *Introduction to Islamic Law*; and Coulson, *History of Islamic Law*.

59. Ann Mayer, "Islam and Human Rights," p. 36.

60. Wilfred Cantwell Smith, *The Meaning and End of Religion*, 2d ed. (Harper and Row, 1978), p. 117. See also the discussion of this issue in Tibi, "Iranian Revolution and the Arabs," especially pp. 36–37.

old and new ideas are still being debated, even where constitutional changes have been introduced.

In other words, the Islamic revivalism that is taking place today, particularly in the Middle East, is a call for Islamic law and government, but it is being sounded by groups that do not always see eye to eye on the concepts involved. In Egypt, for example, article 2 of the 1971 constitution stated that the principles of shariʿa are "a major source of legislation." In 1980 the indefinite article *a* was changed to *the* to appease the country's Islamic opposition, which, however, remained dissatisfied because it contested that this merely amounted to a symbolic gesture.[61] Yet the Islamic revivalists were unable to provide a clear definition of the legal system they assumed was ready to be implemented.

One of the reasons for the ambiguity and the continuing debate is that Islamic revivalists want the Qur'an to be the basis for the legal system, but the term shariʿa is never used in the Qur'an in the sense referred to in the political writings of Islamic revivalism.[62] Moreover, as already mentioned, there are no consistent codified Islamic norms that can be referred to as Islamic law. What is known as Islamic law consists of interpretations of Islamic scripture.

Before revivalism took hold, some Arab and Islamic jurists had tried to combine various European precepts with what they considered to be Islamic norms.[63] This effort gave rise to the existing legal systems, which are by and large secular even though several constitutions stipulate that they should be based primarily on Islamic law. Some of the jurists who had an Islamic education and had received legal training in the West sought to establish a modern Islamic legal tradition based on a new reading of Islamic legal sources in the light of modern European law. One Islamic work that has contributed to this end is *The Principles of Government in Islam Compared with the Principles of Modern Constitutional Law*, first published in 1966.[64] Many refer to this book in claiming that

61. Ann Mayer, "Law and Religion in the Muslim Middle East," p. 138.

62. It does appear in the Qur'an (only three verses) in three places: *al-shura*, v. 13: *al-ma'ida*, v. 48; and, most important, *al-jathiya*, v. 18, "And now we have set you on the right path (*shariʿa*) follow it."

63. See Schacht, *Introduction to Islamic Law*, pp. 100–111.

64. Abdulhamid Mutawalli, *mabadi niẓam al-ḥukm fi al-islam ma-ʿa al-muqarana bi al-mabadi' al-dusṭuriyya al-ḥaditha* (The Principles of the System of Governing in Islam Compared with the Principles of Modern Constitutionalism) (Alexandria: Dar al-Maarif, 1966). See in particular the lengthy chapter "The Sources of Constitutional Legislation in Islamic Shariʿa," pp. 17–266. The *shura* chapter (pp. 659–89) indicates that justice, freedom, and equality were always authentic Islamic principles.

Islam provides a constitutional framework for a system of government that guarantees the rights of participation, justice, freedom, and equality.[65]

A prominent Egyptian jurist has pointed out that *shariʿa* originally meant "source of water" or "the mouth," and that the term itself occurs literally only once in the Qur'an, where it in no way refers to legislation or law.[66] In the course of history, however, it came to be applied to all Islamic precepts, both religious and legal. To add to the confusion, most Muslims fail to distinguish between religion as the revelation of God and religious thought as the human understanding of religion expressed in a wide variety of interpretations. Thus, Ashmawi says, "the call for the implementation of the *shariʿa* is not to *shariʿa* as it is used in the Qur'an itself. It refers instead to the meaning the term has acquired in traditional religious thought. . . . Ultimately the implementation of the shariʿa, in this sense, is the implementation of a system of Islamic thought (p. 53). Furthermore, a close inspection of the Qur'an reveals that its precepts, now interpreted as a legal system named *shariʿa*, have always been related to specific historical situations:

> The *shariʿa* was not revealed all at once nor did it descend as an absolute command. Rather it was tied to reality, revolved around it, and was interwoven with it. *Shariʿa* derived its own rules from prevailing traditions and customs. These rules were modified in keeping with the development of those traditions and customs [Ashmawi, p. 89].

I believe that the *shariʿa* must be interpreted in this way if the spirit of Islam is to be preserved at the same time that Islamic law is adjusted to the current standards of human rights, which it conflicts with in several respects. For example, the *shariʿa* discriminates against women and non-Muslims.[67] This discrimination is incompatible with the principles of the Universal Declaration of Human Rights. Before Islamic *shariʿa* can be reconciled with the concept of the universality of human rights,

65. See, for example, al-ʿAwwa, *fi al-niẓam al-siyasi*, pp. 132, 138, 161.

66. See Muhammad Saʿid al-Ashmawi, *Usul al-Shariʿa*, (The Sources of Shariʿa), 2d ed. (Cairo: Madbuli Press and Beirut: Iqra' Press, 1983), pp. 31, 34.

67. See Abdullahi Ahmed An-Naʿim, "Islamic Law, International Relations, and Human Rights: Challenge and Response," *Cornell International Law Journal*, vol. 20, no. 2 (1987), p. 317; and chap. 7 in An-Naʿim, *Toward an Islamic Reformation: Civil Liberties, Human Rights and International Law* (Syracuse University Press, 1990).

this conflict must be resolved. Muslims have to learn to speak the language of human rights in their own tongue. Although such "enlightenment" does not seem to be in sight at present, things may yet change if the fact that a few Muslim lawyers have begun to speak this language is any indication of what the future holds.

For the time being, Islamic revivalists are preoccupied with pushing for a system of government that is based on the Qur'an. The legal principle of the *shura* is part and parcel of this system. The revivalists boast that the Qur'an contains the first theory of democracy known to humanity, albeit in two short verses:

[Those] who avoid gross sins and indecencies and, when angered, are willing to forgive, [those] who obey their Lord, attend to their prayers, and conduct their affairs by mutual consent/*wa amruhum shura baynahum* [*Surat Al-Shura,* verses 37–38].

Take counsel with them in the conduct of affairs/*wa shawiruhum fi al-amr* [*Surat Al-Imran,* verse 159].

Historically, this latter precept can be traced to the pre-Islamic system of tribal consultation among the leaders of ethnic groups. The Prophet Muhammad consulted with his close colleagues and followers, the foremost being Abu Bakr and Umar. The four righteous caliphs of early Islam maintained this tradition, and then Caliph Umar increased the number of counselors to six.

What the political writings of the Islamic revivalists tell us, however, seems to wander from the historical truth. One recent book of some renown, *fann al-hukm fi al-islam,* contains a long chapter on *shura* that projects modernity into Islam entirely on the basis of the two aforementioned Qur'anic verses.[68] In this book *shura* (counsel) is interpreted as a democratic system that guarantees its citizens all human rights within a participatory framework of freedom. Islam is said to be final divine revelation, which therefore embodies par excellence intellectual progress in all realms of life—in religious rituals, public affairs, and politics, which encompasses human rights: "With regard to progress in any realm of life no human thought can aspire to the standards set by Islam. Thus the correct interpretation of the Qur'an guarantees the individuals

68. Mustafa Abu-Zaid Fahmi, *fann al-hukm fi al-islam* (The Art of Governing in Islam) (Cairo: al-maktab al-misri al-hadith, 1981).

in all epochs the ultimate freedom, the ultimate dignity and the ultimate security" (Fahmi, p. 200). Furthermore,

> if political democracy simply means government of the people, by the people, and that the people are the source of the state's sovereignty and of its powers . . . then Islam must be the first democracy established on earth. . . . I wonder why scholars no longer write on this subject to demonstrate how Islam protects the individual from tyranny no less than any of the most developed modern constitutions [Fahmi, p. 201].

This is a typical example of the arguments put forth by the Islamic revivalists.

For all its problems, Islamic revivalism has added a new dimension to Islamic political thought with regard to human rights that departs from the traditional Islamic viewpoint on this question. Most Islamic fundamentalists believe that God is the only sovereign and thus the sovereignty of a state is based on the will of God. Therefore the function of the individual is to perform God's will, in other words, religious duties, and not to seek rights for the individual. In this traditionalist view, the *ulama* (Islamic religious scholars) are the only people qualified to interpret the will of God and to act as a legislature. Revivalists do not all share this view. Many believe that legislation must be enacted by human beings in accordance with the principle of the *shura* in a conspicuously modern interpretation of popular sovereignty:

> The *shariʿa* has admitted the *shura* as a major pillar in this field [system of government] which means that the legislative power must be set in accordance with the *shura* provision. The people can practice *shura* as they want: either directly, if their small number makes direct democracy in the sense of modern constitutional theory feasible, or indirectly through elected deputies as in parliamentary democracy. . . . In the revelation [Qur'an], Islam has instituted *shura* as a major principle of government: Muslims "conduct their public affairs in mutual consent." Thus, legislative power has to be organized along the lines of the *shura*. No minority is eligible to govern—not even if this minority were to be composed of legal scholars and *muftis* [*ulama*] of Islam.[69]

69. Fahmi, *fann al-ḥukm fi al-islam*, p. 212. Compare this with the totalitarian views of Maudoodi in M. M. Sharif, ed., *A History of Muslim Philosophy*, vol. 1 (Wiesbaden 1963).

In this view, an Islamic constitution is a product of the practice of *shura* and not the result of a divine decree. It is formulated by the people and approved by them. Some would go a step further and say that Islamic *shura*-democracy is the only true democracy in the world: "The Islamic system of government is the most advanced that humanity has ever known. Islam established democracy and instituted *shura* as one of the major elements of state rule. . . . In this way Islam's achievement is unprecedented in the history of mankind."[70] If one asks why, in spite of this alleged achievement, Muslims have been ruled by hateful tyrants throughout their history and thus deprived of their human rights, one is given the stock answer: it is not Islam but Muslims that are to blame.

The political literature of Islamic revivalism calls for an Islamic system of government, but, as noted, no concrete system has been defined. Revivalists merely say the system must be based on the *shariʿa* and on *shura*, its political component. Admittedly, some revivalists read modern ideas into Islam, sometimes with interesting results—most notably, the recognition of human rights and of popular sovereignty.[71] These thinkers pose a challenge to the traditional view that God is the only sovereign and hence the only legislator in an Islamic state. Their interpretation of the Qur'an as being the true source of democracy runs counter to the traditional belief that divine law, the *shariʿa*, provides the binding precepts that humans must live by and that amount to religious duties, not human rights. *Al-niẓam al-islami*, they argue, is the custodian of Islamic *shariʿa*. It is difficult to see how the revivalists can escape these implications and tie this system of government to the freedoms included in the Universal Declaration of Human Rights.[72]

---

70. Fahmi, *fann al-ḥukm fi al-islam*, p. 248.

71. See Hinsley, *Sovereignty*, chap. 6. The modern concept of sovereignty is related to the definition of human rights as natural rights. On an international level, state sovereignty poses the problem of intervention and international enforcement of human rights. See the discussion of these issues in Falk, *Human Rights and State Sovereignty*.

72. The emphasis on the liberal concept of human rights should not be interpreted as if these rights were immutable and absolute. Human rights, too, are historical products and they are subject to evolution. However, they are always the point of departure. For further details, see Ian Shapiro, *The Evolution of Rights in Liberal Theory* (Cambridge University Press, 1986), especially pts. 1 and 4. Western political theory has to be rethought with regard to its "capacity to direct us in the face of the world which now confronts us." John Dunn, *Western Political Theory in the Face of the Future* (Cambridge University Press, 1979), p. 7.

Conclusion

The concept of human rights has evolved in an interesting way since the Age of Enlightenment. From its birthplace in Europe it traveled to other parts of the world, ironically, on the heels of European conquerors. Although non-Westerners were reluctant to accept the foreign culture that they were exposed to, they began to reassess their own cultural heritage in the light of European values and to read new meaning into their indigenous norms and values. To be sure, the primary objective of European colonialists was not to disseminate their humanitarian heritage, but to make economic gains.

Since then, the societies of the world have come into closer contact because of technological advances in communication and transportation. Interestingly, "'the shrinking of the globe,' while it has brought societies to a degree of mutual awareness and interaction that they have not had before, does not in itself create a unity of outlook and has not in fact done so." As Zbigniew Brzesinski put it, "Humanity is becoming simultaneously more unified and more fragmented."[73] That is to say, not all societies subscribe to the same values. The situation is even more complicated in the case of human rights, because many states appear to be in formal agreement with the Universal Declaration of Human Rights and yet deny these rights to their citizens.[74]

The fragmentation that is taking place is particularly evident in the Middle East. This part of the world has been exposed to modern Western political, economic, and cultural practices, but instead of seeking a "unity of outlook," the states there are intensifying their efforts to return to pure Islam.[75] However, it is not Islam in the traditional sense. These states are mobilizing forces against the very Western culture that has caused the revivalists to search for evidence of Western

73. Quotations from Hedley Bull, *The Anarchical Society: A Study of Order in World Politics* (Columbia University Press, 1977), p. 273. See also the newly reprinted study of F. S. C. Northrop, *The Taming of Nations: A Study of the Cultural Bases of International Policy,* 2d ed. (Woodbridge, Conn.: Ox Bow Press, 1987; the first printing was 1952). Northrop points out that owing to cultural diversity, international relations are also intercultural relations.

74. See, for example, the survey in Raymond D. Gastil, ed., *Freedom in the World: Political Rights and Civil Liberties, 1985–1986* (Westport, Conn.: Greenwood Press, 1986). The country summaries are in pt. 5, pp. 251–400.

75. See Tibi, *Crisis of Modern Islam,* and "The Renewed Role of Islam in the Political and Social Development of the Middle East," *Middle East Journal,* vol. 37, no. 1 (1983), pp. 3–13.

precepts (that is, concerning democracy and human rights) in the Qur'an.

These findings oblige us to reformulate our assumption concerning the possibility of using European culture as a frame of reference for other cultures and concerning the globalization of the European heritage. The problem is that, although the structural unity of the present international system is increasing, cultural fragmentation is intensifying in the sense that we are further from a consensus on common values than ever. Thus it is necessary to accept cultural pluralism—as opposed to cultural relativism, which must not be allowed to sanction violations of human rights, such as torture. There can be no compromise as far as these ends are concerned. Otherwise, it looks as though we may have to settle for the universality of human rights coexisting with various cultural efforts at creating these rights on different cultural foundations. In other words, cultural pluralism in the realm of human rights cannot mean more than a cultural indigenization of basic human rights established in the more advanced Western societies since the French Revolution. The rejection of this view by many governments in Asia and Africa has always been an ideological justification for arbitrary rule and for denying humans the very basic human rights criticized as Western values that, in Khomeini's words, "the Westernized intellectuals are imitating."

I suppose that the new interpretations of Islamic scripture and the move to formulate a Universal Islamic Declaration of Human Rights can be considered progress of sorts. Even the belief in the Islamic origin of these rights can be tolerated if we accept cultural pluralism and say that the same values may be arrived at from different foundations. However, without a system of institutional control there can be no guarantee that human rights will be safeguarded. The mere existence of norms means nothing unless there are institutions to enforce them.

Muslim revivalists argue that the Islamic system of government offers such a guarantee, which is embodied in the *shari'a*. But the *shari'a* does not constitute a unitary legal system backed up by an institutional framework. Islamic revivalists do not go much beyond a formal endorsement of human rights. Because Muslims are reluctant to build such a framework, they are unable to establish an Islamic tradition of human rights that is compatible with universal standards. I do not think the situation will change much in the immediate future. Muslims will not be able to guarantee human rights adequately as long as they overlook the historical character of Islamic revelation.

Although Muslims belong to many diverse groups, they all face the same two options, namely, traditionalism or historicism.[76] As long as they are unwilling to apply the method of historicism to their understanding of their own religion, they will continue to accept the literal interpretation of the scripture, and thus to believe that Muslims are superior to others. This is one of the great obstacles preventing them from learning to speak the universal language of human rights in their own tongue. In part this problem can be attributed to the inability of Muslims to cope culturally with rapid social change, which in turn is related to their complete reliance on the scripture for all their social and political norms. Thus, for the time being, the Islamic debate on human rights will probably do little to promote human rights in the universal sense.

76. See Abdallah Laroui, *The Crisis of the Arab Intellectual: Traditionalism or Historicism?* (University of California Press, 1976).

CHAPTER SIX

Current Muslim Thinking on Human Rights

Ann Elizabeth Mayer

MUSLIM VIEWS on the relationship of Islam and human rights are so complex that it is extremely difficult to make valid generalizations about this subject. Shaken by a sudden and as yet incomplete modernization process, the Islamic tradition is in a state of ferment. Exposure to diverse intellectual currents, including liberalism and Marxism, has given rise to different interpretations of Islamic scripture and a range of opinions on any given rights issue. To understand these developments, one must critically examine a variety of positions that Muslims have taken on Islam and human rights.

To begin with, there is widespread enthusiasm for reviving Islamic law to replace the laws and legal institutions borrowed from the West since the onset of its powerful influence in the nineteenth century. Many Muslims see this revival as a form of political resistance to imperialism. Demands for the Islamization of law dovetail with the currents of cultural nationalism that have condemned the Western influences on dress, music, education, the family, and other aspects of life. Campaigns have been launched in the Muslim world to effectuate an "Islamization of modernity," which entails subjecting institutions borrowed from the West to Islamic critiques and reforming them along Islamic lines. Advocates of Islamization have also called upon Muslims to reject international human rights, which they associate with the West, and to replace them with Islamic rights principles. But what are these Islamic rights principles? Where are they set forth? And what is one to make of the fact that many Muslims enthusiastically support the international human rights norms apparently without seeing any conflict between these rights and their religion?

In the premodern era, Islamic thought on human rights, like the Judeo-Christian tradition, emphasized the duties of the believer vis-à-vis the deity, not the protection of individual freedoms. The rules of the

133

premodern *shari'a* were elaborated primarily in treatises written by jurists between the ninth and thirteenth centuries. These rules mandated various types of inequality and restricted freedoms in ways that broadly coincided with the social structure and customary law of traditional Arabian society and the societies that were incorporated into the Islamic community in the early centuries of the Islamic conquests. Islamic legal thought reflected the values and priorities characteristic of traditional societies (see chapter 7), whose main concern was to safeguard social solidarity and traditional family structure. As a result, the importance of individual freedoms was downgraded. Not surprisingly, the *shari'a* rules elaborated in this context were at odds with those codified many centuries later in the International Bill of Human Rights.

There are Muslims who still adhere to the rules set down by the premodern jurists and do not believe their validity has been affected by changed social and economic circumstances. Their religious beliefs prevent them from endorsing many international human rights norms. But there are also Muslims who dismiss the ideas of the premodern jurists as products of the time and circumstances in which they were elaborated and who call for updated interpretations of Islamic texts that take into account advances in knowledge and the present needs and problems of the Muslim community. In addition, the monopoly over interpretation formerly enjoyed by religious scholars has eroded, as expanded opportunities for education and exposure to new ideas have prompted many Muslims who are not clerical specialists in religious law to participate in debates on the contemporary meaning of the Islamic legacy. Many of the influential works on Islam in relation to the problems of contemporary society are by Muslims who are not themselves members of the religious establishment. As I explain in this chapter, Muslims who are not adverse to updating and reforming their tradition in the light of changed social realities and modern ideas tend to welcome fresh interpretations of Islamic requirements that harmonize Islam and international human rights principles.

Because Muslim attitudes toward international human rights vary greatly and therefore are difficult to survey, it is tempting when writing on this topic simply to refer to the Islamic sources. These seem finite and concrete. Indeed, both Western and Muslim authors have concentrated primarily on Islamic sources (the Qur'an and *sunna* of the Prophet), or sometimes on their interpretations in the works of jurists, in their search for direct counterparts or rejections of modern rights norms. Thus many works on the topic of Islam and human rights are burdened with long quotations from these sources, followed by conclusory assertions of whether they correspond to or conflict with international rights norms, as if the implications of these ancient texts for human rights were self-evident. In reality, of course, these texts can be interpreted in many ways and by themselves prove nothing.

I attempt to shed some light on Muslim attitudes toward human rights by examining some representative Muslim opinions. Islam should be treated not as a static entity embodied in texts with fixed meanings, but as an evolving phenomenon that is manifested in the day-to-day lives and conduct of Muslims. Therefore it is important to look at the conduct of actual governments, even though state practice does not have normative force in Islamic law. I discuss the functions of Islam as a component of contemporary legal systems and of state-sponsored ideologies, where it has had great impact on rights.[1] By showing how governmental policies that apply Islamic law affect rights, I hope to correct some of the trends in the literature on Islam and human rights—particularly the emphasis on textually derived, idealized visions of a perfect Islamic society in which no rights abuses are possible.

Westerners writing on Islam and rights have been reluctant to pass judgment on whether the Islamic tradition as embodied in state policies and applied by Muslim governments conforms to relevant international norms on human rights. I take issue with the notion that the canons of cultural relativism should preclude using international human rights standards for any critical review of de jure and de facto treatments of human rights standards that are officially justified by reference to Islamic criteria. Indeed, because the International Bill of Human Rights is itself being adopted by more and more Muslims as the normative standard for rights, the international human rights standards should be treated as part—admittedly only one part—of the evolving Islamic tradition and the complex Islamic response to human rights issues. I concentrate on civil and political rights, because these are currently the most hotly contested issues in the disputes about international versus Islamic versions of human rights. They are also the rights that people living in Muslim countries have come to take particularly seriously because they are so frequently and egregiously violated.

1. Scholars who share the view that one must look at the conduct of Muslim governments in this connection include Abdullahi An-Naʿim, whose work is discussed later in the chapter, and Sami Aldeeb Abu Sahlieh, "Les droits de l'homme et l'Islam," *Revue générale de droit international public*, vol. 89 (1985), pp. 625–716.

Tensions between the Islamic Tradition and International Law

Islam is both a religion and a scheme of law that includes its own rules of international law, known as the *siyar*.[2] Since Muslims believe Islamic law is divinely inspired, in theory it has to be treated as though it superseded all man-made laws. Thus, whenever there is a conflict between Islamic and international law, Muslims are bound to follow their religious law. Of course, according to international law, where there are applicable international legal norms, these are supreme and override laws that conflict with them.

In their international relations, contemporary Muslim governments defer to public international law. It would be impractical to rely on Islamic law because the relations between countries are not amenable to being managed according to the scheme of the premodern *siyar*. In internal matters, however, Muslim governments do not consistently defer to public international law. When it comes to those international principles that are designed to regulate the way governments exercise their power over persons subject to their domestic jurisdiction, premodern *shari'a* rules may be applied. The premodern *shari'a* personal status law has persisted in somewhat modified form in the legal systems of most Muslim countries.[3]

Many Muslim countries are signatories to the international human rights conventions. Formally, at least, they acknowledge the authority of international human rights standards. However, some Muslim countries have refused to sign international human rights conventions. Saudi Arabia and postrevolutionary Iran have maintained that their religious obligations compel them to uphold the supremacy of Islamic law in their domestic legal systems. Here the latent tensions between Islamic and international law become, at least ostensibly, the cause of conflict — but there may be other reasons for rejecting international law. An official policy of repudiating international human rights standards in order to follow *shari'a* law may not necessarily be dictated by the religious piety of the persons who wield power, but may merely be a convenient pre-

2. Aspects of these rules are outlined in Majid Khadduri, *War and Peace in the Law of Islam* (Johns Hopkins University Press, 1955).

3. Saudi Arabia retains the premodern rules as the law of the land. For the general patterns of *shari'a* influence on legal systems today, see Ann Elizabeth Mayer, "Law and Religion in the Muslim Middle East," *American Journal of Comparative Law*, vol. 35, no. 1 (1987), pp. 127–84.

text for denying freedoms that the government wishes to curtail for reasons of self-interest.

Muslim opinion seems divided on whether Islamic law should take precedence over public international law. Some Muslims who are committed to the premodern *shari'a* still follow the older *siyar* rules and therefore reject the authority of public international law. Many more seem eager to find ways to reconcile the competing claims of Islamic and international law. Still others argue that international law is itself a product of Islamic influences, even though neutral historical scholarship has not so far established this proposition.[4] Some Muslims simply treat Islamic law and international law as complementary legal orders and ignore the possibility of conflict.[5] There seems to be a growing tendency in the Muslim world to assume that public international law is part of the heritage of humankind, so that no special Islamic justification is required for adhering to it.

This movement toward a reconciliation of Islam and international law can serve as a foundation for crafting schemes of human rights that fit both international and Islamic criteria, provided a genuine effort is made to eliminate potential conflicts by offering new interpretations of the Islamic sources that accommodate a modern rights philosophy.

Competing Visions of Human Rights in the Islamic Tradition

The unsettled nature of the relationship between Islamic and public international law has repercussions in the area of human rights. Muslims who still follow the premodern jurists associate international human rights concepts with Christian and European tradition, which they consider to be alien to and therefore incompatible with Islam. Reluctant to say that following Islam means denying human rights, Muslims who

4. The argument that Islam shaped international law has also recently been put forward by a Western scholar. Marcel A. Boisard, "On the Probable Influence of Islam on Western Public and International Law," *International Journal of Middle Eastern Studies,* vol. 11, no. 4 (1980), pp. 429–50. The article demonstrates ways that such influence was possible rather than proves it was probable.

5. A good example of this approach is Sobhi Mahmassani, "The Principles of International Law in the Light of Islamic Doctrine," *Académie de droit international, Recueil des cours,* vol. 117 (1966, I), pp. 201–328. How Muslims view the relationship between Islamic and public international law is reviewed succinctly in Rudolph Peters, *Islam and Colonialism: The Doctrine of Jihad in Modern History* (The Hague: Mouton, 1979), pp. 137–45.

reject the international norms now argue for the substitution of Islamic human rights, or rights that Islamic sources have supposedly authorized. Islamic schemes of human rights are a recent innovation that appeared only after the articulation of human rights principles in international documents like the Universal Declaration of Human Rights of 1948. Especially in the last two decades, the impetus to conjoin Islamic law and human rights principles has spawned many new theories and publications.

The literature on Islamic human rights commonly suggests that Islam has had its own human rights tradition ever since it came into being in the seventh century. The fabrication of Islamic pedigrees for modern human rights principles, while involving a distortion of legal history, has twofold significance. It demonstrates the extent to which ideas of identifiably Western, Christian provenance remain unacceptable in some Muslim milieus. It also bears witness to the appeal and prestige that human rights ideals enjoy in the Muslim world.

One might see in Muslim claims that human rights originated in the Islamic tradition a kind of benign fiction designed to facilitate their adoption in Muslim countries. Although this may indeed be the motive for fostering this fiction in some instances, the ramifications are not always benign. The idea of the Islamic origins of human rights can also be used to undermine the authority of the international models. Islamic models that do not offer rights protections equivalent to those in the corresponding international norms can be used to justify violating the international norms.

The Universal Islamic Declaration of Human Rights of 1981, discussed by Bassam Tibi in this volume, is a case in point. It articulates in its foreword the proposition that "Islam gave to mankind an ideal code of human rights fourteen centuries ago," a code that the declaration purports to restate.[6] In fact, the model is patently derivative: it is obvious from the similarities between the terminology and format of this Islamic Declaration and the 1948 Universal Declaration of Human Rights that the intention is to persuade Muslims that the protections offered in the Islamic version will be the substantial equivalent of those offered in international law. However, when one examines the substance of individual provisions, one discovers noteworthy discrepancies between the rights offered in the two schemes. For example, the Islamic declaration, most clearly in the authoritative Arabic version, states that all rights are

6. *Universal Islamic Declaration of Human Rights* (London: Islamic Council, 1981).

guaranteed only to the extent that they are protected by Islamic law.[7] This ambiguous document—which shows a strong formal resemblance to the 1948 declaration but actually treats Islamic law as the controlling standard—reflects the lack of critical analysis of the relationship between the Islamic and Western traditions.

However, one also finds Muslims who believe that the Islamic tradition, interpreted in an enlightened and progressive spirit, is broadly or even entirely congruent with the principles of modern international human rights. Thus, when such Muslims speak of Islamic human rights, they are in fact offering a theological endorsement of the principles in the International Bill. They acknowledge the historical contingency of the premodern *shari'a* rules and stress the elements in the rich and complex Islamic tradition that embody values and concepts analogous to those underlying international human rights schemes. In their view, a harmonization of the Islamic tradition and respect for human rights is eminently feasible.

In addition, some Muslims ground their belief in human rights in their Islamic creed. One might compare them to the Reverend Martin Luther King, Jr., whose strong Baptist faith nourished his commitment to the crusade for civil rights. For example, a Sudanese Muslim legal scholar, Professor Abdullahi An-Na'im, has gained international recognition for his involvement in the campaign for human rights in the Sudan, particularly during 1983–85, the worst phase of Nimeiri's repressive regime, in which Islam provided the pretext for egregious human rights violations. An-Na'im's new approach includes exceptionally honest discussions of the problems in reconciling elements of the premodern *shari'a* and modern rights principles. He has also presented thoughtful proposals for new interpretations of Islamic scripture that help to eliminate conflicts that stand in the way of a synthesis of Islam and human rights.[8]

7. Rights are qualified throughout by references to "the Law" in the English version. The Explanatory Notes state that "the Law" denotes the *shari'a*. Section XII of the Preamble says that the Islamic order is one "wherein no one shall be deprived of the rights assured to him by the Law except by its authority and to the extent permitted by it." Therefore, it is the *shari'a* that sets the limits on rights in this scheme, not international principles. The use of the *shari'a* to qualify rights is much more apparent in the Arabic version.

8. His work includes Abdullahi Ahmed El Naiem, "A Modern Approach to Human Rights in Islam: Foundations and Implications for Africa," in Claude E. Welch, Jr., and Ronald I. Meltzer, eds., *Human Rights and Development in Africa* (Albany: State University of New York Press, 1984), pp. 75–89; and Abdullahi Ahmed An-Na'im, "Religious Free-

Another devout Muslim who has worked on behalf of democratic freedoms is Mehdi Bazargan, the former prime minister of Iran. Bazargan struggled bravely to promote human rights under the late Shah of Iran, whose rule was marked by systematic violations of human rights and brutal repression of both the secular and religious opposition. Bazargan viewed Islam and the Islamic clergy as natural allies in this struggle, and after the Islamic Revolution his piety and credentials as a rights activist enabled him to win the support of both the clerical and liberal-leftist factions in the new regime. Later, after a falling out with the increasingly powerful and antidemocratic clerical faction, Bazargan was forced to leave the government, but he continued a lonely fight in Iran for democratic freedom as the leader of an opposition party and one of the few politicians of stature in Iran who has been a consistently outspoken critic of the denial of human rights under the Khomeini regime.

These and other Muslims feel that there can be a natural synergism of human rights and their own religious tradition, but they have also had to confront the painful reality that Islam may be used not only to inspire those who struggle against political oppression, but also to provide official justification for denying rights and freedoms.

The State and Islamic Human Rights Schemes

There is a sharp dichotomy between the attitudes of private Muslims toward rights and the policies implicit in Islamic human rights schemes endorsed by states. The Iranian government has probably gone further than any other in openly adopting Islam as the rationale for the de jure denial of rights, and Iran's 1979 constitution may be taken as a model of the thesis that Islamic law mandates restrictions on rights, with the

---

dom in Egypt: Under the Shadow of the Islamic Dhimma System," in Leonard Swidler, ed., *Religious Liberty and Human Rights in Nations and Religions* (Philadelphia: Ecumenical Press, 1986), pp. 43–59. An-Na'im has drawn inspiration from the ideas of Mahmud Muhammad Taha, the leader of the Republican movement in the Sudan and a proponent of new interpretations of Islam that brought its teachings in harmony with modern human rights principles. Taha's execution by Nimeiri as an "apostate" on January 18, 1985, for opposing Nimeiri and his Islamization program is now annually commemorated as Arab Human Rights Day. An-Na'im discussed Taha's trial and execution in "The Islamic Law of Apostasy and Its Modern Applicability: A Case from the Sudan," *Religion*, vol. 16 (1986), pp. 197–224. For his translation of Taha's interpretations of the Qur'an, see Abdullahi An-Na'im, trans., *The Second Message of Islam: Mahmoud Mohamed Taha* (Syracuse University Press, 1987).

result that its Islamic version of rights is much narrower than those in the International Bill.

Iran's constitution elevates religious tradition over otherwise applicable secular rights principles.[9] Some of its specific rights provisions have separate Islamic qualifications, as in article 27, which allows unarmed assemblies and marches provided "they are not detrimental to the fundamental principles of Islam" (p. 38), but there are broader Islamic qualifications as well. For example, article 4 states:

All civil, penal, financial, economic, administrative, cultural, military, political, and other laws and regulations must be based on Islamic criteria. This principle applies absolutely and generally to all articles of the Constitution as well as to all laws and regulations, and the *fuqaha* on the Council of Guardians have the duty of supervising its implementation [p. 29].

This means that all of the rights provisions in the Iranian constitution, even those not expressly subject to Islamic conditions, are subject to qualification by Islamic principles, which constitute the supreme law of the land and can even override the constitution itself.

Article 20 stipulates how Islamic criteria affect rights: "All citizens of the nation, both women and men, equally enjoy the protection of the law and enjoy all human, political, economic, social, and cultural rights, in conformity with Islamic criteria" (p. 36).

The provision allowing human rights to be enjoyed "according to Islamic standards" does not specifically say that Islamic criteria are to be used to restrict rights and freedoms. Could not these "Islamic standards" be understood to mandate a higher, rather than lower, standard of rights protections? While this is a theoretical possibility, the record of conduct by the Iranian regime provides a gloss regarding how these principles are in fact interpreted by the Iranian government. The extensive human rights abuses perpetrated in the years since the Islamic Revolution indicate that the regime has consistently applied "Islamic standards" to curb and even entirely negate the rights and freedoms available under international human rights standards. Furthermore, the institutional framework for protecting rights has been deliberately dismantled in the course of establishing the Iranian version of Islamic jus-

9. Hamid Algar, trans., *Constitution of the Islamic Republic of Iran* (Berkeley: Mizan Press, 1980).

tice, thereby disabling people from seeking redress for violations of rights. The Iranian Bar Association has been destroyed and the judiciary replaced by clerics and new judicial trainees who are prepared to carry out the regime's policies and to mete out summary justice in proceedings from which any semblance of due process has been eliminated.[10]

Muslims' reactions to Khomeini's Islamization program have varied widely. Muslims who supported Ayatollah Khomeini politically do not appear troubled by the human rights violations, but other Muslims find these violations to be monstrous perversions of central Islamic values.[11] Even some of Iran's high-ranking clerics have publicly denounced the official interpretations of Islamic law, the cruelty of the Islamic courts, and the suppression of democratic freedoms.[12]

Given the dissension that the Iranian record of rights violations has provoked among Muslims, should it be treated as a local Shi'a or Iranian aberration? The answer seems to be negative. The treatment of rights in postrevolutionary Iran has broader significance, because analogous developments have taken place elsewhere in Sunni environments like the Sudan and may be brewing in other countries, such as Afghanistan, where there are strong Islamic fundamentalist forces that may favor using Islam to deny or circumscribe rights and freedoms.

The example of Pakistan also merits brief consideration here. Islamization in Pakistan after the coup by General Mohammad Zia in 1977 meant the effective abrogation of many civil and political rights and gave the conservative but politically compliant clerics greater influence in the judiciary. President Zia pursued his Islamization program via martial law from 1977 to 1985, and during this period the rights provisions of Pakistan's constitution were suspended. The end of martial law in 1985 was initially taken by some to signal a relaxation of dictatorial military rule, but in May 1988, impatient with the watered-down form of democracy he had tolerated since 1986, President Zia dismissed the government and disbanded the relatively tame National Assembly. On June 15, 1988, he issued a presidential decree, the Islamic Law En-

10. Extensive evidence of rights violations has been collected by Amnesty International and has been published in Amnesty's annual reports, newsletters, and special reports on Iran, such as *Iran: Violations of Human Rights: Documents Sent by Amnesty International to the Government of the Islamic Republic of Iran* (London, 1987).

11. For example, see the reactions of Suroosh Irfani, *Iran's Islamic Revolution: Popular Liberation or Religious Dictatorship?* (London: Zed Books, 1983).

12. Irfani, *Iran's Islamic Revolution*, pp. 214–17, 220–21; Sepehr Zabih, *Iran since the Revolution* (Johns Hopkins University Press, 1982), p. 79; and Amnesty International, *Law and Human Rights in the Islamic Republic of Iran* (London, February 1980), pp. 52, 54–55.

forcement Ordinance, making the *shariʿa* the supreme law of the land—thereby allowing it to supersede provisions in the constitution, just as the government had done in postrevolutionary Iran. He also planned to intensify and accelerate Islamization by giving Islamic clerics the right to interpret the requirements of the *shariʿa*, which would have enabled some of the most reactionary elements in Pakistani society to impose their political and social views in the guise of applying the *shariʿa*. Pakistani women were thereby threatened with losing the rights that ameliorative legislation and progressive court rulings had afforded them over several decades. Of course, the sudden death of Zia in an accident in August 1988 and the remarkable subsequent transition to a democratically elected government have obviated the fears that Zia would further exploit Islamic criteria to dismantle protection for civil and political rights.

As these examples clearly show, Muslim governments that are philosophically disposed to diminish the autonomy of their citizens and to subvert rights protections find in the application of Islamic law a pretext for curbing democratic freedoms and denying human rights. At the same time, Muslims are becoming more disposed to hold that Islam mandates protections of the same human rights. This divergence creates enormous tensions.

Human Rights—a Political or a Religious Issue for Muslims?

In view of the present trend toward Islamization and the limited progress of secularization in Muslim societies, political discourse, including the debates on human rights, will inevitably revolve around the use of Islamic concepts, principles, and symbols.[13] This does not mean that all human rights controversies among Muslims or in the Muslim world necessarily begin and end at the level of Islamic discourse. Far from it. As already noted, some Muslims have begun to treat the human rights principles of international law as part of the common heritage of humankind that Muslims can utilize without requiring any special religious dispensation. This is a significant development, because Muslims still live in cultures that are permeated by religion in a way that Western culture has not been for centuries. Treating political life as a domain

13. The lack of progress of secularization in the Muslim world is analyzed by Bassam Tibi, "Islam and Secularization: Religion and the Functional Differentiation of the Social System," *Archiv für Rechts- und Sozialphilosophie*, vol. 66 (1980), pp. 207–22.

independent of religious constraints reflects a new, modern perspective on the role of religion in society.

Despite the recent tendency in Islamic thought to ideologize Islam — that is, to treat it as an all-encompassing program of regulations—there are Muslims who believe that the scope of Islamic law is more limited. This view is not new: in much of the premodern Islamic jurisprudence, private law matters were emphasized and Islamic law was by and large undeveloped in the area of politics and public law.[14] Moreover, Muslims are currently offering some telling critiques of what they view as a present tendency to exaggerate the domain of Islamic law and to make political issues theological ones without offering an adequate analysis of the governmental or political problems in Muslim societies.[15] They find an Islamic warrant for a separate secular sphere.[16] They may find that treating rights issues as a matter of secular politics is more consonant with authentic Islamic tradition than are the contemporary ideologized versions of Islam, which sacralize all political questions, including human rights issues. As Bassam Tibi has noted elsewhere in this volume, many Muslims have criticized injecting Islam into the political sphere, where it inevitably becomes the tool of secular, political factions.

Many of the human rights groups that are proliferating in the Muslim world have practical agendas and are focusing on projects designed to protect individuals against the rights abuses prevalent in Muslim coun-

14. See, for example, Yadh Ben Achour, "Structure de la pensée politique islamique classique," *Pouvoirs*, vol. 12 (1980), pp. 15–26.

15. In this connection, I expect that the scholarship of Professor Mohammed Arkoun of the Sorbonne is destined to have far-reaching and lasting impact. His recent works include *Pour une critique de la raison islamique* (Paris: Maisonneuve et Larose, 1984) and *L'Islam, morale et politique* (Paris: Desclée de Brouwer, 1986). Provocative analyses of this topic are also offered in Muhammad El Shakankiri, "Loi divine, loi humaine et droit dans l'histoire juridique de l'Islam," *Revue historique de droit français et étranger,* vol. 59 (1981), pp. 161–82, and Hisham Djaït, "Islam et politique," in Ernest Gellner and Jean-Claude Vatin, eds., *Islam et politique au Maghreb* (Paris: Centre National de la Recherche Scientifique, 1981), pp. 141–49.

16. There are interesting parallels with debates on religion and state in early American history. I am grateful to David Little for educating me about aspects of Roger Williams's ideas formulated in a period when Christian thought was wrestling with whether there could be a religious warrant for a secular sphere. See David Little, "Roger Williams and the Separation of Church and State," in James E. Wood, Jr., ed., *Religion and the State: Essays in Honor of Leo Pfeffer* (Waco: Baylor University Press, 1985). In the contemporary Islamic environment there are Muslims who are fighting battles very similar to the ones that Williams fought in the seventeenth century in Rhode Island.

tries.[17] Bassam Tibi, a cofounder of the Arab Organization for Human Rights and one of its most articulate spokespersons, demonstrates this practical orientation and its corollary—impatience with the idealized, abstract schemes of the Islamic order and with the comprehensiveness that proponents of Islamization endlessly extol while refusing to offer detailed solutions to specific problems, such as how to institutionalize human rights protections in contemporary political systems.

Pragmatically oriented Muslim rights activists may choose not to participate personally in theological debates. Viewed from the standpoint of Muslims whose first priority is to develop mechanisms to protect democratic freedoms, the ongoing theological disputes about where Islamic doctrine stands on questions of human rights may appear academic. Nonetheless, the work of such Muslims should not be dismissed when one looks at where the Islamic tradition stands vis-à-vis human rights. By their commitment to work for human rights as defined by international law, these Muslim rights activists are implicitly taking a position on a highly contentious point of Islamic doctrine that is opposed to that of Muslims who insist that Islam mandates a distinctive, comprehensive blueprint for all human activities, including politics.

One must be careful not to treat the views that are radically antimodern, especially the pronouncements of reactionary clerics, as more authentically "Islamic" than the ideas of liberal or progressive Muslims that correspond more closely to the values behind modern international human rights principles.

Some Muslims who are opposed to international human rights principles—and, indeed, to any ideas that come from the West—would tend to support the idea that the farther an "Islamic" position diverges from modern, Western norms or the more it resembles the views propounded by premodern Islamic jurists, the closer it comes to representing authentic Islamic doctrine. However, looking for what is maximally opposed to Western norms has not normally been the method used in the Islamic legal tradition as the way to measure the validity of competing interpretations of Islamic requirements! Furthermore, the humanism, moderation, rationality, flexibility, and openness that characterize much of the Islamic tradition are highly prized by Muslims and leave many of them

17. As an introduction to the local human rights organizations working in the Middle East, see MERIP (Middle East Research and Information Project), *Middle East Report*, vol. 17 (November–December 1987), which contains a number of articles on this subject.

disinclined to accept arguments that their religion is a static body of doctrine impervious to change that obliges them to reject ideas from the West, even where the latter are of demonstrable value. Thus, outside observers can easily be misled if they assume that the average Muslim considers the more exotic, reactionary "Islamic" views to be more consonant with his own Islamic tradition than ones that correspond to the aspirations of contemporary Muslims for enhanced rights and freedoms along international lines.

Therefore, when Muslims present ideas on rights that are similar to modern, Western ones, these should not be dismissed out of hand on the theory that any similarities to Western ideas mean that the ideas are inherently "un-Islamic" or that their proponents are necessarily alienated from their own tradition. It would be particularly hard to justify dismissing one segment of Muslim views on rights as insufficiently "Islamic" in character in the face of the dissension among Muslims on where the Islamic tradition stands on rights issues.

An example that current news reports bring to mind is that of the recently excommunicated Archbishop Lefebvre, who appears to represent an extreme form of Catholicism that is untouched by the inroads of modernity and farthest removed from the model of Protestantism. His position resembles that of the pre–Vatican II Church in its ambitions to dominate government and politics. If one were surveying the Catholic tradition, one would be ill-advised to consider his views more authentically "Catholic" than those of the Vatican or to claim that the views of leftist priests in Latin America and of liberal lay Catholics in Northern Europe and America should be automatically discounted. Treating Archbishop Lefebvre's views as more inherently "Catholic" would also mean taking at face value his claim that he stands for the true Church, which is incompatible with the wariness one should employ in evaluating such self-serving characterizations. Furthermore, to do so would effectively be to take sides in an internal church dispute and to delegitimize the views of Catholic critics of Lefebvre. In a survey of Catholic ideas, Lefebvre's views should simply be acknowledged as constituting one among many points along the broad spectrum of contemporary Catholic opinion.

If one should not use the ideas of Archbishop Lefebvre as benchmarks for determining where pure or authentic Catholicism stands on contested questions, it seems that one should also go beyond the ideas of premodern Islamic jurists and the opinions of the more obscurantist and reactionary elements in the Islamic clergy and give consideration to the full range of Muslim opinion on a disputed issue like human rights, including Muslim opinion at the other end of the political spectrum. Thus, I would argue that the wholehearted endorsement of international human rights standards has to be recognized as one part of the Islamic tradition.

Comparing Islamic Cultural Norms and International Human Rights

In examining human rights in cross-cultural perspectives, one necessarily supposes that such comparisons are valid. But should such comparisons treat the International Bill of Human Rights as a normative standard? Is it legitimate to criticize Islamization schemes where these entail derogations from rights guaranteed under the International Bill?

Strong objections are raised when rights concepts bearing "Islamic" labels are judged in relation to their international counterparts, where the latter are treated as the norm. The typical charge is that such assessments violate the canons of cultural relativism or that they are vitiated by an inevitable association with the imperialist enterprise, since they use Western norms to establish deficiencies in the products of third world cultures. I have come to the conclusion that such objections rest on flawed premises.[18]

When speaking of the need for cultural relativism, I believe that one generally has in mind the image of an anthropologist from a modern Western culture attempting to study a traditional society that is organized along quite different lines. There must be some concern lest the anthropologist bring along the baggage of preconceptions taken from the advanced Western culture that will lead him or her to misread the traditional society and dismiss it as defective or inferior simply because it functions in different ways and has different goals. A respect for cultural relativism would mean that the anthropologist would be careful to avoid referring to the Western culture as a universal normative model and would bear in mind that societies may define and solve problems and set priorities in different ways. The investigation would be improved, since elements in the traditional society would be viewed in the

---

18. In pondering this issue, I have found the work of An-Naʿim very stimulating. See also Jack Donnelly, "Cultural Relativism and Universal Human Rights," *Human Rights Quarterly*, vol. 6 (1984), pp. 400–19; and Fernando R. Tesón, "International Human Rights and Cultural Relativism," *Virginia Journal of International Law*, vol. 25 (1985), pp. 869–98.

context of that society, and not in relation to modern Western societies, where they might not fit or where they might have a different meaning. In particular, the investigator would not criticize the traditional culture simply because its institutions and priorities did not correspond to modern Western models.

Should this scheme, in which cultural relativism admittedly makes sense, have any bearing on the comparison between Islamic versions of human rights norms and those in public international law? There are several reasons why it should not. Human rights principles are not creations of a traditional culture like ritual circumcisions, tribal social organization, or bride prices. They are principles that were developed in Western culture from the eighteenth century onward and later via their formulations after World War II in the International Bill of Human Rights. The civil and political rights they afford are not designed to deal with the communitarian or tribal structures of traditional societies but with the problems of the rights and freedoms of the individual in modern nation states, where the state is in a position to exert centralized control over the society, dominating and oppressing those subject to its great coercive power.

Rather than being products of the indigenous culture, Islamic versions of human rights represent legal transplants that have been taken from Western and international human rights principles. One of the ways that legal cultures have historically grown is by borrowing laws and institutions. Comparative legal history studies legal transplants in a variety of contexts.[19] Whether the transplants stay the same or undergo permutations in their new environments, research on their fate should not be barred simply because the legal culture into which they have been transplanted is one bearing the imprint of an Islamic legacy.

Those who argue against using modern human rights norms to measure distinctive, "Islamic" rights ideas on the grounds of cultural relativism may think that Muslims' ideas are shaped by the values of traditional societies in the Muslim world. But Muslims' ideas on human rights today are rarely the products of immersion in traditional culture, which is rapidly eroding under the impact of urbanization, industrialization, the expanding mass media, and other forces. Although the ideas of Muslims who write about the hypothetical *nizam islami* do bear the

---

19. Alan Watson, *Legal Transplants: An Approach to Comparative Law* (University Press of Virginia, 1974).

imprint of a dissimilar cultural tradition, the debates about actual civil and political rights in Muslim societies do not revolve around exotic issues. Instead, the clash is over the same competing claims—by the state for obedience and control and by the individual for freedom—that are characteristic of struggles for rights elsewhere. This is the very kind of struggle that gave rise to the international human rights principles, which were specifically designed to protect the weaker party in the contest, the individual. Private Muslims' ideas on human rights are shaped largely by personal experience with the oppressive power of dictatorial regimes that employ the security apparatus and other resources available to the modern nation state to punish and inhibit dissent, curb individual freedoms, reinforce hierarchies of privilege, and undermine the independence and integrity of the judiciary and the legal profession. These governmental strategies are designed to maximize state power and control at the expense of rights and freedoms of individuals and are not in any way distinctively "Islamic," regardless of the exotic nomenclature and rationales that Muslim governments may employ to try to legitimize them.

One should also consider the political significance of allowing the canons of cultural relativism to preclude the criticisms of human rights schemes that purport to rest on an Islamic basis. Insofar as Islamic criteria have been used by governments in the Muslim world to shape rights, Islamic law has been exploited in countries like the Sudan, Iran, and Pakistan to provide an official rationale for circumscribing democratic freedoms and human rights. Muslims who exploit the name of Islam to legitimize oppression may characterize any condemnations of the rights consequences of governmental Islamization measures as being motivated by "anti-Islamic" sentiment. But does it make sense to say that official rationalizations that have been consistently used for consolidating the power of the state at the expense of individual freedoms should insulate governmental denials of rights from critical scrutiny? In particular, does it make sense to say that the mere invocation of the authority of the Islamic tradition should preclude such scrutiny? The answer must be no if one believes that governments in the Muslim world should not have carte blanche to ignore international human rights principles. Private Muslims are widely supportive of the International Bill, and Muslims who are victimized by rights violations that are officially justified as applications of Islamic law do not beg the international community to ignore their oppression and sufferings. Indeed, they tend to recognize that governmental schemes for applying Islamic law tend to be designed to serve the particular political goals of the regimes involved.

One example of the response to such schemes can be seen in the January 31, 1987, report of the Board of Trustees to the General Assembly of the Arab Organization for Human Rights, which reflects a pragmatic, secular approach to human rights. The *shariʿa* is referred to in a summary of pretexts that Arab governments have used to deny rights and fundamental freedoms. The report notes that governments have used the *shariʿa* to support their "one-sided and self-serving interpretation of the Islamic doctrine."[20]

Similarly, the reaction of Pakistani Muslims to President Zia's aforementioned presidential ordinance calling for the immediate application of Islamic law was that his version of "Islam" was a predictably one-sided and self-serving one. Benazir Bhutto, the charismatic leader of the opposition, responded, "General Zia is once again using Islam to perpetuate an oppressive rule in the country."[21] The All Parties Conference in Lahore on June 17, 1988, denounced the ordinance as "a blatant violation of the Constitution," human rights, and democratic principles. The ordinance was, it stated, "based on dishonesty and smacks of Gen. Zia's plan to perpetuate his rule."[22] Even many Islamic clerics and Islamic fundamentalists who originally supported Zia's Islamization policy feared that Zia's ordinance was simply another tactic for delaying democratic elections.[23] With Zia gone from the scene, Benazir Bhutto was able to run for election as a strong opponent of Zia's Islamization program and its attendant human rights violations.[24] That Bhutto won more votes than any other candidate, despite political circumstances under the caretaker regime favoring those candidates pledged to follow Zia's policies, can be taken as something of a popular referendum by

20. This report has been published under the caption "Human Rights in the Arab World," *IFDA Dossier* 62 (November–December 1987), pp. 63–72; quotation is on p. 70.

21. "Zia Takes Line of the Ayatollahs," *Times* (London), June 16, 1988, p. 1.

22. "Rejects Shariah Ordinance," *The Muslim* (Islamabad), June 18, 1988, p. 1.

23. Elections had been tentatively scheduled for November 1988, but it was uncertain whether Zia actually intended to allow them to proceed and whether he was planning to allow Benazir Bhutto, his most formidable opponent, to run as a candidate. It is entirely possible that he intended to have her declared ineligible to run on the grounds that "Islam" did not permit a woman to run for high office. (This was a tactic that had been used once before in Pakistan's history, in order to undermine the candidacy of Fatimah Jinnah.)

24. Such reactions were reported in articles in *The Muslim* (Islamabad), June 17, 1988, and *Dawn* (Karachi), June 17, 1988.

Pakistani Muslims on whether they believed that Islamic criteria obliged them to acquiesce in Zia's dictatorial policies denying them human rights and democratic freedoms.

Cultural relativists who accept Islamic criteria as the justification for governments' violation of human rights are making assumptions about the good faith of the governments involved that are not shared by Muslims who are oppressed by the same governments. This does not mean that one should automatically take the words of critics of government policies at face value either, but only that official "Islamic" pretexts for rights violations should not be allowed to insulate these from critical appraisals.

Western criticism of the human rights records of Muslim countries is problematic to many people because they remember the way that rights concerns were exploited for the aims of imperialism in the past. Westerners may feel that the Western record of hypocritical and self-serving policies of "protecting" various groups from tyranny and injustice in the Muslim world must taint any contemporary Western critiques of rights abuses. This same record may make Muslims feel that their own criticism of the rights problems in their societies somehow serves the imperialist cause or retroactively rehabilitates it.

The premises underlying the treatment of rights in the old, Eurocentric international law can be used to demonstrate that those who today object to the use of international standards in judging rights violations in Muslim countries are the very ones who are resurrecting old imperialist ideas. Well into the nineteenth century, European scholars viewed international law as an instrument for regulating the relations between Christian powers. Western jurists in the era of European imperialism believed that public international law was the product of a Christian and European tradition and that it could be formulated to serve the expansionary objectives of European powers at the expense of the Muslim world.

In the late nineteenth century, the Institut de Droit International of Paris found it necessary to address certain questions, the mere asking of which today would be taken to reveal an outrageous Eurocentric bias. It was asked, for example, whether "Oriental" countries could be part of the scheme of public international law or whether the ideas of non-Christian peoples were so unlike the principles on which international law rested that "Oriental" countries had to be excluded. At that time, the countries that came under this label included the Ottoman Empire, Algeria, and Egypt. The Treaty of Paris of 1856 had brought the predominantly Muslim Ottoman Empire into the Concert of Europe. Colonial ambitions in the Middle East and North Africa raised questions about which law applied to European expatriates and different groups in the native populations. Also, the collaboration between the imperialist enterprise and aggressive Christian missionary activities had heightened the tension between the largely Muslim colonized peoples and their Christian colonizers.

One expert reporting on an examination of the legal issues in 1875 rejected some of the more extreme positions that were being advocated. He argued that international law did not give Christian nations the right to impose Christianity on non-Christians and that Christians who were subjects of "Oriental" governments owed allegiance to those governments, and not to the Western powers that were seeking a warrant under international law to "protect" them against their own rulers. His report concluded that, while "Oriental" countries could join the international legal system, they could not exercise jurisdiction over any individuals in their territories who were subjects of Christian countries. The latter were entitled to extraterritorial status under international law.[25] Of course, this meant that international law supported the scheme of capitulations whereby Western powers had for centuries obtained from Middle Eastern governments special exemptions for their subjects from the jurisdiction of local courts and the application of Islamic law.

The idea that Westerners needed a higher standard of legal protection than that available under "Oriental" systems of justice emerged before there were any international human rights norms. However, underlying the capitulatory exemptions for Westerners when on "Oriental" soil was the assumption that international law did set a certain minimum standard of justice that was unlikely to be realized if citizens of Western nations were subject to the jurisdiction of inadequate "Oriental" legal systems, which were presumed to fall below this standard.[26] Consistent with the mentality of the European imperialists, the protection available under what was in effect an international minimum standard was not accorded to "Oriental" subjects of "Oriental" countries—although, as

25. This report by David Dudley Field is summarized in "VIme Commission: Applicabilité du droit des gens européen aux nations orientales," *Revue de droit international et de legislation comparée*, vol. 7 (1875), pp. 657–68.

26. Because Western legal systems were presumed to embody the higher norms of international law, no one asked whether the subjects of "Oriental" states when on Western territory might require exemptions from Western legal systems on the model of the capitulations.

noted, the idea that "Oriental" Christians might deserve the protection of international law was at least considered, even if ultimately rejected. Therefore, the subjects of "Oriental" countries had no recourse under the international law of this period to the higher standards of justice associated with the West when they were deprived of rights by their own governments. As "Orientals," they could claim no more than those inferior rights afforded them under their own legal systems, ones that in the nineteenth century were still heavily influenced by Islamic law. The treatment of rights in international law was an expression of the biases and imperialist mentalities of the Christian Westerners who articulated the law. That is to say, they were not concerned with protecting the rights of Muslim subjects of "Oriental" countries.

Do contemporary Western expressions of concern for the protection of rights according to international law necessarily have the same inherent bias and political slant? Should they be considered disguised attempts to undermine local sovereignty under the pretext of "protecting" people from the deficiencies of local systems of justice? I would argue that they do not because of the present state of international human rights law and its objectives.

International law is no longer the artifact of imperialism. It has evolved a great deal, particularly since the United Nations was established and the former European colonies gained their independence. Third world countries, including the countries of the Muslim world, have had an opportunity to contribute to the reformulation of international legal principles in ways that have removed much of the former Eurocentric bias of these rules and paved the way for their universal acceptance. Indeed, on some issues of international law, the views of third world countries have dominated. The rights of "Oriental" subjects of "Oriental" governments, which were of no interest to the jurists in Paris in 1875, have in the interim become an important issue. Today, modern human rights theories are considered to be applicable to all humankind, and the rights of Muslims are given the same recognition as those of Westerners.

Now that international law has lost its former Christian, Eurocentric bias, events have taken a curious twist. Some governments in the Muslim world have asserted that international law may not govern the rights of the subjects of Muslim countries and that their rights should be determined exclusively by reference to local standards, in which Islamic law is purportedly incorporated. In 1984 Iran's representative at the United Nations stated that "the Universal Declaration of Human Rights, which represented secular understanding of the Judaeo-Christian tradition, could not be implemented by Muslims and did not accord with the system of values recognized by the Islamic Republic of Iran; his country would therefore not hesitate to violate its provisions, since it had to choose between violating the divine law of the country and violating secular conventions."[27] This is tantamount to saying that the higher standard of rights available under international law is binding on the West, while Muslim countries may deny the rights of persons subject to their jurisdiction, because the latter are not protected by the guarantees afforded by international law.

Although the Iranian argument resurrects the Eurocentric vision of international law that prevailed in the age of imperialism, Iran can hardly invoke the names of the old imperialists as the authority for its position. But what is the authority for this position? Muslims who apply Islamic rights principles to curtail the rights protections available under international law have yet to offer the international community a coherent explanation of how relegating the people of the Muslim world to a system of substandard rights protections can be reconciled with the modern philosophy of public international law. The international community is entitled to an explanation of why the people who live in the Muslim world, like the "Orientals" of yore, do not deserve the same protections that international law affords Westerners. I doubt that an adequate justification can be articulated.

Conclusion

Although some Muslims are undoubtedly wary of adopting international human rights standards as the norm lest in so doing they may forsake their obligation to follow Islamic law, it is highly significant that Muslims are showing a growing eagerness to incorporate international human rights protections in their legal systems and that the resistance to this in the name of applying Islamic law is largely emanating from governments and ideologues of movements aspiring to governmental power. When one discards the abstract rubric "Islam" and moves from a preoccupation with texts and clerical views—which studying "Islam" seems to entail—toward a study of Muslim behavior and manifest attitudes, the doctrinal obstacles to incorporating human rights in the Islamic tradition seem to become surmountable.

27. UN General Assembly, Thirty-ninth Session, Third Committee, "Summary Record of the 65th Meeting," December 7, 1984, A/C.3/39/SR.65, English, p. 20.

To return to the Iranian example yet again, shortly after the Islamic Revolution in Iran, when Islamic sentiment was intense, the Iranian Lawyers Association and the Iranian Committee for the Defense of Freedom and Human Rights pressed to have the text of the Universal Declaration of Human Rights included in the text of the new Iranian constitution, along with provisions for the intervention of international human rights organizations and foreign lawyers in Iranian courts on behalf of Iranian nationals.[28] Although their efforts were ultimately unsuccessful, these Iranians demonstrated their belief that the people of Iran were as deserving of the guarantees of international human rights protections as any other people and that internationalizing rights cases was a means of advancing human rights protections for Iranians. These Iranians also seem to have understood that the internationalization of human rights claims today has an entirely different meaning from the one it had in the late nineteenth century.

Ayatollah Khomeini's opposition to any attempt to internationalize rights cases in Iran is well documented. Among other things, he characterized Amnesty International as an organization whose activities are inimical to Islam. In a 1981 speech he fulminated:

> Be aware that all satanic powers and all their allied agencies such as Amnesty International and other organizations have all been united to stifle this Islamic Republic here and not to allow it to blossom. . . . We are well aware that this Amnesty International, which has requested to come to Iran and find out what is going on here, is commissioned to come to Iran and condemn our country. These people are all commissioned to become united and to suppress this Islamic movement, that is to suppress Islam. They are afraid of Islam. They were also afraid of Islam from the very beginning, but now that they have been slapped in the face by Islam, they fear it much more.[29]

It is noteworthy that the Iranian demands that the Universal Declaration of Human Rights be incorporated in the Iranian constitution were

28. Responding to such proposals, Ayatollah Khomeini resorted to his usual means of discrediting advocates of human rights, saying that he wanted an Islamic constitution, not one made by foreign-influenced intellectuals who had no faith in Islam. Shaul Bakhash, *The Reign of the Ayatollahs: Iran and the Islamic Revolution* (Basic Books, 1984), p. 77.

29. Reported in *The Cry of Justice: A Collection of the Statements of Imam Khumayni on Human Rights*, pamphlet issued by the Islamic Propagation Organization in connection with a conference on Human Rights in Islam held in Iran in 1988, pp. 23–24.

issued in the brief period of openness and democracy that immediately followed the Islamic Revolution. In the Muslim world, the public demand for the observance of international human rights norms seems to correlate with periods of democratization in which Muslims are permitted freely to express their views. Thus, such demands were also voiced after the democratization of the Pakistani system in late 1988. One might also point to the recent developments in Tunisia, where democratic reforms have been rapidly instituted since President Habib Bourguiba, ailing and increasingly despotic, was removed in November 1987. The Tunisian government in April 1988 became the first government in the Arab world to authorize the establishment of a chapter of Amnesty International. This was not because Tunisians or those who governed them had suddenly abandoned Islam, but because Tunisian Muslims at last had a government that was becoming responsive to their aspirations to have international human rights standards observed in their own country.

I believe that the Tunisian example provides an instructive contrast to the treatment of rights in the Islamization programs instituted by countries like Pakistan, Iran, and the Sudan. The Tunisian experience demonstrates that it is not necessarily religious adherence which stands between Muslims and the realization of a political and legal order that guarantees respect for international human rights norms.

Part Three
The Context of the Nation-State

CHAPTER SEVEN

Group versus Individual Identity in the African Debate on Human Rights

Rhoda E. Howard

IN THE ACADEMIC debate of the last two decades on international human rights, the question of Western intellectual ethnocentrism has often been raised. In objection to the liberal concept that one has human rights simply by virtue of being human, and that human rights entail claims that the individual can make against the state and against society as a whole, some scholars have posited a relativist approach, suggesting that each continent or religious tradition has generated its own concept of human rights.[1] In this body of literature some African authors have argued for an "African" concept of human rights.[2] A major theme of this

I am most grateful to Jack Donnelly for his rigorous comments on a draft of this paper.

1. A classic article arguing for relativism is Adamantia Pollis and Peter Schwab, "Human Rights: A Western Construct with Limited Applicability," in Pollis and Schwab, eds., *Human Rights: Cultural and Ideological Perspectives* (Praeger, 1979), pp. 1–18. For my views on universalism, see Rhoda E. Howard and Jack Donnelly, "Introduction," in Donnelly and Howard, eds., *International Handbook of Human Rights* (Westport, Conn.: Greenwood Press, 1987), pp. 1–28.

2. References cited to represent this point of view include Josiah A.M. Cobbah, "African Values and the Human Rights Debate: An African Perspective," *Human Rights Quarterly*, vol. 9 (August 1987), pp. 309–31; Joseph Ki-Zerbo, "African Personality and the New African Society," in William John Hanna, ed., *Independent Black Africa: The Politics of Freedom* (Chicago: Rand McNally, 1964), pp. 46–59; Asmarom Legesse, "Human Rights in African Political Culture," in Kenneth W. Thompson, ed., *The Moral Imperatives of Human Rights: A World Survey* (Washington, D.C.: University Press of America, 1980), pp. 123–38; Chris C. Mojekwu, "International Human Rights: The African Perspective," in Jack L. Nelson and Vera M. Green, eds., *International Human Rights: Contemporary Issues* (Stanfordville, N.Y.: Human Rights Publishing Group, 1980), pp. 85–95; Fasil Nahum, "African Contribution to Human Rights," paper presented at the Seminar on Law and Human Rights in Development, Gaborone, Botswana, May 24–28, 1982; Benoit Ngom, "Reflexions sur la Notion de Droits" (June 1981); and Dunstan M. Wai, "Human Rights in Sub-Saharan Africa," in Pollis and Schwab, eds., *Human Rights*, pp. 115–44.

argument is that Africans are community or group oriented rather than individualistic, and hence the rights of the individual are not relevant to them. This chapter argues that even if Africans are far more group than individualistically oriented, the conclusion that human rights are therefore irrelevant to African societies does not follow.

Not all African scholars of human rights contend that there is a specifically African version of rights; rather, as among thinkers from any continent, there is a diversity of views. Many adopt a liberal approach and concur with the universal consensus reflected in the International Bill of Human Rights.[3] It is probably fair to say that many African commentators who favor this approach are Western-trained lawyers or political scientists.[4] This does not justify, however, the comment made by Josiah Cobbah, himself a Western-trained academic, who asserts that "African social scientists, politicians, human rights scholars, activists, and lawyers are seriously handicapped . . . through their Western training and have to liberate themselves."[5] To take this approach suggests that such scholars have no capacity for independent thought or analysis, that they are, in fact, mere pawns of their (presumably) Western teachers. Those African scholars who argue for the applicability of human rights to Africa are not merely members of an ideologically captured, Westernized elite. They are people who have thought about the nature of society and politics in contemporary Africa and who in some cases have suffered imprisonment, exile, or threats on their lives as a consequence of the articulation of their beliefs.

The terms "African" and "Western" that dominate much of the international debate on human rights erroneously imply a homogeneity of thought based on the presumed geographical origins of the participant; they also imply that one (African) individual can speak on behalf of a continent. Hence Chris Mojekwu subtitles his contribution to the debate "The African Perspective."[6] In the context of the imperialist historical and ideological baggage that influences this debate, the mere articulation of one body of thought as African can have the effect of rendering

3. The list of such scholars is too large to enumerate in this article but includes many of those mentioned in the bibliography in Rhoda E. Howard, *Human Rights in Commonwealth Africa* (Totowa, N.J.: Rowman and Littlefield, 1986).

4. For example, Olusola Ojo and Amadu Sesay, "The O.A.U. and Human Rights: Prospects for the 1980s and Beyond," *Human Rights Quarterly,* vol. 8 (February 1986), pp. 89–103.

5. Cobbah, "African Values and the Human Rights Debate," p. 327.

6. Mojekwu, "International Human Rights."

illegitimate both African and non-African disagreement. Many Westerners, sensitive to the history of cultural imperialism, hesitate to argue against anyone who claims to be the spokesperson for African culture. But not to hold to the same standards of evidence and logic when debating human rights elsewhere as one would when debating human rights in the Western world can also be considered a form of condescending cultural imperialism, especially when it is easy to identify internal debate among Africans themselves.

This chapter does not discuss all thinking by Africans on human rights. Rather it addresses one part of a body of thought—more or less coherent—that is frequently claimed to represent the allegedly "African" approach to human rights. This approach stresses three interrelated factors.

—The international system: the argument that violations of human rights in Africa are mainly the result of historical and systematic economic exploitation, hence that the most relevant right for Africa is the right to development.

—Africa's poverty: the argument that a very poor country cannot afford "Western" (civil and political) rights and/or that very poor people have no interest in these rights.

—The communalism of African society: the notion that human rights are inappropriate to a communal society; if anything, group rights should be stressed over individual rights.

I have dealt with arguments one and two elsewhere. With regard to the first argument, I acknowledge the historical causes of Africa's present underdevelopment, as well as the detrimental consequences for rights-protection of Africa's weak position in the contemporary world-system. These two aspects justify the proposition that responsibility for Africa's present problems is international. They also justify expansion of the content of human rights, at least at the normative level, to include a right to development, which imposes obligations on the richer nations for a more equitable distribution of the world's resources.[7]

As for the second argument, I maintain that the economic rights in which the poverty stricken are presumably interested cannot be protected without those civil and political liberties that enable people to demand their rights from the state.[8] Further, I argue that even very poor

7. On the right to development, see Rhoda E. Howard, "Human Rights, Development, and Foreign Policy," in David P. Forsythe, ed., *Human Rights and Development: International Views* (London: Macmillan, 1989).

8. Rhoda E. Howard, "The Full-Belly Thesis: Should Economic Rights Take Priority

people are social beings, and that civil and political rights are guarantors that social aspects of their lives will not be pulverized by the state. Human rights can protect the poor as well as the rich.

The third aspect of the African perspective on human rights is one with which I have some disagreements and to which I direct my attention here. The rest of this chapter argues that even if—as those who defend an "African" concept of human rights often argue—Africans value their group identity more than their individual identity, this does not invalidate the applicability of human rights to present-day African society. I refer to the "African" approach to rights as the communalist argument, that is, the argument that individual rights are irrelevant in a communal setting.

Rights, Dignity, and Social Justice

The communalist argument claims that human rights are irrelevant in Africa, since they are grounded in individual claims against the state or society, while people in Africa do not normally view themselves as individuals. The argument that Africans do not, on the whole, possess an individualistic psychology is made forcefully by several spokesmen. Fasil Nahum, for example, argues: "African humanism does not alienate the individual by seeing him as an entity all by himself, having an existence more or less independent of society. . . . The individual does not stand in contradistinction to society but as part of it. Neither should he be considered as alienated from and at war with society." Similarly Asmarom Legesse claims that "no aspect of Western civilization makes an African more uncomfortable than the concept of the sacralized individual whose private wars against society are celebrated." Benoit Ngom further contends that Africans have no notion of private (individual) life; even lovemaking has a ritualized, public nature to it. Olusola Ojo agrees that "the Africans assume harmony, not divergence of interests . . . and are more inclined to think of their obligations to other members of society rather than their claims against them."[9]

On the whole, the argument that Africans are communally inclined is correct. Although there is much social change in the direction of psy-

over Civil and Poltical Rights? Evidence from Sub-Saharan Africa," *Human Rights Quarterly*, vol. 5 (November 1983), pp. 467–90.

9. Nahum, "African Contribution," pp. 2, 5; Legesse, "Human Rights," p. 124; Ngom, "Reflexions," p. 8; and Olusola Ojo, "Understanding Human Rights in Africa," paper presented at the Preparatory Conference on Human Rights: Individual Rights or Collective Rights, University of Limburg, Maastricht, Netherlands, September 18–20, 1987, p. 10.

chological modernization in the Africa of the late twentieth century,[10] Africans on the whole are not as individualistic as Westerners, especially perhaps as Americans. Nevertheless, the corollaries of the argument for African collectivism are both empirically questionable and irrelevant to the argument that Africans do not need human rights. These corollaries can be summarized as having three strands: that African economies were or are redistributive, not acquisitive in orientation; that African politics were or are consensual, not competitive; and that there was or is no social stratification in Africa. The present and the past tenses are used interchangeably in the literature; traditional African society is frequently referred to as if it still exists in unaltered form.[11]

With regard to the first assertion about distributive economics, Joseph Ki-Zerbo argues that two ethical bases of African societies were the principles of solidarity and egalitarianism and that the latter was possible because accumulation of property to the point of "reduc[ing] others to the state of mere tenancy" was unknown. Legesse, writing about the Amhara of Ethiopia, states that peasants could not be deprived of their land and that kings or chiefs had the obligation to share their wealth with their subjects. With regard to the second assertion about consensual politics, Dunstan Wai notes the example of Ashanti chiefs who could be deprived of their power by the elders if they abused their authority. Benoit Ngom agrees that African societies were founded on consensus and group cultural values, although he admits that consensual politics can work only for small-scale polities and are not easily transferable to modern state societies.[12] With regard to the third assertion about social stratification, a number of authors note that most African societies were gerontocracies, based on the rule of elders, but contend that there was otherwise little stratification, although Ngom does mention slaves in order to argue that even they were not excluded from the consultative process.[13]

Taken together, the above three propositions constitute an accurate depiction of the *values* held by many African societies in the past and in the present, and of the ethic that still guides many Africans' thinking. But they are a misleading picture of the *practice*. The picture does not

10. Howard, *Human Rights in Commonwealth Africa*, pp. 27–33.
11. For an extended discussion of these three corollaries, see Howard, *Human Rights in Commonwealth Africa*, pp. 17–23.
12. Ki-Zerbo, "African Personality," pp. 48–49; Legesse, "Human Rights," pp. 125–26; Wai, "Human Rights," p. 116; and Ngom, "Reflexions," pp. 5–6.
13. Ngom, "Reflexions," p. 8.

take into account the existence of expansionist African states and of class- or caste-stratified societies of the past. It is, in fact, a version of the "myth of Merrie Africa," cited by John Iliffe as a cause of the "widespread belief that until recently there were no poor in Africa, because economic differentiation was slight, resources were freely available, and the 'extended family' supported its less fortunate members."[14] In fact, Iliffe argues, there were many poor in precolonial African societies, especially incapacitated people who had no family support, slaves and pawns (debt-peons), outcasts of various kinds, and unsupported women, especially childless women and widows in Islamic society. Mojekwu indirectly confirms this viewpoint, noting that "the concept of human rights in Africa was fundamentally based on ascribed status. . . . Only those who 'belonged' to the community would have their human rights protected by the kinship authorities."[15]

In general, status differentiation based on age and sex pervaded all African societies, and some societies further differentiated between freemen and slaves and between members and aliens. The "traditional" African society to which proponents of the "African" concept of human rights refer is partly an ideological creation by the more powerful groups in African societies to justify the authority and control based upon such status differences.

> Elders tended to appeal to "tradition" in order to defend their dominance . . . against challenge by the young. Men tended to appeal to "tradition" in order to ensure that . . . [there was no] diminution of male control over women. . . . Paramount chiefs and ruling aristocracies . . . appealed to "tradition" in order to maintain or extend their control over their subjects. Indigenous populations appealed to "tradition" in order to ensure that the migrants who settled amongst them did not achieve political or economic rights.[16]

Authors who rely on traditional values to argue against the relevance of human rights to Africa obscure the actual practice of modern societies. Perhaps the greatest weakness of the "myth of Merrie Africa" is

14. John Iliffe, *The African Poor: A History* (Cambridge University Press, 1987), p. 3; see generally chaps. 1–6.

15. Mojekwu, "International Human Rights," pp. 86, 93.

16. Terence Ranger, "The Invention of Tradition in Colonial Africa," in Eric Hobsbawm and Terence Ranger, eds., *The Invention of Tradition* (Cambridge University Press, 1983), p. 254.

not exaggeration of precolonial democracy and egalitarianism, but unwillingness to acknowledge social change in Africa. Such change includes rising rates of landlessness that, coupled with burgeoning populations, impel permanent urbanization and reliance on nonagricultural employment, and accompanying social-psychological aspects of "modernization," especially an increasing trend toward individualism. Although the ethic of communalism still has a strong hold on many Africans, as witnessed for example by urban "hometown" associations dedicated to funding improvements such as schools and clinics in members' home villages, the practice is changing in the face of the realities of economic crisis, urban under- and unemployment, and highly inegalitarian social stratification. The practice is also affected by the political reality of frequently abusive personalist, one-party, or military rule. Nothing in the present political economy of black Africa suggests that a move back to a simpler, more communitarian time is possible.

Nevertheless, some African thinkers still maintain that human rights are inappropriate for Africa insofar as social change has certainly not (yet) converted black Africa into a mainly urbanized, industrialized society. It is certain that in most of independent Africa the majority of the population still lives in rural areas and still has ties to the land. It is also certainly sure that Africans are on the whole less individualistic and more tied to their extended family and kinship groups than Westerners are. But the continued existence of a communitarian ethic among many (not all) Africans does not obviate the relevance of human rights to Africa. Human rights are meant to protect individuals—either on their own or in groups—against such abuses as state-induced starvation, deprivation of one's means of livelihood, or torture. These protections are necessary in any state society. Communally oriented systems of social justice, based on ascribed and differentiated memberships in small-scale pastoral or agricultural societies, unfortunately cannot be transferred to the modern, large-scale state arena.

The African concept of human rights is actually a concept of human dignity, of what defines "the inner (moral) nature and worth of the human person and his or her proper (political) relations with society."[17] Despite the twinning of human rights and human dignity in the Preamble to the Universal Declaration of Human Rights and elsewhere, dignity can be protected in a society that is not based on rights. The

17. Rhoda E. Howard and Jack Donnelly, "Human Dignity, Human Rights, and Political Regimes," *American Political Science Review,* vol. 80 (September 1986), p. 802.

notion of African communalism, which stresses the dignity of membership in, and fulfillment of one's prescribed social role in a group (family, kinship group, "tribe"), still represents accurately how many Africans appear to view their personal relationship to society.

This notion of dignity implies a different notion of justice than does the version based on human rights. The African concept of justice is rooted not in individual claims against the state, but in the physical and psychic security of group membership. In such societies in the past, social justice was based on the premise that responsibility for fulfilling one's role carried certain privileges—that is (as the African Charter on Human and Peoples' Rights reflects in its stress on duties as well as rights), privileges were contingent upon fulfillment of responsibility.[18] Such privileges also reflected social inequality. These were certainly not societies based on rights, yet both dignity and justice were served. For many Africans, unequal allocation of responsibility and privilege according to age, gender, or social status is still a fundamental and valued way of ordering the world; and to assert their human rights as individuals would be unthinkable and would undercut their dignity as group members. Thus many African women, even when aware of their own severe burden of agricultural work, domestic duties, and child care, prefer to stress their families' problems, not their own.[19]

The two contributions to this volume on the Akan and Dinka perspectives on human rights are actually discussions of the Akan and Dinka ethics of human dignity and social justice. Francis Deng's presentation of the Dinka ideal of human rights paints a picture of group membership differentiated by descent, age, and gender. Yet despite the "stratifications and inequities," the "supportive values of unity and harmony . . . reinforce idealized human relations and communal cooperation . . . and a sense of individual and collective dignity." While the Dinka opposed slavery, they did not accord to outsiders "the same standards of dignity normally associated with being Dinka."[20]

The Akan, according to Kwasi Wiredu, had notions of human rights

18. See "Chapter II: Duties" of "The African Charter on Human and Peoples' Rights," in Claude E. Welch, Jr., and Robert I. Meltzer, eds., *Human Rights and Development in Africa* (Albany: State University of New York Press, 1984), pp. 322–23.

19. Joyce Olenja, "Gender and Agricultural Production in Samiya, Kenya," oral presentation to the Canadian Association of African Studies, Kingston, Ontario, May 12, 1988.

20. See chapter 11 in this volume. The quotations are from the abstract of the chapter presented at the Conference on Human Rights in Cross-Cultural Perspectives, June 23–24, 1988.

(privileges) that depended on their fulfillment of social obligations. The Akan viewed people as social beings highly reliant on others, especially on their kinship group. All Akan had rights to land through their lineage; and all Akan could participate, through their lineage and their elders, in democratic consensual politics that included the right to criticize or depose chiefs. Yet while Wiredu acknowledges the changes that have occurred in Akan society since contact with Europeans—for example, the tendency of some chiefs to take over lineage land for their own use—he does not note the indigenous age and gender stratification of Akan society. Nor does he discuss the system of indigenous slavery among the Ashanti, one Akan group, a system that by the late nineteenth century was quite brutally exploitative.[21]

These chapters by Deng and Wiredu could be taken to support the viewpoint of those who argue for an African concept of rights based on the differences between "traditional" African and "modern" Western culture and values. But they actually confirm the view that traditional Africa protected a system of obligations and privileges based on ascribed statuses, not a system of human rights to which one was entitled merely by virtue of being human. The cultures and values characteristic of indigenous African societies do not negate the need for rights in Africa. If anything, the importance of family and community to Africans warrants far more attention to individual rights (to speak their own language, to practice their own religion, to educate their children in schools of their own choosing) than was, unfortunately, paid to the rights of individual Western citizens torn abruptly from their rural communities and forced into cities and factories at similar stages of economic change in Europe and North America. Immediate protection of rights in Africa could stem the emergence of some of those anomic characteristics of Western social psychology, which some ethnic African critics of rights (along with many Westerners, notably Karl Marx in his famous commentary on bourgeois rights), have observed to be characteristic of, and have erroneously deduced to be inevitable consequences of, rights-based societies.[22]

The continued existence of the ethic of communalism should not be taken as an argument against human rights in Africa, but rather as an

21. See A. Norman Klein, "The Two Asantes: Competing Interpretations of Slavery in Akan-Asante Culture and Society," in Paul E. Lovejoy, ed., *The Ideology of Slavery in Africa* (Beverly Hills: Sage, 1981), p. 152.

22. Karl Marx, "On the Jewish Question," in Robert C. Tucker, ed., *The Marx-Engels Reader* (Norton, 1972), pp. 40–44.

argument for them. Abdullahi An-Na'im has stressed the need for human rights to be grounded in the indigenous cultural traditions of every society. G. O. Olusanya makes the same point: "For any law to grow and be productive, it must be rooted in the culture and tradition as well as the realities of the people for whom it is made."[23] In African communal societies, there were many features well worth preserving, and many that could buttress the present international consensus on human rights. Many societies, for example, practiced a "palaver" political system in which chiefs routinely consulted with male (and frequently female) elders.[24] In many societies a chief's power could be greatly restrained.[25] Both these practices provide an ethical support for the right to political participation, which is under such severe challenge in Africa today.[26] With regard to economic rights, in many societies chiefs were responsible for a system of food storage that protected their communities against famine. The ethic of sharing among family and offering hospitality to strangers also protected unlucky individuals against hunger. These practices could buttress the internationally recognized right to food.

Thus these communal practices do not mean that human rights are irrelevant to Africa. They mean rather that the communal concept of social justice had many elements that could buttress a human rights–based approach, and could be adapted to enable the individual to make enforceable claims against the state in newly emergent, often politically and economically abusive African societies. Rights-based protections of African individuals against the state also mean protections against the group, the same group that is so idealized in the argument claiming the irrelevance of human rights to Africa. But rights can also protect groups of individuals against the state—and this is no mean aim when so many groups are at risk as a consequence of abusive state policies.

23. Abdullahi A. An-Na'im, "Religious Minorities under Islamic Law and the Limits of Cultural Relativism," *Human Rights Quarterly*, vol. 9 (February 1987), p. 3; and G. O. Olusanya, "African Charter on Human and Peoples' Rights, History and Development," paper presented at the Seminar marking the Centenary of the Legal Profession in Nigeria, in Lagos, February 21, 1986, cited in Ojo, "Understanding Human Rights in Africa," p. 8.

24. Kamene Okonjo, "The Dual-Sex Political System in Operation: Igbo Women and Community Politics in Midwestern Nigeria," in Nancy J. Hafkin and Edna G. Bay, eds., *Women in Africa: Studies in Social and Economic Change* (Stanford University Press, 1976), pp. 45–58.

25. On the Mosi, see Ki-Zerbo, "African Personality," p. 49.

26. Howard, *Human Rights in Commonwealth Africa*, chap. 6.

Human Dignity and Social Change

The "African concept of human rights" is an empirically accurate description of the way many Africans—especially those still living in rural peasant society—view dignity and social justice. But it is a descriptive, not a categorical term: it describes Africa, but it does not designate a category unique to Africa. If one were to rename the "African" concept of rights the "communal" concept, then many other societies could fit into the same category. The communal version of dignity and justice describes the way most rural societies, including most European societies until two centuries ago or even later, view or viewed social justice.

Late feudal, early industrial England, for example, was a status-based society in which custom and community regulated social relations, and in which the wealthy were expected to share their resources by supporting extended families that included apprentices, servants, and hangers-on from poorer families. The group, not the individual, was the ideal social unit: marriage and morals were strictly controlled, deviance was severely punished, church attendance was obligatory, and private life was frowned upon.[27] Similarly, under the *obshchina* system in Czarist Russia, social relations, distribution of land, and use of communal resources were regulated at the village level by local elders.[28] The extent to which such precapitalist worldviews persisted, even after industrialization and the emergence of political liberalism, is even clearer in literary sources such as the late-nineteenth-century novels of Thomas Hardy or Laurie Lee's description of village life in Britain in the 1920s.[29]

The "African" concept of dignity and social justice is thus typical of the small-scale peasant worldview. In any nonindustrialized society, especially relatively homogeneous societies still insulated from the international economy, one will find that people identify themselves not as individuals but as part of their community, and that, for the most part, they consider the ethical life to be one spent fulfilling their ascribed social roles. But in almost all these societies except perhaps the simplest hunting and gathering groups, one will also find social stratification based on age and sex, differential treatment of outsiders, and (in the

27. Peter Laslett, *The World We Have Lost—Further Explored* (London: Methuen, 1983).

28. Theda Skocpol, *States and Social Revolutions: A Comparative Analysis of France, Russia and China* (Cambridge University Press, 1979), pp. 128–33.

29. Thomas Hardy, *The Mayor of Casterbridge*; and Laurie Lee, *Cider with Rosie* (London: Hogarth Press, 1960).

more complex society) distinctions among slaves, freemen, and nobles. One will also find gradations of wealth, although the use of wealth for the common good will be a stronger principle than it is in developed, urban industrial society.

The peasant worldview has been eroded in the Western world by large-scale social changes, especially by industrialism and urbanization. Wherever such social changes occur, the communalist, role-oriented notion of personhood breaks down (especially among males), to be replaced by the values of secularism, personal privacy, and individualism. This process is easily observable in the more developed economies of contemporary Africa, such as in Nigeria and Kenya. There, as elsewhere in the last two or three centuries, the traditional concept of solidarity is giving way to individualism.

The change from the "African" (peasant, traditional) worldview to the "Western" (urban, modern) is well recognized in sociological literature. In very broad terms, it is the transition from Emile Durkheim's "mechanically organized" societies, those based on homogeneity and a very simple division of labor, to those that are "organically organized," based on social heterogeneity and a very complex division of labor that ideally includes individual freedom of choice regarding occupation. In Max Weber's terms, it is a change from traditional to rational-legal forms of social organization—that is, from authority based on well-established social norms administered by chiefs or judges whose position is sanctioned by religious tradition, to authority based on formal rules administered by any individual whose office (as opposed to personal legitimacy) entitles him to do so. In the vocabulary of Sir Henry Maine, the change can be summarized as a transition from a society based on status to one based on contract.[30] In the case of Africa and the debate about the communal notion of group membership, Maine's terminology is the most apt. What many defenders of the communal ethic are implicitly concerned about is the breakdown of ascribed statuses and the change to a society in which contract (choice) is more prevalent. Human rights—the principle, in part, of individual freedom from ascribed social roles within the group—are seen as facilitating social breakdown.

30. Emile Durkheim, *The Division of Labor in Society* (Free Press, 1933); Max Weber, *The Theory of Social and Economic Organization* (Free Press, 1947), pp. 324–63; and Sir Henry Maine, *Ancient Law* (London: Dent and Sons, 1972), pp. 179–215.

In any analysis of social change anywhere in the world, simplistic dichotomizations into "traditional" and "modern" societies—or, in the terms of the present debate, "African" and "Western" societies—should be avoided. The change is not pervasive in the Western world; many remnants of the earlier worldview remain. Many Westerners question the emergence of secular urban society and attempt to return to the values of a perceived simpler way of life. Africa too is changing. Although 75 percent of the inhabitants in sub-Saharan Africa are still classified as rural, the number has declined from 87 percent in 1965; moreover, the average annual growth rate of the urban population in the first half of the 1980s was 5.7 percent a year.[31] This rate of change suggests a momentum that will not stop. In both the African and the Western cases, the tension between the two modes of life, between communalism and individualism, will continue to pervade individual psyches, family living, choice of community, and political decisionmaking.

To note that the "African" perspective on human rights is in fact a perspective common to many if not all traditional societies is to remove the spurious and static geographic and cultural comparisons that feature heavily in the current human rights debate. One cannot simply contrast "Western" with "African" concepts of social justice. Despite the liberalism of many Western legal forms, there are many Western citizens who advocate a more communal notion of justice, based on reciprocal duties and privileges, rather than the allegedly individualist notion of citizen versus state. Many advocate that the state should severely punish deviance and should also uphold restrictive social roles. Debates in Canada, for example, rage over whether capital punishment (now abolished) should be reinstated and whether mothers ought to stay at home with small children. The resurgence of Christian fundamentalism in the United States and Canada is an obvious indicator of the diversity of Western thought and the importance still attached to family and church by many Western citizens.

Awareness of the erroneous descriptive and analytic nature of simplistic dichotomies such as traditional versus modern and African versus Western enables one to look more critically at the cultural relativism debate. Scholars who use such dichotomies without perceiving their nuances and internal inconsistencies frequently defend African culture

---

31. *World Development Report 1988* (Oxford University Press for the World Bank, 1988), p. 285, table 32.

as if it is undifferentiable, unchangeable, and nonpolitical in its impact. The position is advocated that Africa has an entirely different concept of rights from that of the West, rooted in an entirely different culture.[32] But cultures can and do change; indeed, change is part of their nature as they are, above all, social creations. "Culture must be continuously produced and reproduced by man. Its structures are, therefore, inherently precarious and predestined to change."[33] Cultures can change as a result of internal conflicts or normative innovations. They can also change as a result of foreign influence, but that is not always detrimental or of hostile intent. Cultural compulsion (ideological imperialism) has certainly been a feature of African society since contact with Europeans, especially through the propagation of Christian missionary beliefs, but so has cultural diffusion, the willing adoption by Africans of foreign artifacts, ideas, and values.

Most important from the perspective of the human rights debate, it should be noted that cultures are not holistic entities. The functionalist theory of sociology perceived societies as integrated wholes, whose equilibrium could be severely disturbed if one part or another changed.[34] This functionalist perception was also part of much colonial anthropology; British anthropologists in particular defended the functional integrity of African traditional cultures and customs against missionary and government attempts to impose European ways. Jomo Kenyatta, the first president of Kenya and originally an anthropologist, used functionalist theory to defend his Kikuyu people against Scottish missionary attempts to ban female circumcision, arguing that the practice was an integral and indispensable part of the Kikuyu cultural fabric.[35]

But both in the Western world and in Africa, societies frequently change and adapt to new structural conditions without being so severely disturbed as to lose their equilibrium. When some customs die out, others can emerge. The principle of human rights, where (rarely) it is implemented, changes some social practices but does not destroy the social fabric, which is inherently adaptable. For example, in British-

32. For example, by Ki-Zerbo, "African Personality"; Legesse, "Human Rights"; and Mojekwu, "International Human Rights."

33. Peter L. Berger, *The Sacred Canopy: Elements of a Sociological Theory of Religion* (Anchor Books, 1969), p. 6.

34. Talcott Parsons, *The Social System* (Free Press, 1951), especially chap. 2.

35. Jomo Kenyatta, *Facing Mount Kenya* (London: Heinemann, 1979), pp. 131–35.

ruled Africa the legal principle of "natural justice" mandated the abolition of ritual killings of twin babies and also the abolition of indigenous slavery. Today human rights demand not only the abolition of such practices as preventive detention and wide-scale political murder but also the abolition of practices such as private expropriations of land, which deny the basic human right to food to many Africans (especially women and children).[36] If changes in law and practice were made in accordance with such human rights demands, deep-rooted social norms about the nature of group membership and appropriate social behavior in African societies would not necessarily be destroyed. Rather, the principles of human rights would be grafted onto prevailing belief systems, altered, and debated by individuals and groups.

If human rights analysts rid themselves both of spuriously dichotomous analytical categories and of spurious perceptions of homogeneity in both "traditional" and "modern"—in the context of this chapter "African" and "Western"—societies, then it will be easier to see both the pertinence of rights for all state societies, and the fact that in all societies some cultural trends such as status differentiation militate against rights-protection, while others such as wealth redistribution militate in its favor. In particular, it should be noted that while human rights are a means to social justice suited to modern states, they do not demand conformity to the atomized individualism erroneously assumed to be universal in developed, capitalist society.

The Nigerian political scientist Claude Ake contends that human rights presuppose "a society which is atomized and individualistic, a society of endemic conflict . . . [and] of people conscious of their separateness."[37] This is an exaggerated view both of the societies in which the principle of human rights originated and of the liberal Western societies in which human rights play an important legal role today. The liberal concept of human rights was first articulated in a Europe just beginning to emerge from peasant and feudal society and suffering under absolutist kingships. Human rights as a philosophy was thus engendered in a society much like that which characterizes many parts of Africa today. One reason for the rise of early demands for rights was absolutist control on the rising bourgeois class. But another was notions

36. Howard, *Human Rights in Commonwealth Africa*, chap. 7.
37. Claude Ake, "The African Context of Human Rights," *Africa Today*, 1st/2nd Quarters (1987), p. 5.

of social justice embedded both in some versions of Christianity and in the norms regulating preabsolutist obligations of feudal lords to peasants, which are similar to contemporary African norms regarding the obligations of traditional chiefs and even modern "big men" to the ordinary citizen.

Just as European society in the transition to capitalism engendered demands for rights, so in Africa today the abrupt transitions to political independence, fragile nationhood, and economies characterized by widespread mismanagement and corruption generate an internal discussion of rights. These discussions are often grounded in perceptions of traditional systems of rights (social justice), and in perceptions of extreme differences between the old and the new ways. In particular, there is a fear that group membership and commitment will disappear, and anomic individualism take hold, if a principle of human rights displaces older concepts of dignity and social justice.

This fear of anomie, exemplified in the quotation from Ake, is based on exaggerated misperceptions of the nature of social life in the Western world. Anomie implies normlessness, rootlessness, and disconnection from the community as a whole. It was first identified as a social phenomenon by Durkheim in his classic study of the pattern of suicide in nineteenth-century Europe.[38]

Anomie is certainly a phenomenon characteristic of industrial societies that attempt to protect human rights. However, it is even more a characteristic of societies that deny human rights. For example, in the contemporary Soviet Union individuals have very little sense of connection to the wider society or of obligation to fellow citizens; rather, social life is characterized by "wild individualism, which recognizes obligation to nobody."[39] This cultural phenomenon could be attributed to the dominance of the state over all aspects of social life and the forbidding (until very recently) of all private voluntary organizations and of all religious communities that do not acknowledge the state's ultimate authority. It could also be traced to the fact that the present generation of adults includes millions whose parents were abruptly torn from their home to be executed or imprisoned in labor camps. In a society in which one cannot even count on the basic right to a family, the individual learns to rely entirely on himself or herself. Anomie is more char-

38. Emile Durkheim, *Suicide: A Study in Sociology* (Free Press, 1951), pp. 241–76.
39. Vladimir Shlapentokh, "Fighting to Warm Up the Cold Soviet Heart," *Globe and Mail* (Toronto), April 26, 1988, p. A7.

acteristic of a totalitarian rights-abusive society than of a democratic rights-protective society.

Community life and a sense of obligation to others are strong aspects of modern North American life, despite common misperceptions to the contrary. Many commentators from the less developed world decry the lack of religious commitment in North America. But a good 40 percent of Americans attend religious services weekly, and 60 percent identify themselves as members of a religious community. Although the prevalent social ethic in the United States among the culturally dominant white middle class is indeed identified by American sociologists as individualism, this individualism takes a number of forms, including the "expressive" individualism that is sometimes realized in empathetic commitment to the public good. Furthermore, the biblical and republican traditions—the one based on Christianity and the other on conceptions of the obligations of the citizen to society—are also strong strands in American culture. It has frequently been noted that the United States is a "nation of joiners" in which many people belong to voluntary organizations dedicated to the improvement of the welfare of their own community or of the wider public.[40] That the participation in voluntary organizations is by choice, rather than by ascriptive social role, does not lessen the sense of obligation to the community that it entails.

It should also be noted that the loss of family and community in Western society is often the result of structural factors such as international and internal migration, not of values that favor anomie. This is something that Josiah Cobbah, for example, fails to understand in his reference to the "hullabaloo" in the West over child care.[41] Most children of working mothers in Canada are cared for by relatives or friends as they are in Africa; but for some families separated by geographic mobility, this is not possible. The same problem is now occurring among nonelite African women. Now that many African women are household heads who must assist in the cultivation of (male-owned) cash crops as well as cultivate subsistence crops, and now that they are deprived of the labor of older daughters now at school, the need for day care is widely recognized.[42] Another misperception of North American society

40. Robert N. Bellah and others, *Habits of the Heart: Individualism and Commitment in American Life* (Harper and Row, 1985), pp. 219, 28–31, 167.

41. Cobbah, "African Values," p. 322.

42. For example, Barbara Lewis, "The Impact of Development Policies on Women," in Margaret Jean Hay and Sharon Stichter, eds., *African Women South of the Sahara* (New York: Longman, 1984), p. 185; and Margaret W. Kenyatta, "Women—Equality, Devel-

found among Africans is that "the aged grandparent is . . . thrown into a 'home for the aged' as in a refuse heap."[43] Nine percent of Canadians over the age of sixty-five resided in such homes in 1981,[44] one of the higher rates in the Western world. Many of these residents were the "old old" (persons over the age of 80 requiring full-time care), who were childless or whose children were themselves elderly. The alleged disregard of the family in North America reflects variables such as higher female work-force participation and increased longevity rather than an ethic of individualist disregard for others.

The discussion above of the nature of commitments to family and community in North American society does not negate the many rights-abusive features of both Canada and the United States. In Canada, the indigenous peoples are particularly badly treated, and the poverty of single mothers and their children is emerging as a growing problem. As for the United States, one can argue that it systematically ignores many key economic rights. The rights to food, health care, and shelter are consistently abused, especially for the poor and members of nonwhite ethnic groups.[45] But it is the abuse, not the protection, of human rights that produces the alienation, competition, and crime which are sometimes seen as symptomatic of rights-based societies. A disservice is done to human rights by constant reference to the United States as the model of a rights-protective society. More reference should be made to the smaller Western social democracies that have longer traditions of protection of both civil-political and economic rights.

Thus the belief that the principle of human rights implies anomic individualism is based on misperceptions of the empirical reality of Western rights-oriented societies. It is also based on a fundamental logical error—namely the assumption that because both rights-based philosophies and individualism emerged at roughly the same time in Western history, the former caused the latter. In fact, both were effects of large-scale social change from peasant and feudal to urban industrial society. Nor were both these value changes (toward human rights and

opment and Peace," *Public Enterprise*, vol. 5 (May 1985), p. 284. For a good fictional account of the problems of women in modernizing Africa, see Buchi Emecheta, *The Joys of Motherhood* (London: Allison and Busby, 1979).

43. Nahum, "African Contribution," p. 3.

44. Second Canadian Conference on Aging, October 24–27, 1983, *Fact Book on Aging in Canada* (Ottawa: Minister of Supply and Services Canada, 1983), pp. 68–70.

45. See Robert Justin Goldstein, "The United States," in Donnelly and Howard, *International Handbook*, pp. 436–50.

individualism) inevitable consequences of industrialism. Japan is often cited as an urban, industrial society that has retained a strong sense of family and group membership, although in politics human rights have been an acknowledged principle since the end of World War II.[46]

Neither in the West nor in Africa is it, or will it be, possible to preserve indigenous peasant cultures from the effects of large-scale social and economic change. Social change in Africa is a fairly obvious phenomenon. Yet in the human rights debate, some African commentators illogically suppose that those who note the existence of social change in a direction that resembles "Western" individualism therefore advocate it, or assert its moral value over the collective memberships of an earlier era.[47] But those who advocate human rights as a universal philosophy do not necessarily suggest that "West is best." Rather, many suggest merely that the recent Western history of massive social change, disruptions of rural life, and creation of pervasive, extremely powerful class-based, centralized states required a new philosophy of human rights, which is now required in other geographic areas undergoing similar changes. Human rights do protect atomized individuals torn from their communities. But they also protect families and communities, for example, from arbitrary invasion and dissolution by the state and its coercive organs, as occurred in Ethiopia in the mid-1980s during its enforced resettlement campaign.[48]

The human rights perspective does imply that the individual should be free to choose to stay in or to leave his or her community. To allow people to make such a choice is of course offensive to some cultural traditions. What seems to be particularly offensive to some commentators is the notion that women should be allowed such a choice. Cobbah, for example, comments that "Western scholars and Westernized scholars are increasingly analyzing the human rights abuses of the African woman," but he does not refer to any literature on women in Africa to assess whether the perceptions of such scholars are in fact correct.[49] Few African authors on human rights note the existence and the significance of gender stratification in traditional or in modern African society. This

46. Lawrence W. Beer, "Japan," in Donnelly and Howard, *International Handbook*, pp. 214–15.

47. Cobbah, "African Values," p. 326.

48. Jason W. Clay and Bonnie K. Holcomb, *Politics and the Ethiopian Famine, 1984–1985*, Cultural Survival Report 20 (Cambridge, Mass.: Cultural Survival, 1986).

49. Cobbah, "African Values," p. 328.

is true even though by the time the debate on human rights in Africa began, a large academic literature existed on the effects of social change on African women.[50]

In any case, if women step out of their prescribed social roles in Africa, they will not do so because of the philosophy of human rights. The existence of human rights as a philosophy has a marginal effect on large-scale social structural change, which it cannot in and of itself either stem or impel. But the principle of human rights can modify the effects of social change in manners compatible with the wishes of individuals who define themselves both as members of communities and as persons with their own particular wants and needs. It can also protect individuals and communities against abuses by ruling classes and the state; this is its chief and most compelling object.

Rights against Society, Rights against the State

In the debate on the "African" versus "Western" conception of human rights, what is needed is not merely cultural comparison, but structural and historical comparison and a recognition that no society is static or based on unchanging cultural norms. All societies, traditional or modern, rural or urban, have moral systems, and much of the underlying notion of justice is the same. Most people in most societies disapprove of random murder; most people disapprove of elites who tolerate starvation when resources for redistribution are available.[51] The fundamental difference however between the "African" (read communal) and the "Western" (read individual) notion of justice is that under the Western tradition one can claim a right. Rights have the particular advantage of protecting individuals both against abusive political and economic structures and against social norms that they may find invidious. Rights can be claimed both against the state and against the prevailing social norms of society—for example, religious deviants, women, or even homosexuals in some societies can now claim rights.

In the debate on rights from the "African perspective," it often appears as if the chief item of contention is the right to separate oneself from family or community. The protections that human rights afford

50. For references see Howard, *Human Rights in Commonwealth Africa*, chap. 8. See also "Current Research on African Women," *Canadian Journal of African Studies* (special issue), vol. 22, no. 3 (1988).

51. Barrington Moore, Jr., *Injustice: The Social Bases of Obedience and Revolt* (White Plains, N.Y.: M. E. Sharpe, 1978), pp. 37–45.

against the state are almost ignored. For example, Cobbah dismisses without discussion the problem of elite deprivation of rights.[52] Others go so far, despite mountains of evidence to the contrary, including that offered by African scholars of human rights, as to assert that African politics still reflect the allegedly consensual decisionmaking of small-scale, homogeneous, precontact African tribal groupings.[53]

The chief preoccupation of African scholars who advocate a distinct African concept of human rights seems to be the right of the individual to separate him- (or, as noted, frequently her-) self from the group, not to assert claims against the state. In effect, it is claimed that a war of all against all exists in the Western world, and should not be imported, through the concept of individual human rights, into Africa. The assertion of the "African" concept of rights thus is the assertion of a notion of dignity and justice typical of many rural, nonindustrialized societies and, indeed, of many Westerners who value family, church, and folk over the individual, secular, and cosmopolitan culture. In political terms, this concept of rights is most clearly reflected in the populist socialist trend in some African states.[54] It is well known, however, that under certain political circumstances populist socialism can turn to fascism—that is, the enforcement of group membership and loyalty to the state through coercive corporatism.[55] Human rights provide one check against the perversion of communal beliefs about dignity and social justice into state-centric fascism.

Unfortunately, many African analysts who advocate the communal perspective do not concern themselves with the possibility of political perversion of these notions of dignity and justice, preferring to concentrate more on the social disruptions to which, they allege, human rights contribute. The problem for these analysts is how to preserve the inclusive model of society, in which family and kinship groups take precedence over individual desires, in large African state societies in which rates of urbanization, industrialization, individualization, and anomie are growing.

52. Cobbah, "African Values," p. 326.
53. See Legesse, "Human Rights"; and Mojekwu, "International Human Rights." The contrary evidence from African scholars can be found, for example, in Claude Ake, *A Political Economy of Africa* (Harlow, Essex: Longman, 1981); and Ojo and Sesay, "The O.A.U. and Human Rights," p. 102.
54. Crawford Young, *Ideology and Development in Africa* (Yale University Press, 1982), chap. 3.
55. Howard, *Human Rights in Commonwealth Africa*, p. 228.

One method to preserve the inclusive model of society is of course to deny human rights; for example, to expel unmarried women (universally characterized as prostitutes) from the cities, as is periodically tried in black Africa,[56] or to follow a policy of coercive ethnic membership, as in South Africa. A better means of preserving family and group membership is to consider the protections offered by the classic civil, political, economic, social, and cultural human rights. Human rights are a good tactic for obtaining social justice. Human rights do not mean complete imitation of all that is, or is perceived to be, Western, individualist, and antithetical to African traditional values. Human rights do not mean that kinship bonds must be loosened; indeed, some specifically protect the family against arbitrary dissolution by the state.[57] Human rights do not mean that everyone must be individualistic and self-seeking; they mean rather that, in a world in which the right to health, food, and basic education is protected, a sense of social justice and obligation to the community pervades even secular modern thought, as it does in the social democratic parties of Canada and Western Europe, and in the populist wing of the American Democratic party.

The protections that human rights offer to individuals against their families or communities are secondary to the protections they offer to individuals and groups against the state. It is not accurate to argue, as Claude Ake does, that "rights . . . are not very interesting in the context of African realities . . . the right to peaceful assembly, free speech and thought, fair trial, etc. . . . appeal to people with a full stomach."[58] Although human rights may not be relevant to African peasants in their day-to-day lives—as long as the state is not interested in them or in their particular group—they often become relevant in the breach. In contradiction of his own argument, Ake himself notes: "The willful brutalization of people occurring among us is appalling. Human life is taken lightly especially if it is that of the underprivileged. . . . Ordinary people are terrorized daily by wanton display of state power and its instruments of violence."[59] The real question is not whether people ought to have

56. Howard, *Human Rights in Commonwealth Africa*, p. 194.

57. Jack Donnelly and Rhoda E. Howard, "Assessing National Human Rights Performance: A Theoretical Framework," *Human Rights Quarterly*, vol. 10 (May 1988), pp. 224–28.

58. Ake, "African Context," p. 5. For my views on this assertion, see Howard, "The Full-Belly Thesis."

59. Ake, "African Context," p. 8.

human rights, but whether they will be able to obtain them when they need them, in African as in any other society.

There is no need to worry that "African" concepts of dignity and social justice mean that there is no cultural legitimacy for the notion of human rights in the modern African nation-state. Quite the opposite. The expanded concept of rights found in the International Bill of Human Rights, the African Charter on Human and Peoples' Rights (despite some deviations from the International Bill), and in many African constitutions accords quite nicely with traditional notions of human dignity, in Africa as elsewhere.[60] In particular, the expanded international consensus on human rights explicitly protects both families and social groups.[61] The International Bill also protects the rights to food and work, traditional values now under considerable attack as a result of class formation and state coercion in contemporary Africa.[62]

Human rights do not necessarily favor one mode of life over another. Although individual rights do presuppose the right of any person to remove himself or herself from family or community controls and to "reject generally accepted morality," the existence of human rights in themselves does not impel such rejection.[63] Rather, human rights are designed to protect from the depredations of the state those families and groups in which individuals choose to define themselves (either unconsciously or consciously). Human rights do not imply family or group disintegration. A belief in the protection of the individual against the state makes no moral presumptions about the kind of life worth living, either individualistic or family and group oriented.

And human rights can and do protect groups. Ake maintains that "it is necessary to extend the idea of human rights to include collective human rights for corporate social groups such as the family, the lineage,

60. For comments on the charter, see Ojo and Sesay, "The O.A.U. and Human Rights"; B. Obinna Okere, "The Protection of Human Rights in Africa and the African Charter on Human and Peoples' Rights: A Comparative Analysis with the European and American Systems," *Human Rights Quarterly*, vol. 6 (May 1984), pp. 141–59; and Richard Gittleman, "The Banjul Charter on Human and Peoples' Rights: A Legal Analysis," in Welch and Meltzer, eds., *Human Rights and Development in Africa*, pp. 152–76.

61. See the International Covenant on Economic, Social and Cultural Rights, article 10; the International Covenant on Civil and Political Rights, articles 17, 18, 20, and, especially, 27; and the African Charter on Human and Peoples' Rights, article 18.

62. International Covenant on Economic, Social and Cultural Rights, articles 6 (work) and 11 (food).

63. Quotation from Ojo and Sesay, "The O.A.U. and Human Rights," p. 99.

the ethnic group." Legesse goes further, arguing that "if Africans . . . [had been] the sole authors of the Universal Declaration of Human Rights, they might have ranked the rights of communities above those of individuals."[64] As already noted, the concerns expressed by Legesse and Ake have been acknowledged and addressed for some time, both in the international debate and in international law. Much scholarly and legal attention is being paid at present to the possibility of drafting new international covenants to protect the rights of collectivities. But even as the international legal and moral consensus on rights now stands, family and group rights are protected. Individuals who claim, alone or as part of larger entities, the right to protection of their family, the right to speak their own language or practice their own religion, or the right to have their children educated in their own cultural milieu are claiming group rights.

Human rights do not necessarily imply possessive individualism. Rather, they imply an ethical individualism: a concern with the rights of individuals, either on their own or as members of families, kinship groups, and religious or other groups that they value.[65] Reports in 1988 about the very Dinka tribesmen whom Francis Deng discusses in this book make the need for this concern tragically clear. Dinka were enslaved by nomadic Missiriya Arabs and suffered genocidal attacks upon them by hostile tribes, possibly with the support of the Sudanese army, which apparently perceived the Dinka to be the backbone of the southern rebel movement.[66]

The purpose of human rights is above all to protect people—individually or in groups—against the state. But it is also to protect people against other groups or, if necessary, against their own social group. Individuals are and always will be products and members of their own societies. But social change in the modern world implies a more complex division of labor, urbanization, and removal of many individuals from the restrictive social roles of the past. To deny Africans the protec-

64. Ake, "African Context," p. 9; and Legesse, "Human Rights," p. 128.

65. On possessive versus ethical individualism see Guy Haarscher, "European Culture, Individual Rights, Collective Rights," paper presented at a conference on Human Rights— Rights of Individuals, Rights of Collectivities, Middleburg, The Netherlands, May 31–June 3, 1988.

66. Carol Berger, "Sudan's Dinka Tribesmen 'Facing Extermination,'" *Independent* (London), May 31, 1988, p. 14; and Robert M. Press, "Sudan: Refugee Wave Flows North to Ethiopia," *Christian Science Monitor,* July 4–10, 1988, p. 10. See also many reports throughout the latter half of 1988 in the *Christian Science Monitor* and the *New York Times*.

tion that human rights can provide against both the state and other members of their society, because of fear of the individualism thought to be consequent to the breakdown of the old social order, is both to ignore historical and sociological reality and to deny social justice in the modern world.

CHAPTER EIGHT

Human Rights in Francophone West Africa

Claude E. Welch, Jr.

THE FOLLOWING four vignettes from 1987 to 1988 typify civil and political rights in much of Africa. In Burkina Faso, while the recently installed military government struggled to define its political objectives,
police closed down a new private radio station after a few days on the
air. Although the station manager explicitly limited his programming to
music, the regime feared that the broadcasting facilities could become a
target for a future coup maker, and thus represented a danger. In Côte
d'Ivoire, one-time officials of the teachers' union pressed unsuccessfully
through the court system for restoration of their positions, which were
stripped from them as a result of a rump, government-supported convention; eleven were forcibly conscripted into the army, and the union
ceased its criticism of national austerity policies. In Guinea, after years
of rumors and pressure from Amnesty International, the regime of Colonel (now General) Lansana Conté admitted that several opponents
had been executed, but conspicuously failed to mention when and
where the trials and executions had occurred. In Senegal, leading opposition politicians were clapped into jail and charged with felonious
conduct following national elections, which were enlivened by urban
crowds calling for "change" from the policies of economic retrenchment
encouraged by the International Monetary Fund (IMF); yet a few weeks
later they were released and the most prominent opposition politician
was invited to meet directly with the president.

Apart from their common subjugation to French colonialism, these
four states may seem to share little politically. Burkina Faso and Guinea
are governed by members of the military, Côte d'Ivoire and Senegal by
civilians. Those ruled by soldiers have at various times been identified
with "radical" approaches to politics; those ruled by men in mufti have
usually been classified as "moderate" or "conservative" countries. Only
Senegal is currently marked by an explicitly multiparty system; Côte

184

d'Ivoire has permitted a modest degree of competition within the governing single party; Burkina Faso and Guinea are trying to channel participation through "revolutionary committees" or local groups. Opponents of the current regime have been executed in Guinea following secret trials; in Côte d'Ivoire and Senegal, by contrast, one-time opposition members have been welcomed, on occasion, into cabinet positions.

All have been adversely affected by externally imposed economic constraints—starting from different points. Burkina Faso, one of the world's poorest states, fell even further into arrears with its accumulated debt in the late 1980s; the relative absence of easily developed resources apart from its abundant manpower made hope for development quixotic. Côte d'Ivoire, deemed by many to have achieved an economic miracle, unexpectedly suspended debt repayments and was forced to reschedule its international obligations in the mid-1980s and restructure the parastatal sector. Guinea, with immense mineral resources and an almost collapsed infrastructure, looked unsuccessfully for help to revive its mining industry. Senegal, with an essentially monoculture economy, reeled under the impact of drought and plummeting world demand and prices for peanuts, the chief export crop.

Class awareness and mobilization have differed markedly. In all four countries, trade union activity in the capitals has aroused government suspicion and in some cases repression; in all, rural awareness of economic disparities has grown. In some of these countries, *syndicats* have traditionally played important political roles, in others negligible ones. Socially, Burkina Faso and Senegal appear relatively free of ethnically based tensions, with substantial portions of the populace drawn from a single group; Côte d'Ivoire and Guinea, with more complex ethnic mosaics, seem prone to further fragmentation, with members of certain groups (notably the Bété and Foulah) regarded by national leaders as untrustworthy.

These contrasts must not be pushed too far, however. Common factors, to which this exploratory paper is devoted, exist in all four states. First, personal leadership—centralization of political power in the hands of the president—characterizes Burkina Faso, Côte d'Ivoire, Guinea, and Senegal. Whether the head of state is an army major under forty or a seasoned politician over eighty, he holds the reins of control tightly, isolating or eliminating opponents. Second, despite ratification of some international human rights agreements, the respective leaders have not hesitated to use their powers against these opponents—albeit in differing degrees. Third, they have relied on a French-style legal superstructure supplemented by special courts, which fosters further centralization and personalization of power. Though contrasts will be evident in the more detailed material that follows, my arguments are as follows:

—the imported "French" apparatus of government has yet to be fully "Africanized" in ways that reflect the cultural roots of the respective societies;

—this apparatus reflects long-standing French proclivities toward centralization of power, significantly compounded by the leaders' desire for control;

—though forcible seizures of political control have, in Africa on the whole, been the most frequent causes of restrictions on civil and political rights, single-party and one-man dominance of power has also led to restrictions;

—adherence to international human rights agreements provides a clue but not a definitive index to governmental protection of human rights of all sorts; and

—in the current context, the attitudes and actions of national leaders have greater immediate impact on civil and political rights than do underlying social attitudes, although the latter impose an outer limit of acceptability.

While recognizing that civil and political rights may be viewed as examples of ethnocentrism, I have deliberately focused on them in preparing this chapter. Current international standards of human rights and the machinery for their promotion and protection appear to many to be based on Western concepts of human rights. Though largely correct in historical terms, this assertion overlooks the considerable "domestication" of international norms that has occurred since the end of World War II. Responsibility for civil and political rights in former French colonies in Africa rests in the hands of indigenous leaders. Through their adherence to international agreements on human rights, the four states in West Africa have, in varying degrees, accepted what are now globally recognized standards.

Whatever these standards may be, however, performance shows notable gaps. To bring about change, a combination of bottom-up and top-down strategies for improvement must be pursued. A bottom-up strategy entails struggle for human rights by the relatively disadvantaged (relative, that is, to the political elite) and by the chief victims of social injustice, for human rights (as Scoble noted) represent potential threats to ruling elites, and thus must be entrenched through pressure from organized groups.[1] A top-down strategy relies on the major beneficiaries of the existing distribution of power. The former has been historically far more important than the latter. However, recognizing the personalist nature of governments in francophone Africa (as indeed in tropical Africa as a whole) suggests that choices made by presidents can affect human rights immediately and significantly. They can, in making their choices, draw upon indigenous conceptions of responsibilities as well as international standards established by various documents.

In order to put flesh on these academic bones, civil and political rights in the four countries must first be looked at in their historical context, then in specific detail.

Historical Background

The student of human rights in Africa will find information more readily available for English-speaking than for French-speaking countries. The following paragraphs summarize, in necessarily cursory form, patterns of French colonialism, constitutional, legal, and political frameworks, and the context for civil and political rights at the time of independence.

Colonial rule à la française was marked by centralization of power in Paris. In contrast with the more centrifugal forms of British rule—in which self-government early became an objective of imperial policy—French rule was far more centripetal. Closer links to the métropole, rather than greater political and cultural distance, were desirable. In the words of a noted 1944 statement on the objectives of French rule:

The objectives of the civilizing work accomplished by France in the colonies *preclude any idea of autonomy, any possibility of evolution outside the French empire; the eventual constitution, even in the long term, of self-governments in the colonies is to be avoided.*[2]

1. "'Rights' as enforceable claims are not given. They are taken, through successful struggle, by the relatively less powerful against the political elite." Harry M. Scoble, "Human Rights Non-governmental Organizations in Black Africa: Their Problems and Prospects in the Wake of the Banjul Charter," in Claude E. Welch, Jr., and Ronald I. Meltzer, eds., *Human Rights and Development in Africa* (Albany: State University of New York Press, 1984), p. 177.

2. *La Conférence Africaine Française* (Paris: Ministère des Colonies, 1945), p. 35; emphasis as in original, author's translation.

The Fourth Republic, which emerged after World War II, was initially characterized by major reforms. Successive governments dramatically expanded civil and political rights within the empire. From the perspective of the local populace, the abolition in 1945 of the *indigénat*—a system of summary punishment by French administration—ended one of the glaring contrasts between the slogan of liberty, equality, fraternity, and the reality of the colonial situation. The first elections ever held in which large numbers of Africans were involved took place in 1945 and 1946, for the two constituent assemblies; the franchise was expanded in fits and starts, becoming universal for adults by the mid-1950s. France also took steps to channel the swelling tide of African nationalism by drawing individual territories closer to the métropole. A so-called framework law of 1956 (the *loi-cadre*) effectively eliminated the federal level of administration; this legislation was perceived by many African politicians as a type of "balkanization" designed to undercut the likelihood of independence.

With these exceptions, however, the overall colonial policy of the Fourth Republic can best be described as immobilism. The high costs incurred in the unsuccessful repression of Vietnamese nationalism, and the start of the Algerian revolution, had significant repercussions: France was willing to fight to maintain its imperial presence. In its tropical African empire, France seemed determined to maintain its facade of global power. Under these circumstances, self-determination—arguably the broadest of the collective social, civil, and political rights—continued to be actively discouraged.

The Fourth Republic was severely tested by the Algerian revolution. It collapsed in May 1958 as a result of colonists' resentment and breakdowns of military discipline. Its successor republic made no constitutional provision for easy evolution to independence. The government of the Fifth Republic, under the leadership of Charles de Gaulle, sought to maintain its African colonies within a French framework, a "Community." Any leader seeking to opt out would be punished. Stand as it might against the push for self-determination, and threaten retribution against those who wanted independence, the French government was, however, pushing against an irreversible tide.

Independence was granted to Burkina Faso (then called Upper Volta), Côte d'Ivoire, and Senegal (then part of the Mali Federation) in the summer of 1960, as part of a reasonably amicable constitutional evolution. Guinea, by contrast, received self-government in a brusque manner in 1958. Its rejection of the Fifth Republic constitution (ratified by referendum elsewhere in the empire, dubbed the "French Union" at the time) brought immediate retribution from France. Guinea's leader Sékou Touré proclaimed, "We prefer poverty in liberty to riches in slavery." The electorate followed his lead, and Guinea quickly found itself thrust outside the French protective mantle. The situation was fraught with tension. Within a few months, pressure from then prime minister Leopold Sédar Senghor of Senegal, among others, led the French to rethink their policies. A constitutional amendment made independence possible—an opportunity taken by essentially all French-ruled territories in Africa during 1960.

Within the individual states, centralization was the order of the day once self-government was obtained. Inherited institutions—the civil service, court systems, local administration—were subject to rhetorical flourishes and relatively limited immediate change.[3] Dominant parties were rapidly transformed into de jure single parties: the Parti Démocratique Voltaïque (PDV) in Burkina Faso, the Parti Démocratique de la Côte d'Ivoire (PDCI), the Parti Démocratique de Guinea (PDG), and the Union Progressiste Sénégalaise (UPS). The governments increased their economic roles.

At independence the men at the helm were all characterized by a sense of strong personal leadership, though a powerful state and party was essential. In the apt words of Coleman and Rosberg, written in the early 1960s:

> The political culture of the new African elites has probably been the decisive factor in the general trend toward the one-party polity . . . there are at least three rather common elements in [this] political culture . . . : elitism, statism, and nationalism. These are all interrelated and mutually reinforcing, and each is supportive of one or another aspect of the one-party syndrome.[4]

Benefiting from a bandwagon of popular support, and able to draw upon an expanding panoply of government powers, the leaders of French-speaking West Africa moved to implement their respective po-

3. A major exception occurred in Guinea, where indigenous leaders who had been co-opted by the French administration as "chefs de canton" were removed and a major reform of local government undertaken, under the auspices, naturally, of the Parti Démocratique de Guinea.

4. James S. Coleman and Carl G. Rosberg, Jr., *Political Parties and National Integration in Tropical Africa* (University of California Press, 1964), pp. 661–62.

litical programs. All faced similar challenges: popular economic and social aspirations (for example, education and health services) that were
in many cases beyond government resources; pockets of disaffection,
based on varying combinations of regional and ethnic sentiment; the
choice of appropriate development strategy, notably the choice between
further reliance on export of a small number of agricultural commodities with fluctuating world market prices, further development of mineral exports, or efforts to create a domestic industrial base in the face of
small, poor domestic markets; and maintaining the loyalty or obedience
of the armed forces. To meet these challenges, the leaders chose—without exception—to enhance the powers of the government and the party
that, in turn, controlled the government.

By the mid-1980s, a quarter-century after independence, the political scene had changed dramatically in two states, modestly in the others. New presidents ruled in three. Although Félix Houphouët-Boigny,
"the old man," had maintained his grip on power in Côte d'Ivoire, a
succession of military leaders had paraded across the political stage in
Burkina Faso, an army officer had risen to the top in Guinea shortly
after Touré's death (by natural causes), and President Senghor's right-
hand man had become president of Senegal after Senghor's voluntary
resignation. A high degree of political stability thus marked Côte
d'Ivoire and Senegal, while far greater turbulence characterized Burkina
Faso and Guinea. What were the effects on civil and political rights in
the four states? What factors influenced their enforcement? It is appropriate to look at these issues in greater detail by providing vignettes of
the four states.

Survey of Civil and Political Rights in the Four States

Before I discuss the individual countries, some preliminary points
must be made. First, the establishment of single parties reflected several
factors. Coleman and Rosberg have identified some, with which I concur: the "heavy functional load" taken on by governing parties in an
effort to achieve rapid change, the relative power of traditional political
authorities,[5] the inherited system of colonial administration which pro-

5. As is well known, French colonial administrative policies undercut the power of
"traditional" chiefs far more markedly than did British policy. On the other hand, alliances
with respected chiefs or religious leaders were consciously pursued by Félix Houphouët-
Boigny (a Baoulé chief as well as president of Côte d'Ivoire), Senghor, and Maurice Yameogo (Upper Volta's prime minister from independence until January 1966).

vided both an authoritarian heritage and little exposure to pluralistic democracy, the "political culture" of leaders, to which reference has already been made, and the aura of legitimacy with which these parties surrounded themselves.[6] To view declining electoral competition as the result of a single cause, such as leaders' desires or the communal heritage, does violence to the facts.

Second, the heads of state adopted ambivalent attitudes toward "traditional" values. All were ready to extol deep-seated beliefs in the purportedly traditional value of consensus—so long as they benefited—yet they were also ready to take steps against ethnic or regional consciousness that seemed to threaten national unity. With pride they periodically cited historic documents such as the Declaration of the Rights of Man and of the Citizen or the Universal Declaration of Human Rights, meanwhile pursuing policies that tended to restrict rights. In other words, their outlooks and actions were shaped by both "communitarian" and "universal" values, with a strong tinge of pragmatism.

Third, except for Senegal under presidents Senghor and Abdou Diouf, the policies followed in the four states tended toward greater emphasis on development and the concomitant economic steps than upon rights defined in narrow civil and political terms. Tensions between collective needs for group or national advancement on the one hand, and individual-based liberties on the other, were resolved more commonly in terms of the former.[7]

Burkina Faso

Burkina Faso holds a dubious distinction. Among the French-speaking states of Africa, it stands at the top in terms of the number of forcible changes of government. Coups d'état—notably since 1978— have served as the chief means of shuffling political personnel. Although most military figures have promised to reintroduce civilian leaders— and, in fact, one of them attempted twice to return the armed services to the barracks following open elections—the more common result has been another round of military intervention. In the process, civil and political rights have been trampled upon.

The initial intervention of the armed forces resulted from widespread popular discontent. General Sangoulé Lamizana's seizure of power in

6. Coleman and Rosberg, *Political Parties and National Integration*, pp. 658–60.
7. I have explored this general issue more broadly in Claude E. Welch, Jr., "Human Rights as a Problem in Contemporary Africa," in Welch and Meltzer, eds., *Human Rights and Development*, especially pp. 22–27.

January 1966 was widely welcomed.[8] His rule was easy (if his burden was not light). Lamizana tried on two occasions to reintroduce competitive politics. His 1970 attempt at democratization was aborted in 1974, when he took control back into his own hands; his 1976 effort was ended in 1980 by the intervention of an aspirant colonel. A cycle of increasing military involvement in politics was thereby initiated.

The most recent chapter in this parade of army figures across the political stage occurred with Burkina Faso's fifth coup d'état in October 1987. The flamboyant, radical head of state, Captain Thomas Sankara, and several members of his immediate entourage were killed in internecine fighting; Captain Blaise Compaore assumed power and sought to create a political base.[9] Whether Burkina Faso can escape the self-perpetuating cycle of military involvement is seriously doubted by most scholars of the country.

While Lamizana had been content in the 1970s to allow—indeed, to encourage—civilian politicians to create their own political movements, his successors kept a far tighter grip. The short-lived regimes of Colonel Sayé Zerbo, Major Jean-Baptiste Ouedraogo, and Sankara distrusted most Burkinabe politicians. Only Sankara sought to build a new, single foundation for popular mobilization and control through Committees for the Defense of the Revolution (CDRs). His idiosyncratic style (such as wearing combat fatigues to meetings of heads of state), his strong rhetoric about the need for new directions, his change of the country's name, and the like, brought far greater international attention than the country would otherwise have received.[10] Burkina Faso was perceived

8. For details, see W. A. E. Skurnik, "The Military and Politics: Dahomey and Upper Volta," in Claude E. Welch, Jr., ed., *Soldier and State in Africa* (Northwestern University Press, 1970), pp. 68–71.

9. Details can be found in Claude E. Welch, Jr., "Obstacles to Disengagement and Democratization: Military Regimes in Benin and Burkina Faso," in Constantine P. Danopoulos, ed., *The Decline of Military Regimes: The Civilian Influence* (Boulder, Colo.: Westview, 1988), pp. 25–43.

10. Burkina Faso was called Upper Volta (Haute-Volta) under French colonial rule. The new name (loosely translated as "land of the incorruptible men") was adopted in August 1984, a year after Sankara's coup d'état: the adjectival form is Burkinabe. The following remarks by Sankara illustrate his ideas: "I do not think that to build up a nation it is necessary to fill up certain structures; that is that after choosing a flag, one must have this and that and a constitution in order to be considered a fully-fledged, normal stage. We have no complex about not having a constitution compared with states that do. We do not feel we live in a lawless state compared to other states which have a well-written constitution. We want our constitution to be the people's conscience shared by the majority of the masses . . . I want to take this opportunity to make a clarification. We have

by many as an example of Africans seizing control of their own destiny. Hence Sankara's death during a palace coup led by his former right-hand man, and his hasty burial with only a twig to mark his grave, elicited a strong international and a somewhat more muted domestic response.[11]

The fragility of power and the personal risks of leadership have thus been underscored in Burkina Faso during the past decade. The new Compaore government does not dare to resurrect the limited cooperation with political movements that marked the two attempts by Lamizana to liberalize, nor to continue the widespread popular mobilization that characterized Sankara's frenetic rule. Repression of *all* political or potentially political activity seems the safer course. It was in this respect that two noteworthy developments occurred in March 1988. The first was the silencing of Horizon FM, a pop music station launched less than three months earlier and on the air for only five days. Its owner, taking a lesson from American cultural and commercial mores, promised "lots of music, lots of commercials, lots of dancing and lots of laughter. But absolutely no politics. People are tired of all that stuff. State radio in Africa is constipated. It's time to horizonise, look farther than your nose. Find new horizons."[12]

The station had conformed with all legal requirements, yet six government ministers (including the minister of defense) had to "study the workings of the radio" for several weeks before granting the operating license. On March 11 the Popular Front (Compaore's junta) issued an "Action Plan" guaranteeing freedom of speech; at the same time, how-

omitted the words people's, democratic and republic from Burkina Faso. That is because that is a kind of tautology which can create confusion. For us the word state was designated by Burkina which has a geographical meaning, while the judicial organization is designated by the word Faso which takes into account an institution's republican value. . . . We acknowledge that a republic is a more elaborate and advanced form of society than other forms of social organisations. However, since the republic could not fully express what we had in mind, we had to look for another word. Unfortunately, the dictionary could not help. So we have had to return to our language to say what we mean." *Africa Research Bulletin,* vol. 21 (August 15, 1984), p. 7337.

11. By May 1988, however, the new regime had relented and placed a concrete marker on Sankara's final resting place.

12. *West Africa,* March 28, 1988, p. 573. Such pandering to popular taste contrasted strongly with the didactic tone of radio broadcasts under Sankara. On the other hand, the Sankara government "encouraged the creation of 'Radio Entrez Parlez,' a weekend FM station that invited anyone to 'come in and speak'" over the public airwaves. Interestingly, the relatively authoritarian government of Omar Bongo in Gabon has encouraged grilling of government ministers about their departments on television; Bongo himself has allegedly appeared incognito in the studio while the questioning was going on.

ever, the Popular Front demanded that the managers of Horizon FM guarantee the station's security by posting costly armed guards. The condition was economically impossible to meet and the station was forced to close. Why? The regime was concerned that a possible intruder might seize a live microphone and thereby sow discontent or rebellion among Burkinabe citizens. At the present time, the venture in capitalist entrepreneurship and popular culture remains silenced.

The second series of actions, which indicated a growing authoritarianism, came with respect to the CDRs. These had been created by the Sankara government for popular mobilization, for curbing the power of traditional chiefs in rural areas, and for undercutting the influence of pre-1984 political movements. The Compaore government officially abolished the CDRs in March 1988, since "their actions were marred by serious shortcomings due to the fact that their role was not clearly stated." Yet the regime's goals seem no more clearly obvious.[13] Those who govern in Ouagadougou, with their military backgrounds, have scant willingness to permit political organizing among the masses.

The picture is not altogether grim. Although it has attacked some excesses of the popular tribunals established by the Sankara regime, freed from jail nineteen members of a magistrates' union, and released political prisoners, the Compaore government appears uncertain how to restructure the civil justice system. Defendants cannot be represented by counsel in the People's Revolutionary Courts; military courts continue to be used extensively for alleged political and security offenses.[14] The fate of the revolutionary and military courts, which coexist with the regular, French-modeled judicial system, will say a great deal about the future of civil and political liberties in Burkina Faso. Compaore's attempts in late 1988 for rapprochement with the powerful trade unions may portend greater willingness to work with what have historically been the most organized groups in Burkinabe society.

13. Officially, these goals are listed as "the achievement of unity among the people; the improvement of living conditions for all social strata and classes; the consolidation of political independence; the achievement of economic independence; the maintaining and strengthening of democratic freedoms; the strengthening of ties between the Popular Front's member organizations; the creation of conditions for the settlement of the problem of women's emancipation; the development of a national culture; and the promotion of cooperation ties with all countries and states as specified in the political orientation speech." *West Africa*, March 28, 1988, p. 573.

14. *Country Reports on Human Rights Practices for 1986*, report submitted to the Senate Committee on Foreign Relations and the House Committee on Foreign Affairs (U.S. Department of State, 1987), p. 26.

The government of Burkina Faso continues to maintain its strongly military character. The would-be Revolutionary Committees have been disbanded, and no comparable means of popular political mobilization have been established.[15] Trade unions are groping to regain their influence. But the man on whose head power rests uneasily remains wary. In the face of severe economic adversity, limited public support, and uncertain political goals, Compaore has yet to take major steps to liberalize the system. Many of those imprisoned in his October 1987 coup remain behind bars, and only among civil servants and trade unionists is there any opportunity for political involvement.

Côte d'Ivoire

U.S. Secretary of State George P. Shultz had little but praise for Côte d'Ivoire, an "oasis of African economic development," during a January 1987 tour through tropical Africa. Although nations that have tried Marxism have suffered economic decline and "massive violations of common human rights," Shultz continued, private enterprise and President Félix Houphouët-Boigny's leadership had made a significant difference.[16]

Shultz was impressed, and perhaps seduced, by the glitter of Abidjan. He was incorrect in both his economic and his political observations. The veneer of prosperity wore thin; indeed, four months after the secretary of state's visit, Côte d'Ivoire suspended payments of its foreign debt. The depressed world market prices for cocoa and coffee, the country's leading exports, dealt an unparalleled blow to hopes for national development.

But it is not the economic situation of Côte d'Ivoire that is in question here; it is the context for civil and political rights. The shadow of Houphouët-Boigny lies across the entire Ivorian political scene. To Jackson and Rosberg, Houphouët-Boigny typifies the "African autocrat." He is "an anti-politician, an administrator's politician and not a politician's politician. During the long and successful tenure of his rule he has virtually suspended public politics in Ivory Coast and subjected what re-

15. The replacements for the CDRs, the Revolutionary Committees (CRs), had a far more limited role. For example, the May 1988 "elections" for members of the CR bureaus were limited to the civil service and state enterprises; voters lined up behind the candidate of their choice. *Africa Research Bulletin*, vol. 25 (June 15, 1988), p. 8881.

16. Dispatch from Abidjan, "Shultz Praises Economic Development of Ivory Coast," AM cycle, January 13, 1987.

mains to his stern and unrelenting control."[17] Little of note occurs in Côte d'Ivoire, domestically or internationally, without the direct approval of "Le Vieux."

Take, for example, the Organization of African Unity (OAU), parent body of the African Commission on Human and Peoples' Rights. Houphouët-Boigny clearly disdains both: he was among a minority of heads of state who did not attend the twenty-fifth anniversary celebrations of the OAU in May 1988; Côte d'Ivoire is among the fifteen of the OAU's fifty member states that have yet to ratify the Banjul Charter on Human and Peoples' Rights.[18] Since the National Assembly is "a passive instrument that consents automatically to executive decrees and instructions,"[19] a brief statement from the presidential palace at Yamoussoukro (Houphouët-Boigny's native village, which he is trying to convert into the national capital) *could* result in Ivorian ratification of the charter. Similarly, by a simple nod of the president's head, Côte d'Ivoire could adhere to many more international human rights documents than are contained in the country's present meager record.

The U.S. Department of State deems the human rights situation in Côte d'Ivoire "generally satisfactory."[20] I disagree, in absolute terms; only by comparison with its immediate neighbors (Burkina Faso, Ghana, Guinea, Liberia, and Mali) could the situation in Côte d'Ivoire be so deemed. To illustrate, the 1987 crisis over the National Union of Secondary School Teachers (SYNESCI) is instructive. In this contest between the personal authority vested in Houphouët-Boigny and the pressures for competition and pluralism represented by the union, the president's views have been clear:

> Do not make us choose between disorder and injustice. . . . I will not hesitate to choose injustice. One always has the time to redress an injustice, but when disorder takes over it is the life of the regime, the life of men, that is at stake. . . . I am warning all those who think that we can tolerate indefinitely taking liberties with freedom . . . we do not tolerate that. It is finished. . . . The PDCI (Parti démocratique de

17. Robert H. Jackson and Carl G. Rosberg, *Personal Rule in Black Africa: Prince, Autocrat, Prophet, Tyrant* (University of California Press, 1982), p. 145.

18. Dispatch from Addis Ababa, Inter Press Service, May 27, 1988. The other non-ratifiers are Angola, Benin, Burundi, Cameroon, Djibouti, Ethiopia, Ghana, Kenya, Lesotho, Madagascar, Malawi, Mauritius, Seychelles, and Swaziland.

19. Jackson and Rosberg, *Personal Rule in Black Africa*, p. 147.

20. *Country Reports on Human Rights Practices for 1986*, p. 83.

la Côte d'Ivoire) is the framework in which all Ivorians, as long as there is only one party, must evolve. In the future, there will perhaps be several parties, as is provided for in the constitution, but the precondition must first be realised: national unity.[21]

Leaders of the teachers' union had taken an active role in a 1983 strike, which paralyzed secondary education for a fortnight and which was clearly perceived by the Ivorian government as one of its most severe post-independence challenges. The leaders were marked men thereafter. When the July 1987 union conference was held, a large group of teachers and school heads, many of them not card-holding members, forced their way in, elected new leaders, and received immediate government recognition: the new executive promised to end its opposition to national policies. The deposed SYNESCI leaders were arrested in early September, and eleven of these "troublemakers" were transferred to a military camp without being charged. "They have been sent to the army for national service and for civic and moral education for the better interest of the country," the minister of national education averred, with their national service to "last as long as it takes to train a citizen worthy of the name."[22] Three were sentenced to varying prison terms on grounds of embezzlement of union resources but were released without fanfare in July 1988. L'affaire SYNESCI provides a clearer glimpse of the realities of Ivorian politics than could a secretary of state's whirlwind visit to a clean-scrubbed national capital. The future of civil and political rights in Côte d'Ivoire rests in the hands of Houphouët-Boigny—or, more likely, of the successor to the eighty-five-year-old head of state. Indigenous belief systems have had little impact on the autocrat of Yamoussoukro. The worsening economic situation has escalated tensions, for which there are few, if any, legitimate means of relief.

Guinea

An answer came in December 1987 to the question Amnesty International had been posing for several months: what was the fate of twenty prisoners who disappeared following an abortive coup d'état in July 1985, and of other persons imprisoned following a successful, bloodless coup d'état in April 1984? In his first press conference since

21. Quoted in *Africa Research Bulletin*, vol. 24 (October 15, 1987), pp. 8640–41. See also *West Africa*, September 21, 1987, p. 1869.

22. *Africa Research Bulletin*, vol. 24 (December 15, 1987), p. 8703.

seizing power, General Lansana Conté admitted that some had died in detention before coming to trial—to trial, it should be added, *in camera*.[23]

Guinea suffered under the authoritarian rule of President Sékou Touré for close to thirty years. Jackson and Rosberg called his government "one of the most durable personal regimes in independent Africa and one of the most despotic."[24] The low ratings given by Raymond Gastil for political rights and civil liberties accurately reflect the country's condition (see table A-2 and figure A-1). When Touré died of heart failure in Cleveland in March 1984, hopes ran high that a just, open government could be installed. Within a matter of days, however, the provisional civilian cabinet was swept aside and the armed forces under Conté took control. The new Military Committee for National Redress (CMRN) clapped officials of the former Touré regime into jail, while promising positive change. In the words of the U.S. State Department,

[the CMRN] has sought to portray itself as the antithesis of the previous regime led by Ahmed Sekou Touré. Its positive approach on human rights practices has in fact provided the CMRN with much of its legitimacy so far. While this approach is represented more in the relaxation of authoritarian controls than in the establishment of functioning due process or political participation, the government's actions and attitudes in 1985 created an atmosphere in which human rights considerations were commanding greater attention.[25]

Two factors are commonly cited to explain the current condition of civil and political rights in Guinea. First is the economic situation. When even touted success stories like Côte d'Ivoire fall victim to tumbling commodity prices and inflated expectations of creditworthiness, resource-rich but infrastructure-poor countries like Guinea suffer more. IMF conditionalities have affected the Conté government and the people of Guinea markedly. Rising tensions have been hard to contain; liberalization could uncork further problems. (See the following section on Senegal for illustration.) Hence continued restrictions on civil and po-

23. *Africa Research Bulletin*, vol. 24 (January 15, 1988), p. 8731.
24. Jackson and Rosberg, *Personal Rule in Black Africa*, p. 208.
25. *Country Reports on Human Rights Practices for 1985*, report for the House Committee on Foreign Affairs and the Senate Committee on Foreign Relations (U.S. Department of State, 1986).

litical rights appear necessary to the government in view of the national "crisis."

The second factor generally advanced as an explanation arises from the inherent nature of military regimes. They are held to be authoritarian, often fragile in their popular underpinnings and hence willing to use greater violence than their civilian analogues. The professional training of military officers disposes them to employ coercion rather than negotiations. They favor top-down approaches to change, as aptly described several years ago by Huntington:

> Their goal is community without politics, consensus by command. By criticizing and downgrading the role of politics the military prevent society from achieving the community which it needs and they value . . . their tendency is to attempt to fill the vacuum of political institutions by the creation of nonpolitical or at least nonpartisan organizations such as national associations and conciliar hierarchies. . . . Theirs is a "non-political model of nation-building" which fails to recognize the conflicts of interests and values inherent in any society, but particularly prevalent in one undergoing rapid social change.[26]

In the specific context of Guinea, the preceding Touré government was assuredly civilian, and even more assuredly violent in its retention of power. Yet the Conté regime (CMRN) has had to backtrack to a significant extent on the human rights promises with which it assumed control. An attempted coup, tinged by ethnic factors, rocked the junta in July 1985 and led to secret trials before the specially established State Security Court and before the military court. In May 1987 a CMRN communiqué confirmed that death sentences had been meted out to fifty-eight persons (including nine former cabinet ministers and thirty military officers). It should be noted that the government did permit the entry of a team from Amnesty International, which has a local Guinean affiliate, shortly after this announcement.

Somewhat at variance with Huntington's prescription, the government has announced plans for strengthening local government and for decentralizing some administrative functions. All elections are to be on nonpartisan bases. Key administrative personnel must be changed

26. Samuel P. Huntington, *Political Order in Changing Societies* (Yale University Press, 1968), pp. 244–45.

down to the provincial level, and several years (and perhaps a few more coups d'état) will have to pass before the civil and political rights that the citizens of Guinea have never enjoyed at a national level can be established.

Senegal

Senegal has in most respects led other French-speaking African states in official commitment to human rights. It adheres to a large number of major conventions. As both Coulon and Klein argue, Senegal is "such a free place" because of its long tradition of modern politics, its large bourgeoisie, and the political domination of the intellectual Senghor (who retired as president at the end of 1980) and his successor, Abdou Diouf. However, Klein also notes the menace of economic stagnation, which "restricts the government and threatens the human rights situation."[27] His prognostication has proved accurate. The state of emergency following electoral violence was rooted directly in the country's financial woes.

In terms of opportunities for political party organizing, Senegal is unique in Africa—although, in reality, political mobilization in rural areas depends largely on clientele networks controlled by local notables. Seventeen parties campaigned in the February 1988 presidential and National Assembly elections. The real contest, however, lay between President Diouf and his governing Parti Socialiste (PS), and long-time opposition leader Abdoulaye Wade and his Parti Démocratique Sénégalais (PDS). Political suspicions flared while popular economic discontent grew. Conditionalities imposed by the IMF have had severe effects on the population of Dakar, heavily dependent for decades on government employment, and (to a lesser extent) on the rural population, heavily dependent on peanut cultivation and afflicted by both drought conditions and precipitous declines in world prices and demand. Wade appealed for "change" (*sopi* in Wolof, the dominant Senegalese language), touching a responsive chord. He promised to provide the staple food, rice, for 60 CFA francs per kilo rather than its official 160 CFA francs per kilo.

27. See Christian Coulon, "Senegal: The Development and Fragility of Semi-democracy," in Larry Diamond, Juan J. Linz, and Seymour Martin Lipset, eds., *Democracy in Developing Countries: Africa* (Boulder, Colo.: Lynne Rienner, 1988), pp. 141–78; and Martin A. Klein, "Senegal," in Jack Donnelly and Rhoda E. Howard, eds., *International Handbook of Human Rights* (Westport, Conn.: Greenwood Press, 1987), pp. 323–37; quotation from p. 334.

The Parti Socialiste was highly unlikely to lose the election, but its leaders were loathe to permit the opposition a significant share of the vote.[28] However, since the 1983 election had been marred by widespread allegations of fraud, the PDS was particularly watchful.[29] Students were mobilized for action, practically all high schools in the country having gone on strike nine days before the election. There was thus an explosive atmosphere of striking high schoolers, disaffected urban employed, active politicians from often quixotic splinter groups, a governing party uncertain how to balance its desire for a veneer of electoral openness with its need for a continued grip on power, and national police, paramilitary, and military units on alert.

When the election results were announced—not by the Supreme Court, as had been promised in a concession to the opposition parties, but by the distrusted Ministry of the Interior—disturbances broke out. The announced result was not unexpected: Diouf retained the presidency, with 73 percent of the popular vote. Wade's supporters, however, had clearly expected victory. A state of emergency was proclaimed. The university campus seethed and was occupied by riot police; Wade and close associates were arrested and charged with attacking state security. The situation remained tense for several weeks. But reason and conciliation prevailed. Wade was released after two months' imprisonment and his one-year jail sentence suspended, restrictions were lifted on May 22, an amnesty was announced for all those arrested in the preelection and postelection disturbance, and, most surprisingly, President Diouf called on Wade to discuss ways of calming the situation, without preconditions imposed by either party. Although no agreement resulted from their negotiations, the fact that bitter opponents met face-to-face outside prison walls spoke well—relatively—of Senegal's position.

The economic situation of Senegal is parlous. Discontent stemming from the retrenchments, low peanut prices, high costs of food, and the like, will not abate in the near future. The country faces major structural economic problems. The Diouf government has adhered relatively well to the challenge of both elections and IMF conditionalities in the face of these problems. Its openness, especially by contrast with the stop-

28. I base this assertion largely on personal observation of Senegal in the past twenty-five years. I was in Dakar for several days before the February 28 election and followed subsequent events through the press and personal contact with specialists both inside and outside Senegal.

29. In these elections the PDS won less than 15 percent of the popular vote and 8 of the 120 seats in the National Assembly.

and-start radicalism in Burkina Faso, the personalistic authoritarianism of Côte d'Ivoire, and the hesitant quasi-liberalization in Guinea, remains remarkable. Nonetheless, comparisons must be hedged with caution. As Coulon aptly comments, "Democracy [by mid-1988] had not become part of everyone's belief system in Senegal. . . . The authoritarian and clientelist, but inert, state counted on middlemen to preserve stability. The new technocratic, democratic, and more ambitious state can no longer call upon these local resources to maintain itself. That makes it all the more vulnerable."[30]

Does the example of Senegal suggest that indigenous values of toleration and pluralism enhance recognition and protection of human rights? The answer is yes—but in combination with other factors. In seeking to explain Senegal's "semidemocracy," Coulon cites nine factors, only two of which directly reflect indigenous values. These nine are (1) political culture (a mixture of liberalism, a propensity for accumulation of power, and the desire to convey a favorable image to the outside); (2) historical developments (including the "softening" of colonial rule by indirect rule around the Muslim brotherhoods, and the existence of democratic institutions in the urban areas); (3) class structure, whose negative consequences have been overridden by patronage networks and redistribution of wealth; (4) ethnicity and religion (including the significant position of the Wolof, with 41 percent of the population, and Islam, to which over 90 percent adhere); (5) state-society relations, in which the state is omnipresent but removed from impact on society; (6) political institutions, with the proviso that "politics is much more an arena for politicians than a channel for the expression and defense of new social interests and forces"; (7) political leadership; (8) socioeconomic development; and (9) international factors.[31] In turn, three critical issues confront the Senegalese government: economic survival, the potential for Islamic mobilization and protest, and separatist sentiment in the Casamance region. Thus while civil and political rights in Senegal have gained governmental protection significantly beyond the levels of the other francophone states, they could be reduced with a change in regime or further worsening of the economic situation.

To return to the overall theme of this book, it is appropriate now to

---

30. Coulon, "Senegal," p. 159. See also Robert Fatton, Jr., *The Making of a Liberal Democracy: Senegal's Passive Revolution* (Boulder, Colo.: Lynne Rienner, 1987).

31. Coulon, "Senegal," p. 168.

review the external factors influencing civil and political rights, notably the use of internationally drafted agreements by the four states in guiding their domestic protection of rights.

Adherence to International Human Rights Agreements

Can the contrasts between the theory and practice of human rights in these four countries be traced in any direct fashion to *international* norms and values? Since the adoption of the United Nations' Universal Declaration of Human Rights, various declarations have been drafted to serve as standard setters. Human rights are defined by a series of important documents, which individual states are free to ratify. In so doing, however, they assume new obligations. In the words of the Proclamation of Teheran, the Universal Declaration "states a common understanding of the peoples of the world concerning the inalienable and inviolable rights of all members of the human family and constitutes an obligation for the members of the international community," while the successor covenants, conventions, and declarations "have created new standards and obligations to which States should conform."[32] A government ratifying the International Covenant on Civil and Political Rights must submit reports to the UN Human Rights Committee "on the measures they have adopted which give effect to the rights recognized herein and on the progress made in the enjoyment of these rights" (article 40); a government adopting the optional protocol recognizes the right of individuals to communicate directly with the Human Rights Committee (article 1). Do states adhere to binding conventions because of domestic pressure? desire by national leaders? the example of neighboring or linked states? influence from international organizations?

A varied picture emerges from the pattern of accession to international human rights agreements. Of the 70 major international human rights instruments listed by Jean-Bernard Marie, Burkina Faso had ratified 19, Côte d'Ivoire 18, Guinea 22, and Senegal 25 as of January 1, 1988 (table A-1).[33]

Ratification of a convention is not difficult—notably when a single party controls the legislature and the presidency is held by a man endowed with significant personal power. The differential performance of

32. "Proclamation of Teheran," in *Human Rights: A Compilation of International Instruments* (United Nations, 1983), p. 18.

33. Jean-Bernard Marie, "International Instruments Relating to Human Rights," *Human Rights Law Journal*, vol. 9, pt. 1 (1988), pp. 113–40.

the francophone states of West Africa, I believe, can be attributed directly to the relative interest taken by heads of state—whether to promote and protect human rights within their states or, in a Machiavellian fashion, to offer a facade rather than a reality of support. The proclivities of Presidents Diouf and Senghor account in large measure for Senegal's numerous ratifications. The adherence of Guinea to nearly as many international human rights instruments is more puzzling—for, as will be shown below, one Western source has ranked Guinea as the worst among the four in terms of its performance in civil and political rights. The governments of President Touré and of Colonel-turned-President Conté have not matched treaty commitments with effective protection; they have sought the symbol rather than the substance of rights, as defined within the International Bill of Human Rights. Passivity rather than activity appears to be the norm for Burkina Faso and Côte d'Ivoire. In neither case have the many leaders of Burkina Faso or the single ruler of Côte d'Ivoire shown any marked interest in ratifying these agreements. And, for all states, ratification of agreements has tended to occur as clusters of temporary activity. For example, almost all the six International Labour Organization (ILO) conventions listed in the table were approved by the four states early in their independence.[34] Acceptance of an international treaty does not provide insight into actual performance. It is necessary to turn to other measures. Unfortunately, no widely accepted source exists free of political or ideological commitment. The following paragraphs provide evidence of trends, but they are not conclusive in themselves.

For several years Freedom House, an American conservative foundation concerned with civil and political rights, has published an annual comparative survey of "freedom." The methodology and normative characterizations of the organization have often been called into question. Despite its weaknesses, the survey, prepared by Raymond Gastil, provides a baseline, even if from a particularly Western perspective. Table A-2 shows the scores from 1972 through 1988—with a range from 1 (free) to 7 (not free), and with an intermediate category, partly free. Figure A-1 shows the criteria for the scores.

By presenting this material, I do not wish to endorse Gastil's methodology; however, the trends are interesting. Gastil clearly was most

34. *List of Ratifications of Conventions (as of 31 December 1987)* (Geneva: International Labour Organization, 1988). Of the twenty-four instruments of ratification, all were deposited with the ILO before the end of 1962 except Guinea's approval of Convention no. 100 and Senegal's approval of Convention no. 111.

impressed by Burkina Faso (then Upper Volta) in the late 1970s, when General Lamizana presided over a multiparty parliament. That the government was paralyzed into inaction by squabbles among the politicians, whose ineffectiveness led to a series of armed forces' seizures of power, did not enter the Freedom House estimates. As made clear in the criteria employed for the ratings, it is far more the trappings of formal democracy for political rights than the substance or effectiveness of government policies that is of concern. No direct mention is made of relevant international documents in Gastil's survey; yet surely acceptance of the Optional Protocol to the International Covenant on Civil and Political Rights (ICCPR), to take one obvious example, or submission of reports should be noted favorably.

Concluding Observations

Thus far I have sketched the historical background and recent conditions of civil and political rights in four French-speaking West African states, examined their adherence to international agreements and maintenance of the rights listed in the ICCPR, and suggested that the interest of national leaders provides the most cogent explanation for the differing levels of performance. It still remains, however, to explore alternative reasons.

African societies, many have argued, are characterized by strong emphasis on group membership. According to Chris Mojekwu, "The concept of human rights in Africa was fundamentally based on ascribed status. . . . One who had lost his membership in a social unit or one who did not belong—an outcast or a stranger—lived outside the range of human rights protection by the social unit." [35] In other words, rights were tied directly to group membership: those outsiders differed in status and hence in the rights they enjoyed; within the group, ascription resulted in lower levels of liberties and privileges. The point is that "traditional" African societies had limited conceptions of rights inherent in

35. Chris C. Mojekwu, "International Human Rights: The African Perspective," in Jack L. Nelson and Vera M. Green, eds., *International Human Rights: Contemporary Issues* (Stanfordville, N.Y.: Human Rights Publishing Group, 1980), p. 86. See also Latif O. Adegbite, "African Attitudes to the International Protection of Human Rights," in Asbjörn Eide and August Schou, eds., *International Protection of Human Rights* (New York: Interscience Publishers, 1968), pp. 69–81; and Kéba M'Baye, "Les réalités du monde noir et les droits de l'homme," *Human Rights Journal*, vol. 2 (1969), pp. 382–94.

individuals. As Howard has observed, this is a conception of human dignity, not of inalienable or innate human rights.[36]

Speaking generally, inequalities exist in all societies. Many persons are excluded from full participation on the basis of categorical differences. Most notably, women and resident aliens are liable to unequal treatment on the simple basis of gender, citizenship, or culture. The noble words of the United Nations Charter—that the UN shall promote "universal respect for, and observance of, human rights and fundamental freedoms for all *without distinction as to race, sex, language, or religion"*—remain unrealized. For change to come, efforts will be necessary both from inside particular societies and from outside them.

Within individual African cultures, as shown in other chapters in this volume, opportunity exists for employing indigenous values in the interest of universally defined human rights. Conceptions essential to human rights—for example, responsibility toward others, participation, or respect for ways of life—exist in contemporary African societies. Civil and political rights are influenced by the underlying social values of compromise, harmony without concurrent uniformity, and tolerance of diversity. Grafts on local roots of this sort seem destined to mature and flower more robustly than alien transplants into inhospitable soil.

Several steps can be taken in building from the bottom up—that is to say, on the basis of cultural factors. First, individual societies must be closely examined to uncover *concepts* relevant to human rights: the worth and dignity of individuals, and obligations or duties to others (both within and outside the particular group). Second, indigenous *institutions* merit study: means of conflict resolution, sanction and rehabilitation, selection of leaders, responsibility for decisionmaking, and implementation of decisions. Third, the *patterns* uncovered widely throughout an entire African state should be compared to find elements of commonality, which form part of the national as contrasted with the ethnic sets of values.

Top-down actions must complement these efforts. The studies just advocated will require encouragement from individual governments. Human rights issues should be adopted within curricula, using ex-

36. Rhoda E. Howard, *Human Rights in Commonwealth Africa* (Totowa, N.J.: Rowman and Littlefield, 1986), pp. 17–23. "There is no specifically African concept of human rights. The argument for such a concept is based on a philosophical confusion of human dignity with human rights, and on an inadequate understanding of structural organization and social changes in African society" (p. 23).

amples appropriate to the age level and cultural backgrounds of pupils. Ministries dealing with likely problem areas in human rights—for example, portfolios on women's affairs, labor, education, justice, and interior—should be headed by leaders who are aware of internationally accepted human rights standards and cultural norms and practices. Encouragement ought to be given from nongovernmental and intergovernmental organizations on behalf of human rights. There have been some recent noteworthy accomplishments. Amnesty International has had discernible effects on conditions of imprisonment, notably in Guinea, through the spotlight of publicity and the carefully checked information it brought to bear on particular governments. Representatives of the International Commission of Jurists encouraged African governments to ratify the Banjul Charter, and the African Commission on Human and Peoples' Rights, whose members were elected at the 1987 OAU summit, can take a leading role in its promotion.[37] Regional organizations, like the Economic Community of West African States, (ECOWAS), could examine such issues as refugees, which afflict large numbers of African countries. And though the experience has been highly mixed in terms of success, the aid-linked and market-linked human rights provisions of the Lome agreements between the European Community and the ACP (African, Caribbean, and Pacific states) merit attention.

New approaches to human rights must ultimately be built on these foundations. In the short run, civil and political rights in contemporary West Africa are affected far more by persons in power than by values held within the social communities or by pressures brought to bear from external governments and organizations. In other words, reform begins at home. The ultimate focus must be the establishment of a government of laws, not of men. The observation made by Feinberg bears quoting here: "Men associated with the executive branch [of governments in Africa] have tended to emphasize subordination of the courts and judges to the needs of the political party, the nation (as interpreted by the leaders), or an ideology (such as socialism in Tanzania), rather than

---

37. Article 45 of the Banjul Charter defines the commission's functions. In a nutshell, the commission seems to have been designed far more as a body for promotion than for protection of human rights. For discussion of the commission's weakness in protection, resulting from the wording of the charter, see Richard Gittleman, "The Banjul Charter on Human and Peoples' Rights: A Legal Analysis," in Welch and Meltzer, eds., *Human Rights and Development in Africa*, pp. 152–76.

to the rule of law."[38] Such conditions are inherently inimical to civil and political rights.

The enhancement of human rights in francophone Africa, as elsewhere south of the Sahara, requires effective support from those in power. Cultural roots are important; they are necessary, but not sufficient. Regional and international pressures have seemingly been counterproductive in almost as many instances as they have been beneficial. While struggles from the bottom up will be necessary, and while external pushes for change will be attempted, extensions from the top down seem most likely to bring change in the immediate future. As for civil and political liberties, the personalized nature of leadership in francophone Africa makes it appropriate to focus on a small number of individuals as being potentially the greatest obstacles or the strongest advocates.

38. Harvey M. Feinberg, "Africa," in Alan N. Katz, *Legal Traditions and Systems: An International Handbook* (Westport, Conn: Greenwood Press, 1986), p. 21.

TABLE A-1. RATIFICATIONS OF MAJOR HUMAN RIGHTS TREATIES

Title of treaty	Burkina Faso	Côte d'Ivoire	Guinea	Senegal	Global total
1. International Covenant on Civil and Political Rights (ICCPR)			X	X	87
2. Optional Protocol to the ICCPR				X	39
3. International Covenant on Economic, Social and Cultural Rights			X	X	91
4. International Convention on the Elimination of All Forms of Racial Discrimination	X	X	X	X	124
5. International Convention on the Suppression and Punishment of the Crime of Apartheid	X		X	X	86
6. International Convention against Apartheid in Sports				X	23
7. Convention on the Elimination of All Forms of Discrimination against Women	X		X	X	94
8. Convention on the Prevention and Punishment of the Crime of Genocide	X			X	97
9. Slavery Convention of 1926, amended by 1953 Protocol		X	X	X	93
10. Convention for the Suppression of the Traffic in Persons and of the Exploitation of the Prostitution of Others	X		X	X	59
11. Convention relating to the Status of Refugees	X	X	X	X	100
12. Protocol relating to the Status of Refugees	X	X	X	X	101
13. Convention on the Political Rights of Women			X	X	94
14. Convention on Consent to Marriage, Minimum Age for Marriages and Registration of Marriages	X		X		35
15. International Labour Organization Convention (no. 100) concerning Equal Remuneration for Women and Women Workers for Work of Equal Value	X	X	X	X	108
16. ILO Convention (no. 111) concerning Discrimination in Respect of Employment and Occupation	X	X	X	X	108

TABLE A-1 (continued)

Title of treaty	Burkina Faso	Côte d'Ivoire	Guinea	Senegal	Global total
17. ILO Convention (no. 29) concerning Forced Labour	X	X	X	X	129
18. Convention relating to the Status of Refugees	X	X	X	X	100
19. ILO Convention (no. 11) concerning the Rights of Association and Combination of Agricultural Workers	X	X	X	X	107
20. ILO Convention (no. 87) concerning Freedom of Association and Protection of the Right to Organize	X	X	X	X	98
21. ILO Convention (no. 98) concerning the Application of the Principles of the Right to Organize and Bargain Collectively	X	X	X	X	114
22. Protocol I Additional to the Geneva Conventions of 12 August 1949, and relating to the Protection of Victims of International Armed Conflict	X		X	X	71
23. Protocol II Additional to the Geneva Conventions of 12 August 1949, and relating to the Protection of Victims of Non-International Armed Conflicts	X		X	X	64
24. Convention against Torture and Other Cruel, Inhuman, or Degrading Treatment or Punishment				X	28
25. African Charter of Human and Peoples' Rights	X		X	X	35
26. OAU Convention Governing the Specific Aspects of Refugee Problems in Africa	X		X	X	34
Four-country total	19	11	22	25	. . .

SOURCE: Jean-Bernard Marie, "International Instruments Relating to Human Rights," *Human Rights Law Journal*, vol. 9 (1988), pt. 1, pp. 113–40.

TABLE A-2. FREEDOM RATINGS FOR FOUR WEST AFRICAN COUNTRIES, 1973–87[a]

Year	Burkina Faso		Côte d'Ivoire		Guinea		Senegal	
	Score	Category	Score	Category	Score	Category	Score	Category
1973	3, 4	PF	6, 6	NF	7, 7	NF	6, 5	NF
1975	6, 4	PF	6, 6	NF	7, 7	NF	6, 5	NF
1976	6, 4	PF	6, 5	NF	7, 7	NF	6, 4	PF
1977	5, 5	PF	6, 5	NF	7, 7	NF	6, 4	PF
1978	5, 4	PF	6, 5	NF	7, 7	NF	5, 3	PF
1979	2, 3	F	6, 5	NF	7, 7	NF	4, 3	PF
1980	2, 3	F	6, 5	PF	7, 7	NF	4, 3	PF
1981	6, 5	PF	6, 5	PF	7, 7	NF	4, 4	PF
1982	6, 5	PF	5, 5	PF	7, 7	NF	4, 4	PF
1983	6, 5	PF	5, 5	PF	7, 7	NF	4, 4	PF
1984	7, 5	NF	6, 5	PF	7, 5	NF	3, 4	PF
1985	7, 6	NF	6, 5	PF	7, 5	NF	3, 4	PF
1986	7, 6	NF	6, 5	PF	7, 5	NF	3, 4	PF
1987	7, 6	NF	6, 5	PF	7, 6	NF	3, 4	PF

SOURCE: Figures for 1973–86 are from Raymond D. Gastil, *Freedom in the World: Political and Civil Liberties, 1986–1987* (Greenwood Press, 1987); figures for 1987 are from *Freedom in the World, 1987–88* version, pp. 55–62.

a. The lower the number, the higher the freedom score; the first number refers to civil liberties; the second to political rights. F = free; NF = not free; PF = partly free. See figure A-1 for the factors that enter into the judgments made by Gastil.

FIGURE A-1. FACTORS CONSIDERED BY RAYMOND GASTIL IN ASSIGNING FREEDOM SCORES IN TABLE A-2

Civil Liberties

1. Media/literature free of political censorship
    a. Press independent of government
    b. Broadcasting independent of government
2. Open public discussion
3. Freedom of assembly and demonstration
4. Freedom of political or quasi-political organization
5. Nondiscriminatory rule of law in politically relevant cases
    a. independent judiciary
    b. security forces respect individuals
6. Free from unjustified political terror or imprisonment
    a. free from imprisonment or exile for reason of conscience
    b. free from torture
    c. free from terror by groups not opposed to the system
    d. free from government-organized terror

212   CLAUDE E. WELCH, JR.

FIGURE A-1 (continued)

Civil Liberties (*continued*)

7. Free trade unions, peasant organizations, or equivalents
8. Free businesses or cooperatives
9. Free professional or other private organizations
10. Free religious institutions
11. Personal social rights: including those to property, internal and external travel, choice of residence, marriage, and family
12. Socioeconomic rights: including freedom from dependency on landlords, bosses, union leaders or bureaucrats
13. Freedom from gross socioeconomic inequality
14. Freedom from gross government indifference or corruption

Political Rights

1. Chief authority recently elected by a meaningful process
2. Legislature recently elected by a meaningful process
   Alternatives for (1) and (2):
   a. no choice and possibility of rejection
   b. no choice but some possibility of rejection
   c. choice possible only among government-approved candidates
   d. government or single-party selected candidates
   e. relatively open choices possible only in local elections
   f. open choice possible within a restricted range
   g. relatively open choices possible in all elections
3. Fair election laws, campaigning opportunity, polling and tabulation
4. Fair reflection of voter preference in distribution of power
   —parliament, for example, has effective power
5. Multiple political parties
   —only dominant party allowed effective opportunity
   —open to rise and fall of competing parties
6. Recent shifts in power through elections
7. Significant opposition vote
8. Free of military or foreign control
9. Major group or groups denied reasonable self-determination
10. Decentralized political power
11. Informal consensus; de facto opposition power

SOURCE: Gastil, *Freedom in the World, 1986–1987*, pp. 9–10.

CHAPTER NINE

Participatory Approaches to Human Rights in Sub-Saharan Africa

James C. N. Paul

IT IS SOMETIMES argued that in many developing countries, notably in sub-Saharan Africa (SSA), there are serious contradictions between the goals of promoting universal human rights, generating economic development, and respecting indigenous cultures. From some perspectives— particularly those of elites in power—the proposition may seem attractive. But it appears flawed if one focuses on the role of human rights in promoting people-centered, self-reliant development and in protecting endogenous, popular cultures—and if one emphasizes participatory strategies to develop rights that empower people (notably the rural poor, who are most of the people) to achieve these ends.

This essay explores the role of human rights in the development of economies and societies geared to the cultures and needs of rural people in SSA. The focus is on rural societies because, as noted, most people in SSA live in rural environments and depend on agriculture or agrarian-related activities for their livelihood. The development of sustainable, democratic constitutional orders greatly depends on the development, in rural areas, of new forms and structures to enable both more effective political participation and the imposition of accountability on power-wielders—so that rural people can have the means to assert and protect their interests, which are often very different from those of urban elites. Similarly, sustainable and equitable economic development in SSA de-

Many of the ideas in this paper grow out of my association with the International Center for Law in Development in New York. ICLD is a third world–oriented nongovernmental organization that collaborates with other organizations working with the rural poor. Its interests center on the development of human rights as legal resources for the rural poor and on the role of human rights in development processes. I am grateful to Clarence J. Dias, president of ICLD, for providing much of the intellectual inspiration for this paper.

pends significantly on development of smallholder agriculture and improvement of the conditions of life in rural communities. Obviously strategies to promote these kinds of development must find resonance in rural cultures, just as rural people must find ways of adapting traditional beliefs and patterns of behavior to the exigencies of social change.

The participatory approach to human rights development discussed here emphasizes the importance of developing new processes that will enable people to understand the general principles of universal human rights law and relate them to their needs. It is also premised on the assumption that universal rights can come into meaningful existence only when they are seen to be related to the protection and advancement of important interests, and when they are asserted and exercised through participatory structures that express widely shared, deeply felt popular concerns and values. The importance of generating these structures is the central message of this chapter.

The first section examines some universal rights (now guaranteed by international law to all people everywhere) that are of particular relevance to the great mass of rural people in most SSA countries. The second section examines the historical development of "modern" states in SSA, their political and economic characteristics, and their effect on rural societies. The imposition of these exogenous states (and their alien legal orders, political structures, economies, cultures, and capacities to use force) has produced profound changes in many countries: the danger of increased ethnic, cultural, and class tensions; and the deterioration of rural economies, making it urgent to generate sustainable rural development that builds on the energies of small farmers and traditional units of production. The third section focuses on the relationship between human rights and various rural development objectives widely stressed today. Abundant evidence shows that the *exercise* of human rights is essential both to protect those interests of rural people that are directly affected by development projects and to realize more benefits from those projects. The fourth section discusses relationships between rights and cultures. Again, abundant evidence shows the importance of enabling people to use rights not only to protect their basic cultural interests but also to facilitate endogenous adaptation of cultures to social change and the realization of the basic rights of all within those cultures, notably women. The final section examines some elements of a participatory approach to the development of human rights in SSA and some strategies to promote it.

International Human Rights Law in the African Context

International human rights law is slowly, painfully revolutionizing the international order by imposing new obligations on all states to promote and protect rights deemed to be the universal entitlement of all peoples everywhere. The promotion of human rights has always been a central task of the United Nations system and a solemn obligation imposed by the UN Charter on each member.

From its beginnings in the 1940s, but especially during the last two decades, the UN system has been used to construct a substantial edifice of human rights law. The Universal Declaration, promulgated in 1948, is the centerpiece, setting out broad principles that define the field. The two international covenants, drafted in the 1960s and now widely ratified, elaborate many of these principles: together these instruments constitute the International Bill of Human Rights. Other important additions, particularly from third world perspectives, include the Convention on the Elimination of All Forms of Racial Discrimination and the 1979 Convention on the Elimination of All Forms of Discrimination against Women (CEDAW), both now ratified by more than 100 countries. Very important, too, are a number of International Labour Organization (ILO) conventions, setting out, often in explicit detail, the rights of different categories of "workers," including smallholders and rural women in their capacity as workers within households. Recent additions are the UN Convention on the Rights of the Child (1989), the evolving Human Right to Development, now set out in the General Assembly Declaration of 1986, and a proposed Declaration on the Rights of Ethnic and Cultural Minorities.[1]

African governments explicitly stated their adherence to the Universal Declaration when they ratified the Charter of the Organization of African Unity (OAU), and they reaffirmed that allegiance as well as recognized the validity of the covenants in the International African Charter of Human and Peoples' Rights (Banjul Charter), adopted by the

1. An excellent book that reviews the history and development of international human rights law and sets forth the content of the international instruments discussed here is *United Nations Action in the Field of Human Rights* (United Nations, 1988). See also Theodor Meron, ed., *Human Rights in International Law: Legal and Policy Issues* (Oxford: Clarendon Press, 1984). A good collection of international instruments highly relevant to the third world rural poor is Katarina Tomasevski, ed., *The Right to Food: A Guide through Applicable International Law* (Hingham, Mass.: Kluwer Academic Publishers, 1987).

OAU in 1981. African governments have participated, sometimes extensively, in the drafting of international rights instruments from the international covenants onward.

Yet African political leaders and some African intellectuals have displayed ambivalence, and sometimes hostility, toward the principle that all states must now be governed by a regime of universal human rights law. Perhaps the Banjul Charter reflects this ambivalence (some say cynicism). Arguably, the source of this lack of commitment may be found in the nature of many SSA states: universal rights, if taken seriously, pose a clear and present challenge to the existing constitutional orders of these states. But the reasons often officially avowed have to do with the alleged incompatibility of many universal rights with social conditions in African societies.

Thus it has been argued that international human rights law is grounded in an alien "Western" (some say bourgeois) jurisprudence. These rights (it is said) exalt principles of individual freedom at the cost of collective values rooted in African cultures. They are also incompatible with the imperatives of "development," which require an active interventionist state. Indeed, the state is sometimes portrayed as the protector of its peoples from the threat of neocolonialism and other subtle but profound forms of external domination. African governments have helped to create the concept of "peoples' rights," now used as a term of art in some circles: "peoples' rights" are collective rights to national sovereignty free from external influence (sometimes said to be grounded in a nation-state's right to self-determination) and rights to national "control over the country's natural resources"; and the state is seen as a surrogate of "the people"—a protector of their culture, liberty, and development.[2]

In view of the legacies of colonialism, racism, and the continuing attempts of external powers to manipulate (sometimes "destabilize") African governments, and in view of the vulnerability of African economies, one can readily appreciate the appeal of some of these arguments. But they are founded on flawed assumptions. One can question whether many SSA states, as now constituted, are authentic surrogates of their people, notably rural people, when these people seem to lack meaningful powers to participate in their governments and impose ac-

2. For discussions of these and related issues, see various chapters in Rhoda E. Howard, *Human Rights in Commonwealth Africa* (Totowa, N.J.: Rowman and Littlefield, 1986); and Claude E. Welch, Jr., and Ronald I. Meltzer, eds., *Human Rights and Development in Africa* (Albany: State University of New York Press, 1984).

countability on them. One can question whether many SSA states, as now constituted, have brought "development" to rural peoples—particularly since it is now widely conceded that most have often promulgated policies and programs which have seriously harmed the economies of the rural poor. One might argue that many SSA states, as now constituted, pose a risk to those cultural and ethnic minorities that lack both political power in the state and rights to protect themselves from various forms of domination, sometimes brutal, by the state.

These questions are examined in succeeding sections. But a starting point in this debate, often ignored by the skeptics, should be an examination of those rights that have come today to be seen as universal, because they protect those basic interests of people that are not only universally shared but also essential to the realization of the dignity we now ascribe to the human person.

From the perspective of the rural poor in SSA, the development of several basic rights seems important, namely, rights relating to participation, basic human needs, security in land, equality, and "development processes."[3]

Participation. Rights of participation are central not only to the development of democratic systems of governance but also to the development of human rights systems geared to local needs and cultures. The essence of any basic right is the power it bestows on people, acting individually or collectively, to demand recognition and protection of the interests guaranteed by the right. Participation is a way of exercising that power. The empowerment of people with capacities to identify, assert, and protect their vital interests (that is, their basic rights) requires

3. The discussion that follows draws from James C. N. Paul, "International Development Agencies, Human Rights and Humane Development Projects," in Irving Brecher, ed., *Human Rights Development and Foreign Policy: Canadian Perspectives* (Halifax: Institute for Research on Public Policy, 1989), pp. 275–325. See also: for rights of participation, Ved P. Nanda, "Development and Human Rights: The Role of International Law and Organizations," in George W. Shepherd, Jr., and Ved P. Nanda, eds., *Human Rights and Third World Development* (Westport, Conn.: Greenwood Press, 1985), pp. 287–307; for the "right to food," Clarence J. Dias and James C. N. Paul, "Developing the Human Right to Food as a Legal Resource for the Rural Poor," in Philip Alston and Katarina Tomasevski, eds., *The Right to Food* (Boston: M. Nijhoff, 1984); for women and use of the CEDAW convention, Katarina Tomasevski, "Women-in-Development Cooperation: A Human Rights Perspective," *SIM Newsletter and Netherlands Human Rights Quarterly,* vol. 6 (1988), pp. 29–54; for the human right to development, Philip Alston, "Making Space for New Human Rights: The Case for the Right to Development," *Harvard Human Rights Yearbook,* vol. 1 (Spring 1988), pp. 3–40. There is an urgent need for an intensive study of international human rights law and rights to "security in land."

recognition of many component rights, such as access to information; freedom to form and finance different kinds of self-managed organizations and use them as vehicles for many different kinds of collective action; freedom of communication and access to the media; access to officials, government agencies, the courts, and other forums; and often freedom to form organizations to provide assistance, including legal assistance to help others realize the rights noted here (and others). These rights are guaranteed by the International Covenant on Political and Civil Rights and by many ILO conventions, notably Convention 141, which guarantees rights of association and collective action for small farmers, peasants, self-employed rural women, and other agrarian workers. A number of international instruments have called for the incorporation of these rights into development processes.

Basic human needs. Rights to food, health, and education (including functional civic and human rights education) are guaranteed by the International Covenant on Economic, Social and Cultural Rights. The scope of these rights remains to be developed. No one suggests that people can demand that governments provide free food or doctors for all. But they can demand that governments take steps, appropriate to the circumstances, to provide essential services at a basic level; they can demand protections against practices that exacerbate risks of hunger, disease, and ignorance, including ignorance of the information people need to protect other basic interests; and they can demand protections against unjustifiable discrimination in the allocation of resources and services to provide for those needs. All these kinds of legitimate demands are highly relevant to the situation of the rural poor in SSA. All too often development programs inflict harms that violate "basic needs" rights: dams may create risks of bilharzia, malaria, and salinization of water resources leading to degradation of land and food sources; export commercial crop programs may disrupt local food production; and other policies may affect the distribution and availability of food. Ministries that are supposed to supply essential services, such as health care, often seem to ignore the needs of rural areas, or they downgrade bureaucratic failures causing the breakdown of services they are supposed to be providing. When the victims of such wrongs are powerless to protest and demand redress, it is unlikely that those responsible will be held accountable or that the damage done will be compensated. Through the exercise of rights of participation, rural people can begin to assert and enforce basic needs rights.

Security in land. This right is obviously important to smallholder rural families, indeed to groups that hold land collectively, not only because land is a crucial source of food supply and income but also because it is a source of identity and political status, and integral to culture. Protecting that security is becoming increasingly important in areas where the political economy of development threatens the tenure of vulnerable smallholders. Rights to demand such protections can be drawn from provisions of the Universal Declaration, the International Covenant on Economic and Social Rights, and now from the recently enacted ILO Convention 169, which protects the rights of ethnic and tribal groups that hold land collectively. Yet it also seems apparent that rights to security in land need to be developed to fit SSA contexts, a task that will clearly require participation.

Equality. These rights may also be central, particularly if one tries to understand the interests of rural women and other historically vulnerable groups. Article 14 of the 1979 UN Convention on the Elimination of All Forms of Discrimination against Women (a convention now ratified by most SSA countries) speaks directly to the situation of rural women; it prohibits discrimination in the allocation of goods and services, in control of land, and in access to cooperatives and other public agencies and the courts. The convention makes it possible for rural women to challenge and significantly change the position and roles now so often ascribed to them by custom or practice. The possibility of their doing so may depend on the extent to which rural women are helped to perceive, and believe in, their rights and to organize efforts to demand them—that is, on their capacity to realize rights of participation.

The human right to development. This right is important, too, because it entitles rural people to demand that those who do development—international agencies like the World Bank as well as government departments and parastatal organizations—operate through structures that *promote* (as well as protect) the basic rights of those particularly and directly affected by a development program.

The right to "development" as a "right of *people*" has been incorporated in the Banjul Charter. A further recent step has been the drafting and adoption of the 1986 UN Declaration on the Human Right to Development as a *human* right. The impetus for the declaration came from third world countries, and the purpose was to give content and focus to the right. It was approved by the UN General Assembly by a vote of 146 to 1 (the United States stood alone in opposition and eight western governments abstained). The 1986 Declaration is hardly a model of clarity. It combines many quite different propositions, and insofar as it purports to grant "rights" to states to demand a "new international economic order," it is controversial, even problematic, as a *human* rights instrument. But some other essential propositions of the declaration seem clear, and on these there may be little disagreement about the value and importance of the declaration to rural people in SSA. The declaration quite clearly

—affirms the principle of "people-centered" development; people should be the active subjects as well as the objects of "development" efforts;

—confirms the principle that human rights are means as well as ends of this kind of development;

—underscores (as have so many other General Assembly resolutions) the central importance of "participation" as both a basic right (or bundle of rights) and a means to realize other rights in people-centered development;

—imposes the obligation on governments and international development agencies to respect and promote human rights in the processes of development;

—empowers people, notably the intended beneficiaries of development activities, to demand accountability to these principles through processes of participation.[4]

Thus the human right to development is in part *process oriented* and perhaps comparable to the right to "due process." It focuses on processes and institutions used to promote social change. It calls for participation of people, notably those most affected, in the design and management of change. It recognizes that rights of participation are an essential precondition if people are to gain the capacity to understand their situation, assert themselves, and win recognition of other rights. Participation is the vehicle by which other, very general, rights set out in the Universal Declaration and the covenants can be converted into specific, context-related claims for the protections and entitlements promised by the International Bill of Human Rights.

This summary listing of different categories of basic human rights relevant to rural peoples is suggestive, not exhaustive. Other categories of rights could be noted, and group rights to retain and protect indigenous cultures are discussed later in the chapter. The point here is to demonstrate that international human rights law *does* provide rights

4. United Nations, General Assembly Resolution 41/128 (December 4, 1986).

that can be used by the rural poor in SSA to protect and advance their interests. Exercise of those rights is not incompatible with traditional values. The rights noted protect the shared interests of groups as well as those of individuals. The development of capacities to understand and claim these rights may indeed be crucial to the future welfare and progress of rural societies. That proposition becomes even more clear if one examines the nature of SSA states on the one hand and the centrality of human rights to the realization of people-centered (as opposed to state-centered) development on the other.

Historical Development of Modern States in Africa

A starting point in any discussion of the importance and role of universal human rights in SSA is to examine the nature of states in that region and see how it has affected the rural populations.[5]

Of course, generalizations on this subject must be qualified. States in SSA, like states everywhere, are social variables. A few may be characterized by relatively free, democratic political systems and an absence of cultural and ethnic cleavage and conflict. Some may seem to be democratic, but participation is controlled in them (for example, by a one-party system). Most SSA states are essentially authoritarian—autonomous from and unaccountable to the people governed. That seems particularly true if one views the state from the perspective of rural people.

5. Discussion here draws from James C. N. Paul, "The International Third World Legal Studies Association Project on Developing Constitutional Orders in Sub-Saharan African States: An Unofficial Report," *Third World Legal Studies* (forthcoming). The literature on the characteristics and pathologies of the states in SSA has grown extensively over the last dozen years. Discussion in this section draws on "The State and the Crisis in Africa: In Search of a Second Liberation," *Development Dialogue,* vol. 2 (1987), pp. 5–29 (a report of a seminar organized by the Dag Hammarskjöld Foundation and largely composed of prominent African scholars); Robert H. Jackson and Carl G. Rosberg, "Sovereignty and Underdevelopment: Juridical Statehood in the African Crisis," *Journal of Modern African Studies,* vol. 24 (March 1986), pp. 1–13; Robert H. Jackson and Carl G. Rosberg, *Personal Rule in Black Africa: Prince, Autocrat, Prophet, Tyrant* (University of California Press, 1982); Robert H. Jackson and Carl G. Rosberg, "Popular Legitimacy in African Multi-Ethnic States," *Journal of Modern African Studies,* vol. 22 (June 1984), pp. 177–98; Richard Sandbrook and Judith Barker, *The Politics of Africa's Economic Stagnation* (Cambridge University Press, 1985); Robert H. Bates, *Markets and States in Tropical Africa: The Political Basis of Agricultural Policies* (University of California Press, 1981); Larry Diamond, "Class Formation in the Swollen African State," *Journal of Modern African Studies,* vol. 25 (December 1987), pp. 567–96; and Richard L. Sklar, "The Nature of Class Domination in Africa," *Journal of Modern African Studies,* vol. 17 (December 1979), pp. 531–32.

SSA states are products of recent and exogenous historical processes. The colonial powers drew territorial boundaries without much reference to indigenous factors, and they arbitrarily aggregated different ethnic and cultural groups under the sovereignty of an alien government. These regimes expropriated indigenous structures of governance or subverted and converted them into institutions of colonial control. People were treated as subjects of the state, not citizens—until the eve of independence. Those who lived in regions that were environmentally capable of producing export commodities and that were accessible to transport were integrated (sometimes by force) into a "modern" money economy. Those who were more remotely situated (or who lived in less fertile environments) were left "undeveloped," weakly linked to the emerging "modern" economy. Similarly, because of geography and culture, some ethnic groups were given more opportunity for education and employment in subordinate positions in government and the security forces.

The colonial state built the foundations—legal, economic, and political—of the postcolonial state. To legitimize its boundaries and sovereignty, the colonial state used a repertoire of law, not European but colonial law and international law. To maintain political control, it used "emergency powers," preventive detention, broadly defined crimes of sedition, and controls over education, communications, formation of associations, meetings, and collective activities. To convert subsistence farmers into cash crop producers or wage workers, it used laws dealing with taxation, employment, credit, and regulation of agricultural practices. To stimulate and maintain economies based on export production, it created state corporations and regimes of regulation. Outside of agriculture, the colonial state used regulatory law to deter the development of indigenous capitalism, at least on any significant scale.

The state became the major employer of salaried workers; the incomes and perks of its higher officials were extraordinarily large, relative to the local economy, and the status ascribed to these offices was great. Independence did not signal a reduction in the pay scales. On the eve of independence the state was potentially the dominant economic enterprise, the main source of well-paid employment and civic status for educated, urban-oriented elites. Indeed, for those who controlled it, the state provided a large domain of patronage and power. There existed no economic base, independent of the state, that could be used to organize and sustain political opposition to the government in power.

As independence neared, the colonial powers promulgated new constitutions—exogenous laws with no continuities to past experience—purporting to convert the state into a more democratic polity. In anglophonic Africa, British-style constitutions envisioned a parliamentary system and cabinet government, chosen through competitive elections with universal suffrage. Bills of rights enforceable in independent courts guaranteed new rights unknown to colonial law; other provisions were designed to ensure the political neutrality of a professional civil service subordinate to the rule of law. The incongruence between these constitutions and both past experience and the real nature of the powers of state soon became apparent. The struggle for independence also became a struggle for power to control the state and the resources it commanded once independence was achieved.

Political leaders often used ethnic-based or regional parties to win elections; electoral victories were used to convert parliamentary constitutions into executive systems; and other measures, notably the repertoire of colonial law that was still in place, were used to entrench the regime in power. Military intervention took place when some combination of political conflict, widespread corruption, and maladministration produced a crisis in government or when a faction of soldiers decided to impose its own rule.

From the 1960s on, governments, including security organizations, increased rapidly in size, functions, and powers. Governments also monopolized or closely regulated the media. They used the old colonial laws as well as new measures to limit or repress opposition. Opportunities for, and rights of, autonomous political participation, notably space for nongovernmental activities, were limited. During much of this period it was generally believed that states could plan and manage "development," a term that often meant "economic growth." The role of the state in the economy became more and more extensive. By the latter 1970s, as agricultural production declined and economies deteriorated, with a worsening of the conditions of rural life, the concept of "development" and the role of the state in producing it became much more problematic.

Certainly that seems true if the state is viewed from the perspectives of rural people. Over past decades they have become ever more dependent on the state as well as increasingly ruled by it. Social and cultural changes have created community needs for health, educational, and protective services; for access to information, credit, and inputs all controlled by the state; for efficient systems of milling, storage, transport, and markets that can provide goods now deemed essential, including food to supplement subsistence production; and for a legal system that provides access and engenders confidence. The state has monopolized or regulated all these sectors, and often the results have been unfortunate if the interests of rural people are the criteria. The state has often depressed prices of cash crops and taxed producers directly and indirectly by monopolizing and profiting from the marketing of agricultural commodities. It has imposed development programs on communities that often fail to benefit the rural poor and that sometimes inflict particular harm on women and other vulnerable groups.

These and other powers are exercised by governmental organizations that are usually highly centralized, hierarchical, and largely managed by urban-oriented professionals. Entry into higher positions in bureaucracies depends on educational attainments largely unavailable to rural populations and often unrelated to their circumstances. Political incentives to delegate authority, especially in ways that empower people, are usually lacking. Indeed, dealings between agencies and local communities are often characterized by negligence, arbitrary decisions, and corruption.

The social gap between governments and rural people is said to be growing. It is widely argued that the state has become a means of accumulation as well as power for those who are well positioned within it. The state thus provides the basis for the formation of a new, essentially urban class that has a vested interest in maintaining the existing political economy. Irrespective of the validity of this thesis, the state is probably viewed with increasing suspicion, if not hostility, by rural peoples. This aversion is regularly reflected in studies of popular attitudes toward state institutions, including the courts.[6]

The effect of SSA states on historic cultures is sometimes overlooked. These cultures, after all, are rooted in the ethnic and linguistic groups that make up the state and in the historic lands and environments of those groups. Indigenous cultures are important, in part, because they provide rural people with a set of identities and loyalties as well as with a means of understanding and relating to the world; they are important because they satisfy deep-seated psychological and social needs.

Because indigenous cultures are partly group-related phenomena,

6. See, for example, Paul Richards, *Indigenous Agricultural Revolution: Ecology and Food Production in West Africa* (Boulder, Colo.: Westview Press, 1985); David W. Brokensha and Peter D. Little, eds., *Anthropology of Development and Change in East Africa* (Westview Press, 1988); and R. E. Downs and S. P. Reyna, eds., *Land and Society in Contemporary Africa* (University Press of New England, 1988).

how the state relates to quite different ethnic and other cultural and religious groups should be understood. Generalizations here may be difficult, but clearly in countries characterized by cultural and ethnic pluralism and historic cleavages, the state is often perceived as a threat to groups that lack power within it. The threat is exacerbated when it is believed the state monopolizes power and is unaccountable to any rule of law that protects the rights and group interests of those excluded.[7]

Human Rights and Rural Development

Rural development, as the term is used here, focuses on multidimensional development geared to smallholder households: on ways to increase their production of both food and other cash crops and on ways to increase new forms of income-generating employment to support households. The human dimension of rural development focuses not only on efforts to improve access to services and resources essential to well-being and human productivity, but also on efforts to help the rural poor become economically more self-reliant, aggressive, and innovative. The political dimension (emphasized in other literature) focuses on efforts to help the poor change their relationships with state agencies, local elites, and the legal system. The educational dimension focuses on ways to generate and share knowledge and skills that enable people, notably women, to engage in these tasks, especially through new forms of collective activities. These objectives are obviously interdependent.[8]

The importance of rural development in Sub-Saharan Africa has been repeatedly recognized in recent development literature: in reports of the World Bank, UN agencies, the UN special session on Africa, and SSA governments. Although of course other development strategies, such as industrialization, regional integration, and restructuring, are important, rural development for several reasons is seen as critical. First, most people in most SSA countries live in smallholder households. Second, smallholder households produce, overwhelmingly, most of the food consumed within SSA countries, as well as many of the cash crops that are mainstays of national economies. And third, efforts to alleviate

7. See, for example, Dunstan N. Wai, "Human Rights in Sub Saharan Africa," in Adamantia Pollis and Peter Schwab, eds., *Human Rights: Cultural and Ideological Perspectives* (Praeger, 1979), pp. 115–44.

8. The text in this section draws from James C. N. Paul, "Rural Development, Human Rights and Constitutional Orders in Sub-Saharan Africa," *Third World Legal Studies* (forthcoming), which contains an extensive annotated bibliography.

poverty and create markets for local industrialization may ultimately depend on raising living standards through rural development.

Recent Experience

Although the importance of rural development is now stressed in official rhetoric, strategies to promote it must take account of trends now affecting smallholder agriculture, trends that underscore the importance of the political, hence human, rights dimensions of rural development. Here are a few examples.

—During the last two decades, especially in the period 1978–86, agriculture deteriorated and production, notably food production per capita, declined. Despite increasing food imports, nutrition levels, particularly among the rural poor, declined. It is estimated that at least 20 percent of the rural people in most countries are undernourished; the long-term consequences of this trend, if it persists, are grim to contemplate. Even though observers disagree about the causes of food deficits (for example, to what extent malnutrition reflects problems of production shortages as opposed to problems of distribution or access to food in rural areas) and disagree about strategies to meet food shortages (for example, over the role of food imports), they largely agree that development strategies must emphasize greater local food self-sufficiency, increases in household earnings, and improved systems of storage and distribution.[9] A report from the Southern African Development Coordinating Conference summarizes the new view: "Present food production is largely in the hands of small farmers . . . and the failure of general policies to address the problems of the small farmer has been a major part of the more general problem of declining agricultural production."[10] It is also clear that the problems of the small farmer can never be properly defined, let alone addressed, without his—and, today, her—participation in the effort.

—The rapid growth of female-headed, smallholder households has been widely noted—as growing numbers of adult males migrate to larger towns and other areas to seek wage employment. Although women have often been traditionally responsible (to varying degrees) for household food production, the migration of males frequently imposes new labor demands on women that are difficult, sometimes im-

9. See World Bank, *The Challenge of Hunger in Africa: A Call to Action* (Washington, 1988).
10. SADCC, *Food and Agricultural Conference Report* (Gaborone, Botswana, 1986).

possible, to meet. The position of women smallholders is further handicapped if they lack control over the land they farm and lack access to extension, credit, inputs, cooperatives, and other markets. When needs for labor, inputs, and other resources are unmet, productivity and income decline. When, in these circumstances, absent husbands fail to remit adequate funds, and when other sources of family earning fail, the result may be hunger and other forms of immiserization. These conditions reflect women's lack of power—within families, land tenure systems, cooperatives, development agencies, courts, and other forums.[11]

—There appear to be growing inequalities among households in terms of land, incomes, and access to resources. In some rural communities there is a growing "presence" of absentee, urban landholders— elites who invest in productive land in periurban areas. Where land is scarce and productive, the development of new or competing types of land tenure systems also seems to create new risks for more vulnerable households. Of course these patterns vary, and they are complex. But it is important to recognize that socioeconomic stasis is not the condition of many rural areas; the picture is often one of change, coupled with a growing, but perhaps still inchoate, politicization of groups and communities that have suffered from, or are threatened by, the changes taking place.[12]

—Another trend has been a deterioration of infrastructure and services in more remote rural regions. Deterioration of roads and transport contributes to lack of access to markets, including lack of access to consumer goods needed by rural families, conditions that contribute to lack of incentives to produce for the market. Deterioration in services may be reflected in such areas as extension or primary health—in services that may profoundly affect household productivity and the welfare of women and children. Again, these trends may in part be attributed to the political impotence of the rural poor.[13]

—Deterioration of environments is another trend, and it is probably far more serious than is yet generally recognized. The situations and

11. For an excellent collection of papers and reports on rural women in Africa, see the entire volume of *Canadian Journal of African Studies*, vol. 22, no. 3 (1988), especially Kathleen Staudt, "Women Farmers in Africa: Research and Institutional Action, 1972–1987," pp. 567–82.

12. See, for example, Brokensha and Little, *Ecology and Food Production*; Downs and Reyna, *Land and Society*; and Wayne E. Nafziger, *Inequality in Africa: Political Elites, Proletariat, Peasants, and the Poor* (Cambridge University Press, 1988).

13. See, for example, World Bank, *Sub-Saharan Africa: From Crisis to Sustainable Development* (Washington, 1989).

causes of degradation differ. In many areas there may be an increasing failure to follow ecologically sound crop rotation schemes as pressures on land intensify. Some environmentally vulnerable regions are threatened by new settlements and the introduction of unsuitable cultivation. And many other areas are being put at risk by the introduction of monocropping, overgrazing, deforestation, or other harmful practices. Obviously, many of these harmful practices cannot be arrested simply by enacting legislation and creating regimes of government regulation; appropriate remedies (and their enforcement) must come from within communities affected, through processes of popular participation.[14]

—Another trend in many countries is the increasing rate of population growth, with attendant needs for more food and basic services, and the increasing pressure on land, notably where there are declining opportunities for other productive employment. Indeed, although population growth still tends to be ignored in national planning or in the administration of health and education programs in many countries, the need to reckon with current fertility rates, particularly in rural areas, is widely stressed in the development literature. The evidence is growing that when appropriate health education and family planning services are made available, people use contraceptives and other controls. Awareness of these services, and demands for them, can be increased by helping women to organize and learn. Indeed, efforts to generate demand for health and family planning services are probably essential.[15]

Explanations for the Trends

External calamities like severe droughts, debt or restructuring difficulties, and declining terms of trade and other crises that impoverish governments may of course be major causes of distress. But ameliorating those conditions will not in itself arrest the trends noted, let alone produce rural development. Changes in agricultural and rural development policies and programs must also take place.

One effort must be a careful review of the measures needed to promote food security for rural households (that is, their capacity to meet

---

14. See, for example, Lloyd Timberlake, "Guarding Africa's Renewable Resources," in Robert J. Berg and Jennifer Seymour Whitaker, eds., *Strategies for African Development*, Study for the Committee on African Development Strategies (University of California Press, 1986), pp. 111–28; and World Bank, *Sub-Saharan Africa*.

15. See World Bank, *Population Growth and Policies in Sub-Saharan Africa* (Washington, 1986); and Fred T. Sai, "Population and Health: Africa's Most Basic Problem," in Berg and Whitaker, eds., *Strategies for African Development*, pp. 129–52.

basic needs from some combination of self-provisioning and purchase of food in accessible markets, including imported food when necessary). The political will to mount such efforts, and their effectiveness, may depend largely on local capacities to demand them. Increasingly the problem of food security is seen as partly a problem of political empowerment and not simply one of economics. State regulation of producer prices and state practices that tend to monopolize marketing, transport, food storage and distribution, and other activities affecting producer incentives should be rigorously reviewed and revised. Allocational policies favoring large-scale farmers and export agriculture at the cost of services to smallholders and food production should also be reviewed. In many regions programs to protect or rehabilitate physical environments must be put in place. And clearly the needs of rural women in respect to all their multiple roles must be addressed. It is usually conceded that appropriate measures to understand, define, and secure these objectives require a much greater involvement of those whose interests are most at stake, and that nongovernmental organizations of various kinds, working with rural communities, should play a greater role in helping to identify and articulate the concerns, needs, and requirements of smallholder households.

Many of the government agencies responsible for designing and administering programs directly affecting rural development are afflicted with pathologies that limit their capacity to reach, work with, and benefit the rural poor. These pathologies are reflected in hierarchical, stratified, and overcentralized forms of organization; in official behavior characterized by elitist and etatist attitudes, patron-client relationships, and discrimination against women farmers; in abuses of power and, often enough, corrupt dealings; and in processes for decisionmaking characterized by secrecy, limited access, and even less accountability.[16]

Some kinds of development projects have inflicted serious wrongs on vulnerable groups in rural communities, harms that go unredressed and that exacerbate the hardships. Among these risk-prone measures are projects to build major dams and highways, to introduce large-scale agriculture or new systems of production of export crops, to extract timber resources, and to resettle rural people in new environments. "Modernization of agriculture" schemes have, in effect, transformed self-provisioning farmers into debt-ridden producers of export crops, dependent

16. See, for example, Goran Hyden, *No Shortcuts to Progress: African Development Management in Perspective* (University of California Press, 1983).

on private firms or parastatal agencies for inputs, credit, and prices. The introduction of mechanized farming and other kinds of cash crop projects often seriously harms environments and food systems. Resettlement projects have often produced disease, hunger, and other deprivations through faulty planning and management sometimes characterized by gross negligence. If project-affected people are to be protected from these and other harms, they must obviously be empowered with rights and aided by nongovernmental organizations that can help them to understand and exercise their rights.

Strategies for Rural Development

To address these problems, new policies must be developed and, at the microeconomic level, some combination of measures (depending on social and physical environments) must be designed to provide for the following:[17]

increased smallholder production of food and cash crops through research and extension geared to community knowledge and concerns (that is, through local group-managed projects); and provision of accessible inputs, credit, improved storage, transport, and marketing through arrangements that are made responsive to the needs of smallholders by new accountability procedures;

construction or rehabilitation of essential infrastructure such as rural roads and communications;

water resources for agriculture through small-scale irrigation or water conservation (that is, catchment) facilities for farmers in low rainfall areas;

essential services and facilities, for example to provide primary health care, family planning, and more accessible potable water;

protection or rehabilitation of degraded environments through reforestation, controls on land use, and conservation of water and of lands threatened with erosion;

support (credit, knowledge, and skills training) for small-scale, income-generating enterprises, notably participatory group enterprises, such as the manufacturing of butter, soap, or charcoal, the processing of fish or crops, and household industries; and

the inclusion of women in all these measures.

The importance of "participation" in rural development is, of course, now recognized. The World Bank has recently promulgated official pol-

---

17. See, for example, World Bank, *Sub-Saharan Africa.*

icies favoring participation, notably through official collaboration with nongovernmental organizations acting as intermediaries or as agents for official organizations. But no clear consensus exists on the multiple functions of participation, and even less clarity about the kinds of organizations and structural changes needed to promote them. There is also a bewildering silence (among both development experts and many lawyers) about the kinds of legal changes that must be put in place if participatory activities essential to rural development are to be encouraged, protected, and institutionalized and thus made sustainable.[18]

These activities may vary greatly in purpose. They may include efforts of community organizers (supported by external nongovernmental organizations) to catalyze groups within communities; to provide, generate, and share knowledge needed by groups to promote and protect their interests; and to train local paraprofessionals. They may entail formation and use of local self-managed organizations to pursue economic purposes (such as marketing, credit, and processing), or political objectives (pressuring officials, electioneering) at both local and regional levels. They may entail efforts to influence agencies or impose accountability for official negligence or wrongdoing, including recourse to the courts. They may entail various forms of collaboration between local, national, and even international organizations. They may result in various kinds of relationships between nongovernmental organizations and official agencies, ranging from joint enterprise collaborations to conflict and confrontation.

If these kinds of activities are to be undertaken effectively, those who engage in them must enjoy empowering rights not generally accorded to citizens of many SSA states today. Some examples would be powers to meet together without hindrance from local officials and the police; to form self-managed, autonomous associations; to organize a wide variety of collective activities (such as those already noted); to

18. The literature on participation is extensive. World Bank staff members, notably Michael Cernea, have produced some of the best. See, for example, Michael Cernea, *Putting People First: Sociological Variables in Rural Development* (Oxford University Press, 1985); and Cernea, *Nongovernmental Organizations and Local Development* (Washington: World Bank, 1988). The Bank has recently developed new policies and strategies favoring cooperation with nongovernmental organizations in rural development projects. For an instructive review of some of the assumptions, experience, and interesting issues to be resolved, see Lawrence F. Salmen and A. Paige-Evans, "World Bank Work with Nongovernmental Organizations," World Bank Working Paper (Washington, 1989). See also Pearl T. Robinson, "Transnational NGOS: A New Direction for US Policy," *Issues: A Journal of Opinion* (African Studies Association), vol. 18 (Winter 1989), pp. 41–46.

enjoy a corporate type of legal status and group capacity to make contracts, bring legal actions, and raise money through local solicitations and grants from external agencies; to have access to the media and rights to organize their own communication systems; to engage in nonviolent demonstrations and other peaceful protest activity in order to make grievances known and visible; to seek and secure official information from development agencies—especially information that is crucial to enable meaningful participation; and to have access to legal resources.

Human Rights and the Development of Human Cultures

Much has been written about the relationships between "traditional" African cultures and the cultural assumptions sometimes said to underlie international human rights law. Yet the subject appears fraught with difficulties.[19]

The concept of culture is hard to define, particularly for purposes of addressing the questions of interest here. It is linked to a person's language, ethnic identity, and other loyalties. Although for some purposes one may talk of *an* African culture, clearly in most SSA states a plurality of cultures exists: different ethnic groups and polities have had strikingly different political histories, traditions, and structures, and the extent to which these have been modified or expropriated by the colonial or postcolonial state may vary. Other forces of change, which vary with the locale, may be at work: the growth, penetration, and impact of the state and the increasing dependency on it; the introduction of new crops and new economic concerns; the influence of education, and the media and religious spheres; the changing position of women in the economy and the changing character of households and families; the evolution of new classes, both local and national; and the perceived threat of political domination by other ethnic groups. All of these, and other factors, may affect the way people may come to appreciate and use human rights law when they have the opportunity to understand it.

Skeptics argue that it is difficult for rural people to relate to this law. Some have noted that the very concept of a "right" empowering one to assert superior claims against the collective decisions of the community (or the state) may be both difficult to express in many African languages

19. For some general discussions on this subject, see Theodore E. Downing and Gilbert Kushner, eds., *Human Rights and Anthropology* (Cambridge, Mass.: Cultural Survival, 1988); and Howard, *Human Rights in Commonwealth Africa*, chap. 2.

and alien to local experience. The value of collective decisions, community consensus, loyalties to one's group, and respect for leaders has been stressed, as a common element of African cultures. These and other phenomena may make it difficult for communities to accept and act on human rights principles.

The participatory approach emphasized here is not concerned with efforts to atomize communities by promoting individualism. Rather, it is concerned with helping groups threatened or victimized by the state or other groups to act themselves to protect their basic interests. The role of professional outsiders is not to co-opt and assert the claims of victims, but to help victims understand that they do have basic, "universal" rights, and that these can legitimate their efforts to protect their interests. The victims must decide for themselves whether and how to assert their claims. The process of developing awareness and assertion of rights must be endogenous, derived from the group's sense of justice and expressed in its terms and pressed through strategies adopted by the group.

The concept of a "right," as it has been developed in Western jurisprudence, may be in some respects alien to African cultures. But the underlying interests that universal rights are designed to protect are not alien to SSA cultures, and they are surely of paramount importance today. The value of human rights law as a resource and method to legitimize claims may come to be appreciated once the link between rights and essential interests is understood.

As already emphasized, it is the imposition of the "modern" but culturally "alien" state, with its panoply of alien laws and alien organizations, and its pervasive and often abused powers of social control, that creates the need for efforts to entrench human rights, not only in the legal orders of SSA but also in popular cultures. The imposition of the "modern" state without the protections of rights may indeed have characterized the history of state formation in many countries throughout the world in earlier times, but that is a condition which the world community, organized through the UN system, now condemns. Lawless states produce human misery and threats to peace and economic burdens on the international community, as well as wrongs that can no longer be condoned by silence and abstention.

The imposition of economic change and the effect of development programs force the issue even more, as already noted. Development has often heavily affected women, undermining the security provided by "traditional" cultures. Even the most benign, "poverty-centered" development projects have often entailed some forcible external intervention into the lives of people; and often, as noted, they have produced adverse effects. In these contexts it seems misleading to suggest that rights are somehow irrelevant to rural people because they have lacked the traditions, knowledge, and means to assert them.

The pluralistic, cultural, and ethnic character of SSA states also suggests not only that it is inaccurate to speak of a single, common "African" political culture but also that recognition of the basic interests and rights emphasized in this chapter are one essential way to preserve the political unity of those states by ensuring the protections of rights to cultural and ethnic minorities within them. Ethnic conflict in SSA politics may well be (in part at least) a product of the present autonomy and unregulated power of the state. The state's power to control the people, land, and other resources of those groups that are politically weak can be coveted by those that are strong; the more conditions of cleavage and mistrust exist between the groups, the more people may be manipulated to see the state in terms of ethnic politics, and the more resentment there may be if they perceive themselves as losers in this game. The state, uncommitted to and unregulated by human rights law, fosters the "we versus they" syndrome.

The emplacement of human rights in the political order is one way (along with others) of trying to mitigate this kind of rivalry and mistrust by limiting the power of the state. Rights of participation are crucial to this process, for they legitimize efforts of people to demand appropriate protections for their interests. The International Covenant on Economic, Social and Cultural Rights guarantees rights of cultural groups to maintain their language and protect their cultures. The Convention on Racial Discrimination (ratified by virtually all SSA states) provides additional protections. The newly adopted ILO Convention 169 is designed to protect the lands, held through customary group-tenure systems, of cultural and ethnic minorities; and the use of this convention in SSA contexts presents interesting challenges to human rights activists working with relevant groups. Indeed, in view of the tragic experiences of ethnic and cultural conflict in most parts of the world, efforts are now being pressed within the UN system to develop a more coherent, systematic body of law that will protect groups from forcible assimilation, political domination, and discrimination.

A further challenge relates to the position of women, youth, and minorities within cultural groups. African cultures have usually defined distinct roles for women; they have often restricted or excluded their rights to hold land, have limited their participation, and have imposed other disabilities. Some argue that attempts to use law to force changes in these customs will be unavailing if not counterproductive.

Indeed, as noted earlier, the disabilities imposed on rural women are increasingly harmful in the results they produce; women now constitute significant victim groups within rural communities, and there is evidence that they increasingly perceive themselves as such. Economic and social changes may be forcing cultural changes. The participatory approach emphasizes processes rather than the use of state force to change these conditions. The assumption is that as women are helped through participatory activities to understand that they do have basic rights to protect their increasingly important interests, they will devise ways to demand these protections. Once again, victims must be helped to decide for themselves whether and how to enforce their rights. Probably there is no other way to change cultural assumptions and norms. The challenge to human rights activists is to develop strategies to promote these processes.[20]

Strategies for Developing Participatory Approaches

The basic theory and assumptions of the participatory approach have, it is hoped, been made apparent. The attempt here is to discuss ways to develop and use that approach. The text draws on Asian experiences, reflected in a growing literature produced by scholar-activists of that region.[21]

The formation of groups, activities, and causes. The participatory approach emphasizes the need to help widely different kinds of groups to form self-managed organizations and engage in self-reliant, collective efforts. Many of these local activities may not seem at first glance to be connected with human rights issues. But in fact all grass-roots activities that promote free association and self-managed activities are experi-

20. See Margaret Schuler, ed., *Empowerment and the Law: Strategies of Third World Women* (Washington: OEF International, 1986). See also *Canadian Journal of African Studies*, vol. 22, no. 3 (1988).

21. For a collection of papers on this subject, see, for example, *Third World Legal Studies, 1985: Developing Legal Resources with the Third World's Poor* (Valparaiso, Ind.: Valparaiso University School of Law, 1985). See also Asian Cultural Forum on Development, *Empowerment and Social Change: A Shared Struggle,* Report of the Chiangmai Workshop on Middle Level Leadership in Asian NGOs (Bangkok, 1989). The "explosive" development of nongovernmental organizations in the third world is discussed in Cernea, *Nongovernmental Organizations.*

ences in participation; they usually help to teach ways to exercise rights of participation, and they may provide opportunities for generating greater knowledge and appreciation of other rights. Groups organized to promote self-help projects among peasants and rural women by creating new structures to provide credit or marketing cooperatives and to address health care needs or environmental concerns, such as overgrazing or deforestation—groups organized for people-centered development objectives—can provide a foundation for other kinds of collective efforts to promote and protect basic interests.

The generation of grass-roots activity may require, or at least be greatly aided by, support groups operating at national levels. Over the long haul this national-level activity seems crucial. But again there are many kinds of support-type nongovernmental organizations, ranging from those that assist more conventional local, self-help activities to those concerned with victims of maldevelopment, displacement, or official discrimination or repression. Churches, women's associations, environmental, and other kinds of public interest organizations, as well as legal assistance groups, may provide the structures for these kinds of support activities. Thus the development of participatory approaches should be seen to encompass a wide range of nongovernmental activities. Human rights law provides a legal infrastructure that protects and legitimates these efforts.

The roles of law and legal resources.   The participatory approach requires us to transcend the traditional, positivistic notion of law and lawyer roles. If communities and groups are to be helped in their efforts to use human rights law, they must be helped to develop legal resources of their own, and not be made dependent on the professional domination and other limitations that often characterize conventional "legal aid" programs.

The concept of legal resources emphasizes the development, *within groups,* of functional knowledge and skills that enable people working collectively to understand relevant law and generate the capacity to use it to protect and promote their shared interests as they perceive them. The concept of law means far more than official legislation and rules. The "law" that people need for these purposes may include widely shared notions of justice and customs that can be used to animate endogenous groups as well as universal human rights instruments and official constitutions, legislation, and judge-made law.

Further, the concept of law used here is a dynamic one. The very general guarantees that constitute "universal rights" must, in any setting, be interpreted and given content by creating component rights geared to the needs and concerns of people in very different environments, who are confronting very different problems and threats. Moreover, the struggle to generate participatory approaches to achieve those ends may mean that groups may be forced to pit law against law: local officials may invoke penal and related legislation to prohibit formation of "unlicensed" groups or meetings, to jail organizers and leaders as disorderly persons, and to use other sanctions to deter collective activities and bar outside groups from aiding them; grass-roots organizers and leaders—and lawyers and others lending them support—must be prepared to invoke other bodies of law such as constitutional guarantees, official policy statements extolling participation, and widely ratified international conventions (notably ILO conventions), to expose the fundamental contradictions in, and illegality of, official practices that use state law to frustrate realization of these rights. There is nothing really novel about this; historically, struggles to bring rights into real existence in all parts of the world have often entailed processes of pitting rights law against repressive forms of positive law.

The aggressive use of forums. Lawyers may overemphasize the role of courts in struggles for rights. Of course courts are sometimes important—at least when the judges are independent and capable of escaping the tyranny of the kind of narrow, legalistic, and positivistic outlook that has too often characterized the jurisprudence of African courts, and that is antithetical to the growth of rights. Indeed, lawyers and judges in Africa might study with profit the development of social action litigation (SAL) recently fostered by the Supreme Court of India. SAL jurisprudence holds that, in third world countries, courts must become much more accessible to grass-roots organizations; they must proactively develop processes that enable them to entertain the petitions of groups, however crudely phrased, whenever these allege facts that can be converted into human rights claims. In India, the Supreme Court invented new processes to facilitate full investigation of these kinds of claims, for example, by appointing lawyers and court-sponsored commissions to hear all the parties, make findings, and submit appropriate proposals for relief to the Court. The very concept of judicial power is, in this jurisprudence, revised to reform a legal system that has historically frustrated participation by imposing unrealistic barriers to access and limitations on judicial jurisdiction.

Yet the courts are only one forum. Others range from organizing mass meetings, demonstrations, and boycotts to using less confrontational tactics to persuade agencies and officials. The participatory approach emphasizes, too, efforts to open the media to grass-roots organizations and their surrogates. In some situations international forums may provide strategic opportunities. Presumably, international development assistance agencies, such as the World Bank (and also bilateral agencies), are now obligated under international law to promote as well as protect universal human rights in the development projects they finance. National and international nongovernmental human rights groups can properly put pressure on those agencies (as environmental groups already have) to meet their obligations by incorporating appropriate standards and procedures into loan and other aid agreements. The ILO and other UN agencies also can provide forums that can be used by third world nongovernmental organizations to promote participatory initiatives.

A new breed of activists and scholars. The participatory approach probably calls for the creation and development of groups of people who are trained to help processes of local mobilization and organization. It calls for activists who can provide relevant and functional knowledge and training at local levels. It calls for fund raisers and activists. It plainly requires the assistance of lawyers capable of developing legal resources with and for rural groups and for the nongovernmental organizations working with them. If such activities are to be pursued, activists and nongovernmental organizations may need "shields" from hostile governments. Perhaps churches, educational institutions, progressive UN agencies, or international nongovernmental organizations can help to provide both the protection and encouragement needed to nurture these kinds of human resources.

But the agenda sketched here, and the constraints, are formidable. Much may depend on whether African-oriented human rights scholars will begin to expand their horizons and concern themselves more with action-oriented strategies geared to the needs of people. If they do so, human rights law can develop a content and process that will reflect, indeed protect, both cultural values and other vital interests.

IN FEBRUARY 1990 representatives of 150 African nongovernmental organizations (from 40 countries) plus observers from African governments and international development agencies met in conference at Arusha, Tanzania. This International Conference on Popular Participation in the Recovery and Development Process in Africa was cosponsored by the UN Economic Commission for Africa and other UN agencies and a consortium of nongovernmental organizations. The UN Non Governmental Liaison Service reported:

> After four days of intensive, lively debate and dialogue in workshops and plenary sessions, the *African Charter for Popular Participation in Development and Transformation* was adopted by acclamation. The Charter asserts that "there must be an opening up of the political process to accommodate freedom of opinions, tolerate differences . . . as well as ensure the effective participation of the people and their organizations and associations in designing policies and pro-grammes." It urges African governments to "yield space to the people" and to "promote accountability by the State to the people." It calls upon the people themselves to press for democratic partici-pation and to "establish independent people's organizations that are genuinely grassroot, democratically administered and self-reliant." It recommends the establishment of national fora for "honest and open dialogue" between Governments, NGOs and people's organizations.
>
> A significant portion of the Charter is devoted to analyzing the pivotal contribution made to development by women. It urges that attainment of equal rights by women in social, economic and politi-cal spheres must be a central feature of any democratic and partici-patory pattern of development.[22]

22. *NGLS News*, March 1990, pp. 3–4.

Part Four
African Cultural Perspectives

CHAPTER TEN

An Akan Perspective on Human Rights

Kwasi Wiredu

A RIGHT is a claim that people are entitled to make on others or on society at large by virtue of their status. Human rights are claims that people are entitled to make simply by virtue of their status as human beings. The question naturally arises, what is it about a human being that makes him or her entitled to make the latter kind of claim? I intend to explore the answer to this question, which is found in Akan thought, by looking principally at the Akan conception of a person.

The word *Akan* refers both to a group of intimately related languages found in West Africa and to the people who speak them. This ethnic group lives predominantly in Ghana and in parts of adjoining Côte d'Ivoire. In Ghana they inhabit most of the southern and middle belts and account for about half the national population of 14 million. Best known among the Akan subgroup are the Ashantis. Closely cognate are the Denkyiras, Akims, Akuapims, Fantes, Kwahus, Wassas, Brongs, and Nzimas, among others.[1]

All these groups share the same culture not only in basics but also in many details. Although the cultural affinities of the various Akan subgroups with the other ethnic groups of Ghana are not on the same

1. The Akans have, historically, been the subject of some famous anthropological, linguistic, and philosophical studies by foreign scholars such as R. S. Rattray, *Ashanti* (Oxford University Press, 1923), and *Religion and Art in Ashanti* (Oxford University Press, 1927); J. G. Christaller, *Dictionary of the Asante and Fante Language Called Tshi (Twi)*, 2d ed. (Basel, 1933); and E. L. Mayerowitz, *The Sacred State of the Akan* (London: Faber and Faber, 1951); and native scholars such as Casely Hayford, *Gold Coast Native Institutions* (London: Sweet and Maxwell, 1903); J. B. Danquah, *The Akan Doctrine of God* (London, 1946); and K. A. Busia, *The Position of the Chief in the Modern Political System of Ashanti* (London: Frank Cass, 1951). Two important recent philosophical studies are W. E. Abraham, *The Mind of Africa* (University of Chicago Press, 1962); and Kwame Gyekye, *An Essay on African Philosophical Thought: The Akan Conceptual Scheme* (Cambridge University Press, 1987).

scale as among themselves, any divergences affect only details. Indeed, viewed against the distant cultures of the East and West, Akan culture can be seen to have such fundamental commonalities with other African cultures as to be subsumable under "African culture" as a general cultural type.

The Akan Conception of a Person

The Akan conception of a person has both descriptive and normative aspects that are directly relevant not only to the idea that there are human rights but also to the question of what those rights are. In this conception a person is the result of the union of three elements, not necessarily sharply disparate ontologically though each is different from the other. There is the life principle (*okra*), the blood principle (*mogya*), and what might be called the personality principle (*sunsum*). The first, the *okra*, is held to come directly from God. It is supposed to be an actual speck of God that he gives out of himself as a gift of life along with a specific destiny. The second, the *mogya* (literally, blood) is held to come from the mother and is the basis of lineage, or more extensively, clan identity. The third, the *sunsum*, is supposed to come from the father, but not directly. In the making of a baby, the father contributes *ntoro* (semen), which combines, according to the Akans, with the blood of the mother to constitute, in due course, the frame of the human being to come. The inherited characteristics of the new arrival are, of course, taken to be attributable to both parents. But the father's input is believed to give rise to a certain immanent characteristic of the individual, called the *sunsum*, which is the kind of personal presence that he has, the unique impression that he communicates to others. This is one meaning of the word *sunsum*. In this sense, *sunsum* is not an entity; it is, rather, a manner of being. But it is assumed that there must be something in the person that is the cause of the characteristic in question. It is in this sense that *sunsum* names a constituent of the human person.

By virtue of possessing an *okra*, a divine element, every person has an intrinsic value, the same in each, which he does not owe to any earthly circumstance. Associated with this value is a concept of human dignity, which implies that every human being is entitled in an equal measure to a certain basic respect. In support of this the Akans say, "Every one is the offspring of God; no one the offspring of the earth." Directly implied in the doctrine of *okra* is the right of each person, as the recipient of a destiny, to pursue that unique destiny assigned to him by

God. In more colloquial language everyone has the right to do his own thing, with the understanding, of course, that ultimately one must bear the consequences of one's own choices. This might almost be called the metaphysical right of privacy. It is clinched with the maxim "Nobody was there when I was taking my destiny from my God."

Through the possession of an *okra, mogya,* and *sunsum* a person is situated in a network of kinship relations that generate a system of rights and obligations. Because the Akans are matrilineal, the most important kinship group is the lineage, which may be pictured as a system of concentric circles of matrilineal kinship relationship that, at its outermost reaches, can include people in widely separated geographic regions. In these outermost dimensions a lineage becomes a clan. Its innermost circle comprises the grandmother, the mother, the mother's siblings, her own children, and the children of her sisters. To this group, with the mother as the principal personage, belongs the duty of nursing an Akan newborn. The Akans have an acute sense of the dependency of a human being. On first appearance in this world, one is totally defenseless and dependent. This is the time when there is the greatest need for the care and protection of others and also, to the Akan mind, the time of the greatest right to that help; but this right never deserts a human being, for one is seen at all times as insufficient unto oneself. The logic of this right may be simply phrased: a genuine human need carries the right to satisfaction. The right to be nursed, then, is the first human right. In the fullness of time it will be transformed dialectically into a duty, the duty to nurse one's mother in her old age. "If your mother nurses you to grow your teeth," says an Akan adage, "you nurse her to lose hers." But there is another aspect to the nurturing of a human being—he or she needs to be instructed in the arts of gainful living—and this function the Akans ascribe to the father. To the father, then, attaches the duty to provide the child with character training, general education, and career preparation.

Through an individual's *ntoro,* the element contributed to each biological makeup by the father, one acquires a certain social link to a patrilineal kinship group, which, however, is much less important than one's matrilineal affiliations except for this: from the father's sister the child has the right to receive sexual education.

Earning a livelihood in traditional Akan society presupposed the possession of one basic resource: land. In an agricultural society like traditional Akan society, education profited a person little unless he could count on some land, land to till and land on which to build. It is in this connection that we see an Akan person's most cherished positive right, the right to land. This right he has by virtue of his membership in a lineage; it is a claim that he has primarily on his lineage, but because of the statewide significance of land, it is also, as I will explain later, a right that he could claim against the state.

We have already mentioned some quite important rights. These are rights, in the Akan perception of things, that people have simply because they are human beings. They are entitlements entailed by the intrinsic sociality of the human status. In viewing a human being in this light, the Akans perhaps went beyond Aristotle's maxim that man is by nature a political animal. To the Akans, a human being is already social at conception, for the union of the blood principle and the personality principle already defines a social identity. A person is social in a further sense. The social identity just alluded to is a kinship identity. But a person lives, moves, and has his being in an environment that includes people outside the kin group. He lives in a town and has to relate to that environment in definite ways. A well-known Akan maxim asserts that when a human being descends upon the earth from above, he lands in a town. Membership in town and state brings with it a wider set of rights and obligations embracing the whole race of humankind, for the possession of the *okra*, the speck of God in man, is taken to link all human beings together in one universal family. The immediate concerns here, however, are with the rights of man in the context of Akan society. In that society an individual's status as a person is predicated upon the fulfillment of certain roles that have a reference to circles of relationships transcending the kin group. There is an ambiguity here in the use of the word *person*, the resolution of which will bring us to the normative conception of a person.

In one sense the Akan word *onipa* translates into the English word *person* in the sense of a human being, the possessor of *okra, mogya,* and *sunsum.* In this sense everyone is born as a person, an *onipa.* This is the descriptive sense of the word. But there is a further sense of the word *onipa* in which to call an individual a person is to commend him; it implies the recognition that he has attained a certain status in the community. Specifically, it implies that he has demonstrated an ability through hard work and sober thinking to sustain a household and make contributions to the communal welfare. In traditional Akan society, public works were always done through communal labor. Moreover, the defense of the state against external attack was the responsibility of all. Good contributions toward these ends stamped an individual in the community as an *onipa*. Inversely, consistent default distanced him from that title. In this sense, personhood is not something you are born with but something you may achieve, and it is subject to degrees, so that some are more *onipa* than others, depending on the degree of fulfillment of one's obligations to self, household, and community.

On the face of it, the normative layer in the Akan concept of person brings only obligations to the individual. In fact, however, these obligations are matched by a whole series of rights that accrue to the individual simply because he lives in a society in which everyone has those obligations. It is useful in this regard to recall the fact, noted earlier, that the Akans viewed a human being as essentially dependent. From this point of view, human society is seen as a necessary framework of mutual aid for survival and, beyond that, for the attainment of reasonable levels of well-being. A number of Akan sayings testify to this conception, which is at the root of Akan communalism. One is to the effect that a human being is not a palm tree so as to be sufficient unto himself. (The Akans were highly impressed by the number of things that could be got from a palm tree, not the least memorable among them being palm nut soup and palm wine.) A second saying points out that to be human is to be in need of help. Literally it says simply "a human being needs help" (*onipa hyia mmoa*). The Akan verb *hyia* means "is in need of." In this context it also has the connotation of merits, "is entitled to," so that the maxim may also be interpreted as asserting that a human being, simply because he is a human being, is entitled to help from others. A further saying explains that it is because of the need to have someone blow out the speck of dust in one's eye that antelopes go in twos. This saying obviously puts forward mutual aid as the rationale of society.

Although the rights deriving from the general human entitlement to the help of their kind did not have the backing of state sanctions, they were deeply enough felt in Akan society. In consequence, such rights may be said to have enjoyed the strong backing of public opinion, which in communalistic societies cannot be taken lightly. However, at this stage rights that appertain to political existence must be looked at. If, as the Akans said, when a human being descends upon the earth, he lands in a town, the point is that he becomes integrated into a particular social and political structure. The specifics of that structure will determine his rights and obligations.

The Akan Political System

The importance of kinship relations in Akan society has already been noted. This grouping provides the basic units of political organization. These units are the lineages. A lineage, to be sure, is all the individuals in a town who are descended from one ancestress. A clan includes all the lineages united by a common maternal ancestry. It is too large and too scattered to be the unit of political organization in spite of the real feelings of brotherhood (and sisterhood) that exist among its members. In every town there would be quite a manageable number of lineages. Each of them had a head, called *Abusuapanyin* (elder of the lineage), who was elected by the adult members of the group. Age was an important qualification for this position—just reflect on the title "elder"— but so also was wisdom, eloquence, integrity, and, in earlier times, fighting competence. The last qualification calls for a word of explanation. Every head of lineage was, ex officio, a military leader who led his lineage in a particular position in the battle formation of the Akan army. This was not a professional army but rather a citizen force. In battle formation the Akan army had the following pattern. The first line consisted of a number of small units of scouts. Behind them was a large column of advance guard. Next to it came the main body of infantrymen grouped in two large columns. Following after them came the rear guard, which was a very large column. If the chief himself was taking the field, his company occupied the position between the second main infantry column and the rear guard. Flanking this array of forces on both sides were the left and right wings, which were long columns of fighting men.[2] All these battle positions were manned by distinct lineages commanded by their heads. In view of the military significance of the lineage headship, it was natural, in electing someone to that position, to bear in mind the question of his probable prowess in battle. More recently, however, this particular consideration has lost its urgency. The military-sounding names of the headships persist, though, to the present day. (For example, the head of one of the lineages is called *Kyidomhene. Akyi* means rear, *dom* means troops, and *hene* means chief; thus the title means chief of the rear guard.)

It is clear from this description, by the way, that not just military service but military service in a particular battle position or war capacity

2. W. E. Abraham has a memorable description of the Ashanti army in battle deployment in *Mind of Africa*, pp. 83–84. K. A. Busia gives an illustrated description in *Position of the Chief*, p. 14.

was a birth obligation in Akan society. Everyone had a part in the war effort. Even those able-bodied men who stayed behind in times of war while others marched to the front did so for a military reason—namely, to guard home. The chief of the home-guard lineage, called *Ankobeahene* (literally, did-not-go-anywhere chief), was quite an important leader. It did not escape the Akans that to commit every able-bodied man to the fray would be to guarantee a field day to any band of marauders on the home front. Also it struck them very forcibly that a situation in which a group of healthy men remained together with a very great number of women, temporarily unattended by their husbands, required wise governance. Women, as a rule, did not go into battle, though it should be recalled that at least one major Ashanti war with the British, the Yaa Asantewaa War of 1900, was fought under the inspiration of a woman. For their part, the women prayed for the success of their men in the field, a function that was quite appreciated. Besides, they acted beforehand as motivators for their men, especially for the reluctant warriors among them.

But if every Akan was thus obligated by birth to contribute to defense in one way or another, there was also the complementary fact that he had a right to the protection of his person, property, and dignity, not only in his own state but also outside it. And states were known to go to war to secure the freedom of their citizens abroad or avenge their mistreatment.

The ruling body of an Akan town was a council consisting of the lineage heads with the chief of the town in the capacity of chairman. The functions of the council were to preserve law, order, and peace in the town, to ensure its safety, and to promote its welfare. The office of a chief is hereditary but also partly elective. Some sort of an election is necessary because at any one time there are several people belonging to the royal lineage who are qualified by birth to be considered. The queen of the town (strictly, the queen mother) has the prerogative of selecting the best-qualified candidate, all things considered, but the final decision does not come until the council has assessed the candidate and indicated its approval. Such an approval, if forthcoming, seals the election, provided an objection is not voiced by the populace.

This last proviso is of special significance for the question of human rights, as shown later. In every town there was an unofficial personage recognized as the chief of the general populace. He was called *Nkwankwaahene* (literally, the chief of the young men) and functioned as the spokesman of the populace. His position is described here as unofficial simply because unlike most Akan political offices, it had nothing to do with his lineage; moreover, he was not a member of the chief's council. However, he had the right to make representations before the council on behalf of the young men of the town. In particular, if there were objections to a proposed chief among the populace, he made very forthright representations that, as a rule, prevailed. This is in conformity with the Akan principle that royals do not install a chief; it is those who have to serve him who do.

Beyond the political organization of the Akan town, a certain collection of towns constituted a division (*Oman*, literally, state) with a divisional council consisting of paramount chiefs. In an Akan territory of the proportions of Ashanti, paramount chiefs from a number of divisional councils served also as members of a confederacy council, which held sway over the whole nation.

Rights of Political Participation

This brings us, naturally, to political rights. It is clear from the foregoing that in principle citizens had a say, first in the question of who would exercise political power over them, and second in the issue of what specific policies were to be implemented in the town and, derivatively, in the state and nation. They had two avenues in this matter. They could work through their lineage head, who was in duty bound to consult them on all matters due for decision at the council, and they could work through the spokesman of the populace. The chief had absolutely no right to impose his own wishes on the elders of the council. On the contrary, all decisions of the council were based on consensus. The elders would keep on discussing an issue till consensus was reached, a method that contrasts with the decision by majority vote that prevails in modern democracies. The rationale of decision by consensus, as can easily be inferred, was to forestall the trivialization of the right of the minority to have an effect on decisionmaking.

Once a decision had been reached in council by consensus, it became officially the decision of the chief, regardless of his own opinion. That opinion would already have been given consideration at the discussion stage, but no one encouraged him in any illusions of infallibility. Nevertheless, the chief was never contradicted in public, since he was a symbol of the unity of the council and was also perceived as the link between the community and its hallowed ancestors. Because of the great pains taken to achieve consensus, the council took a very severe view of a member who subjected any of its decisions to criticism in public. The leader of the populace was in a different position. Not being privy to the deliberations of the council, he had the fullest right to criticize any decisions unacceptable to his constituency, as did the members of that constituency. One thing then is clear here. The people's freedom of thought and expression went beyond the devices of any chief or council.

Nor was there ever a doubt about the right of the people, including the elders, to dismiss a chief who tried to be oppressive. A cherished principle of Akan politics was that those who served the chief could also destool him. (The stool was the symbol of chiefly status, and so the installation of a chief was called enstoolment and his dismissal destoolment.) This was a process governed by well-defined rules. Charges had to be filed before appropriate bodies and thorough investigations made before a decision to destool or retain a chief was reached. Actually, as Abraham remarked, among the Akans "kingship was more a sacred office than a political one."[3] The chief was regarded as the spiritual link between the people and their ancestors and was for this reason approached with virtual awe. But this did not translate into abject subservience when it came to political matters. Here the chief had to play the game according to the rules whereby he was always to act in conformity with the decisions of the council and eschew any wayward style of life. So long as he did so, he was held to be sacrosanct, but as soon as he violated this compact, he lost that status and could experience a rough time. When this factor is taken into account, the representative character of the Akan system looms even larger. The real power was in the hands of the elected elders of the various lineages. This conforms to the principle that people have a right to determine who shall exercise political power over them and for how long.

That principle links up with another important feature of the Akan constitution: its decentralization. At every level of political organization, the groups involved enjoyed self-government. Thus the lineage, together with its head, conducted its affairs without interference from any higher authorities so long as the issues did not have townwide or statewide reverberations. Similarly, the town and the division handled all issues pertaining exclusively to their domains. Apparent here is the Akan conception of a right due to all human beings, that is, the right of self-government.

This right of self-government was particularly important in the ad-

3. Abraham, *Mind of Africa*, p. 77.

ministration of justice. Because all kinds of cases arising in the internal affairs of a lineage or sometimes in interlineage affairs were left to lineage personnel to settle on a household-to-household basis rather than in the more formalized and adversarial atmosphere of a chief's court, many potentially divisive problems between people could be solved painlessly, often through mere verbal apologies or minor compensations. A salutary by-product of this personalized way of settling cases was that it often brought a reinforcement of neighborhood good will. This is not to suggest, though, that the official, state-level reaction to issues of wrongdoing and the like was excessively retributive. On the contrary, often the aim was to reestablish satisfactory relations between person and person or person and the ancestors through compensatory settlements and pacificatory rituals.

The Right to a Trial

There are some interesting aspects of the Akan approach to punishment and related issues that could be gone into here, but from the point of view of human rights, the most important observation is that it was an absolute principle of Akan justice that no human being could be punished without trial. Neither at the lineage level nor at any other level of Akan society could a citizen be subjected to any sort of sanctions without proof of wrongdoing. This principle was so strongly adhered to that even a dead body was tried before posthumous punishment was symbolically meted out to him. The best-known example of this sort of procedure was the reaction to a suicide apparently committed to evade the consequences of evil conduct. The dead person was meticulously tried. If guilt was established, the body was decapitated. If the motive behind the suicide remained obscure, it was assumed to be bad and had the same result.[4] If the right of the dead to trial before punishment was recognized, could the living have been entitled to less courtesy? The modern misdeeds, on the part of certain governments both inside and outside Africa, of imprisoning citizens without trial would have been inconceivable in a traditional Akan setting, not only because there were no such institutions as prisons but also because the principle of such a practice would have been totally repugnant to the Akan mentality.

Perhaps I ought not to leave the topic of suicide without an Akan-

4. See for example, Busia, *Position of the Chief*, pp. 66, 70–71.

oriented comment on the question of the right to die. This question is becoming increasingly urgent because of the technological facilities now available for prolonging life amid the terminal impairment of body and sometimes mind. It might be thought from the drastic treatment of suicide just noted and from the Akan belief that the life principle in man is divine that the Akan mind would recoil from the idea that human beings might have a right to terminate their own lives under the circumstances in question. But the contrary is true. Death, in the traditional Akan understanding of the matter, cannot adversely affect the life principle, which is immortal; death only means the separation of that principle from the rest of the human system. The whole point of life consists in the pursuit of human well-being both in one's own case and in concord with the well-being of others. When any such prospects are permanently eliminated by deleterious conditions, the artificial prolongation of painful life or, worse, of vegetative existence can make no sense to man, ancestor, or God. In such circumstances respect for human beings would dictate the right to die in dignity. As for suicide, it was only those committed with known or presumed evil motives that elicited symbolic punishment. Such a thing as suicide committed from noble motives was not unknown in Akan society, and exculpatory maxims were not hard to find. According to one of the most characteristic of Akan sayings, "Disgrace does not befit an Akan-born" (*Animguase nfata okanniba*). The allusion is, of course, to disgrace not arising from wrongdoing. More explicitly, the Akans often say, "Death is preferable to disgrace" (*Animguase de afanyinam owuo*). Defeated generals were known to take this to heart. Rather than return home in disgrace, they frequently elected to commit suicide in the field.

The Right to Land

As noted earlier, any human being was held, by virtue of his blood principle (*mogya*), to be entitled to some land. For the duration of his life any Akan had the right to the use of a piece of the lineage land. However, land was supposed to belong to the whole lineage, conceived as including the ancestors, the living members, and those as yet to be born. For this reason, in traditional times the sale of land was prohibited. And the prohibition was effective. But our ancestors reckoned without the conquering power of modern commercialism. Land sale is now a thriving racket in which chiefs yield no ground to commoners.

As a foreseeable consequence, there are now many Akans and others who have no land to till. Here then, sadly, is a human right, recognized of old, that seems to have been devoured by advancing time.

In traditional times land was regarded as so important an issue that matters relating to its ownership were not left to individual lineages alone. The chief, acting as usual on the advice of his council, had a certain right of redistribution. Normally, no lineage could be dispossessed of any of its land. But if large tracts of land in the possession of a given lineage remained untilled for a considerable time while another lineage by reason, say, of preeminent fertility was hard pressed for land to feed on, the chief could acquire a part of the unused land and allocate it to the group in need. The seeming inconsistency of this practice of land transfer with the notion that land ownership could not be changed because the land of the lineage belonged to past, present, and future members was resolved doctrinally as follows. The ancestors, indeed, retain prima facie entitlement to the land of their lineages. In general, lineage ancestors oversee the affairs of their living descendants. But just as in life the chief has the duty to see to the general welfare of the entire town or state, so also in the world of the dead, the ancestors of the lineage of the chief, who remain chiefs even in their postmortem state, have townwide or statewide concerns. In particular, they have an interest in seeing to the equitable use of the available land. Hence in redistributing land as indicated, the living chief, who is supposed to be a link between the people and the ancestors, would be carrying out the wishes of the latter. Note that this does not empower a chief to acquire land belonging to a given lineage for his own personal purposes. No Akan doctrine countenances that. A chief always had a liberal allotment of land from the original landholdings of his lineage in the first place, and from extensive plots set aside especially for the office of the stool in the second place. The first he could use in his own name; the second in the name of the stool. Notwithstanding the redistributive rider just outlined, therefore, the right to land was a very solid right. At all events, no justifiable redistribution could leave an originally well-endowed lineage short of land for its own livelihood. This right, then, conceived in Akan terms as a human right, was claimed within the lineage, but for the reasons indicated it could also be claimed against the state.

The right to land was one of the deepest bases of attachment to particular locations. However, in spite of all the culturally ingrained love of consensus, there were times in the past when dissensions, even within a lineage, proved irresolvable. In the face of this kind of situation some sections of the lineage preferred to move on in search of land and peace of mind. This was one of the ways in which some ethnic groups, the Akans in particular, became spread over great expanses of territory in the geographic area now called Ghana. Given this history, it is easy to understand that the right to remain in or leave a town or state would not be an issue for debate among the Akans. It was taken for granted.

Religious Freedom

My previous mention of the right to freedom of thought and expression referred to political issues. It is relevant, however, to ask whether the Akan system supported freedom of thought and expression in such areas as religion and metaphysics.

To consider religion first, there was no such thing as an institutionalized religion in Akan land. Religion consisted simply of belief and trust in and reverence for a Supreme Being regarded as the architect of the cosmos. The Akans took it to be obvious even to children that such a being existed—witness the saying: "No one shows God to a child" (*Obi nykyere akwadaa Nyame*). However, I know of no sentiment in the Akan corpus of proverbs, epigrams, tales, and explicit doctrines that lends the slightest support to any abridgement of the freedom of thought or expression. As a matter of fact, skeptics with respect to religious and other issues (*akyinyefo*, literally, debater) were known in Akan society, but no harm seems to have befallen them.

The belief in the assortment of extrahuman forces (including the ancestors) that is so often mentioned in connection with Akan, and in general with African, religion does not seem to me to belong properly to the field of religion. Be that as it may, one must concede that any person in Akan traditional society disagreeing fundamentally with this worldview would have had a serious sense of isolation. Almost every custom or cultural practice presupposed beliefs of that sort. Yet if he was prepared to perform his civic duties without bothering about any underlying beliefs, he could live in harmony with his kinsmen in spite of his philosophical nonconformism. Here again, one may observe that persecution on grounds of belief is unheard of in Akan society.

The conflict between Christian missionaries and the chiefs of Ashanti in the early years of this century, when the campaign to convert the people of Ghana to the Christian faith was getting under way, provides an illuminating case study. In that conflict the Ashanti chiefs remained remarkably forbearing, merely insisting that all Ashantis, irrespective of their religious persuasion, should obey customary law. By contrast, the missionaries, without challenging the authority of the chiefs over the Ashanti people, objected to the participation of Ashanti Christians in any activities that seemed to be based on beliefs they regarded as incompatible with their faith, beliefs which they called fetish. Intellectually this issue has not been resolved even to this day, but the force of circumstances has seemed to give the upper hand now to one party, now to the other. By the 1930s and 1940s Christianity was in the ascendancy, and many of the chiefs themselves, including, a little later, the king of Ashanti, had become converts. Neither the psychology, nor the logic, nor the theology of such conversions was free from paradox. But it ensured the easing of the conflict by virtue of accommodations from the side of the Ashanti authorities. Then came political independence, and with it a certain reassertion of cultural identity on the part of the people and, complementarily, greater tolerance for African ways on the part of the Christian dignitaries, both foreign and native. As a result, practices like traditional drumming and the pouring of libation to the ancestors, which a few decades ago were proscribed by the missionaries for being fetish, are now commonplace among Christians, sometimes even on occasions of Christian worship. In fact, one even hears of the Africanization of Christianity from some high-minded church circles. Evidently the wheel has turned 180 degrees, or nearly so.

In all this, two things stand out as indicative of the Ashanti (and, generally, Ghanaian) tolerance for different beliefs. First, there is the fact that a great many Ashantis, commoners and chiefs alike, found a way to embrace the new beliefs, while not erasing the older ones from their consciousness.[5] But second, and even more important, the Ashantis from the beginning were not much exercised about what actually went on in the minds of people in matters having to do with such things as their worldview. Their main concern regarding the early Ashanti converts was simply with their actual civic conduct. You can get people to do or not do specific things, reasoned the Akans, but you cannot guarantee that they will think particular thoughts. Hence the futility, from their point of view, of trying to interfere with freedom of thought. Confronted with any such attempt, an Akan would typically say to himself or to a confidant: *Me kose kose wo mitirm,* meaning "My real thoughts are in my own head," which by interpretation means, "I carry in my own person proof of the futility of any attempt to control people's think-

5. Other Ashantis extended the same courtesy to Islam.

ing." Not only, then, is it wrong from the Akan standpoint to try to curtail freedom of thought; it is by and large futile.

From their tolerant attitude toward other people's religious beliefs, it is sufficiently clear that the Akans made no exceptions about subject matter in the question of the freedom of thought. When they said "two heads are better than one" and "one head does not hold council" in extolling the virtues of consultation, they were not thinking of politics alone. They were aware that other minds always have the potential to bring to light new aspects of things familiar or recondite. In metaphysical matters they left little doubt of their sense of the presumptuousness of dogmatism, for their metaphysicians often spoke in paradoxes and riddles, purposely inviting individual speculative ingenuity. Witness, for example, the following poser from a metaphysical drum text:

Who gave word to Hearing
For Hearing to have told the Spider
For the Spider to have told the maker of the world
For the maker of the world to have made the world?

Conclusion

In summary, one finds a veritable harvest of human rights. Akan thought recognized the right of a newborn to be nursed and educated, the right of an adult to a plot of land from the ancestral holdings, the right of any well-defined unit of political organization to self-government, the right of all to have a say in the enstoolment or destoolment of their chiefs or their elders and to participate in the shaping of governmental policies, the right of all to freedom of thought and expression in all matters, political, religious, and metaphysical, the right of everybody to trial before punishment, the right of a person to remain at any locality or to leave, and so on. Although frequently people who talk of human rights have political rights uppermost in their minds, some human rights do not fall within the purview of any constituted authority. In the last analysis, a people's conception of human rights will reflect their fundamental values, and not all such values will ever acquire the backing of institutional authority. In any case this discussion does not pretend to have disclosed all the human rights generated by Akan values.

Again, it is probably needless to point out that my outline of human rights is a portrayal of Akan principles rather than an assessment of

Akan practice. One can assume, a priori, that in actual practice the reality must have been some sort of a mixture of both the pursuit and the perversion of precept. By way of empirical confirmation, let me mention, on the negative side, two examples—one a premeditated abrogation, the other a situational diminution of a human right. On the grounds that a deceased chief needed the services of attendants during his postmortem journey to the land of the dead, the Akans in former times would ritually kill some people on the death of an important chief for that function. Given the eschatology, the practice was logical. But the belief itself was an appalling contravention of the Akan precept that, as offspring of God, all human beings are entitled to equal respect and dignity. Not that the right to life, which is implicit in this idea of respect for persons, is absolute. In fact, only a little reflection suffices to show that every right is open to qualification in some circumstances. For instance, in certain easily imagined situations the right of self-defense will nullify an attacker's right to life. It is important to note, though, that a right can be overridden only by another right or some other kind of genuine moral principle. As for the specific question of human sacrifice, the principle of it is not unheard of in some other cultures that pride themselves on their belief in the sanctity of human life. Thus Christianity, for example, openly exults in the idea of an omnipotent deity ordaining his "only begotten son" to be killed so that his erring creatures might thereby have the chance of salvation.

What then is so objectionable about the Akan custom in question, which, happily, no one now openly defends? The answer is simple. It is drastically lacking in fairness, and it flies in the face of the golden rule, which is as explicit in indigenous Akan ethical thinking as it is in Christian ethics. Indeed, the principle that all human beings are entitled to equal respect is only a special case of the golden rule. Obviously, equal respect here does not require that a murderer or a swindler be accorded the same deference as, say, an upright benefactor of humankind. What it means, nevertheless, is that in our reactions to the one class of persons *just as much* as to the other we should always imaginatively put ourselves in their shoes. In essence, then, equal respect is a requirement of sympathetic impartiality. Now the fact is that, in spite of the profound respect that the Akans had for their chiefs, few cherished the notion of being killed in order to have the honor of serving their chiefs on their last journey. Accordingly, sympathetic impartiality should have destroyed that custom before birth. In general, no rights can be justifiably superseded in a manner oblivious to the principle of sympathetic impartiality. If there is any absolute principle of human conduct, that is it.

The second traditional Akan situation uncongenial to a human right is seen in the Akan attitude to the freedom of speech of nonadults. It is easy to understand that in a traditional society both knowledge and wisdom would tend to correspond with age. Hence the deliverances of the old would command virtually automatic respect. But an unhappy consequence of this was that the self-expression of minors was apt to be rigorously circumscribed. Dissent on the part of a minor in the face of adult pronouncements was almost equated with disrespect or obstinacy. It would perhaps be excessive to call this a positive invasion of a human right. Indeed, given the traditional ethos, minors usually came to internalize the imperative of acquiescence. But in the modern context such an ethos must take on an aspect distinctly inconsonant with the rights of nonadults in the matter of the freedom of expression.

Probably every culture can be viewed as a matrix of forces and tendencies of thought and practice not always mutually compatible. The characterization of cultural traits, therefore, frequently has to take cognizance of countervailing factors. Nevertheless, the bent of a culture will, if anything, stand out in heightened relief in the full view of such facts. On the question of human rights it can justly be said that, notwithstanding any contrary tendencies, the principles of human rights enumerated here did motivate predominantly favorable practices in traditional Akan society. Moreover, from the perspective of those principles one can check how faithful certain claims in contemporary African politics are to at least one African tradition. Regrettably, I must content myself here with only one, brief, illustration.

Many African governments today are based upon the one-party system. There are both critics and defenders of that system in Africa, and in the resulting controversy human rights have almost always been at issue. In some one-party apologetics the suggestion is made not only that the system is hospitable to all the desirable human rights but also that traditional African systems of government were of the one-party variety, in a full-blown or an embryonic form. As far at least as the Akan tradition is concerned, I hope that this discussion demonstrates that both claims are contrary to fact. Although the Akan system was not of a multiparty type, it was not a one-party type either. The decisive reason that the Akan system is antithetical to the one-party system is that no such system can survive the right of the populace, organized under their own spokesman, to question the decisions of the ruling body or to demand the dismissal of its leader. Since the traditional system featured this right, it was neither a one-party system nor even a simulacrum of it. For the same reason it is not true that the one-party system is compatible with all human rights. On this showing, our traditional systems require close analysis from the point of view of contemporary existential concerns. Human rights are certainly among the most urgent of these concerns. That Africa has suffered human rights deprivations from various causes in the past, including particularly the transatlantic slave trade and colonialism, is well-known history. It is surely an agonizing reflection that, aside from the vexatious case of apartheid, the encroachments on human rights in Africa in recent times have usually come from African governments themselves. To a certain extent the exigencies of postindependence reconstruction may account for this. But they cannot justify it. Nor, as just pointed out in the matter of the one-party system, can they be rationalized by appeal to any authentic aspect of African traditional politics, at least in the Akan instance. How to devise a system of politics that, while being responsive to the developments of the modern world, will reflect the best traditional thinking about human rights (and other values) is one of the profoundest challenges facing modern Africans. A good beginning is to become informed about traditional life and thought.

CHAPTER ELEVEN

A Cultural Approach to Human Rights among the Dinka

Francis M. Deng

THE UNDERLYING postulate presented here takes issue with the view, widely held in the West and accepted or exploited in developing countries, that the concept of human rights is peculiarly Western. Such a view is not only empirically questionable but also does a disservice to the cause of human rights. Whether or not they are articulated, respected, or violated, human rights are, and ought to be, viewed as universally inherent in the very notion of humanity; to hold otherwise would be a contradiction in terms. To arrogate the concept to only certain groups, cultures, or civilizations is to aggravate divisiveness on the issue, to encourage defensiveness or unwarranted self-justification on the part of the excluded, and to impede progress toward a universal consensus on human rights.

To argue for the principle of universality is not to deny the significance of the cultural context for the definition, the scope, and the degree of protection of human rights. In a world that is paradoxically shrinking and proliferating at the same time, it is by seeing human rights concretely manifested in a particular context that we can fully appreciate their form and content in a comparative framework. To understand the diversity of the cultural contexts and their relevance to the conceptualization and protection of human rights is to enhance prospects for cross-cultural enrichment in defending and promoting human rights.

The potential in this regard lies in the hypothesis that every culture has humanitarian ideals or principles that could contribute to the redefinition and promotion of universal standards as the latter are adapted to local and national contexts. In practical terms, societies or cultures do not retain or alter their entire systems of values and institutional practices in the process of change, but rather selectively adopt from, adapt to, and integrate into new situations of cross-cultural interaction. In this process, old and new ideas and practices are favored, modified, or rejected, depending on their appeal and degree of compatibility with preferred values and modes of behavior.

It is with these cross-cultural dynamics and potentials in mind that this essay approaches the subject of human rights among the Dinka. First, I present the concept of human rights in terms of the fundamental values of Dinka society, how they condition the social structures and patterns of behavior and the level of success of traditional ideas and practices. Second, I give an overview of the problems posed by the pluralism of the nation-state context, especially as regards ethnic, cultural, and religious competition for power and national resources and the implications for the protection of human rights. Finally, I comment on the prospects for a cross-cultural approach to human rights among the Dinka and in the wider context of their nation-state, the Sudan.

Dinka Cultural Values

The recent accounts of the civil war that has been raging in the Sudan for the last five years between the government and the rebels, the Sudan People's Liberation Movement (SPLM) and its military wing, the Sudan People's Liberation Army (SPLA), have exposed to the world the devastations and unprecedented suffering that the war has inflicted on the local population.[1] The Dinka, a Nilotic people in the southern part of the country, have been spotlighted as the principal victims of atrocities, massacres, and the deadly use of mass starvation as a weapon. Their current image is that of a people displaced, shattered, and scattered, paradoxically fleeing for security outside the war zone in the South to the hostile but more secure environment of the North, or infiltrating the neighboring countries to the south as refugees. Some observers even see the Dinka as a people threatened not only with massive depopulation but possibly with extinction as a cohesive cultural entity.[2]

While this image is a gruesome reflection of the tragic conditions under which the Dinka and their fellow southern Sudanese live today,

1. A press campaign initially led by the *Atlanta Journal* and the *Atlanta Constitution* gained momentum in the summer of 1988 and continued to intensify into 1989 when international response eventually measured up to the challenge.

2. This theme not only emerges in the popular press but has also emanated from official statements of the Sudan government. Prime Minister Sadiq al-Mahdi has often argued and has indeed written that one of the end results of the war is "a depopulated South." See "Sudan's Peace Initiative: A Working Paper for Peace," in Abdel Ghaffar, M. Ahmed, and Gunnar M. Sorbo, eds., *Management of the Crisis in the Sudan* (University of Bergen, Centre for Development Studies, April 1989).

it tends to overshadow their cultural resilience and vitality and their potential contribution to shaping the future of Sudan. Indeed, the war and its devastating consequences result directly from their determination to shake the foundations of the prevailing structures and to reshape them to promote equality for all Sudanese, irrespective of race, ethnicity, culture, religion, or sex. Whether or not the SPLM-SPLA succeeds in attaining this challenging objective, there is little doubt that it represents a far more dynamic vision for the nation than that of the present establishment. That the nation must evolve along those lines if it is to survive is unquestionable—however long it might take and whatever the forces that eventually bring it about.

It is also unquestionable that, whatever the equations, the Dinka are bound to be significant because of both their numbers and their distinctive characteristics. Numbering several million in a country of about twenty million composed of several hundred tribal groups, they are by far the largest ethnic group in the Sudan. Although they farm and grow a wide variety of crops—sorghum, millet, maize, sesame, beans, groundnuts, pumpkins, okra, tobacco, and others—their culture is dominated by cattle and, to a lesser extent, sheep and goats, to which they attach a social and moral significance far beyond their economic value.

Dinka settlements are spread over a vast territory covering about one-tenth of the nearly one million square miles that make the Sudan the largest country in Africa. There are usually several miles between clusters of huts and cattle byres in settlements or villages, each accommodating only a few families whose homesteads are also well separated. Large in numbers, widespread in settlement, and segmented by the topography of their land, the Dinka are a conglomerate of some twenty-five independent groups that are also segmented into autonomous subgroups, all of which share a striking pride in their race and culture. All this makes for a paradoxical combination of individualism and exclusiveness of interests with an equal emphasis on communalism, a collective sense of purpose, and common cultural values. Every society has a hierarchy of fundamental values around which its social structures and institutional practices are organized. And although it is no longer possible to isolate any cultural context from others with which it interrelates, it is possible to discern a core system of values and institutions in any given society, even if modified by the pluralistic impact of the contemporary world. In this respect the Dinka offer a striking example, in terms of both the particulars of their traditional system and the pluralistic framework of their national context. Since they remain among the African people least touched by Western or Islamic civilization, the Dinka today provide a good model of traditional African society and, though generalizations are dangerous, much of what is said about them can be assumed to be true of their fellow Nilotics, especially the Nuer and the Shilluk, and possibly other southern peoples if not Africans in general.

In my multifaceted studies of the Dinka, I have been struck by the extent to which certain concepts emerge as overriding goals that determine organizational structures, patterns of behavior, and social standing in Dinka society.[3] If a Dinka is asked what the main values of his people are, he or she may not mention these concepts in the precise order in which I present them, but almost every Dinka would recognize them and their importance without hesitation.

The Concept of Immortality

The first value to consider is the Dinka's religious outlook and how it influences their worldview and institutionalized social and moral practices. The fundamental question of human existence and concern of all religions is what happens after death. Although the Dinka are said to be among the most religious people in the Sudan, believing in one God, Nhialic, whose attributes are identical to those identified in Judaism, Christianity, or Islam, they do not believe in the Christian or Muslim concept of heaven or hell.[4] Their belief in some form of existence after death appears to be a projection of this life into the next, with the individual maintaining the identity he or she had at death. Immortality for the Dinka is therefore a form of maintaining the identity of the dead, and rendering that person capable of continuing to participate in the social processes of this world and to influence the affairs of the living. This is achievable through a concept of biological and social procreation

3. See, in particular, Francis M. Deng, *Tradition and Modernization: A Challenge for Law among the Dinka of the Sudan* (Yale University Press, 1971); *The Dinka of the Sudan*, 2d ed. (Holt, Rinehart and Winston, 1972); *Dinka Folktales: African Stories from the Sudan* (New York: Africana Publishing Company, 1974); *The Dinka and Their Songs* (Oxford: Clarendon Press, 1973); *Africans of Two Worlds: The Dinka in Afro-Arab Sudan* (Yale University Press, 1978); *Dinka Cosmology* (London: Ithaca Press, 1980); and *The Man Called Deng Majok: A Biography of Power, Polygyny and Change* (Yale University Press, 1986).

4. In the words of Charles and Brenda Seligman, "The Dinka, and the kindred Nuer, are . . . by far the most religious peoples in the Sudan." See *Pagan Tribes of the Nilotic Sudan* (London: Routledge and Kegan Paul, 1965), p. 178.

known as *koc e nhom*, which literally means "standing the head [of the deceased person] upright." Although the concept applies to both men and women, it is primarily geared toward maintaining the male line as expressed in the lineage and clan systems. In the Dinka system of nomenclature, the Dinka line of descent is usually expressed in the name of every descendant, which is linked to a specific ancestry by the term *de* or *d'*, depending on whether the name that follows begins with a consonant or a vowel. In my case, since Francis is a Christian name I acquired on conversion, Mading, my Dinka name, and Deng, my father's name, I should be called Francis Mading de [son of] Deng, according to Dinka usage.

The worst thing that can happen to a person, which every Dinka dreads, is dying without a child, particularly a son, to "stand his [the parent's] head upright."[5] Conversely, the death of a person who has begotten sons, especially if they are grown up, is said to be the kind of death that people should not mourn, since the man will have immortalized himself.

Ideally, every Dinka male should be immortalized through procreation, whether the children are begotten by him or by others through proxy procreation. This accounts for the institution of the levitate, by which a widow of childbearing age, without sons who are old enough to be initiated as men or daughters who have reached marriageable age, cohabits with a senior son (by another wife) of her deceased husband, or with his close relative (a brother) to continue to have children in the name of the deceased. Accordingly, a senior son of the dead man can beget a child whom all, including the biological father, would regard as his brother or sister. This child grows up seeing the biological father as his or her brother. When a man dies before marrying, even as an infant, he leaves his kinsmen with a religious obligation to marry on his behalf and beget children to his name. In Dinka customary law, some of the cattle paid as compensation for homicide must be kept and eventually used to marry a wife who will bear children for the dead man.

What is crucial about this overriding principle of immortality is that it determines the relative position of a person in the social hierarchy, the shaping of values, and the sharing of resources. As the father of all,

5. In the words of the Oxford anthropologist, Godfrey Lienhardt: "Dinka greatly fear to die without issue, in whom the survival of their names—the only kind of immortality they know—will be assured." *Divinity and Experience: The Religion of the Dinka* (Oxford: Clarendon Press, 1961), p. 26.

God reigns supreme, followed by other deities, clan spirits, and the ancestors. Among the living, the spiritual hierarchy of authority is headed by the eldest male member of the family or the lineage, with the rest of the members stratified according to descent, age, and gender, which subordinates children to elders and women to men.

The Concept of Human Relations

The second overriding goal of the Dinka is the idealized concept of human relations known as *cieng*. As a verb, *cieng* means to live together, to look after, to put in order, to inhabit, to treat a person well, and to be generous, hospitable, kind, and compassionate toward others. In addition to the noun form of these verbs, *cieng* as a noun also means morals, behavior, habit, conduct, nature of, custom, rule, law, way of life, or culture.

Although the word is also used descriptively, *cieng* is essentially normative and implies a judgment of values. Appropriate adjectives and adverbs may be added to emphasize the judgment, such as "good" or "bad" *cieng*, "to *cieng* well" or "to *cieng* badly." To say that "this is *cieng*" or that a person "knows *cieng*" is to evaluate the behavior or the person positively; to say that "it is not *cieng*" or that a person "does not know *cieng*" is a negative judgment. Whether it is a way of life or a set of standards, *cieng* implies people living together in a community, as in the standard expression *cieng baai, baai* being family, home, village, tribe, or country.

Cieng places emphasis on such human values as dignity, integrity, honor, and respect for self and for others, loyalty and piety, compassion and generosity, and unity and harmony. *Cieng* does not merely advocate attuning individual interests to the interests of others; it requires positive assistance to one's fellow human beings. Good *cieng* is opposed to coercion and violence, for solidarity, harmony, and mutual cooperation are more fittingly achieved voluntarily and by persuasion.

Cieng, as the Dinka see it, has the sanctity of a good moral order not only inherited from the ancestors, who had in turn received it from God and clan spirits, but also fortified and policed by them. Not only is failure to adhere to its principles disapproved of as an antisocial act warranting punitive measures from the community, but, more important, it is seen as a violation of the moral code, which may invite spiritual retribution manifest in illness and even death, according to the gravity of the violation. Conversely, a distinguished adherence to the ideals of *cieng* receives appropriate recognition and reward, both social and spiritual.

Individual and Collective Dignity

Although the continuity of the lineage is a common objective and the values of unity and harmony are beneficial to all in varying degrees, Dinka social morals ensure the mutual interest of all the members by providing them with varied avenues to individual and collective pride, honor, and dignity, expressed in yet another concept called *dheng*. Among the many positive meanings of *dheng* are nobility, beauty, handsomeness, elegance, charm, grace, gentleness, hospitality, generosity, good manners, discretion, and kindness. The adjective form of *dheng* is *adheng*. When a man matures and undergoes a ceremony of initiation into adulthood, he becomes an *adheng*, which can appropriately be translated as "gentleman" in a positive sense. Although the noun is used only for men, the adjective form applies to both sexes. The virtue an *adheng* man or woman is assumed to possess is *dheng*. Indeed, any display of an aesthetic nature is considered *dheng*. The way a man or woman walks, talks, eats, or dresses, and the way he or she behaves toward fellow men and women are all factors in determining a person's *dheng*.

Although *dheng* relates to social relations, it should not be confused with *cieng*: *cieng* provides standards for evaluating conduct, while *dheng* classifies people according to that conduct; *cieng* requires that one should behave in a certain way, while *dheng* labels one virtuous for behaving in that way; *cieng* is a normative concept, a means, while *dheng* is a concept of status, an end.

A remarkable feature of Dinka culture is that it gives virtually everybody some avenue to dignity, honor, and pride. The degree varies, and the means are diverse: there are the sensuous means concerned mostly with appearance, bearing, and sex appeal; there are the qualities of virtue in one's relations to others; and there are the ascribed or achieved values, material or spiritual, that help to determine one's social standing. Some people distinguish themselves by their sensuous gifts; most people try to win some recognition by adherence to the norms of *cieng*; yet others depend to some extent on the social class that they are born into or that they achieve. These means are interrelated and cannot really be pursued separately; they represent alternative modes of gaining some share in the values of self-respect, inner pride, and human dignity.

One of the ways in which the Dinka traditionally achieved a high degree of cohesiveness and tranquillity before the disruptive effect of modernity was to balance material and human values. Wealth and status carried with them voluntary social consciousness and a sense of personal responsibility toward the needy. This tended to diffuse the tension or animosity between socioeconomic classes. One is an *adheng* by having an indulgent disposition or by having material means in abundance; but an ideal *adheng* is one who combines generosity with wealth. A generous but poor person is an *adheng*; it is good enough that he does his best. A rich and miserly man is not an *adheng*; he is on the threshold of *yuur* or *ayur*, the opposite of *dheng* and *adheng*. It is not enough that he gives if he does so reluctantly or not in proportion to his wealth. The ideal *adheng* is one who will open his door and be hospitable to anyone at any time, derive pleasure from doing so, and be able to afford it.

To be truly an *adheng*, it is not enough to fall suddenly into wealth by a stroke of luck. Conversely, to fall suddenly into poverty from a known wealthy background does not entirely diminish the attributes of *adheng*. Something of an inherited status is always considered.

Spiritual Principles

The Dinka believe their value system is ordained and ultimately sanctioned by God and the ancestral spirits. Despite the martial culture of the Dinka as herders and warriors, killing, even in fair fight, is believed to be spiritually contaminating and dangerous and must be redressed according to certain ritual practices. Killing by stealth or ambush is particularly hated and requires even more elaborate procedures of redress and rites of atonement. Theft was hardly heard of in traditional society and, when it occurred, was met with degrading sanctions that were severely damaging to one's social standing. Virtually every wrong is a sin that requires religious or spiritual remedies to restore harmony and tranquillity; otherwise it threatens the wrongdoer with misfortune and even death. As Godfrey Lienhardt observed:

> Divinity [God] is held ultimately to reveal truth and falsehood, and in doing so provides a sanction for justice between men. Cruelty, lying, cheating, and all other forms of injustice are hated by Divinity, and the Dinka suppose that, in some way, if concealed by men they will be revealed by him. . . . Divinity is made the final judge of right and wrong, even when men feel sure that they are in the right. Divinity is thus the guardian of truth—and sometimes signifies to men what really *is* the case, behind or beyond their errors and falsehoods. The Dinka have no problem of the prospering sinner, for they are sure that Divinity will ultimately bring justice. Since among them every

man at some time must meet with suffering or misfortune, death or disease among his family or his cattle, there is always evidence, for those who wish to refer to it, of divine justice. It is a serious matter when a man calls on Divinity to judge between him and another, so serious that only a fool would take the risks involved if he knew he was in the wrong, and to call upon Divinity as witness gives the man who does so an initial presumption of being in the right.[6]

As one chief expressed it:

Even if a right is hidden, God will always uncover the right of a person. It doesn't matter how much it might be covered; even if the covering be heaped as high as this house and the right is there, it will appear. It may be covered for ten years, and God will uncover it for ten years, until it reappears. . . . If a man is not given his right, God never loses sight of the right.[7]

Political and Legal Principles

These moral and spiritual principles are also applied to guide and control the exercise of political and legal authority by divine leaders. Dinka law is not a dictate of the Augustinian sovereign, with coercive sanctions. Rather, it is an expression of the collective will of the community, inherited from the ancestors, generally respected and observed, sanctioned largely through persuasion or, if need be, spiritual curse as an ultimate resort. Until the advent of colonial rule, there were no police or prisons; the effectiveness of the controlling authority depended largely on the moral force of his character, which was, in turn, dependent on the degree of adherence to the values subsumed in the overriding principles that guided Dinka society.

Contrary to general assumptions, the lineage system placed considerable emphasis on the individual as a crucial element in the ancestral line and therefore as a vital spark in the collective interest of the community. The individual's sense of justice was as important to the group as was the interest of the group to the individual. The society ultimately rested on the sum total of the cooperation of the individuals. Sanctions against the individual were resorted to only when the individual disregarded the community sense of right and wrong, and after a lengthy attempt at persuasion.

6. Lienhardt, *Divinity and Experience*, pp. 46–47.
7. Chief Thon Wai, in Deng, *Africans of Two Worlds*, p. 66.

Also conducive to legal persuasion were kinship loyalties behind individual disputants. To impose a judgment without exhaustive persuasion might provoke not only the person concerned but also his or her group and all those loyal to the individual member. Furthermore, conflicts usually concerned personal matters and involved people who must nevertheless live together. Therefore, persuasion and reconciliation were traditionally a pragmatic necessity.

In order to reconcile people, the chief himself must not be hot-tempered or impatient, but should be a model of purity, righteousness, and, in Dinka terms, "a man with a cool heart," whose divine enlightenment and wisdom formed the point of consensus. In carrying out his duties, and in accordance with the overriding goals of Dinka society, the chief was supposed to emphasize persuasion rather than coercion. *Luk*, to persuade, also means "court" or "trial." Lienhardt made the following observation about the Nilotic procedure of settling disputes:

> I suppose everyone would agree that one of the most decisive marks of a society we should call in a spiritual sense "civilized" is a highly developed sense and practice of justice, and here the Nilotes, with their intense respect for the personal independence and dignity of themselves and of others, may be superior to societies more civilized in the material sense. . . . The Dinka and Nuer are a warlike people, and have never been slow to assert their rights, as they see them, by physical force. Yet if one sees Dinka trying to resolve a dispute, according to their own customary law, there is often a reasonableness and gentleness in their demeanour, a courtesy and quietness in the speech of those older men superior in status and wisdom, an attempt to get at the whole truth of the situation before them.[8]

In another context, Lienhardt explains the role of divine leadership in conflict resolution:

> The centrally important gift which masters of the fishing-spear [Divine Chiefs] are thought to have had transmitted to them by their ancestors is the gift of insight into truth, and of speaking "the true word," that is, of representing a situation as it really and absolutely *is*. . . . [I]n ordinary secular disputes points of difference between the disputants, and many other matters are represented at length before any gathering which will attend to them.

8. *Listener and BBC Review,* vol. 69 (1963), p. 828.

... [T]he traditional purpose of *luk* was the presentation of the whole of a situation to the disputants and to the community, so that its rights and wrongs ... were apparent in such a way as to transcend the individual views of truth held by those in conflict [and to be seen as such by them].[9]

The Dinka of course never claim to live up to the ideals of their cultural values. Quite the contrary, it is by reference to both the successes and the failures, an appraisal often expressed in songs, that these values are reaffirmed. As Lienhardt noted, *cieng* for the Dinka embodies "notions ... of what [the] society ought, ideally, to be like."[10]

Implications for Human Rights

Dinka cultural values and patterns of behavior have both positive and negative implications for the protection of human rights. Positively, semblances of rights were observed before the modern nation-state. But the same principles that guaranteed respect for those rights limited the scope of their realization, both in terms of the substance and of the people benefited.

There can be hardly any doubt that some notions of human rights are defined and observed by the Dinka as part of their total value system. Respect for human dignity as they see it is an integral part of the principles of conduct that guide and regulate human relationships and constitutes the sum total of the moral code and the social order.

By and large, responsibility in the observance of these principles is apportioned according to one's relative position in the social hierarchy or structure as determined by descent, leadership position, age, or gender, even though certain obligations toward fellow human beings are universally prescribed. How else, but as indigenous principles of human rights, can we interpret these words from a Dinka chief, describing his people's moral values?

If you see a man walking on his two legs, do not despise him; he is a human being. Bring him close to you and treat him like a human being. That is how you will secure your own life. But if you push him

9. Lienhardt, *Divinity and Experience*, pp. 247–48.

10. Godfrey Lienhardt, "The Western Dinka," in John Middleton and David Tait, eds., *Tribes without Rulers*, Studies in African Segmentary Systems (London: Routledge and Kegan Paul, 1967), p. 106.

onto the ground and do not give him what he needs, things will spoil and even your big share, which you guard with care, will be destroyed. . . . Even the tree which cannot speak has the nature of a human being. It is a human being to God, the person who created it. Do not despise it.[11]

Needless to say, what is said about men in this context applies to women with equal moral force.

Another chief, referring to what he saw as the disdain the Arab-Muslim North has toward the people of the South, said:

Our brothers [the northerners] thought that we should be treated that way because we were in their eyes like fools. I have never heard of a man being such a fool. A human being who speaks with his mouth cannot be such a fool. Whatever way he lives, he remains a human being. And whatever he does must be thought of as the behavior of a human being.[12]

Rights Accruing from the Value System

Here I give a few examples of the kind of rights that accrued in accordance with the priorities of the value system. Marriage, for instance, being directly related to the goal of permanent identity and influence, was the right of every individual; it imposed the duty on a man's family to provide the requisite social and financial means for marrying—even if the individual should be dead. And so great was the demand for women or marriage partners that every woman was married sooner or later. Any man whose family was too poor to acquire a wife for him could approach a wealthier person and ultimately the chief to offer him help, even if that meant herding for him or otherwise rendering services for some time before he got the cattle wealth he needed for marriage.

The sanctity of life and of the human body was well established and appropriate measures were taken to remedy any violation. Even in tribal fights, for which the Nilotic peoples are known, war ethics dictated that an enemy outside the battlefield must not be attacked; an injured warrior, physically sheltered by a woman for protection, must not be killed or subjected to any torture.

During emergency situations of need, the more fortunate were com-

11. Deng, *Africans of Two Worlds*, pp. 64–65.
12. Deng, *Africans of Two Worlds*, pp. 64–65.

pelled to assist their less fortunate kinsfolk with relief provisions. Where famine threatened a family with starvation, the victims were entitled to seize the property of a relative, and if necessary, of anybody, so as to relieve hunger, on the implied understanding that appropriate compensation would eventually be provided when conditions went back to normal. The same principle applied where illness threatened death and required an animal sacrifice to ancestral spirits to bring relief. If a family had no animal to sacrifice, relatives were called upon to assist. And if the pressures of the situation required acting promptly, the relatives of the sick person were authorized to seize any animal within easy reach for the sacrifice, on the understanding that they would, in due course, compensate the owner. Within his means as the head of the tribe, the chief was ultimately responsible for providing the needy with relief against famine or illness.

All these customs might be labeled positive economic and social rights. The so-called negative civil and political rights were implicit in the values that political and legal authorities were to observe in their exercise of power. This was ensured particularly by the lack of police force behind the authority of the chief, except for the power to curse, which by its moral and spiritual nature could be effective only against a deserving wrongdoer. These are only examples of what the Dinka would consider the rights of belonging to a lineage or a clan: the proper way to live together in good *cieng*, and with the dignity (*dheng*) that every Dinka expects as a birthright. The ultimate responsibility for ensuring their protection rests with the chief, as the father of all.

Shortcomings of the Value System

There are, however, severe constraints on the Dinka cultural system of values in terms of objective universal human rights standards. One set of negative effects derives from the inequities inherent in the logic of the lineage system and its stratification on the basis of descent, age, and sex. Another set of negative characteristics lies in the conservative nature of the system and its resistance to change or cross-cultural assimilation. And yet another shortcoming of the system lies in the fact that its human rights values weaken as one goes away from the structural center of Dinka community.

Inequities in the system. The problem lies not only in the injustices of the system but also in the fact that those who are less favored by it tend to react to the inequities, thereby creating paradoxes in the social system. For instance, although women are the least favored by the ancestral values, society depends on them not only as sources of income through the custom of marriage with cattle wealth but also as mothers who perform the educational role of inculcating ancestral values in their children at an early age. Yet women have no legitimate voice in the open channels of decisionmaking and can participate only through indirect influence on their sons and husbands. But because of the close association between mothers and children and the considerable influence wives have over their husbands, women are regarded as most influential in the affairs of men. Nevertheless, because of their general subordination, and especially because of the inequities of polygyny, women are known for jealousies, divisiveness, and even disloyalty to clan ideals. Their influence, especially on the children, must therefore be curtailed.

The Dinka reconcile these conflicting realities by recognizing the love and affection for the mother as functions of the heart, while those feelings for the father are functions of the mind. One's feelings for the mother are recognized as natural, but should not be openly displayed and indeed should be controlled, concealed, and only discreetly expressed. Since the father is the symbol of family unity and solidarity, love and affection for him are recognized as objective and should be actively fostered, encouraged, and openly displayed. Although a Dinka will address his mother by name, he should always address his father deferentially as "father" and observe the highest standards of filial piety toward him.

As a result of these contradictions, the position of women among the Dinka is a complex one in which deprivations and inequities are compensated by devices that ensure a degree of conformity and stability, despite ambivalences.

The position of male youth is equally fraught with paradoxes, though less threatening to the system. Youth, especially men, are tomorrow's beneficiaries of the ancestral ideals and their succession to their elders is considered as only a function of time and patience. The process by which they get to that objective is regulated by a system of age-grades or age-sets, which every Dinka joins at about the age of sixteen to eighteen. Initiation into the age-set entails elaborate rituals and in some tribes an operation of cutting the forehead with deep marks that cicatrize and become quite prominent. This operation is perhaps the most painful ritual in Dinka society.

After graduating from initiation, a man becomes a member of his age-set, a corporate entity that provides a lifelong comradeship and mutual dependency on the members. They move from being warriors to being family men, and on to being tribal elders with a legitimate voice in public affairs. Young women are also classified into age-sets that correspond with male age-sets, for whom they play a supportive role. But in most Dinka tribes, women are not subjected to the painful physical operation that men must endure to qualify as adults.

Although the young men are the ultimate beneficiaries of the values of ancestral continuity, they are subordinated in a way that is only ameliorated by considerable compensation devices, in essence a division of functions and roles. For instance, while the choice or at least the consent of the father for a marriage partner is pivotal and all the social and legal formalities of marriage are performed by him, a young man and his age-mates preoccupy themselves with the aesthetics of courtship and winning the girl's love or consent. Indeed, although the power of decisionmaking lies with their father, the cooperation of the young couple is essential, if only as a practical consideration. Furthermore, although the control of family wealth lies with their elders, the youth preoccupy themselves with the aesthetics of cattle-complex, including displaying and singing over "personality oxen," which are usually adorned with objects of beautification and with which young men identify themselves as symbols of their virility and wealth. Young men particularly relish the euphoric life of the cattle camps to which they move in search of grazings and water and in which they otherwise engage themselves in courtship, singing, and dancing. But perhaps one of the most critical divisions of functions between the generations is that while the elders are the peacemakers who will endeavor to settle disputes amicably and restore unity and harmony through mediation and reconciliation, male youth age-sets, supported by their female counterparts, are essentially warriors whose role is to defend society against the aggression of wild animals, cultivate the fields of the chiefs, and build their houses, or otherwise perform other community services that require physical courage, strength, and endurance.

Although the roles of the elders and the youth are complementary, their relationships are fraught with tension and potential conflict, which are inherent in the nature of procreational stratification. After all, it is the son who will step into the shoes of the father, and among the Dinka the eldest son does in fact inherit his father's shoes. According to the custom of levitate, the son inherits his father's junior wives of childbearing age and begets children with them as sons and daughters of his dead father—his own half-brothers and half-sisters. While this relationship must await the father's death, the potential is threatening to the father and can be a cause of conflict.

Generational competition for young women and overall dominance is implicit in a custom known as *biok*, in which the dominant warrior age-set provokes the newly graduated age-set into a play fight that can result in severe casualties. Since fighting is perhaps the most conspicuous way in which youth warrior age-sets assert their power and foster their subjective sense of identity and dignity, they tend to be aggressive and find cause for war in the slightest provocation. Consequently, their role is fundamentally counter to that of the peacemaking elders. The Dinka reputation as warlike largely emanates from this disposition of its youth. By the same token, these compensational devices sublimate the energies of youths in activities that might seem rebellious but that never threaten the foundations of the social system of which they are the eventual heirs.

The sublimation of aggressive dispositions in young men is remarkably evident in the way they sharpen the horns of their bulls and encourage them to fight. Castrated bulls, which are used as personality oxen, symbolize the qualities of gentleness and submissiveness on the one hand and of aggressiveness and physical courage on the other. In their ox songs, young men and women praise their oxen or the oxen of their husbands or boyfriends for their aggressiveness and valor even as they criticize them for the same.

To a young man or woman, an ox symbolizes wealth. The pride in one's family wealth is usually expressed in ox songs and in relations to one's ox. The hardships of herding in distant camps are always justified by young men in terms of slaving for the love of one's personality ox. Thus by owning an ox or a few oxen, a young man feels as rich as his father who controls the herd. The fact that oxen, though castrated and subdued, are pivotal in the aesthetics of cattle is symbolic of the fact that young men, though subordinated to elders, occupy a high position in the aesthetics of Dinka society.

The significance of aesthetic values as compensational or alternative avenues to material *dheng* is evident in Dinka terminology. A man is said to be *alueth*, a liar (though not in the usual sense of the word), if he is not particularly good at singing or dancing, not really handsome or wealthy, or otherwise not socially known, but puts on an impressive show of being a good singer or dancer, bears himself with such exaggerated style as though strikingly handsome, shows excessive hospitality as though wealthy, or is otherwise pompous in any *dheng* situation.

At the same time, a man who is distinguished in singing, dancing, handsomeness, wealth, or any attribute of *dheng* and acts in accordance with his awareness of, and pride in, this distinction is also referred to as *alueth*—liar. Every young man and woman is considered essentially vain by virtue of a preoccupation with aesthetic values. And to the Dinka this is not really a criticism; quite the contrary, it is a paradoxical compliment or praise.

Singing is seen in the same light. To compose a song is "to create" a song (*cak dit*); to tell a lie is also "to create" words (*cak wel*). *Cak* is also applied to God's act of creation, and although it might be pushing the analogy too far to consider such a creation "telling a lie," there is the common denominator of making something that was formerly nonexistent. In the case of songs, "telling a lie" may indicate the usual exaggeration and distortion, but this does not discredit the positive values of song, which give to young men and women the standard values used by elders to embody the acceptable ideals of the system. Songs mean much to all Dinkas of both sexes and of all ages; otherwise, their significance to youth would be much less meaningful. It is, however, significant that this is the group most conspicuously preoccupied with them. So ritualized, mystified, and glorified are the values of young people that their forms and their effect on society are more conspicuous and attention drawing than those of their elders. The result is a purposeful, proud, gratified, and socially integrated youth, delighted with the pleasures of today yet aspiring to the utilitarian promises of later age. Generally satisfied with their status, they conform to the fundamental norms of the system, the dictates of their male elders.

Resistance to change or cross-cultural assimilation. The Dinka value system is essentially backward-looking in that the idealized view of the ancestral past forms and reinforces the present value system so as to facilitate the future. The Dinka never claim to have done better than their fathers, and even if they have, they never voice pride in that achievement. On the contrary, they tend to glorify the achievements of the forefathers; after all, the continued participation of the forebears in the affairs of the living is largely dependent on their being remembered for positive virtues, in turn dependent on continued exaltation and glorification.[13] A frequently heard comment among the Dinka is that "in

---

13. In these lines from an ox song, for instance, a relative whose good conduct supposedly attracted a man with high-quality cattle to marry her (as a result of which he, the singer, acquired his ox) is praised with reference to the old Dinka ways: "The girl named

the past, people listened to each other and words would unite and flow in one direction."

Until recently, when the coming of modernity began to have a visible effect on the Dinka, the notion of development, now widely accepted among them, was nonexistent. This is quite apparent from the principles that the Dinka associate with the role of leadership. When a man succeeds to a position of leadership and proves himself a worthy leader, he is said to have established control over the situation, *dom baai*. If there are particular problems that need solutions, such as conflicts between community members or when God and the ancestral spirits have, for one reason or another, been provoked into punishing the community with natural disasters, then the leader has the duty to take appropriate measures to resolve the conflicts, propitiate the supernatural powers, and restore a state of unity, harmony, and functional prosperity. That is *guier baai*. When that state is achieved, the task of the leader is to ensure that it is maintained, *muk baai*. The notion of endeavoring to elevate society or individuals to a yet unrealized higher and better level of existence through a process similar to "development" was, I believe, foreign to the Dinka. Individual and societal goals, even to the optimum degree, were considered part of experience, achievable and, indeed, at one time or another, actually achieved. Godfrey Lienhardt provides an insight into the Dinka perspective in this respect:

> To traditional Dinka, that idea of progress was quite foreign. There was little evidence that life had ever been different from what it was today, nor, until the coming of the Europeans, that it was ever going to change in the future. But by the 1940s, it had become apparent to many thoughtful Dinka that in lacking education their people were lacking some of the essential skills for political survival in the modern Sudan, and they came to accept the idea that they were in some ways which put them at a disadvantage in the modern world, backward. This idea was suggested to them, with no disrespect for their own culture, by missionaries and government officials alike, since both were anxious that the Dinka should be able to speak for themselves in councils of state outside their own homeland when the Sudan became independent.[14]

after my grandmother, mother of Deng de Bong, / her conduct is as good as that of the ancient Dinka." Deng, *Dinka and Their Songs*, p. 113.

14. Godfrey Lienhardt, "The Dinka and Catholicism," in J. Davis, ed., *Religious Organization and Religious Experience* (Academic Press, 1982), p. 88.

Cultural exclusiveness. Because of the family orientation of the system, Dinka cultural values tend to weaken as the community widens, and they become minimal in relations with foreigners. The Dinka do not believe the principles of *koc e nhom, cieng,* or *dheng* apply only to the Dinka. All peoples seek or ought to seek immortality through procreation; and all people have their own *cieng,* whether or not they live up to the objective standards of the ideal *cieng* as the Dinka see it. Nor is the notion of human dignity as embodied in *dheng* a Dinka prerogative. But in all these areas the Dinka believe that their conceptualization of the principles involved and the behavioral ways of applying them are superior to those of others—the foreigners. As they see it, the best possible procreation is one that ensures the continuation of the Dinka race, religious beliefs, and cultural patterns.

In 1949 Trimingham observed:

One of the determinants of the rapid or slow spread of Christianity in the South has been provided by the contrast between the semi-nomadic cattle-breeding Nilotic tribes (Shilluk, Nuer and Dinka) and the settled agriculturists. The life of the former is bound up with a cow economy, this animal being a veritable god. They are intensely conservative and very proud of their civilization. They have acted as a bastion against the penetration of Islam by having proved impervious to its seductions. Christian work amongst them demanded from the first a distinctive treatment and they have only just begun to respond in some degree to the treasures of the Christian Gospel. Consequently, it is very important, now the barriers are beginning to be broken down to the penetration of new ideas and ways of life, that the missionary effort should be intensified amongst them, so that with the Christianizing of their civilization their unique ethnic qualities may still be preserved and they may find a true sphere within the structure of the wider Sudan.[15]

Trimingham's observation is widely shared by observers of Nilotic peoples. As Audrey Butt wrote in 1952:

They consider their country the best in the world and everyone inferior to themselves. For this reason they . . . scorn European and Arab cultures. . . . Their attitude toward any authority that would

15. J. Spencer Trimingham, *The Christian Church in Post-War Sudan* (London: World Dominion Press, 1949), p. 34.

coerce them is one of touchiness, pride, and reckless disobedience. [A Nilote] is ready to defend himself and his property from the inroads of others. They are thus self-reliant, brave fighters, turbulent and aggressive, and are extremely conservative in their aversion from innovation and interference.[16]

The implications of the Dinka value system for the respect and protection of human rights among the Dinka are complex. On the one hand, there would seem to be a high regard for the human being and human dignity in the moral code of the Dinka as defined by their value system. On the other hand, that value system stratifies those within it according to descent, age, and sex. The Dinka also have a condescending view of the world beyond them. Although non-Dinkas are critically appraised by the yardstick of the Dinka code, they are considered almost by definition incapable of living up to those standards and are also recognized as disadvantaged in their sharing the benefits of Dinka cultural values. Traditionally, the Dinka code not only stratified and discriminated internally but also was essentially circumscribed to exclude non-Dinkas, whose behavior was inadequate since it was not in accordance with Dinka ideas. Whether the Dinka attributed these inferior qualities to an inherent incapability or to a choice to remain morally depraved is not clear.

The Pluralism of the Nation-State

The emergence of the nation-state with its ethnic and cultural pluralism affected the Dinka value system in several ways. In certain respects, and especially through the exercise of coercive state power, Dinka ideals of persuasive authority were violated. But paradoxically the establishment of law and order under the British was viewed as a reaffirmation and an approximation of the Dinka ideals. Concomitantly, the diversification of the cultural value systems placed the stratifications of the traditional society in question and offered opportunities for education and economic, social, and cultural self-enhancement, which began to undermine the old order. Furthermore, as ethnic and cultural groups battled over the shaping of national identity and the sharing of

16. Audrey Butt, *The Nilotes of the Sudan and Uganda* (London: International African Institute, 1964), p. 41.

power and wealth, both the Dinka ideals and the newly acquired standards of human rights suffered gross violations not only through the state machinery but also in intergroup relations.

The emergence of the nation-state as a coercive force came to the Dinka first under the Turko-Egyptian rule of 1821–85, during which the ineffectiveness of the administration combined with the terrorism of state-assisted slavery. This was followed by the Mahdist state of 1885–98, which overthrew the Turko-Egyptian administration and plunged the country as a whole into a devastating state of anarchy, aggravated by famine and disease. The Anglo-Egyptian reconquest of 1898 reestablished colonial control, which lasted until independence in 1956 and was the most effective in consolidating the framework of the modern nation-state.

Initially the Dinka viewed colonial intervention, as did all the Sudanese, as a gross violation of their fundamental human rights, manifested in the mere fact of military conquest and maintained through the threat of the police and the army, elements of authority that were alien to the Dinka political system. But paradoxically this coercive force was also used to enforce law and order and to establish conditions of peace and security that contrasted sharply with the level of violence and devastation that had prevailed under all previous administrations. The introduction of the Western concept of the rule of law and the protection of fundamental human rights, though modified by the coercive nature of colonial rule as a system of foreign domination, became one of the most significant accomplishments of the British administration. Colonialism also introduced into the state machinery a welfare system of services in such fields as health, education, and employment which, though limited and inequitable, was roughly in tune with traditional expectations about the responsibility of leadership toward the community. Furthermore, through the system of indirect rule, the British governed by remote control, which did not seem oppressive to the people, but on the contrary permitted them to run their own affairs under their traditional leadership.

Because of these experiences with the British, Dinka favor them over the Arabs and even go so far as regarding the Europeans, as represented by the British, to be closer to the Dinka system of values than the Arabs, as represented by the northern Sudanese. One chief echoed a familiar Dinka appreciation of the European as *adheng* in comparison with the Arab and went on to say: "This . . . race [meaning the English as a synonym for the white race] ... [a]nd we, these people who are so black, so different from them, so different in colour, we are similar." Another chief explained: "The Dinka saw the English as a good man [adheng]. He would not cheat you on your thing. . . . The English, if he sees your thing fallen among his things, he will pick it out and give it to you. But if it were these neighbours of ours, instead of giving it back, they would cover it with many things in order to cheat you." [17]

But the Dinka viewed the effect of British rule on their society with ambivalence when it came to the exercise of police force behind the administrative and judicial powers of the chiefs, who had previously relied on the persuasive power of divine authority. The Dinka saw the coercive power of the chiefs, now expressed in flogging, fines, or imprisonment, not only as oppressive but as totally repugnant to Dinka notions of human dignity. Because policemen among the Dinka were mostly Arab or northern, and the British rules remote and invisible, the symbols of oppression were seen as Arab. The Dinka word for the government is *jur*, which, at least among the Ngok Dinka, is used to mean Arab. An abundance of songs by former prisoners illustrate the reaction of the Dinka to this aspect of state power.

The following song is quoted at length because it covers the various aspects of power transformation in Dinka society. Because the singer had not responded to a court summons, a policeman was sent to summon him or seize his personality ox to compel his appearance. On appearance, he was committed to jail to await trial. Later, the case was settled in his favor.

> I went and sat under the [Court] tree . . .
> Of all the people that gathered
> Not a single man said, "Good morning."
> So I sat with a twisted heart . . .
> A court order was written in silence
> Even my name was not asked . . .
> Why do all people get angry when I state my case?
> Do they mean to put me in jail?
> "Yes, the law is strong
> You will go into jail."

17. First quotation by Chief Ayeny Aleu, second by Chief Giir Thiik, in Deng, *Dinka Cosmology,* pp. 114, 47.

Is that why people threaten me with anger?
Only jail? . . .
I will go myself right now
Without being driven by the police.
Even if there is a crocodile in jail which catches people,
I'll go inside.
I am locked in jail, I am locked in jail
And sweat hurts our eyes,
Sweat hurts our eyes, while bats stink . . .
Son of Pakir clan, Mayon de Dan de Kir [an elder prisoner]
The Government is not like the ancient times
Do not get angry when the police send you
You will be beaten, and there the face of great shame
Shame for the beating of an elder
While young men watch him beaten . . .
A victim of law cannot be replaced . . .
Let's tie our hearts, father of Nyannuer,
And go to grow cotton.
When we were driven to the field
I walked, tilting my head like a canoe;
I almost refused to work.
"The pain of initiation," came back to my heart[18]
I almost did what I almost did . . .
Mijang de Dak [a Dinka policeman] do not walk behind us
Do not follow us with the whip
People do not enslave one another
When they are both initiated . . .
The vileness of the Arab police
A Dinka must not join
To kill his own people . . .
[For] this case
If the Creator were near
I would call my [deceased] father
I would call my father, the son of Deng,
To come and attend my case;
Each man comes with his father
And I brave the court alone,

18. He supposedly won respect for initiation.

I am lonely in my pleading
Lonely as though I never had a father.[19]

While the administration and judicial effect of the government was initially the most pronounced, a more subtle but equally radical change was effected through missionary schools. Education set in motion a process that was eventually to reverse the traditional hierarchy of knowledge. In traditional society knowledge was presumed to accumulate with age and the proximity to the ancestors. Now, according to the new code of learning, the Dinka as a cultural group not only had a lot to learn but should indeed be ashamed of where they stood in the newly postulated scale of progress and must endeavor to improve their lot.

As Lienhardt has noted:

The Nilotes regarded the missionaries like all foreigners as inferior to themselves in all but technological and medical skills, and were as secure in their own standards as the missionaries in theirs. So the missionary presence was valued above all for one contribution to Dinka well-being which reflective and influential Dinka slowly came to see as necessary for their cultural and political survival—education. The Dinka were made increasingly aware that much though they might have preferred to live without external interference in their traditional mode of life, that interference had already begun to endanger their independence. They saw that they needed enough of their own people capable of thinking in foreign ways, of meeting foreigners on their own ground while remaining Dinka in their loyalties, to understand and circumvent encroachments on their own autonomy.[20]

That encroachment on their autonomy has been the source of the conflict marking the relations between the Arab Muslim North and the African Christianized South since the dawn of independence.

The civil war that is still raging in the country was triggered by a mutiny in a southern battalion in August 1955, four months before independence on January 1, 1956, and continued until 1972, when it was ended by the Addis Ababa Agreement, only to be resumed in 1983 with the violation of that agreement by the president, Jaafer Mohamed Ni-

19. Deng, *Dinka and Their Songs*, pp. 147–49.
20. Lienhardt, "Dinka and Catholicism," p. 86.

meiri. As the South began to assert itself politically and economically, enjoying an autonomy based on parliamentary democracy, while the country was under a presidential military system, Nimeiri in 1983 divided the South into three regions, lowered the powers of the regions, and imposed shari'a, the so-called September laws, whose criminal justice led to frequent floggings and amputation of limbs, most of the victims being poor Muslims from the West and non-Muslim destitutes from the South. Even after Nimeiri's overthrow and the promise of abrogating the September laws, neither the transitional military government nor the civilian government that was formed through parliamentary elections abrogated those laws. On the contrary, the political trend is to replace them with other Islamic laws that will supposedly be more authentic.

The reaction to Nimeiri's violation of the Addis Ababa Agreement was the creation of the Sudan People's Liberation Movement and its military wing, the Sudan People's Liberation Army, which has been fighting not for separation or autonomy for the South, but allegedly to free the entire country from any discrimination based on race, religion, or culture. Although the movement is centered in the South, is led by a Dinka, and is composed mostly of Dinka fighting men, it claims to be national not only in its objectives but also in its composition. (Its northern membership is largely derived from the disadvantaged, mostly non-Arab regions of southern Kordofan and southern Blue Nile.)

As the Islamic fervor in the North becomes increasingly pronounced, the South reacts in an eclectic manner that combines commitment to secularism with the consolidation of a religious identity that has evolved along the lines of traditional African beliefs combined with the adopted Christian faith, both Catholic and Protestant in equal proportions. Indeed, the issue of religion in the South-North conflict has become one of politicized religious identity. The elements of traditional religions and Christianity have become conceptually integrated as essential ingredients of southern identity, which is seen to be in violent confrontation with Islam as an official religion, which the dominant elites in the North seek to promote, if not impose, through the instrumentality of the state.

Gross violations of human rights have always been a conspicuous feature of the civil war as the innocent civilian population falls victim to arbitrary arrests, torture, and murder, with a notable increase in cases of massacre. Recently the establishment of tribal militias among groups that have historically been mutually hostile has aggravated the situation, and well-documented reports of slavery and similar practices have begun to appear in the press, both inside the country and abroad.[21] Given the militant attitude of certain Arab groups now in confrontation with the South, who are being trained, armed, and organized into militias to cheapen the cost of the war for the government, it is easy to see how religious intolerance and fanaticism can fuel an attitude of unscrupulous ruthlessness. How else can one explain eyewitness accounts of the horrible treatment of civilians, including pregnant women being cut open and small babies being thrown into boiling water, not to mention the classic yoke on people's necks. Some conscientious Muslim leaders have confessed to being approached by followers wondering whether killing a Dinka is *halal*, religiously permitted, or *haram*, forbidden.[22]

This is indeed an area in which the Dinka have always claimed moral superiority over the Arabs, believing that God created the Dinka differently from the Arabs. Referring to the allegation that slavery was practiced by all societies, Arab and African alike, one elder, Bulabek-Malith, observed in protest:

A human being created by God was never made a slave by the black man [meaning Dinka]; it was the Arabs who made them slaves. . . . Slavery is not known to us. . . . To capture people to become slaves among us is unknown. . . . A person known to his relatives is the man who stays among us. And he is not treated like a slave; he becomes a member of the family. The treatment I told you before, where people are crippled [tortured] and where people's testicles are pricked, never happened among the black people.

And a chief, Biong Mijak, commented:

What the Arabs have written down is a lie. . . . Even our ancestors tell us they never captured Arab children. People kill themselves in

21. Two University of Khartoum lecturers, Ushari Ahmed Mahmoud and Suleyman Ali Baldo, conducted a study of the practice and published their findings in a booklet called *The Dhein Massacre: Slavery in the Sudan*, Human Rights Abuses in the Sudan 1987 (Sudan Relief and Rehabilitation Association). See also *Sudan Times*, September 23, 1987; September 21, 1987; August 21, 1987; July 23, 1987; and July 21, 1987; *Washington Post*, April 15, 1988; February 16, 1988; November 29, 1987; and November 21, 1987; *New York Times*, July 3, 1988; *Atlanta Constitution*, April 17, 1988; April 15, 1988; *Atlanta Journal–Atlanta Constitution*, March 27, 1988; and *Atlanta Constitution*, March 21, 1988. Intensive coverage was sustained into 1989 and still continues intermittently.

22. Oral report to the author by a prominent leader of one of the leading religious sects.

war, face to face, but we do not go and capture people. . . . We have something God gave us from the ancient past, from the time our ancestors came leading the people. . . . War has always occurred [but we] have war ethics that came with us from the ancient past. We never ambush . . . we kill face to face. It is the Arabs who treat us as slaves and capture us in secrecy.[23]

Dinka reaction to developments in the pluralistic world of the nation-state and its conflicting array of positives and negatives is equally contradictory. On the one hand, they are beginning to reinterpret their value systems to become more universally valid. For instance, the following lines of a song that was composed during the peaceful period of the Addis Ababa Agreement stress the universality of human equality, irrespective of race or religion:

No one was bad when God created us
No one was bad when the Creator made us
No one was bad when we emerged from the Byre of Creation;
We were all equal
I swear by death, we were all children of the one Adam;
Both Mohamed and Deng—Arab and Dinka
I swear by death, we were all children of the one Adam;
The Black Sudan and the Brown Sudan.[24]

On the other hand, the Dinka have become increasingly disillusioned by their relative position in the modern world and in particular their subjection to the dominant Arab Muslim majority of the North. This has created a situation in which they have to reinterpret their relative inferiority in the modern context, while nevertheless upholding their distinctive moral ideals. As the Dinka see the need to pursue their traditional pride and human dignity by the new modern criteria, they reflect a willingness to change that is in sharp contrast to their reputed conservatism. At the same time, fear of assimilation by the Arab Muslim North has aroused in them an intense desire to preserve their traditional ways. "If you, our children, have survived," said an elder, Chief Biong Mijak, "hold to the ways of our ancestors very firmly. Let us be friends with the Arabs, but each man should have his own way." Another elder, Chief Makuei Bilkuei, remarked: "Why don't we promote our [own]

23. Quotations from Deng, *Dinka Cosmology,* pp. 282, 283.
24. Author's translation from his collections.

ways? Why do we take [Arab] ways without our own plan? . . . What have you people done to promote our own ways with the Arabs?" "God did not create at random," Chief Biong Mijak said. "He created some people brown and some black. We cannot say we want to destroy what God has created. . . . God would get angry if we spoiled his work." Chief Makuei Bilkuei gave a dramatic account of his resistance to Arab Islamic influence: "God has refused my speaking Arabic. I asked God, 'Why don't I speak Arabic?' And he said, 'You will turn into a bad man.' . . . I said, 'There is something good in Arabic!' And he said, 'No, there is nothing good in it.'"[25]

Conclusion

The experience of the Dinka suggests that they clearly had notions of human rights that formed an integral part of their value system: its overriding goals for life, its ideals for relationships between people, and its sense of human dignity. However, the logic of this value system stratified people according to descent, age, and sex in a way to create inequities that were recognized but tolerated, since dissidents lacked alternatives. The system was also conservative and oriented away from change and development. Furthermore, the effectiveness of the value system diminished as people moved away from the family and the lineage-oriented sense of the community.

With the emergence of the nation-state, new opportunities for education and employment, and Western ideas of democracy and equality, the old structures and their underlying cultural values became exposed to reassessment and scrutiny. The result was that, while certain ideals and practices continued to be expressed and given wider application, new values and patterns of behavior developed that redefined standards for the promotion and protection of human rights. And yet the competition for power and national resources in the pluralistic context of the nation-state has generated tensions and conflicts leading to gross violations of human rights.

With regard to the Sudan, a cross-cultural approach to developing new ethical values, which uses coexisting or interactive value systems and practices, would not only form a bridge between cultural contexts but would also enrich the process of universalization in the promotion

25. Quotations from Chief Biong Mijak are from Deng, *Africans of Two Worlds*, pp. 76, 75; quotations from Chief Makuei Bilkuei are from Deng, *Dinka Cosmology*, pp. 80, 84–85.

and protection of human rights. This is essentially a function of education, cross-cultural communication, and practical cooperation. Although the long-term result may be viewed as a composite, integrated whole, expressed in some form of universal instruments, in reality the process will continue to reflect an eclectic multiplicity of contents and levels, a complex combination of unity of purpose and diversity of means. As one elder said on a different but related issue: "Man has only one head and one neck, but he has two legs to stand on."[26]

26. Chief Giir Thiik, quoted in Deng, *Dinka Cosmology,* p. 44.

CHAPTER TWELVE

Traditional Culture and the Prospect for Human Rights in Africa

James Silk

THE ACHIEVEMENT of African national independence from colonial rule during the last thirty years has coincided with a period of growing international attention and sensitivity to human rights. In this setting of general concern, Africa's disappointing postcolonial human rights record, marked by notorious abuses, has spawned a literature examining the complex context of human rights in Africa and speculating about the prospects for those rights. This literature consists largely of attempts to respond to one question: why is the African human rights record so bad?

Perhaps the inherently negative nature of this question has determined the tone of a central controversy within this literature about the significance of traditional, or precolonial, African culture. Some have characterized the issue as whether, or to what extent, traditional African societies recognized and protected human rights.[1] The responses, however, suggest less of a debate than a rough consensus around a theme broad enough to embrace several variations. The theme that emerges is that traditional African culture was or is compatible with human rights, but with an African conception of human rights—consistent with the African context—not with the inevitably Western norms embodied in the International Bill of Human Rights. The main obstacles to the observation of human rights lie not in traditional African values, but in problems arising from colonial rule and the imperatives of nation building.

On one level it is difficult to argue with this proposition. It expresses

---

1. See Introduction to section 1, "Roots and Implications of Human Rights in Africa," in Claude E. Welch, Jr., and Ronald I. Meltzer, eds., *Human Rights and Development in Africa* (Albany: State University of New York Press, 1984), p. 7.

a rejection of a kind of cultural imperialism that is, of course, unacceptable and that must be guarded against in the human rights field. It reflects an accurate historical understanding of the development and articulation of international human rights norms by the developed Western nations. It may also provide the basis for the expansion of international human rights norms. However, as most often expressed, the proposition—that international human rights are not universal but Western and that there is an African notion of human rights that is not ultimately consistent with international norms—is troublesome. First, it can be and is used as an apology or an excuse for Africa's poor human rights record: Africa cannot be held to standards that are culturally inappropriate and that Africans had no part in establishing. Also, denying the universality of human rights may effectively destroy the meaning and value of the entire concept of human rights: there can be no basis for international protection if each society can determine its own list of human rights. The very significance of international human rights is in their universality.

These dangers are intertwined with the questions addressed by the literature on human rights in Africa. Focusing on whether specific rights were recognized and protected in traditional African society—and, if so, whether they were rights consistent with Western or African conceptions—has led the discussion away from consideration of a fundamental question. That question may be stated in negative or positive terms: is there something in traditional African culture that is inhospitable to basic international human rights, or is there some fundamental value in African traditional culture that can provide the basis for the protection of such basic human rights? This question sounds similar to that raised in the literature—both are variants of the overarching question "whether human rights are culturally specific" [2]—but the consequences of pursuing the two lines of inquiry are different.

The approach suggested here recognizes differences in culture and in levels of development. But it does not seek, within African traditional culture, broadly defined, the presence or absence of specific rights. Instead, it assumes that underlying the International Bill of Human Rights as a necessary, though not sufficient, source of human rights norms, is some fundamental metaphysical idea (an idea that may well be "Western" *as articulated*). It calls then for a close look at a specific traditional

---

2. Rhoda Howard, "Evaluating Human Rights in Africa: Some Problems of Implicit Comparisons," *Human Rights Quarterly*, vol. 6 (May 1984), p. 165.

culture to see if a substantially similar idea is present. The identification of such an idea in a given culture would suggest that international human rights norms are not fundamentally inconsistent with that culture's values. The inability to locate such an idea would provide more compelling evidence for the conclusion that international human rights are not universal and are not likely to take root in the particular non-Western society in question.

The Literature on Human Rights in Africa

Despite different and even conflicting normative judgments within the extensive literature on human rights in Africa, a remarkably consistent descriptive pattern emerges: traditional African society embodies values that are consistent with and supportive of human rights, but the effects of colonialism and the difficulties of nation building and development have contributed to an erosion of those values or, at least, bred disrespect for and abuse of human rights. Linking disrespect for human rights to authoritarianism, Dunstan Wai, for example, argues that "authoritarianism in modern Africa is not at all in accord with the spirit and practice of traditional political systems, but that its practices are aberrations facilitated by colonial legacies and reinforced by the agonies of 'underdevelopment.'"[3]

Wai's description is paradigmatic of the most frequently recurring explanation of Africa's human rights failings: traditional values are a positive factor, but the colonial legacy and the need for development and national unity have been negative factors for human rights. Closer examination of individual interpretations reveals differences within this pattern. The most important of these differences for the purposes of this essay fall into two categories. First, although there is near unanimity that colonial rule, the need for national unity, and pressures to modernize have fostered human rights abuses, commentators' attitudes toward these factors vary, from criticism of the way those pressures have dam-

3. Dunstan M. Wai, "Human Rights in Sub-Saharan Africa," in Adamantia Pollis and Peter Schwab, eds., *Human Rights: Cultural and Ideological Perspectives* (Praeger, 1979), p. 115. The All Africa Council of Churches/World Council of Churches, among others, has expressed similar views: "There is no doubt that violations of human rights existed in traditional African society. . . . However, our traditional societies do have many elements upon which we may rely today in our efforts to escape often grim present realities." A discussion of the contribution of colonialism to human rights violations in Africa follows. "Factors Responsible for the Violation of Human Rights in Africa," *Issue: A Quarterly Journal of Africanist Opinion*, vol. 6 (Winter, 1976), p. 44 (hereafter *Issue*).

aged human rights, to neutral description, to "realistic" acceptance of violations as necessary evils under the circumstances. Second, writers differ in the way they evaluate traditional society in relation to rights and in the conclusions they make about the character of the rights in question.

The Effects of Colonialism

It is not surprising that the greatest agreement exists about the negative impact of colonialism, both in its direct chilling effect on human rights and in its destruction of traditional institutions. The most noticeable variations here are in the importance this factor is given for the continuing human rights abuses and in the specific explanations offered of colonialism's effects. Taken together, these accounts constitute a rather comprehensive critique of the detrimental role of colonial rule for human rights in Africa. Colonial rule destroyed traditional institutions and relationships that protected people and constrained power; imposed authoritarian governments and reduced the rights exercised by individuals, conditioning Africans to these repressive ways; left behind disastrously ill-structured economies and societies riddled with ethnic, social, economic, and political divisions; and imposed political boundaries that were arbitrary and incompatible with traditional social structures.[4]

Minasse Haile's rendering of the effect of colonial rule provides an example of some of these themes.

Colonialism has contributed to the poor record of human rights in Africa. Human rights were not part of the Western law brought to Africa. The colonial government in Africa was "authoritarian to the

4. See Chris C. Mojekwu, "International Human Rights: The African Perspective," in Jack L. Nelson and Vera M. Green, eds., *International Human Rights: Contemporary Issues* (New York: Human Rights Publishing Group, 1980), pp. 87–88; Claude E. Welch, Jr., "Human Rights as a Problem in Contemporary Africa," in Welch and Meltzer, eds., *Human Rights and Development*, pp. 11–15; S. K. B. Asante, "Nation Building and Human Rights in Emergent African Nations," *Cornell International Law Journal*, vol. 2 (Spring 1969), p. 88; Minasse Haile, "Human Rights, Stability, and Development in Africa: Some Observations on Concept and Reality," *Virginia Journal of International Law*, vol. 24 (Spring 1984), pp. 591–92; Kéba M'Baye, "Human Rights in Africa," in Karel Vasak and Philip Alston, eds., *The International Dimensions of Human Rights*, vol. 2 (Westport, Conn.: Greenwood Press, 1982), p. 587; Richard F. Weisfelder, "The Decline of Human Rights in Lesotho: An Evaluation of Domestic and External Determinants," *Issue*, vol. 6 (Winter 1976), p. 23; Wai, "Human Rights in Sub-Saharan Africa," p. 118; and All Africa Council of Churches, "Factors Responsible for the Violation," pp. 44–45.

core," and its legacies in the areas of civil, political, and personal security rights, and in the administration of judicial rights were clearly undemocratic. . . .

The state and the law were used to regulate and coerce. Colonial courts were used to enforce taxes and impose servitude on the African peoples as part of the apparatus of control. . . .

The colonial state in Africa also created other situations that now militate against the adequate observance of human rights, for example, a very high degree of social stratification and the maintenance and intensification of parochial, tribal identities.[5]

The Significance of Nation Building

The pressures of nation building are also viewed almost unanimously as factors contributing to Africa's poor record on human rights. Within this descriptive unanimity, however, is a somewhat confusing array of opinions about whether these pressures justify or excuse the abuses they contribute to. These views fall roughly into three categories, which, for convenience, might be labeled critical or impatient, neutral or descriptive, and realistic or pessimistic. None of the commentators fall neatly into any of these categories. In particular, none embrace wholeheartedly the "realistic" position that abuses are understandable and necessary evils.

Kéba M'Baye's account exemplifies those that are, to a large extent, neutrally descriptive.[6] He notes that after independence the African states became members of the United Nations, accepting its principles, including the Universal Declaration of Human Rights. They also incorporated references to human rights in their constitutions. "Looking beyond the phrases set down in these constitutions and laws, one discovers an Africa more concerned with achieving economic and social development and maintaining the stability of its government than with recognizing and promoting rights and freedoms" (pp. 591–92). The notion of equality is valued in terms of the right to equal enjoyment of the world's wealth. "Hence the pursuit of development for the sake of which all sacrifices are permissible" (p. 592).

M'Baye describes the concerns of Africans after independence as

5. Haile, "Human Rights, Stability, and Development," pp. 591–92.
6. M'Baye, "Human Rights in Africa," pp. 591–601. Pages for quotations are given in the text.

being very different from those of the Western nations that incorporated human rights into the UN Charter after World War II. Having long suffered from poverty, Africans wanted above all to "make up for their economic backwardness, protect their fragile independence and help the other peoples of the continent to shake off the colonial yoke. . . . They reached a point where they neglected all that did not seem likely to consolidate their sovereignty and ensure their economic progress" (pp. 592–93). M'Baye does not, however, accept this neglect uncritically. He sees this as a "questionable conception" of development. True economic and social development, he says, "must necessarily include respect for the human person and the protection of his rights and freedoms" (p. 593).

Despite his rejection of the development justification for human rights abuses, M'Baye's assessment is balanced by an almost fatalistic realism about the pressures facing African political leaders. They were "faced with the hard facts of reality in the form of the countless difficulties which had arisen," difficulties that placed them in a "position of weakness" allowing imperialist exploitation and fostering internal insecurity (p. 594). Thus, M'Baye says, African governments interpreted the Universal Declaration of Human Rights, along with the international recognition that no country lived up to its mandate perfectly, "in such a way as to justify the infringements required inevitably by the necessities of unity, prosperity, and stability" (pp. 594–95).

M'Baye is troubled by the notion, expressed by a group of jurists meeting in Dakar in 1967 to discuss human rights, that underdevelopment should be considered "a permanent exceptional circumstance" justifying some derogations from human rights. For him, the conference's statement—implying that this circumstance will end once a state is free of its colonial legacy—conceals "the idea of a state of permanent emergency which, as long as it lasts, justifies certain violations of the principle of the rule of law" (p. 597). Yet M'Baye's conclusion reveals an ambivalence about the relationship between the imperatives of nation building and human rights. He says, "Thus, the African governments appear clearly to have sacrificed rights and freedoms for the sake of development and political stability. This situation can be explained and even justified" (p. 599). He summarizes the rationale that, given the need to develop, idleness can be viewed as an infraction and the exercise of rights as "an attack on public order." His final optimism about Africa's eventual tendency toward respect for human rights is based on the perception that in any society, rights are sometimes circumscribed during crisis, "and Africa in fact, is undergoing a crisis" (pp. 599–601).

While M'Baye's analysis shows how the pressures of nation building impinge negatively on human rights, it leaves unanswered the question of whether, despite the obvious obstacles created by current circumstances, Africa is ultimately fertile ground for human rights. Neither his concluding optimistic assumption, that the Universal Declaration of Human Rights is an ideal "common to all mankind," nor his account, discussed below, of rights found in traditional African society, satisfactorily answer this question. M'Baye's concentration on the damage done to human rights by the imperatives of development and national unity obviates the utility of looking at the more fundamental question, a failure symptomatic of the literature.

S. K. B. Asante, too, reflects ambivalence about the nation-building rationale for curtailment of human rights.[7] He ultimately rejects it with some force, but his analysis concedes, in its realism, a great deal to the pressures of nation building. Indeed, Asante describes his section on nation building, "A Realistic Appraisal," as an examination of the validity of the "thesis that the stark realities of nation-building in Africa do not admit of the luxury of human rights" (p. 83). He sets out the "formidable difficulties" in the way of nation building, beginning with the artificially created national boundaries left by the colonial powers.

> This means that upon attaining independence, African governments are confronted with a situation in which the very existence of their respective nations has yet to be established as a meaningful concept. Development is further bedeviled by poverty, disease and illiteracy and a serious dearth of human and material resources. On this fragile foundation, the leaders of an emergent African nation are charged with accomplishing at least four herculean tasks in their lifetime: First, to forge the bonds of unity and nationhood, and to foster wider loyalties beyond parochial, tribal or regional confines. Second, to convert a subsistence economy into a modern cash economy without unleashing social turbulence and economic chaos. Third, to industrialize the country and to introduce a sophisticated system of agriculture. Fourth, to erase poverty, disease and illiteracy, raise the standard of living of the people, and in short create a modern state with

7. Asante, "Nation Building and Human Rights," pp. 83–99.

all its paraphernalia. . . . This unprecedented pace of development and modernization can only be feasible, if at all, within a stable political framework; and there can be no political stability without a national political consensus. Most African nations are yet to attain this consensus; the frequent incidence of coups d'état graphically demonstrates the terrible convulsions through which African nations are passing. Political instability obviously militates against the establishment of any articulate body of social or political values, but further it undermines the inculcation of healthy and meaningful human rights traditions [pp. 83–84].

Asante attributes to "a substantial number of thoughtful Africans" a series of reasons, including those related to nation building, for the unsuitability of fundamental human rights for Africa. First, some argue that the concept of a bill of rights is a bourgeois one, suitable for an affluent society:

But a new African state, confronted with the baffling problems of nation building, the problems of creating political stability, and eradicating disease, poverty and illiteracy, cannot afford the luxury of limited government. . . . The emphasis should be on strong government. . . . A bill of rights . . . might well impede not only social and economic progress but also national unity [p. 85].

Those who make this argument conclude, according to Asante, that "the courts should not be entrusted with the awesome responsibility of determining the extent to which individual rights must give way to the wider considerations of social progress; that responsibility properly belongs to political leaders responsible to the electorate" (pp. 85–86). Asante does not comment on this argument, but it is odd that, in an argument for the legitimacy of curbing individual rights and in the context of African authoritarian regimes, the authority of the electorate is invoked.

Second, Asante cites the argument that "political stability and internal security in a new African state can only be assured at the expense of the fundamental liberties of the individual." He notes that many African states have justified recourse to preventive detention "on the grounds that the critical formative years of a new nation demand firm, indeed, stern measures to avert subversion and political disintegration" (p. 86). Thus freedoms of association and speech cannot be tolerated when used to subvert or disrupt national unity. Due process, too, may endanger state security where, because opposition groups are inclined to use violence, the state must be able to use all its powers to extinguish any threat (pp. 86–87).

Asante recognizes and accepts the need for strong government and "vigorous social discipline" in Africa, but notes that some argue for more, for "a guarantee against a change of government for ten years or so, severe curtailment of fundamental liberties—no trouble-makers or agitators" (pp. 91–92). And he notes that the demands for stability can be and have been manipulated to sustain "despotism and corruption" (p. 92). Asante summarizes the pressure national unity puts on human rights:

> The most pressing problems now facing African leaders revolve around the preservation of the new nations from disintegration and their security against internal and external subversion. It is in the protection against the dangers in these critical areas that the rights of the individual are most likely to be overridden by the compelling claims of the State.
>
> A new African State has to tackle the fundamental problem of welding a heterogeneous conglomeration of tribes and communities into a united nation. . . . [T]he fear of disintegration haunts every African nation [p. 92].

Asante finds, as a matter of fact, that many African governments have resorted to clear violations of classical human rights in order to "avert social and political disintegration" (p. 93). When he shifts to evaluating these justifications for curtailing human rights, Asante reveals his ambivalence.

Asante notes the dilemma. He acknowledges that "most progressive Africans" would not hesitate to subordinate "the concept of free association to that of national unity," but he asserts that "effective participation by all the diverse communities" in the national life is the "key to national unity and stability in Africa" (p. 94). However, Asante says, nation building is a long, difficult process, and to achieve national unity, "divisive forces should be discouraged and prohibited outright wherever feasible. . . . [T]he compelling claims of national security in the formative stages of nationhood may well justify some limitations on freedom of association" (p. 95). From his realist position, the challenges to the establishment and maintenance of government authority, including the possible inability to distinguish political opposition from subversion, must be addressed. Thus the key question becomes: *"To what extent should individual rights be curtailed in the interests of public safety and national security in an emergent African nation?"* (p. 97, emphasis added). This realism carries an irony that is representative of the literature's attitude toward human rights. Although Asante refers to freedoms of association and expression as "fundamental freedoms," he finds it "obvious" that the limits on those freedoms are not the same in a struggling new nation as in a stable democracy (p. 97). The problem is that the word "fundamental" must mean something more than "important" if human rights are to have any significance. For those who can invoke necessity—including the security of the ruling group against dangers real or imagined—to justify encroachments on fundamental freedoms, the freedoms are simply not fundamental at all.

This apparent desire to have it both ways—characteristic of the realist approach—is evident in Asante's discussion of personal liberty. He describes the indiscriminate use of preventive detention without due process as an instrument of terror to protect "corrupt, repressive and irresponsible" regimes.

> Nevertheless, a realist cannot entirely rule out the possibility that preventive detention could, with certain safeguards . . . , be a legitimate exercise of state power in certain situations in any emergent country. Preventive detention may, in certain circumstances, indeed be unavoidable as a means of preserving democracy in the formative stages of some emergent nations, provided it is hedged about with safeguards [pp. 98–99].

Whether this failure to come to terms with the meaning of "fundamental" is simply an understandable by-product of nation building or something more intrinsic to African culture is, in a sense, the question that always remains.

The realist position, with its wistful pessimism, is also reflected in the writing of Rhoda Howard. She describes the building of the nation-state as imposing certain structural limitations, impediments to the realization of human rights. Thus African states, not yet truly nations, cannot afford the right to criticize, which secure nations can afford. A variety of factors lead Howard to conclude that "economic and social conditions are not conducive to human rights": tenuous individual loyalty to the state; the lack of a sense that the state exercises authority legitimately; ethnic, religious, and linguistic differences that contribute to secessionist tendencies; and a lack of "mediating institutions" that can act as "'countervailing powers' to the state."[8] Her pessimism leaves her in a position to make the tepid conclusion that "nevertheless, there is no excuse for *some* of the abuses of power which occur" (p. 747, emphasis added).

For Haile, the critical factor in the realization of human rights is the existence, not of an appropriate philosophical tradition, but of the necessary economic and social conditions.[9] In the West, changes produced those necessary conditions. In Africa, the situation is paradoxical. "Increasingly conditions are being created in Africa, which, on the one hand, necessitate the observance of human rights, while, on the other hand, make their observance difficult in the present social and economic context" (p. 587). Haile lists, with sympathy, the "problems and perceptions" of those who govern postindependence African states: national unity, especially with mistrust and jealousy between ethnic groups; fragile ruling coalitions; the ability of dissidents among urban elites to mobilize unrest; pressure on rulers that results in resource allocation and price and other policies with urban bias; "vulnerable economies, declining terms of trade, increasing energy costs, expanding populations, rising costs of government, demands for increased military expenditure, and high civil service salaries [that] create constant, often conflicting demands on very limited resources"; the "political weakness of the rural sector" and the need for foreign exchange, resulting in resources being allocated at the expense of peasant producers; "internal political instability and . . . external friction between states"; and "still unassimilated peoples with different loyalties and alliances," which contributes to the "fear of secession" and the diversion of a large share of resources from development to security and defense and further frustrates rising social and economic demands (pp. 593–98).

Haile recognizes that "unity in a heterogeneous society requires continued open discussion of the mutuality of interests and emphasis on common goals, aspirations and destiny" and, therefore "a sense of com-

---

8. Rhoda Howard, "The Dilemma of Human Rights in Sub-Saharan Africa," *International Journal*, vol. 35 (1980), pp. 738–42, 747.

9. Haile, "Human Rights, Stability, and Development," pp. 587–98.

monality" among ethnically diverse people as to both the fruits and burdens of independence and development (p. 594). But realism brings him to the conclusion "that in the circumstances in which modernization is taking place in most of the African countries today, democracy is not a viable political institution" because political and economic demands cannot be met and thus must be suppressed by denying civil and political rights. Similarly, personal security rights must yield to the demands for "national cohesion and political stability" when those values are precarious and when guaranteeing such rights requires the use of scarce resources (pp. 599–601).

Haile traps himself in the same inconsistency reflected in Asante and Howard, an inevitably half-hearted appeal for whatever rights are consistent with the needs of nation building in the difficult circumstances present in Africa: "Authoritarian governments in Africa should observe those personal security rights that can co-exist with authoritarianism" (p. 603). It is clear that this means less than the full panoply of rights set forth in the International Bill of Human Rights; it is not clear just who is to determine which ones (although, as discussed below, Haile gives examples of a few rights that should be respected in any circumstances, rights that might be called fundamental). Haile's focus on the conclusion that all these circumstances have created an environment "inhospitable to an adequate observance of human rights" does not get us very far in assessing the ultimate prospects for human rights in Africa. No one would argue that the observance of human rights is easy in this environment. The further question is whether there are conditions that make the setting not just inhospitable, but *incompatible*, with human rights.

More or less the same list of obstacles is catalogued by John K. Ebiasah: problems of national unity, with internal warfare and violent political opposition, brought about by tribal attachments; continuing tribal and ethnic antagonisms; the use by opposition parties of violent methods learned during the anticolonialist period; and the pattern of attempted coups and assassinations.[10] In the newly independent African states, these factors led quickly to a turn away from democracy in favor of one-party governments marked by the suppression of opposition.

10. John K. Ebiasah, "Protecting the Human Rights of Political Detainees: The Contradictions and Paradoxes in the African Experience," *Howard Law Journal*, vol. 22, no. 3 (1979), pp. 257–59.

While Ebiasah recognizes the real threat of "reckless, irresponsible opposition" (p. 259), he finally rejects these difficulties as a justification for a lowered standard of human rights.

> Detention of political opponents cannot hasten the development of the African peoples whose independence dates back only twenty-two years. What the people need are political leaders who are committed to the establishment of democratic institutions based upon the rule of law and respect for the inherent worth of the individual as a human being entitled to the recognition of his fundamental human rights [p. 280].

Wai adamantly rejects the imperatives of nation building as a justification for human rights abuses. He summarizes the arguments advanced by African leaders to support infringements on individual rights[11]—the difficulty of nation building within artificial boundaries imposed by the colonial powers, the lack of the physical means of national security, the overriding concern with "stability, order and authority . . . to bring about prosperity for all citizens," all requiring some sacrifice of rights "for the common good of all" (p. 120). Similarly, he notes, leaders argue that "the priority of African states is economic development and elimination of hunger, disease, and illiteracy" (p. 120). Therefore, opposition to the policies necessary to achieve these ends must be suppressed. Wai finds these arguments unpersuasive.

> The above arguments seem to stem from the beliefs that in the pursuit of political strength and economic development criticism of policy makers is harmful, that there should be no dissent, and that the presidents are immune from doing wrong. . . . [S]tability has been used as a mask—a convenient cover for a lust for power and wealth that has driven African leaders to maximize their powers of detention to perpetuate their rule. That is, it is not so much a concern for protection of society and the fundamental human rights of its members that motivates the banning of opposition parties and the perfection of colonial detention laws. Rather it is a desire for authoritarian power and personal protection of the leaders. *Considerations of stability require a high respect and regard for rights and not their suppression.*

So far, political restrictions in Africa have proved counterproduc-

---

11. Wai, "Human Rights in Sub-Saharan Africa," pp. 120–21.

tive and repression has produced negative results [p. 121, emphasis added].

If Wai is correct that the legitimate needs of nation building cannot account for Africa's poor human rights record, is he also correct in attributing that record to the desire for power and the protection of ruling elites? Or, if true stability requires respect for rights, is there something basic to the African context that, regardless of economic and political circumstances, condemns the continent to a bleak human rights future?

The Role of Traditional Culture

Assessments of the relationship between traditional African culture and human rights are carried on at a high level of generalization and present a remarkably consistent theme. The discussion suggests that there was a monolithic set of values that characterized African traditional society. The paradigmatic assessment begins with an assertion that values associated with human rights norms were present and important in traditional society. An early example of this view is found in the late-eighteenth-century work of an African writer, Ottobah Cugoano, about slaves taken from Africa. "Their freedom and rights are as dear to them as those privileges are to other peole. And it may be said that freedom, and the liberty of enjoying their own privileges, burns with as much zeal and fervor in the breast of an Aethiopian, as in the breast of any inhabitant on the globe." [12]

The next step in the paradigm is to identify these values. Often this takes the form of a list of rights that were respected in traditional society. Almost always, the values presented as positive for human rights are distinguished as uniquely African values, giving rise to a conception of human rights appropriate for Africa, as opposed to those Western values embodied in international human rights norms. Finally, in this paradigm the failure to incorporate these traditional values in the institutions and practices of postcolonial African nations is noted and attributed to the colonial legacy and the problems of nation building.

Most of the writing on this subject finds that human rights were recognized and protected in some significant way in traditional African society. This writing is general and cites very little specific, concrete evi-

---

12. Ottobah Cugoano, *Thoughts and Sentiments on the Evils of Slavery* (1787), pp. 25–29; quoted in Thomas L. Hodgkin, "The Relevance of 'Western' Ideas for the New African States," in J. Roland Pennock, ed., *Self-Government in Modernizing Nations* (Prentice-Hall, 1964), p. 55.

dence. Accounts tend to fall roughly into one of two categories. Some conclude that human rights consistent with universal norms were respected in traditional Africa. Others, the majority, find that human rights were recognized and protected, but that they were part of a uniquely African concept of human rights. Given the generality of these conclusions and the mixing, or blurring, of the two categories in some accounts, it may be somewhat artificial to attempt to put them in categories, but it is important to see the different tendencies and consider their possible implications.

The view that traditional values embodied respect for the equivalent of modern international human rights. Those authors who assert a close kinship between modern universal human rights norms and traditional African values make three kinds of arguments. Again, they often combine these. First, some find and list evidence of the valuation and protection of specific rights in traditional society. Others describe the political structure of traditional society and attempt to show that respect for individual rights was inherent in that structure. Finally, some rely on the presence within traditional societies of a fundamental value that is consistent with or even equivalent to respect for human rights.

Lakshman Marasinghe looks directly to "traditional customs and systems of law" as the ultimate basis for protection of human rights in Africa.[13] Recognizing that traditional conceptions of human rights, unlike modern conceptions, were not universalist but depended on membership in a particular group, Marasinghe claims, "The right to membership, the freedom of thought, speech, belief, and association, and the right to enjoy property have all been recognized by most traditional societies as fundamental human rights" (p. 33). After detailing these rights and explaining some limitations on them, Marasinghe concludes by defining human rights as "powers" held by individuals and finds that they exist in all "civilized systems" and "traditional societies." The right, then, is to have the individual's power enforced against the state or other individuals. It is in nontraditional legal systems that obstacles to such enforcement may occur, he says; the structure of traditional society, without modern limitations on access to justice, provided a more secure guarantee against human rights violations than do the transitory constitutions of nontraditional societies (pp. 42–43). The existence of particular rights in traditional society and the internalization of these rights

---

13. Lakshman Marasinghe, "Traditional Conceptions of Human Rights in Africa," in Welch and Meltzer, eds., *Human Rights and Development*, p. 32.

within the structure of society seem a fragile basis for Marsinghe's confidence in the invulnerability of the traditional African conception of human rights.

M'Baye is a proponent of the notion of an essential difference between the Western and the traditional conceptions of human rights. However, he finds that traditional Africa had a system of rights that, while not formulated like modern conceptions, shows "a definite kinship which undeniably links them to the present system of human rights."[14] M'Baye then describes how traditional African "humanism led to religious respect for others" (p. 589) and the recognition and protection of their rights, including the rights to life, work, and education, and the freedoms of expression, religion, association, and movement. M'Baye oversimplifies in showing the existence of some of these rights. For example, his only argument for the existence of freedom of association is that "Africans formed all kinds of groups among themselves" (p. 590). This confusion of the presence of certain kinds of behavior with the *right* to engage in such behavior is another weakness in the argument based on the protection of specific rights in traditional society.

For some, the list of rights protected in traditional society becomes a more general point. Wai points specifically to the freedoms of expression and association in traditional African life in arguing that "traditional African attitudes, beliefs, institutions, and experiences sustained the 'view that certain rights should be upheld against alleged necessities of state.'"[15] But Wai's real point about traditional African society is that the political system was one of limited government power, with checks on abuses of power and institutionalized participation in decisions. The flaw in Wai's argument that "traditional African societies supported and practiced human rights" is his implicit conflation of human rights and a particular form of government—democratic institutions incorporating checks on the power of rulers.[16] That such a system may have respected

14. M'Baye, "Human Rights in Africa," p. 588.
15. Wai, "Human Rights in Sub-Saharan Africa, pp. 116–17, quoting Weisfelder, "Decline of Human Rights in Lesotho," p. 22.
16. Wai, "Human Rights in Sub-Saharan Africa," p. 117. Compare Osita C. Eze, *Human Rights in Africa: Some Selected Problems* (Lagos: Nigerian Institute of International Affairs, in Cooperation with MacMillan Nigeria Publishers, 1984), pp. 10–13. Eze emphasizes that traditional African legal systems were quite advanced, norms of conduct were not markedly different from modern norms, and human rights existed, but he disputes the idea that these observations can support a broad inference that human rights were recognized and protected in traditional African society.

certain values that we now define as human rights does not imply that those values were viewed as rights that *must* be respected.

Haile also identifies the consensual basis of politics within groups in traditional society, but finds this an entirely inadequate constraint on power in the modern context.[17] He does not take the differences in expression and institutionalization of rights between traditional Africa and the West as evidence of "inherent differences in the concept of human rights" (p. 585). In fact, as evidence that the African and Western conceptions of human rights are not entirely different, he notes that the African Charter on Human and Peoples' Rights incorporates principles of participatory democracy from the Universal Declaration of Human Rights (p. 586). This is an oversimplification that fails to distinguish between cultural tradition and a modern political choice influenced by many factors, including modern Western values. Nevertheless, Haile's ultimate point here is that "the existence of a general philosophical tradition embracing human rights" is not an important concern. His thesis is that, whether or not there was such a tradition in the West, "the practical realization of human rights in Western society . . . [lies] in the economic and social changes that have created the necessary conditions for the protection of those rights" (p. 587).

Haile's almost casual assertion of comparability between Western and traditional African traditions of human rights is a corollary of his argument that what matters is economic and social conditions. His emphasis on those conditions as a prerequisite for realizing human rights is an important contribution to the discussion. But his correct observation that a philosophic tradition does not "*necessarily* preordain that a society will be characterized by the observance of human rights" (p. 587, emphasis added)—that it is not a sufficient cause—seems to lead him to an assumption that such a tradition is also not a necessary cause. As a result, it is not important for him to inquire into the existence of such a tradition. This paper argues, however, that some such conception or value is a necessary condition for respecting human rights. Thus an inquiry into the existence of such a tradition becomes important.

Asante's analysis embodies variations of two of the arguments for finding traditional society consistent with modern human rights norms. He finds respect for human rights inherent in the traditional African legal structure, and he identifies human dignity as a fundamental value in traditional African culture. Although his description of African legal

17. Haile, "Human Rights, Stability, and Development," pp. 584–85.

systems involves what sounds like a list of specific rights, its essential point is about the way structure and process safeguarded human rights.

The notion of due process of law permeated indigenous law; deprivation of personal liberty or property was rare; security of the person was assured, and customary legal process was characterized not by unpredictable and harsh encroachments upon the individual by the sovereign, but by meticulous, if cumbersome, procedures for decision-making. The African conception of human rights was an essential aspect of African humanism sustained by religious doctrine and the principle of accountability to the ancestral spirits. In any case indigenous African culture revolved around the family or the clan; government by the sovereign was essentially limited. The concept of accountability of the chief to the people was well-settled and so there was little opportunity for violation of human rights. Violation of community norms invariably led to the deposition of the chief.[18]

This portrayal is open to the criticism that it equates certain features of limited government with respect for human rights. However, it suggests the importance of a more fundamental cultural concept informing this structure. Asante states the presence of this concept more explicitly when he says that "traditional African concepts of humanism unequivocally asserted the dignity and worth of man" (p. 102). Because, for Asante, the purpose of human rights is the protection of human dignity, the presence of this concept in traditional African society provides the critical link with universal human rights norms.

In his account of the Butare Colloquium on Human Rights and Economic Development in Francophone Africa held in Butare, Rwanda, in 1978, Hurst Hannum reports that a working group of African jurists and other experts identified six "traditional rights which it believed should influence modern human rights concepts: the right to life, the right to education, the right to freedom of movement, the right to receive justice, the right to work and the right to participate in the benefits and decision-making of the community."[19] The group concluded that "many rights now included in the category of 'international human rights' were in fact protected in traditional African societies, usually by

18. Asante, "Nation Building and Human Rights," pp. 73–74.
19. Hurst Hannum, "The Butare Colloquium on Human Rights and Economic Development in Francophone Africa: A Summary and Analysis," *Universal Human Rights*, vol. 1 (April–June 1979), p. 64.

custom and consensus rather than by formal guarantees." But the group went beyond this mere identification of a list of comparable rights, which may tell us very little, to a broader comparison. The group agreed that there must be respect for a traditional "African concept of human rights, which is not, in any event, very different from modern concepts" (p. 69). Hannum does not elaborate on this assertion of similarity. Indeed, when more thorough interpretations of the notion of a unique traditional African concept of human rights are examined, the claim of substantial similarity with modern international concepts seems hard to sustain.

The view that traditional society embodied a uniquely African concept of human rights. The idea that pervades the discussion of human rights in Africa is that there is a unique African concept of human rights based on traditional African values that are fundamentally at odds with the Western values underlying international human rights norms. According to this view, that difference makes international human rights inappropriate for the African context. Even those writers who do not subscribe to this idea often begin by noting their rejection of it. Perhaps more important, this idea is identified with contemporary African leadership. For example, "Civilian leaders of most of the independent English-speaking African states do accept, at least publicly, the Western ideals of civil and political freedom, but in so doing they often stress the unique African context of these ideals." [20] Indeed, when African experts met in Dakar in November 1979 to prepare a draft African charter on human rights, their stated objective was "to prepare an African human rights instrument based upon an African legal philosophy and responsive to African needs." [21]

The notion of appropriateness clearly refers to more than contemporary social and economic conditions. It entails a conviction that Western values are intrinsically incompatible with African culture and cannot be shoehorned into it. [22] For Asmarom Legesse, the effort itself to impose universal human rights norms on Africa is a serious violation of human rights, "an endemic problem that constitutes a threat to the rest of mankind." [23] He articulates a sweeping indictment of the Western lib-

20. Howard, "Dilemma of Human Rights," p. 729.
21. Yougindra Khushalani, "Human Rights in Asia and Africa," *Human Rights Law Journal*, vol. 4, no. 4 (1983), p. 436.
22. See, for example, Mojekwu, "International Human Rights," p. 92.
23. Asmarom Legesse, "Human Rights in African Political Culture," in Kenneth W.

eral democracies for the entire modern international human rights undertaking.

> Their offense is simply the fact that they are still engaged in a civilizing mission vis-à-vis the rest of mankind. They still define the problem of human rights as one of lack of proper political education in the underdeveloped world. They have already succeeded in writing most of their values and code of ethics into the Universal Declaration. Hence, the human rights movement faces the danger of becoming an instrument of cultural imperialism. To the extent that the West fails to realize that other cultural traditions may be as deeply committed to rights, although approaching it from a different ethical perspective, to that extent the movement rests on false premises and tends to legitimize the behavior it seeks to eradicate [p. 130].

This rendition of the conflict between international human rights norms and African values as a violation of human rights is atypical. Nevertheless, the fundamental notion that there is such a conflict, that there is a uniquely African concept of human rights, that cultural differences make international human rights norms inappropriate for the African context is a theme that runs through most of the literature.

What then is the essential difference between African and Western cultures that the authors maintain compels this conclusion? Again, despite different formulations, one primary theme and one subtheme dominate the discussion. The key difference is that African traditional society and culture are characterized as communal or group oriented in contrast to Western individualistic values. According to Legesse:

> One critical difference between African and Western traditions concerns the importance of the human individual. In the liberal democracies of the Western world the ultimate repository of rights is the human person. The individual is held in a virtually sacralized position. There is a perpetual, and in our view obsessive, concern with the dignity of the individual, his worth, personal autonomy, and property.[24]

Thompson, ed., *The Moral Imperatives of Human Rights: A World Survey* (Washington, D.C.: University Press of America, 1980), p. 130.

24. Legesse, "Human Rights in African Political Culture," p. 124. See also Khushalani, "Human Rights in Asia and Africa," p. 414.

In traditional Africa, on the other hand, the community or the group was preeminent, according to these accounts. For example, Yougindra Khushalani asserts:

> African law in general is a law of the group, not only because it applies to micro-societies (lineage, tribe, ethnic group, clan, family) but also because the role of the individual in it is insignificant.
>
> In traditional African societies the importance of the community was emphasized and the individual rights had to be viewed within the context of the community. . . . For that reason, human rights in traditional Africa have their own distinctive cause, aim and function [p. 415].

After describing individual activity in traditional Africa as evidence of the existence of specific rights and freedoms, Khushalani attributes the African respect for rights to traditional society's communal values. He asserts that

> the principle of individual rights within the framework of the legitimate concerns of the community has long been a part of African life. Suffice it to say that African societies stressed the rights of individuals and groups within their social, economic and cultural dimensions. . . .
>
> The prevailing attitude of consensus and understanding resulted in an almost sacred protection of the right to life, liberty and security of person, the right to association and the right to freedom of opinion and expression, even in the religious sphere [p. 418].

The emphatic quality with which Khushalani imbues his account of the group orientation of traditional African society is not present in Asante's account. Although he ultimately finds a strong human rights concept in traditional Africa, Asante observes the difficulty of translating group-based rights norms into the modern developing African state. Still, it is within a value system based on the group that Asante identifies a traditional African concern for human rights.

> Traditional indigenous political systems were predicated on some notion of a rule of law, but the norms prevailing in traditional Africa were essentially concerned with regulating interaction between groups—families, clans and the like—and with ensuring equilibrium

of the whole community. The individual had status and security within his immediate group, but it was unusual for the individual to be involved in a direct confrontation with the sovereign, outside the criminal law.[25]

Asante does not say that the Western human rights concept is wholly incompatible with African traditional culture, but that it is a concept that would have had to be and has not been "assimilated" into the African value system. Although both Africa and the West have basic human rights concepts, they are different, according to Asante, and those differences are significant to a realistic appraisal of the prospects for human rights in Africa.[26]

Virtually inseparable from the notion of group orientation is the subtheme that group membership is crucial to the recognition of individual rights. The integration of these themes can be seen in Welch's account. Recognizing African traditional society's emphasis on collective or communal rights, he notes that individual rights were exercised, but within "the web of kinship." They existed only "in the context of the extended family; they were not inherent in individuals, but latent in ascriptive groups." Liberties "did not exist in the abstract, as rights inherent in *all* human beings," but only within a particular context.[27]

This notion that individual rights existed, but applied only to members of the group, is expressed with only slight variation by these writers. Chris C. Mojekwu observes that

the concept of human rights in Africa was fundamentally based on ascribed status. It was a person's place of birth, his membership or belonging to a particular locality and within a particular social unit that gave content and meaning to his human rights—social, economic, and political. A person had to be born into a social unit or somehow belong to it in order to have any rights which the law of the land could protect. One who had lost his membership in a social unit or one who did not belong—an outcast or a stranger—lived

25. Asante, "Nation Building and Human Rights," p. 100.

26. See also Howard, "Evaluating Human Rights in Africa," pp. 173–74; M'Baye, "Human Rights in Africa," p. 588; Ifeanyi A. Menkiti, "Person and Community in African Thought," in Richard A. Wright, ed., *African Philosophy: An Introduction,* 3d ed. (New York: University Press of America, 1984), pp. 171–80; and Mojekwu, "International Human Rights," pp. 87–92.

27. Welch, "Human Rights as a Problem," pp. 11, 15–17.

outside the range of human rights protection by the social unit. Such strangers to the community had no rights except those which they could negotiate through their hosts or protectors.[28]

This concept of rights dependent upon membership in a particular group is, of course, very different from the modern concept of universal rights. As Latif O. Adegbite notes, the individual's dependence on group membership for protection of his rights had serious consequences for anyone excluded from the relevant group. "Slaves, serfs, aliens, and to some extent, women enjoyed lesser rights." In stratified societies, all but the ruling race were treated as outsiders.[29]

Ifeanyi A. Menkiti's explanation of this difference gives it more substance. The very notion of being a person, thus a being to whom individual rights might apply, is fundamentally different from the Western concept.

> Persons become persons only after a process of incorporation. Without incorporation into this or that community, individuals are considered to be mere danglers to whom the description "person" does not fully apply. For personhood is something which has to be achieved, and is not given simply because one is born of human seed. . . . Thus, it is not enough to have before us the biological organism, with whatever rudimentary psychological characteristics are seen as attaching to it. We must also conceive of this organism as going through a long process of social and ritual transformation until it attains the full complement of excellencies seen as truly definitive of man.[30]

The combination of these two related concepts—the emphasis on collective or communal or group rights over individual rights and the dependence of individual rights on ascribed status within a group—provides the core of the uniquely African concept of human rights proclaimed by these authors. In some form, most of these writers find such a unique concept and view it as an ultimately positive factor for the future of human rights in Africa.

28. Mojekwu, "International Human Rights," p. 86.

29. Latif O. Adegbite, "African Attitudes to the International Protection of Human Rights," in Asbjorn Eide and August Schou, eds., *International Protection of Human Rights,* Proceedings of the Seventh Nobel Symposium, Oslo, September 25–27, 1967 (New York: Interscience Publishers, 1968), p. 69.

30. Menkiti, "Person and Community in African Traditional Thought," p. 172.

Inconsistencies with human rights norms in traditional society. Only quite rarely, and usually as exceptions within accounts otherwise describing general recognition of human rights in traditional society, are traditional values inconsistent with human rights identified in the literature. Asante, for instance, describes traditional African culture as embracing human rights concepts "despite occasional aberrations on the part of a despotic ruler."[31]

Eze criticizes as "rather romantic" the view, represented by M'Baye, that African society was humanist in a way that necessarily led to scrupulous respect for individual rights. He identifies derogations from human rights that were more than "occasional aberrations." In particular, as a form of feudalism emerged in many African societies, with an exploiting class of feudal lords, the exercise of individual rights was "subject to their dictates." Eze acknowledges the existence of human rights in African societies but argues that the extent of their protection depended on the "concrete material living conditions of a given politico-socioeconomic formation." Most important, Eze points out that "traditional African societies knew of *institutionalized derogations* from human rights."[32] These included slavery, a caste system, human sacrifice, and the killing of twins. Eze makes an important contribution to the discussion simply by pointing out that the picture of human rights in traditional African societies is not as bright as most of the accounts suggest.

Other accounts also question the paradigm. Howard challenges the notion that traditional African society was a consensual community "presided over by just elders" with a moral basis for their authority, who guaranteed justice.

> Even within communal groups, there were status divisions which could result in conflicts of interest—between elders and young men, males and females, freemen and slaves. African empires rose and fell, and conquered tribes were subject to their conquerors. . . . Moreover, some of the "integrative" religious customs of traditional societies, such as ritual deaths and the killing of twins, would constitute supreme violations of human rights as they are defined in the twentieth-century context. Thus there is no real evidence that injustice did not exist in traditional African society.[33]

31. Asante, "Nation Building and Human Rights," p. 73, citing Max Gluckman, "Natural Justice in Africa," *Natural Law Forum* (1964), p. 25.
32. Eze, *Human Rights in Africa*, pp. 12–13 (emphasis added).
33. Howard, "Dilemma of Human Rights," pp. 733–34.

Howard concludes her discussion of traditional African human rights values by commenting that appeals to tribal ideology and traditionalism can and have been used to maintain power or "mask the desire to exploit."

Warren Weinstein provides a specific example of the way the importance of traditional group membership translates into human rights difficulties in modern Africa. He describes the reliance of modern leaders in Zaire on family and ethnic groups and the exclusion of others. This, according to Weinstein, "places critical limits on the ability of African leaders to develop institutions that take into account the human rights of those who are outside their family and ethnic group or region."[34]

Jack Donnelly, perhaps exclusively, finds a fundamental lack of a human rights concept in traditional African society. His thesis is that "most non-Western cultural and political traditions lack not only the practice of human rights but the very concept."[35] In the specific context of Africa, Donnelly points out that many who argue that there were human rights in traditional Africa base this conclusion on "little more than a demonstration of the existence of limited government."[36] Similarly, Donnelly says, claims that distributive justice was a central principle in traditional Africa are irrelevant because it is a different concept from that of human rights. He concludes his section on Africa with this statement: "Recognition of human rights simply was not the way of traditional Africa, with obvious and important consequences for political practice" (p. 308). Significantly, although Donnelly is confident that neither concern for, nor recognition of, human rights was present in traditional African society, he recognizes that a concern for human dignity "would appear to be a prerequisite for human rights notions" (p. 307). His point is to challenge claims that non-Western societies, including African traditional society, actually recognized or protected human rights. He does not evaluate the value of the *questions* that these claims purport to answer. Nor does he consider whether general notions

34. Warren Weinstein, "Human Rights and Development in Africa: Dilemmas and Options," *Daedalus*, vol. 112 (Fall 1983), p. 182.

35. Jack Donnelly, "Human Rights and Human Dignity: An Analytic Critique of Non-Western Conceptions of Human Rights," *American Political Science Review*, vol. 76 (June 1982), p. 303.

36. Donnelly, "Human Rights and Human Dignity," p. 308. Donnelly is correct in this assessment. Also, this confusion of limited government with human rights parallels other erroneous equations in the literature. For example, the tolerance for certain types of non-conforming behavior is often mistakenly identified as the existence of a human right to engage in such behavior.

of human dignity are truly meaningful prerequisites for human rights concepts.

Seeking a Basis for a Commitment to the Human Rights Concept

The literature discussing factors that have contributed to postcolonial Africa's poor human rights record has certainly been useful. On the other hand, the search for evidence that traditional African societies protected human rights and respected human dignity may have obscured a question that is important to the future of human rights in Africa. No one doubts that contemporary conditions and the colonial legacy constitute substantial obstacles to the realization of human rights. But it is worth considering whether, even if these problems could be solved, even if the necessary social, political, and economic prerequisites were established, there is something inherent in African cultural values that can be the foundation for a commitment to a human rights concept. Do its traditional values make Africa fertile ground, at least, for the ultimate observance of human rights? Or, asked in the negative, is there something inherent in traditional African society that is radically incompatible with modern international human rights norms?

Perhaps this is the question that writers believe they are answering when they observe that certain rights were respected in traditional African society.[37] But the fact that particular rights were protected does not at all demonstrate the existence of a fundamental belief in the equivalent of a human rights concept. Nor does the uncovering of serious injustices in traditional society mean that such a belief necessarily did not exist. Some suggest that it might be more appropriate to compare Africa today to the West of premodern Europe because of greater comparability of economic and political development.[38] This reflects a proper recognition of the conditions that preceded the relatively recent emergence in the West of international human rights norms. The call for a comparison with an earlier period in European history also recognizes that the long, awful chronicle of Western cruelty—slavery, inquisition, torture, and modern genocide—was not inconsistent with the *eventual* emergence of a human rights concept. This only underscores the importance of looking to traditional African culture for some value,

37. See, for example, All Africa Council of Churches, "Factors Responsible for the Violation," p. 44.
38. See Howard, "Evaluating Human Rights," pp. 165–66, 178.

or cluster of values, equivalent to what must have existed in the West— some seed awaiting the proper conditions to blossom into a concept of universal human rights.

When so many writers have identified what they call a uniquely African concept of human rights, is it necessary to inquire further into the possibility of a value consistent with the development of a human rights concept that is compatible with modern international norms? These writers, after all, claim that the Universal Declaration of Human Rights derives from the Western liberal democracies and so, while universal in intent, is not universal in derivation. Thus Africans should see the norms of the Universal Declaration as an alien system imposed from without.[39] This view is accurate in a superficial, descriptive way. Certainly the documents of the international human rights system, their contents, and their language are Western in origin.[40] But that in itself tells us nothing. That a particular articulation of an idea arises from or in a particular culture does not mean that the idea itself is peculiar to that culture.[41]

The Importance of Universality

The importance of a search for a common value or belief that can be the source of an eventual human rights concept lies in one simple truth: the very idea of human rights means nothing if it does not mean *universal* human rights. The goal of international human rights norms is to establish a standard that disregards national sovereignty in order to protect individuals from abuse. To have human rights at all is to say that there are certain standards below which no state or society can go regardless of its own cultural values. When Marasinghe says, "But if one were to conduct empirical research into the internalized conceptions of human rights recognized by a traditional society, one would find enormous satisfaction as to the basically democratic way in which the society protects its own human values,"[42] he inadvertently discards the entire notion of international human rights, which necessarily entails circumscribing the scope of cultural relativism. The implication of statements like Marasinghe's—that any values are acceptable if they are the values of that society—is so relativist as to make the idea of human

39. Legesse, "Human Rights in African Political Culture," pp. 123, 124.
40. See, for example, Laurie S. Wiseberg, "Human Rights in Africa: Toward the Definition of the Problem of a Double Standard," *Issue,* vol. 6 (Winter 1976), p. 6.
41. See Asante, "Nation Building and Human Rights," p. 102.
42. Marasinghe, "Traditional Conceptions of Human Rights," p. 43.

rights vanish. Donnelly rejects the assumption that the claim of human rights' universality is false. He recognizes the factors that contributed to a human rights concept becoming the modern Western approach to human dignity. But he refuses to assume that the historical fact of the Western evolution of human rights necessarily contradicts their universality.

> At the very least it must be noted in response that if we take seriously the idea of human rights, we must recognize them as both a historical product and of universal validity. As the rights of man, as human rights, they cannot be treated as merely a historical product without destroying the concept. In fact, the idea of human rights would even seem to demand of us a concern for their realization universally, even though we know that the concept was first formulated and institutionalized in a particular civilization at a particular time. Such a demand is a difficult one to be sure, but it is one that seems unavoidable if we are not to renounce human rights in the name of avoiding cultural neo-imperialism.[43]

The argument for a uniquely African concept of human rights seems to begin with the *assumption* that human rights are not universal; therefore, uniquely African values must be embedded in a concept of human rights that is different and separate from the modern international concept. The truth that human rights are not human rights at all unless they are universal points to a fundamental core of rights, basic rights, that must be adhered to all by societies.[44] Peter L. Berger, for example, distinguishes between rights that emerge from an exclusively Western view and those that derive from a wider consensus. The grossest abuses of human rights—genocide, terror, torture, religious persecution, destruction of ethnic institutions—call for condemnation that is based on a consensus much wider than Western civilization, one that emerges from all the major world cultures. For Berger, notions of respect for humans are common to all these cultures and provide the basis for fundamental human rights.[45] Above that basic level, different cultures may

43. Donnelly, "Human Rights and Human Dignity," p. 314.

44. See, for example, Laurie S. Wiseberg and Warren Weinstein, "A Note from the Editors," *Issue,* vol. 6 (Winter 1976), p. 1; and Howard, "Dilemma of Human Rights," pp. 724–25.

45. Peter L. Berger, "Are Human Rights Universal?" *Commentary,* vol. 64 (September 1977), pp. 60–63.

choose to establish different, additional norms that reflect their particular values. Asante endorses the idea that basic human rights are applicable to Africa when he asks whether all human rights deserve equal status.

> There is a strong case for devising some sort of hierarchical scheme for human rights in Africa. . . . Rights pertaining to the enjoyment of material resources or participation in the economic system may vary from country to country; but any advocate of human rights would assert the right to personal liberty in absolute terms. Democratic-minded persons may debate over the merits of free enterprise but *not* the essential validity of the right to freedom of conscience or freedom from inhuman treatment.[46]

In one sense, the notion of basic rights begs the question. By itself, it moves no closer to defining the content of a universal set of rights.

The problem of defining basic rights may, however, be considerably less controversial than that of defining an entire catalog of rights. Maurice Cranston's effort to demarcate the domain of human rights provides some guidance: "A human right, by definition, is something that no one, anywhere, may be deprived of without a grave affront to justice." While Cranston's definition leaves several terms to be defined, the distinction he is aiming at is useful. He says that a human right must be a "sharp, clear imperative," not just a vague wish. It is not an ideal or a standard of achievement and certainly not something that is impossible. In contrast to achieving particular economic or social goals, it is always possible to leave someone alone, which, according to Cranston, is why human rights are mostly negative.[47] Another way of putting this is that basic rights are primary because it is impossible for one to enjoy political, economic, or cultural rights if one is dead, in extreme physical pain from torture, or arbitrarily in prison.

At the very least, then, rights of personal security must be basic. Haile, while making some allowances for the pressures of political stability, sees some rights as, in effect, basic. For him, these are "individual rights the observance of which normally would neither adversely affect political stability nor require large expenditures." Like Cranston, Haile identifies most of these as negative and virtually cost-free, "requir[ing]

---

46. Asante, "Nation Building and Human Rights," p. 105.
47. Maurice Cranston, "Are There Any Human Rights?" *Daedalus*, vol. 112 (Fall 1983), pp. 12–13.

merely that a government abstain from rights-depriving acts." They include "rights against torture, the application of *ex post facto* laws, arbitrary deprivation of life, the proscription of slavery, rights to fair trial (at least in ordinary criminal cases) and freedom of religion."[48] Haile notes, "Those personal security rights, the implementation of which carry no significant political and financial implications, have been given special international status," particularly in article 4 of the International Covenant on Civil and Political Rights.[49] His conclusion, mentioned earlier, that "authoritarian governments in Africa should observe those personal security rights that can co-exist with authoritarianism" (p. 603) has a disturbing circularity, but it rests nonetheless on the acceptance of a core of basic rights that must be universal.

Basic Human Rights

Once the need to accept the universality of basic human rights is established, the problem with arguments that African human rights must be based on communal values becomes clear. The rights that evolve from communal values—people's rights or social, economic, and cultural rights—are simply not *alternatives* to basic human rights. If they are endorsed by the international community or the African community, they must be seen as something above and beyond basic rights. Even Khushalani, who makes perhaps the most emphatic argument against the universality of the "Western" concept of human rights, appears to concede this point even as he seeks to deny it. He criticizes the Western emphasis on individual rights and the resulting neglect of communal rights. He suggests that a culture's understanding of rights will always be particular to that culture. He concludes, "Evidently, there can be no universal understanding of human rights, *save perhaps at the level of certain commonly agreed and generally acceptable norms of State conduct.*"[50] Exactly. And those norms necessarily include the concept of basic human rights.

To show that some basic level of human rights must exist, even within a conception of communal values and rights based on them, does not do away with the insistence that the latter have a superior claim in the African context. Haile summarizes the controversy:

48. Haile, "Human Rights, Stability, and Development," p. 602.
49. Haile, "Human Rights, Stability, and Development," pp. 602–03. See also Wiseberg and Weinstein, "A Note from the Editors," p. 1.
50. Khushalani, "Human Rights in Asia and Africa," pp. 404–05 (emphasis added).

Recently there have been differences of opinion on whether or not priority in implementation should be given to some of the internationally-recognized human rights in preference to some of the other of such rights, in particular, whether the implementation of economic and social rights should be given preference over the realization of civil and political rights by the Third World. There are those who feel that the implementation of civil and political rights in the developing countries is inconsistent with the paramount aspirations of the peoples in those countries for a rapid economic development and political stability.[51]

To demand that no social or political vision can justify the violation of certain basic human rights embodied in modern international norms does not imply a diminished commitment to economic development and just distribution of the world's wealth. To place communal rights ahead of these basic rights of the individual is self-contradictory and has certainly not been shown to be necessary for the achievement of any communal goals.

Simply put, communities do not feel pain. Groups are composed of individuals. Legesse says Africans "might have ranked the rights of communities above those of individuals" if they had written the Universal Declaration. "The worst violations of human rights in history were those directed against entire peoples," Legesse says. He mentions the massacre of native American people, the African slave trade and the colonization of Africa, and the Armenian and Jewish holocausts as examples of "violations of peoples' rights on a massive scale."[52] This is certainly true, but it is not very meaningful. The emphasis on groups is arbitrary. The groups, by their very nature, do not exist without the individuals in them; it was individuals whose lives were lost in the European massacres of native Americans, in the slave trade, and in the death camps. Asante recognizes this in his rejection of the notion that in Africa the need for strong government and the need for human rights are incompatible. "But strong government, rapid economic development, high standards of living, and internal security are *ideas which are meaningful only insofar as they enrich the lives of individual citizens.*"[53]

The insistence, by so many of these writers, on the determinative significance for human rights of the conflict between traditional com-

---

51. Haile, "Human Rights, Stability, and Development," p. 606.
52. Legesse, "Human Rights in African Political Culture," p. 128.
53. Asante, "Nation Building and Human Rights," p. 101 (emphasis added).

munal values and Western individualism remains little more than an assertion based on a cliché. Citing the proposition that African traditional society was communal, they conclude, with little argument, that this fact makes so-called Western individualistic human rights inappropriate for the African context. Donnelly's analysis accepts the truth of this distinction. He says, "One of the key differences between the modern Western and the non-Western approaches to human dignity is the much greater individualism of the Western human-rights approach." But he questions the significance of these differences for human rights. He also finds the geographic origin of a particular approach insignificant.[54] It simply remains unproved that an emphasis on community negates or even opposes a commitment to basic individual human rights.[55] Nor does it seem at all clear that a commitment to basic human rights compels the abstract primacy of the individual over the community.

Identifying a Source of the Human Rights Concept in the West

One must begin, then, by defining the source of the modern human rights concept in the West. Most commentators link such a concept to the development of notions of natural law. Natural law does provide a philosophical or metaphysical basis for the idea of universal human rights, but it is a problem for the purposes of this essay because its vocabulary is so intrinsically Western. Other writers argue that the foundation for human rights is a concern for human dignity.[56] This thesis, however, is seriously flawed. The idea of dignity is so vague as to embrace almost anything. It would be difficult to demonstrate that any culture did not entail some concern for human dignity. As such, it gives

54. Donnelly, "Human Rights and Human Dignity," p. 311.
55. Khushalani's attempt to show that the individualism of the West has no place in developing countries because of the predominance of communalism is, thus, unconvincing. "From the practical experience in many developing states, it is evident that in most states in the world, human rights as defined by the West are rejected or, more accurately, are meaningless. Most states do not have a cultural heritage of individualism, and the doctrines of inalienable human rights have been neither disseminated nor assimilated. The State has become the embodiment of the people, and the individual has no rights or freedoms that are natural and outside the purview of the State." Khushalani, "Human Rights in Asia and Africa," p. 414. Even if the descriptive accuracy of this statement is granted, it remains descriptive. It offers nothing conclusive about the compatability of traditional communal societies and the concept of protecting the individual from violation of basic human rights.
56. See generally, for example, Myres S. McDougal and others, *Human Rights and World Public Order: The Basic Policies of an International Law of Human Dignity* (Yale University Press, 1980); and Asante, "Nation Building and Human Rights," p. 102.

us little to talk about. More important, a concern for human dignity can coexist with values and conduct that are fundamentally hostile to human rights. Donnelly argues that "human rights present only one path to the realization of human dignity. . . . [T]here are conceptions of human dignity which do not imply human rights, and societies and institutions which aim to realize human dignity entirely independent of human rights." Donnelly also says, as noted earlier, that a concern for human dignity "would appear to be a prerequisite for human rights notions."[57] This may be true, but its generality severely limits its usefulness even as a prerequisite.

What must be sought is not a philosophical *justification* for human rights—natural law arguments seek to prove the necessary existence of human rights—but a cultural belief from which a commitment to human rights has a chance to develop. While there are different views of the philosophical basis of human rights in the West (Christian, Judaic, classical, liberal), do all of them have some common, central theme? Do those who attribute Western notions of rights and freedom to the Enlightenment miss some more primal belief that had to be there before changing conditions could bring about a concept of human rights?

For the limited purpose of exploring the possibility of the kind of cultural comparison proposed here, it is enough to postulate, as a good candidate for such a primal belief, the biblical idea that man and woman are created in the image of God. It is not necessary to accept this idea in any literal, religious way. It is, however, at least a powerful metaphor for the notion that to trod on any person is to trod on the "divinity." In a secular version, human reason is a rough equivalent of "in the image of God." An inseparable part of this theme is the fact that man and woman alone possess knowledge of their own mortality. The power of this knowledge links the secular to the spiritual. It is at the heart of the modern psyche as much as it is at the heart of the biblical creation myth. While the implications of this cluster of ideas for human values and conduct are ineffable, some belief akin to it seems a prerequisite for a universal human rights concept. And while secular expressions of the theme are as powerful as religious ones, the phrase "in the image of God" provides the richest material for comparisons to traditional, spiritual societies.

The task then is not to look at African traditional society for a list of inconsistencies with human rights. Nor is it to look for a list of values

57. Donnelly, "Human Rights and Human Dignity," pp. 303, 307.

that merely support respect, in practice, for certain human rights. The task is to look past these, almost as distractions, for a value that constitutes an underlying, if latent, receptivity to the concept of universal human rights. It is not enough that "African academics have demonstrated that a variety of human rights values existed in African traditional society."[58] Nor is it enough, at the other end of the spectrum, to say that traditional African society encompassed practices and values that clash with modern conceptions of human rights. Identifying a basis for the eventual adoption of a concept of respect for international human rights is a difficult task (especially when, given the difficulty of identifying *retrospectively* the basis for this eventual adoption in the West, it is hard even to know what exactly one is looking for). But that is the task: to seek some fundamental value or concept in traditional African society that, coexisting with communalism, might constitute the necessary prerequisite for embracing the basic human rights concept embodied in modern international norms.

Dinka Culture and the Prospects for Human Rights

One of the weaknesses of the literature on African human rights is the tendency to generalize about African traditional society as if it were a single undifferentiated culture. Indeed, it seems ironic that writers who are critical of the international community for promoting a conception of human rights that is insensitive to cultural differences appear so willing to presume the lack of such differences within the continent. There is a need then, in seeking a basis for a human rights concept, to move from such generalizations to an examination of a specific culture.[59] The accounts in this book by Francis Deng and Kwasi Wiredu, for example, seek to do this.

Another example of this kind of inquiry into a particular culture is Richard F. Weisfelder's account of human rights in Lesotho:

What is required is a systematic analysis of the attitudes, beliefs, institutions, and experiences within each society which either sustain

58. Weinstein, "Human Rights and Development in Africa," p. 193.
59. See also Welch, "Human Rights as a Problem," pp. 27–28. Discussing the African Charter of Human and Peoples' Rights, the Banjul Charter, Welch says, "The first significant area for research, it appears, are the relevant traditions that might fall within the Banjul Charter's purview. The problems for investigation are immense. The sources of these practices, and their presuppositions, are diverse and occasionally contradictory."

or repudiate the view that certain rights should be upheld against alleged necessities of state. To be sure, the availability of such information provides no guarantee that civil liberties will be better protected or violations of human rights lessened. What may be achieved is some greater awareness of the beliefs, structures, and groups in a given society which might best be mobilized to forestall gross assaults on human rights and to erode the forces supporting repressive practices.[60]

Weisfelder finds grounds for some optimism in the political traditions of Lesotho, but his evidence, as the research goals he sets out would suggest, goes to the presence of attitudes and practices consistent with respect for particular rights. Despite a society that left "ample room for abuse of power," Weisfelder found that "the myths regarding [the reign of Moshoeshoe I in the nineteenth century]—which may be more politically significant than objective reality—provide the Basotho nation with indigenous concepts of free speech, equal justice, due process of law, tolerance for diversity, and accountability of public officials" (p. 23). His insistence on looking at a specific culture is most valuable. But the need remains to go beyond political traditions that can be identified as equivalent to the protection of specific rights; a concept of human rights requires more than a political system that includes checks on abuses of power and preferences for justice and diversity. The need is to look at a society for a fundamental value that could be the basis for a commitment to the concept of human rights.

It is this goal, then, that informs the following examination of a particular African culture, that of the Dinka. The inquiry here cannot be taken as a thorough assessment of Dinka values. Rather, relying on Deng's accounts,[61] it is merely suggestive of a methodology for answering the question this essay urges. These speculations about the meaning and implications of Dinka traditions are made only with great diffidence and only as a superficial sample of an approach. Certainly, this does not profess to be a full assessment of Dinka values. Nor do these speculations pretend to state truths about traditional society in general.

60. Weisfelder, "Decline of Human Rights in Lesotho," p. 23.
61. Francis M. Deng, *Dinka of the Sudan* (Holt, Rinehart and Winston, 1972); Deng, *Africans of Two Worlds: The Dinka in Afro-Arab Sudan* (Yale University Press, 1978); and Deng, *The Man Called Deng Majok: A Biography of Power, Polygyny, and Change* (Yale University Press, 1986). For a summary of Dinka values and their relationship to human rights, see Deng's chapter in this volume.

One can, of course, make a catalog of aspects of Dinka culture that seem, on the one hand, auspicious, or, on the other, inhospitable for the growth of a universal human rights concept. To do so would involve speculation about whether the direct effect on human rights of a particular custom or value is positive or negative. A few examples will suffice to show both the difficulty and the ultimate futility of making such judgments.

Much is made of the Dinka sense of superiority to "others."[62] This ethnocentrism seems to present the same problem of exclusivity as the general requirement of group membership described in the literature. Similarly, the hierarchies found in Dinka society suggest an obstacle to a concept of universal rights. The importance of the dead also may imply problems for human rights. First, the invocation of ancestors to punish wrongdoers, or of legends and stories about ancestors to explain present conditions, bespeaks a kind of fatalism and, thus, a possible negation of individual responsibility that may work against human rights practice. Second, belief in the potential of the dead to take the life of the living may represent a devaluation of the living that makes it too easy to take life. The violence encouraged in youth and certain specific practices, such as circumcision at the age of six and teeth extraction at ten, can also be pointed to as evidence of a lack of respect for human life. One might also interpret the Dinka preoccupation with cattle as a value that is antithetical to human rights. The celebration of the sacrifice of Acai to avert a natural disaster to the Dinka could be seen as a reflection of the preeminence of communal over individual rights.

For all these possibly "negative" factors in Dinka culture, there are a number of factors that could be seen as evidence of either the protection of certain kinds of rights or attitudes that would support such protection. In a discussion of Dinka reaction to birth control, Deng says that traditional Dinka are shocked by the idea of it as a means to limit family size or population. "Envisaging a human being and slamming the door of life on him on the grounds that the available resources are not sufficient would seem inhuman to the Dinka. . . . They cannot imagine preventing life to improve it."[63] Certainly, if this expresses a general atti-

---

62. Deng, *Dinka of the Sudan*, pp. 2, 6, 14; and Deng, *Africans of Two Worlds*, pp. 66, 70, 76. Although the Dinka treat visitors with hospitality, "once they are given a reason for disrespect by the misconduct of a foreigner, that foreigner barely qualifies as a human being" (*Dinka of the Sudan*, p. 6). The Dinka beliefs and practices mentioned in the rest of this paragraph come from *Dinka of the Sudan*.

63. Deng, *Dinka of the Sudan*, pp. 29–30.

tude toward life, it may signify a commitment to individual life that can transcend the supremacy of the community. There is also evidence of the kind of limited government concept that many of the writers on human rights in Africa find promising. The Dinka notion of a worthy leader is someone who embodies "consensus and reconciliation" and who, therefore, "must be a model of purity [and] righteousness." Because the chief is a "spiritual father," he must help the needy, which often entails self-sacrifice and the need to be generous and "without favoritism." He is "supposed to emphasize persuasion rather than coercion." Although he has spiritual powers that are awesome, "the Dinka know that the Chief should not err and invoke divine power unjustifiably."[64] All these views of authority suggest a predilection for notions of justice and restraint of power that are part of certain fundamental rights. One may also find in the Dinka attitude toward death something that bodes well for respect for the right to life. Death is viewed as "a dreadful end." Although there is fatalism about death, "in no way is it felt that a dead man may be gone to a better life. It is life in this world that really matters to the Dinka."[65] This sort of belief may entail a valuable inconsistency with violations of individual rights.

This inventory of possible negative and positive factors does not really speak to the question of whether there is some fundamental value or belief that could be the basis for a basic universal human rights concept. Things that may sound horrible in a human rights context are not necessarily fatal to the potential for a human rights concept. Violence, cattle devotion, and veneration of the dead suggest a society with some difficult obstacles to overcome, but they are neither different from nor worse than the panoply of horrors and superstitions in the Western tradition.[66] In other words, while some of these factors may be inhospitable to human rights, they do not preclude the potential for achieving a universal human rights concept.

64. Deng, *Dinka of the Sudan*, pp. 113–14. See also Deng, *Africans of Two Worlds*, pp. 117–22.

65. Deng, *Dinka of the Sudan*, p. 136.

66. Howard argues that comparisons should be made between societies at similar stages of development. Thus contemporary Africa should be compared with Western Europe during its "own stage of nation-building, [where] massive violations of what we would now consider elementary human rights occurred." Howard, "Evaluating Human Rights in Africa," p. 167. Donnelly "would argue that pre-modern Western political theory lacks the notion of human rights." Donnelly, "Human Rights and Human Dignity," p. 305, n. 6.

In this regard, the adaptability of the Dinka becomes important. The following comment suggests the possible impermanence of some of these patterns: "The Dinka are thus a submissive people, living in a world they cannot control and subject to the will of a God they do not fully understand."[67] The significance of this lies in its implications for the consequences of development. It suggests that troubling practices may reflect a certain level of understanding and knowledge and thus are susceptible to evolution. The "willingness to change the traditional Dinka ways, including their belief in the aesthetic and social value of cattle" because it is inconsistent with development implies a willingness to adapt, to change things that may seem immutable;[68] this reinforces the conclusion that the factors identified as obstacles to human rights are not insurmountable.

If the inventory of negative factors does not indicate the ultimate impossibility of a human rights concept, neither does the inventory of positive factors ensure the foundations of such a concept. Conventional approaches to the problem would perhaps find the necessary prerequisite in the Dinka concepts of *cieng* and *dheng*, which together form a substantial cultural commitment to human dignity.[69] However, as shown, respect for human dignity is an inadequate creed to rely on as a prerequisite for a concept of basic human rights.

There is, though, in the accounts by Dinka elders of their religious beliefs, a theme that is striking in its similarity to the theme posited above as the necessary precursor in the West for the development of a human rights concept. The Dinka see themselves as the children of God.[70] Furthermore, because God created all of mankind, "every human being, no matter what his race or religion, has a sanctity and a moral or spiritual value that must be respected. To wrong him is to wrong God himself and therefore invite a curse."[71] This notion of every person partaking of the sanctity of God is very close to the notion of "in the image of God."

Although the Dinka sense of superiority is an impediment to the equal treatment of all people, there is also considerable evidence that

67. Deng, *Dinka of the Sudan*, p. 128.
68. Deng, *Africans of Two Worlds*, p. 201.
69. Deng, *Dinka of the Sudan*, pp. 13–14.
70. Deng, *Man Called Deng Majok*, p. 45, n. 13.
71. Deng, *Africans of Two Worlds*, pp. 63–64. The citations that follow are from this book, with page numbers given in the text.

Dinka theology includes the crucial element of universality. "The unity of man and his universe is envisaged to embrace mankind in all its multiplicity of races and cultures" (p. 62). In the words of Chief Thon Wai:

> A man created by God with two legs and two eyes, who urinates and goes to the forest [to empty his bowels], cannot be considered a fool. He is a human being, a part of the human race. . . .
> If you see a man walking on his two legs, do not despise him; he is a human being. Bring him close to you and treat him like a human being. That is how you will secure your own life. But if you push him onto the ground and do not give him what he needs, things will spoil and even your big share, which you guard with care, will be destroyed [pp. 64–65].

Later, discussing the difficulties of achieving harmony with the Arabs and, in particular, of intermarriage, Chief Thon Wai states the key belief: "And we are one people in front of God" (p. 217).

That Dinka are the children of God, that all human beings have the sanctity of God, and that all people must be treated like human beings compose a constellation of beliefs seemingly adequate as a foundation for a human rights concept. The significance of these beliefs is made more concrete by Bulabek-Malith, who reported, "A human being created by God was never made a slave by the black man" (p. 139). This statement, in effect, translates the prerequisite—the sanctity of all humans—into a specific human right.

The similarity noted between Dinka religious myth and the Bible and the Koran (p. 78) suggests that there was contact between the Dinka and the religions that developed just down the Nile—Judaism, Christianity, and Islam (p. 83). One might argue that the influence of those religions accounts for the similarity of Dinka theology to the theme of "in the image of God." But, at the very least, even such an absorption of religious myths indicates a receptivity to the notions the myths embody. The presence of a prerequisite set of values in Dinka traditional society says nothing about the presence or absence of such values in other traditional African societies. It does suggest, though, that Dinka society embodies a fundamental belief that can be the basis for the development of a universal human rights concept.

Part Five
Prospects for a Cross-Cultural Approach

CHAPTER THIRTEEN

Problems of Universal Cultural Legitimacy for Human Rights

Abdullahi Ahmed An-Na'im

IT IS COMMONPLACE now to decry the unacceptable discrepancy between the theory and practice of human rights. Despite the existence of elaborate and enlightened international standards of human rights for several decades, and despite the rhetoric of strong commitment to these standards by governments, which are often supported in or pressured into such commitment by an increasing number of nongovernmental organizations and groups, we continue to witness gross violations of human rights in all parts of the world. If we are to reduce this unacceptable discrepancy and promote and ensure greater respect for the full range of human rights throughout the world, then we must understand and combat not only the immediate causes of the discrepancy but also the underlying factors that contribute to it.

For example, it is often stated that the discrepancy between the theory and practice of human rights results inevitably from ineffective implementation and enforcement procedures under the international human rights instruments. This explanation begs the question—namely, why has the implementation and enforcement process lagged behind the standard-setting achievements?

Other explanations for the discrepancy point to the tendency of official authorities to resist accountability in general, and to resent accountability to external entities as inconsistent with national sovereignty and self-determination. Those in power clearly would prefer to have a free hand to implement their own view of the common good, if not to manipulate power to their own advantage. To avoid accepting this state of

I am grateful to Professor Ken Norman for useful comments on a draft of this chapter. I also wish to acknowledge the research assistance and helpful comments of Charmaine Spencer.

331

affairs as a fait accompli, those in power must be induced to accept internal and external accountability in the interest of implementing and enforcing human rights standards.

Some observers base the discrepancy between human rights theory and practice on the political, social, and economic processes within a given country. Once again, however, the question remains how to adjust or transform the relevant political, social, and economic processes and relationships within a given community so as to promote greater compliance with human rights standards.

Whatever the reason one accepts as the cause of the discrepancy between the theory and practice of human rights, a more positive element needs to be injected into the reform process if this discrepancy is to be reduced. The cultural legitimacy of the full range of human rights standards must be developed—that is, the concern for human rights as they figure in the standards of many different cultures should be enhanced. In particular, I believe it would be useful to challenge representations of some human rights as lacking genuine cultural legitimacy within a given sociological system.

Enhancing the cultural legitimacy for a given human right should mobilize political forces within a community, inducing those in power to accept accountability for the implementation or enforcement of that right. With internal cultural legitimacy, those in power could no longer argue that national sovereignty is demeaned through compliance with standards set for the particular human right as an external value. Compliance with human rights standards would be seen as a legitimate exercise of national sovereignty and not as an external limitation. The continuing processes of change and adjustment of political, social, and economic relationships within a community mean that internal changes can be made to accommodate a given human right, if that right is shown to be legitimate within the culture of the particular community.

The nature and role of cultural legitimacy will be discussed later in this chapter. The term *culture* is used here in its broadest sense of "totality of values, institutions and forms of behaviour transmitted within a society, as well as the material goods produced by man [and woman]. . . . [T]his wide concept of culture covers *Weltanschauung*, ideologies and cognitive behaviour."[1] If, within a given cultural tradition, a certain

1. Roy Preiswerk, "The Place of Intercultural Relations in the Study of International Relations," *Year Book of World Affairs*, vol. 32 (1978), p. 251. On the different senses in

human value or need is believed to be fundamental and is accorded or guaranteed to every human being, then that value has cultural legitimacy. Many factors and forces influence the formulation and content of a purported human right. However, it seems that a necessary prerequisite for a human right is that individuals accept its underlying validity. After all, individual convictions and motivations shape and propel action whether favoring or resisting the recognition and implementation of the claim as a human right. Institutional actors or economic and social forces may appear to be the immediate causes of the result of efforts to recognize and implement a claim as a human right. But in the final analysis institutions emerge from the interaction of individuals; economic and social forces are also the expression of the interests of individuals.

This chapter argues that the difficulties in implementing established human rights effectively, and in recognizing other claims and interests as human rights and implementing them also, derive from the insufficiency of cultural support for the particular right or claim. Culture mediates power and acts as the framework within which self-interest is defined and realized in any community. Cultural legitimacy, moreover, cannot be deduced or assumed from the mere fact of official recognition of the claim as a human right in existing formal documents. As explained later, the process through which the current international human rights standards were formulated and adopted did not address issues of cultural legitimacy in relation to most of the cultural traditions of the world.

To address this fundamental need for universal cultural legitimacy as the basis for international efforts to protect and promote human rights, this chapter begins with a brief explanation of the notion of cultural legitimacy and its impact on public policy and action in relation to human rights. The second section of the chapter reviews the beginning and subsequent stages of modern international efforts to protect and promote human rights in order to assess the nature and quality of such concern with cultural legitimacy as was displayed during those formative and subsequent stages. The third section focuses on the Islamic tradition to illustrate a working model for assessing and enhancing the cultural legitimacy of human rights within indigenous cultural tradi-

---

which the term *culture* is used, see T. S. Eliot, *Notes towards the Definition of Culture* (Harcourt, Brace, 1949); and Raymond Williams, *Keywords: A Vocabulary of Culture and Society* (Oxford University Press, 1976), pp. 76–82.

tions. The possibilities and problems of using the processes of cultural dynamics and change in support of universal standards of human rights are discussed in the final section.

On the Nature and Role of Cultural Legitimacy

Many definitions of *culture* in the wider sense adopted here are found in anthropological or sociological literature, some emphasizing social heritage, others stressing shared ideas or shared (standardized) behavior, and so on.[2] According to one source, culture can generally be seen to comprise the "inherited artifacts, goods, technical processes, ideas, habits, and values" of society, which endow human beings "with an additional extension of [their] anatomical apparatus, with a protective armor of defenses and safeguards, and with mobility and speed." Culture is the cumulative creation of human beings, which "transforms individuals into organized groups and gives these [groups] an almost indefinite continuity."[3]

A more recent approach to the study of culture presents it in terms of symbols and meanings.[4] Geertz, for example, defines culture as "an historically transmitted pattern of meanings embodied in symbols, a system of inherited conceptions expressed in symbolic forms by means of which men [and women] communicate, perpetuate, and develop their knowledge about and attitudes toward life."[5] The proponents of this approach within a number of disciplines would challenge the assumption of the behaviorists who maintain that most things about people—personality, culture, and language—can be understood as a complex of stimulus and response connections, or patterns of behavior.[6] Instead, they view culture as shared information or knowledge encoded in systems of symbols.

2. For a critique of some of these anthropological definitions, see Albert Carl Cafagna, "A Formal Analysis of Definitions of 'Culture,'" in Gertrude E. Dole and Robert L. Carneiro, eds., *Essays in the Science of Culture: In Honor of Leslie A. White* (Thomas Y. Crowell, 1960), pp. 111–32; and A. L. Kroeber and Clyde Kluckhohn, *Culture: A Critical Review of Concepts and Definitions* (Vintage Books, 1963).

3. Bronislaw Malinowski, "Culture," in *Encyclopaedia of the Social Sciences*, vol. 4 (Macmillan, 1931), pp. 621–45.

4. See generally, Richard A. Shweder and Robert A. LeVine, eds., *Culture Theory: Essays on Mind, Self, and Emotion* (Cambridge University Press, 1984).

5. Clifford Geertz, *The Interpretation of Cultures: Selected Essays* (Basic Books, 1973), p. 89.

6. Roy G. D'Andrade, "Cultural Meaning Systems," in Shweder and LeVine, eds., *Culture Theory*, p. 89.

In the context of international relations, Preiswerk has identified four conceptual levels of culture:

Conceptually, we can differentiate between at least four levels of culture: (1) *micro-culture* can be used to describe the particularity of smaller units such as tribes, minorities, village communities, social classes and sub-cultures; (2) one speaks of *national culture*, a very frequently used expression (e.g. "French culture"), mostly in the narrow sense of artistic and intellectual creation. But, insofar as the nationals of a country, despite differentiated micro-cultures, have certain common values, institutions and forms of behavior, one can here also speak of culture in the broad sense; (3) the cultural particularity of a nation is limited to specific cultural characteristics; in other respects it is part of a wider cultural area in so far as it shares other characteristics with neighbouring nations within a *regional culture*; (4) beyond this level one can speak, in the broadest sense, of *macro-culture* to describe characteristics which are common to a number of cultures despite local, national and regional differences.[7]

Cultural legitimacy for human rights might be sought at all these levels and certainly should be discussed in relation to all societies. No society, regardless of material development, has yet been able to demonstrate that it is capable of sustaining the full range of human rights envisaged by the United Nations' International Bill of Human Rights. This failing is particularly true with regard to the so-called third-generation rights, such as a right to development, a right to peace, and a right to the protection of the environment.[8] In other words, the scope and significance of culture should be understood in the broadest sense, with a view to applying the proposed analysis to Western liberal and Marxist societies as well as to societies of the developing world.

It may be argued that this definition of culture is too broad. This would be a valid objection if it is suggested that culture is everything. What is suggested is that there is a cultural dimension to every aspect

7. Preiswerk, "Place of Intercultural Relations," p. 252.
8. The term "third generation rights" was coined to refer to these collective or solidarity rights; civil and political rights are considered "first generation rights," and economic, social, and cultural rights are second generation rights. See, for example, Stephen P. Marks, "Emerging Human Rights: A New Generation for the 1980s?" in Richard Falk, Friedrich Kratochwil, and Saul H. Mendlovitz, eds., *International Law: A Contemporary Perspective*, Studies on a Just World Order, 2 (Boulder, Colo.: Westview Press, 1985), pp. 501–13.

of human consciousness and activity. I understand the phrase quoted earlier, "this wide concept of culture covers *Weltanschauung,* ideologies and cognitive behaviour," to mean that these aspects of human consciousness and activity are anchored in cultural norms and institutions.

Like the term *culture,* the term *legitimacy* can be defined in different ways for different purposes. In relation to the present discussion, legitimacy is the quality or state of being in conformity with recognized principles or accepted rules and standards. Cultural legitimacy may be defined as the quality or state of being in conformity with recognized principles or accepted rules and standards of a given culture.

The prime feature underlying cultural legitimacy is the authority and reverence derived from internal validity. A culturally legitimate norm or value is respected and observed by the members of the particular culture, presumably because it is assumed to bring satisfaction to those members. Because there may be conflicts and tensions between various competing conceptions of individual and collective satisfaction, there is constant change and adjustment of the norms or values in any culture which are accorded respect and observance. Such change and adjustment appears related to prevailing perceptions of whether a specific normative behavior does or does not bring sufficient satisfaction to warrant its continuation.

Cultural Legitimacy and Public Policy and Action

The interdependence and essential compatibility of the individual and society underlie the relationship between cultural legitimacy and public action and policy. As correctly observed by Ruth Benedict:

Society . . . is never an entity separable from the individuals who compose it. No individual can arrive even at the threshold of his potentialities without a culture in which he participates. Conversely, no civilization has in it any element which in the last analysis is not the contribution of an individual. Where else could any trait come from except from the behaviour of a man or a woman or a child?[9]

This suggests two interconnected propositions. Every society is dependent on individual members for the development of its institutions,

9. Ruth Benedict, *Patterns of Culture* (Houghton Mifflin, 1959), p. 253. Alexander Goldenweiser expressed the same notion in *History, Psychology, and Culture* (Gloucester, Mass.: Peter Smith, 1968), p. 59.

norms, values, and action. Each individual is also dependent on society for his or her very existence and for the prospects of realizing a meaningful and gratifying life.

This fundamental interdependence and compatibility does not suggest, however, that there is no tension between individuals and their society. Although there is an overlap between individual perceptions of norms, values, and institutions, these perceptions are by no means identical. The degree of incompatibility and tension varies from person to person, and often between one stage and another in the life of the same person. Although most people find it possible to conform, or are pressured into conforming, with prevailing attitudes and behavioral patterns, others fail or refuse to do so. Depending on many factors, including the personal endowments of the individual and the susceptibility of the culture to change under the particular circumstances, "deviant" individuals may either succeed in bringing about change that favors their perspectives or be branded as abnormal, even psychopathic.[10] Society's great reformers as well as its psychopaths are manifestations of this creative tension.

In addition, society may retrospectively perceive change as positive and beneficial, but such changes can be perceived initially as negative and detrimental by the carriers or guardians of the previous order. In a contemporary debate over social change, appreciating this point enables each side to understand and deal with the other's point of view. Both proponents and opponents of social change are not necessarily malicious, deviant, or reactionary people. Whereas the proponents of change may serve the legitimate needs of their evolving society, opponents may serve the needs of the same society by resisting change until the case for it has been made. These and other elements of the dynamics of cultural change are discussed later in the context of analyzing how a given norm or value attains cultural legitimacy and influences public policy and action.

Cultural norms are not the only determinants of behavior.[11] Cultural habits are conceptualized as ideal norms or patterns of behavior. Since a person behaves in response to his or her perception of the total situa-

10. See Benedict, *Patterns of Culture,* pp. 254–78.

11. Melford E. Spiro, "Some Reflections on Cultural Determinism and Relativism with Special Reference to Emotion and Reason," in Shweder and LeVine, eds., *Culture Theory,* p. 323. See the assumptions underlying cross-cultural studies summarized later in this chapter.

tion, including physical stimuli and psychological factors such as the degree of the person's identification with the cultural model, actual behavior may not necessarily coincide with the ideal norms or patterns of behavior.

Given the individual's dependence on society, and society's formidable capacity to instill or enforce conformity in its members, public policy and action are more likely to accord with ideal cultural norms and patterns of behavior than private action. Whereas the individual may succumb to deviant impulses and drives in private, and may even consider rebellion against the established ideal, open deviance and rebellion are rare. The powerful force of conforming to the established ideal is illustrated by the fact that most people seek to keep their deviant behavior and views secret and, if discovered, try to explain them as temporary lapses in judgment rather than as a deliberate rejection of the ideal norm or pattern of behavior. Even the few who choose to come out in open revolt, whether or not they claim a commitment to an alternative model, would normally attempt to explain or rationalize their position as reflecting a more genuine commitment to the ideals of society, or as resulting from a reinterpretation of those ideals.

Open and systematic nonconformity gravely threatens those in authority over the society—the ruling class or group that over time comes to have a vested interest in the status quo. Using the powers explicitly or implicitly vested in them by society, these people will naturally seek to suppress nonconforming behavior, often in the name of preserving the stability and vital interests of society at large. In other words, the self-interest of those in power in political, economic, religious, or other spheres, who claim a monopoly over the determination of what is in the public good, tends to shape public policy and action in terms of the cultural ideal.

This analysis emphasizes the desirability of seeking the support of the cultural ideal for any proposition of public policy and action, especially for the protection and promotion of human rights. Whether the rights are individual or collective, civil and political, or economic, social, and cultural, their protection requires mobilizing and harnessing the relevant resources of society. That is more likely to be achieved, and more likely to achieve the desired objectives, if the purpose is seen to be consistent with cultural ideals. Because individual action is the ultimate resource at the disposal of any society, it is vital to motivate people to act in favor of a given human right. Such motivation involves a mental attitude that accepts the particular human right as worth working for.

This may require discarding or modifying previously held attitudes or perceptions in order to create or discover new ones.

Basic to this hypothesis is the proposition that all cultural positions have some problems with some human rights, yet where this is so, it is probable that an *internal* value or norm can be used to develop or supplement the cultural legitimacy of any given human right. The goal is to adopt an approach that realistically identifies the lack of cultural support for some human rights and then seeks ways to support and legitimize the particular human right in terms of the values, norms, and processes of change belonging to the relevant cultural tradition.

Cultural Relativism and the Universality of Human Rights

The controversy among anthropologists over cultural relativism can be used to clarify the implications of the need to provide cultural legitimacy for human rights advocated in this chapter. Many scholars have recognized that our perception of the world is conditioned by our pre-existing conceptual categories. Although this generally accepted proposition applies to many facets of life, such as perceptions of beauty, I am concerned here with its ethical implications. Although it may therefore be more appropriate to use the term *ethical relativism*,[12] I use the term *cultural relativism* because it is commonly used in the field with specific reference to ethical issues.

Emphasis on cultural relativism in modern anthropological literature evolved as a reaction against cultural evolutionism—that is to say, the view that human societies tend to progress from "primitive" or "savage" to "modern." With their Eurocentric disposition, nineteenth-century anthropologists ranked Western societies highest and made Western values the standards of their universal model for the "evolution" of societies. Cultural relativism was introduced to combat these Eurocentric and racist notions of progress.[13]

Although there are various formulations of cultural relativism, some perceived to be problematical,[14] the basic thrust of the theory is clear and very useful. "It is aimed at getting people to admit that although it

---

12. See Alison Dundes Renteln, "Relativism and the Search for Human Rights," *American Anthropologist*, vol. 90, no. 1 (1988), p. 59.

13. George W. Stocking, Jr., *Race, Culture, and Evolution: Essays in the History of Anthropology* (Free Press, 1968), pp. 115–17; and Melford E. Spiro, "Culture and Human Nature," in George Spindler, ed., *The Making of Psychological Anthropology* (University of California Press, 1978), p. 336.

14. Renteln, "Relativism and the Search for Human Rights," pp. 58–62.

may *seem* to them that their moral principles are self-evidently true, and hence *seem* to be grounds for passing judgment on other peoples, in fact the self-evidence of these principles is a kind of illusion."[15] According to its strongest proponents, cultural relativism acknowledges the equal validity of diverse patterns of life, and lays "stress on the dignity inherent in every body of custom, and on the need for tolerance of conventions though they may differ from one's own."[16]

The critics of cultural relativism perceive it as undermining the ability to condemn repressive practices in other countries that are sanctioned by the particular culture.[17] For example, some scholars have charged that relativism provides a notion that can be used to justify slavery and genocide.[18]

There is certainly substance to this criticism if one believes cultural relativism implies the complete tolerance of all norms and practices sanctioned by the respective cultures. But some scholars have argued that cultural relativism does not logically entail tolerance, and could entail intolerance.[19] In other words, tolerance of diverse moral practices may be part of a particular culture rather than a necessary consequence of cultural relativism. "It is not the theory of relativism that makes tolerance supreme," Alison Renteln suggested, "but rather the uncritical acceptance of this value by Americans."[20] Although aware that cross-cultural criticism is weakened by being more or less ethnocentric, a relativist may still criticize what violates his or her deeply held beliefs.[21] Despite its ethnocentricity, criticism can be effective in bringing various economic and political pressures to bear on the "offending" culture. In this respect, I agree with Renteln when she says:

15. John Cook, "Cultural Relativism as an Ethnocentric Notion," in Rodger Beehler and Alan R. Drengson, eds., *The Philosophy of Society* (London: Methuen, 1978), p. 294.

16. Melville J. Herskovits, *Man and His Works: The Science of Cultural Anthropology* (Knopf, 1948), p. 76.

17. Barry Barnes and David Bloor, "Relativism, Rationalism and the Sociology of Knowledge," in Martin Hollis and Steven Lukes, eds., *Rationality and Relativism* (MIT Press, 1982), pp. 21, 47; and Elvin Hatch, *Culture and Morality: The Relativity of Values in Anthropology* (Columbia University Press, 1983), p. 12.

18. Frank E. Hartung, "Cultural Relativity and Moral Judgments," *Philosophy of Science*, vol. 21 (1954), pp. 122–23.

19. Robert Redfield, *The Primitive World and Its Transformations* (Cornell University Press, 1953), pp. 146–47.

20. Renteln, "Relativism and the Search for Human Rights," p. 63.

21. David Bidney, "The Concept of Value in Modern Anthropology," in A. L. Kroeber, ed., *Anthropology Today: An Encyclopedic Inventory* (University of Chicago Press, 1953), p. 698.

Although it is appropriate to draw a distinction between criticisms corresponding to internal standards, on the one hand, and external ones, on the other, the theory of relativism blocks neither. It says nothing about the desirability of social criticism. It holds that every society will utilize its own standards. Sometimes there will be a fundamental conflict among the various standards, and sometimes there will be convergence or consensus on standards. What one makes of the conflicting or consensual standards depends not on relativism but on the role one wishes to play in the international community. There is nothing in the theory of relativism that requires one posture as opposed to another.[22]

Moreover, insofar as criticism is based on values accepted by a wide range of cultures, the charge of ethnocentricity is weakened, especially if it can be shown that such criticism is based, even indirectly, on values or norms accepted by the culture being criticized. This would seem to recommend the sort of cross-cultural search for universal human values in support of universal human rights advocated here.

One may ask, why should a proponent of one cultural view accept a judgment of the majority of other cultures? Insofar as a person believes in the validity of a norm, that person is unlikely to accept an opposing norm: the more strongly we believe in our values, the less likely we are to tolerate the values of others.

In response to this point, there appears to be a universal rational principle to the effect that strong evidence of a contrary view should induce a person to reexamine her or his position. In my own culture of northern Sudan, this notion is expressed in this maxim: if two people tell you that your head is missing, you better check to see if it is still there. In other words, the more widely our positions are challenged by others, the more likely we are to reconsider those positions.

As for the dangers of excessive cultural relativism, it is extremely unlikely that any culture will condone an inhumane practice. This may be an article of faith, but it is one worth having. Moreover, probably any inhumane practice that may persist within a given culture can be challenged by an alternative interpretation of the underlying cultural norms. Unless we take this article of faith seriously by looking for its empirical verification, we would prematurely condemn the human experience on this planet to catastrophic failure.

22. Renteln, "Relativism and the Search for Human Rights," p. 64.

As correctly stated by Jack Donnelly, "the problem of cultural relativism and universal human rights cannot be reduced to an either-or choice. Claims of cultural relativism show a great diversity in meaning, substance, and importance."[23] Accordingly, he suggests that a "weak" cultural relativist position may be justified, primarily at the level of form and interpretation, without violating the essential universality of human rights. For example, a weak cultural relativist position would accept a certain degree of practices as legitimate *interpretations* of "the right to political participation," while it would reject other practices as illegitimate and as amounting to a complete denial of the right.[24]

Arguing in terms of the general values sought to be protected by human rights today, and the relative universality of "human nature," Donnelly asserts that basic human rights must at least initially be assumed to be similarly universal. His review of the provisions of the Universal Declaration of Human Rights and the two covenants seems to support this proposition. However, some of the rights recognized by the declaration and covenants may be viewed as "interpretations" or "forms" with which some cultures may differ without necessarily denying universal human rights.[25]

Donnelly proposed the following test for assessing claims of cultural relativism:

Rights are formulated with certain basic violations, or threats to human dignity, in mind. Therefore, the easiest way to overcome the presumption of universality for a widely recognized human right is to demonstrate either that the anticipated violation is not standard in that society, that the value is (justifiably) not considered basic in that society, or that it is protected by an alternative mechanism. In other words, one would have to show that the underlying cultural vision of human nature or society is both morally defensible and incompat-

23. Jack Donnelly, "Cultural Relativism and Universal Human Rights," *Human Rights Quarterly*, vol. 6 (November 1984), p. 410.

24. Donnelly, "Cultural Relativism," p. 408.

25. Donnelly, "Cultural Relativism," pp. 414–18. The two covenants are the Covenant on Economic, Social and Cultural Rights and the Covenant on Civil and Political Rights. Donnelly quotes the "right of free and full consent of intending spouses" under the declaration, and the requirement of segregation of juvenile defendants under the civil and political rights covenant. Since the first right reflects a specific cultural interpretation of marriage, and since the very notion of a juvenile criminal defendant does not exist in many cultures, his version of weak relativism would exclude these rights from the universal scope of human rights.

ible with the implementation of the "universal" human right in question. I would argue that such a test can be met only rarely today, and that permissible exceptions usually are relatively minor and generally consistent with the basic thrust of the Universal Declaration.[26]

In my view, two main conclusions are warranted by the preceding analysis. First, as a manifestation of the right to self-determination and as a safeguard against the dangers of ethnocentrism, the theory of cultural relativism provides a good approach to cross-cultural evaluations without necessarily undermining our ability to criticize and condemn repressive or morally abhorrent practices. Cultural relativism does not necessarily require allowing cultures total autonomy in accepting a given human right as culturally legitimate or rejecting it as culturally illegitimate. As I argue elsewhere, the basic premise of international efforts to protect and promote human rights is the belief that there are limits on cultural relativism.[27] What I find to be at issue, however, is the *manner* in which outsiders can challenge practices that they deem to be in violation of human rights.

Second, cross-cultural evaluations, which are unavoidable for any international effort to protect and promote human rights, are most effective when based on universal human values. The more it can be shown that a particular human right is based on a value or norm accepted by the widest range of cultural traditions, the less our efforts to protect and promote that right will be open to charges of ethnocentricity or cultural imperialism.

Adda Bozeman argues that "ideas . . . are not transferable in their authenticity . . . [and] in the final analysis cultures are different because they are associated with different modes of thought."[28] According to Bozeman, given the difficulty and complexity of perceiving the other in his authenticity, "cross-cultural communications lead to misunderstandings by virtue of their very nature" (p. 27). Although intended to challenge the tenability of international law, Bozeman's thesis has obvious implications for international efforts to protect and promote human rights. In fact, she states expressly in her conclusion:

26. Donnelly, "Cultural Relativism," p. 417.
27. Abdullahi A. An-Na'im, "Religious Minorities under Islamic Law and the Limits of Cultural Relativism," *Human Rights Quarterly*, vol. 9 (February 1987), pp. 1–18.
28. Adda B. Bozeman, *The Future of Law in a Multicultural World* (Princeton University Press, 1971), p. 14. Bozeman's heavy bias against non-Western traditions is revealed very early in her book.

Present efforts aiming at an extension of international law to the sphere of individual life by drafting, for example, universally valid covenants of human rights, appear in this perspective to be exercises in futility—all the more so as most non-Western governments are not constrained by locally dominant moral orders to assure respect for individual liberties within their respective local jurisdictions [pp. 183–84].

It is interesting to note that Bozeman's conception of human rights as exclusively "individual liberties" betrays the reality of her Western ethnocentricity despite the pretense of an effort toward universalism. In her introduction she states that "European peoples escaped the restrictions which came to bind societies in China, India, the Near East, and Africa because they have been continuously responsive to the unsettling forces emanating from biography . . . among them most particularly the commitment to cultivate rational yet daring thought" (p. xv). Nevertheless, I concede the element of truth in what she says but from a constructive perspective. I would take the difficulty and complexity of perceiving the other in his or her authenticity, and the consequent dangers of misunderstanding, as guidelines in searching for cross-cultural support for human rights, and international law in general, rather than as reasons for abandoning the effort. The moral imperative and the practical need for upholding the rule of law in international relations, and protecting and promoting human rights in particular, are too strong to abandon merely because of the complexity and difficulty of the effort. Moreover, each person should work from within her or his own culture precisely in order to avoid the dangers of misunderstanding.

It should be emphasized, however, that in advocating the search for cross-cultural support for human rights, I am not suggesting that universal human rights are only those expressly articulated or overtly supported by existing cultural traditions. I do not believe that universal human rights can only be justified in terms of the least common denominator among the cultural traditions of the world. In my view, human rights should be based on the inherent dignity and integrity of every human being. Cross-cultural studies can be helpful from both substantive and tactical points of view. From a substantive point of view, cross-cultural studies can help to discover the actual content and necessary implications of the inherent dignity and integrity of the human being. It is vital to do this without violating the paramount human right of self-determination by imposing external standards. From a tactical point of view, cross-cultural support for human rights helps to gain legitimacy and efficacy for national as well as international efforts to protect and promote human rights.

It may be necessary, failing internal reinterpretation, to appeal to external standards in order to uphold fundamental human rights against inhumane or seriously objectionable practices sanctioned by any culture. Although this endeavor should not be undertaken lightly, its possibility is the ultimate safeguard against the excesses of cultural relativism. The obvious question here is the criteria by which a given practice may be judged inhumane or seriously objectionable for the purposes of justifying appeal to external standards. In my view, the proper criterion is what may be called the principle of *reciprocity*—namely, that one should not tolerate for another person any treatment that one would not accept for oneself. Placing oneself in the position of the other person, one is able to see if he or she would find the treatment to which the other person is subjected inhumane or seriously objectionable.

In placing oneself in the position of the other, one should not impose one's own perceptions on the other's position. For example, it should not be open to a Muslim to say that since he accepts for himself to be subject to the application of Islamic law (*shari'a*), he would conform with the principle of reciprocity in imposing *shari'a* on non-Muslims. In this context, the principle of reciprocity means that since Muslims would demand the right to decide what law should apply to them, and would not accept being subjected to the religious law of non-Muslims, they should grant the same right to non-Muslims.

As usual, there are clear or strong cases and marginal or weak ones. Whereas appeal to external standards to prevent a culture from sanctioning torture or slavery would be universally accepted as justified and proper, that may not yet be true of some aspects of equality for women. However, to recall that even torture and slavery were not accepted as justification for outside intervention a few decades ago is to appreciate that the scope of protection is expanding. Applying the principle of reciprocity, one can see that as more and more men are faced with the normative imperative of not tolerating for others what they would not accept for themselves, consensus on complete equality for women will grow. In other words, men can be made to concede that women are entitled to the same status and rights men would demand for themselves if they were women. The same normative imperative applies to the status and rights of ethnic, religious, and linguistic minorities and other victims of human rights violations.

Cultural Legitimacy in the Formulation of Current Standards

The degree and quality of concern with cultural legitimacy in the formulation and adoption of current international human rights instruments have been determined by several factors. One is the nature and content of traditional international law as the formal framework for international action generally, including the field of human rights. Another is the reality of national and international relations and differential levels of development, which affect the capacity of participants to articulate an effective cultural perspective in the process of drafting and adopting human rights standards.

This second factor manifests itself in many ways. For example, in an early study on the history and evolution of human rights prepared by the UN Secretariat in 1947, the accessibility of Western perspectives and the presumed inaccessibility of non-Western perspectives were determining elements in excluding the latter.[29] The authors of that study decided to exclude material prior to the Middle Ages because they felt it would be too difficult to go back to antiquity. In doing so, however, they effectively excluded much of the civilizations of African and Asian peoples. Even for its limited time frame, the twelfth to the eighteenth centuries, the study focused on Europe, especially England, because this focus was thought to be particularly interesting and to provide "solid" information. Thus the lack of articulation of non-Western perspectives in manners and languages accessible to officials of the United Nations led to the exclusion of those perspectives at the earliest stages of consultation and conceptualization of human rights.

Related to this factor are the nature and quality of the representation of non-Western countries at the international forums where decisions on international human rights standards and the machinery for their implementation were made. As I suggest later, it seems that the "representatives" of non-Western countries may have been more representative of Western cultural perspectives than of their own. Moreover, different levels of material development may have retarded the efforts of peoples in the developing countries to articulate indigenous cultural perspectives on human rights at home and communicate those perspectives at the international level. Peoples of the developing world lacked both clear articulations of their perspectives and the material resources

29. United Nations, Commission on Human Rights, Second Session, E/CN 4/30 (November 12, 1947).

to contribute significantly to the formulation of the International Bill of Human Rights.

International Law and the Realities of International Relations

Since international efforts for the promotion and protection of human rights were undertaken through either international treaties or state action at the international level, or within established international organizations, it is necessary to consider relevant aspects of international law and relations to assess their effect on the concern with cultural legitimacy during the formulation and adoption of international human rights instruments.[30] In this regard, the primary consideration is that traditional international law recognizes states and organizations of states as its only subjects. In other words, the only entities that have the capacity to acquire rights and obligations under traditional international law are states and organizations of states. Although recent developments support the view that individuals may also acquire some rights and obligations under international law, such rights and obligations have thus far been exclusively enforced through the medium of states.[31]

In accordance with the primary role of states under international law, all *legal* international action, including action in the field of human rights, tends to take the form of communications, agreements, and other actions by a state in relation to other states. Even in political, diplomatic, economic, and other spheres, the state format continues to influence the options and efficacy of action. Private or nonofficial forces within society often have their effect on international action, but mostly through the medium of the national state or through appeals and pressure on other states.[32] The principles and rules of international law on

30. See generally, Robert W. Tucker, *The Inequality of Nations* (Basic Books, 1977); Charles R. Beitz, *Political Theory and International Relations* (Princeton University Press, 1979); M. Donelan, ed., *The Reason of States* (London: Allen and Unwin, 1979); and Stanley Hoffman, *Duties beyond Borders: On the Limits and Possibilities of Ethical International Politics* (Syracuse University Press, 1981).

31. Rosalyn Higgins has argued convincingly that there is no conceptual reason to prevent individuals from being subjects of international law. "Conceptual Thinking about the Individual in International Law," in Falk, Kratochwil, and Mendlovitz, eds., *International Law*, pp. 476–94. Nevertheless, it is still correct to say that individuals are not subjects of international law in the traditional sense of the term.

32. International nongovernmental organizations, such as the International Committee of the Red Cross and Amnesty International, operate through contacts with government officials.

the formulation, interpretation, and enforcement of international treaties are of fundamental importance for human rights, not only because
of the central role of treaties in setting the relevant substantive standards
and procedures but also because international organizations, such as
the United Nations, which play an increasingly important role in the
human rights field, are created and operated in accordance with treaties. Thus the essential format of treaties as instruments negotiated and
ratified by states that have the sole competence to pursue their implementation under international law determines the scope and form of
contributions to the content of such treaties. Therefore, if there is to be
any concern with cultural legitimacy in a human rights treaty, it must
come from or through the action of states party to the negotiation and
ratification of the treaty.

This emphasis on states should not obscure the fact that they are not
completely autonomous entities which act independently from the social and political forces within their populations or from the constraints
of their resources or other factors.[33] In fact, the nature and structure of
the state and its options in international action are very much the product of internal sociological, economic, and political processes. Moreover,
in today's increasingly interdependent world, even the most powerful
states are influenced by the actions of other states. Thus any contribution made by a state to international action for the protection and promotion of human rights would be partly determined by the effect of
internal and external sociological, economic, and political factors on its
domestic and foreign policy. I say "partly determined" because the influence of ideas operating through the personalities of individual state
officials should not be discounted.

To evaluate the degree and quality of concern with cultural legitimacy in the development of the current human rights instruments, it is
necessary to look at the states involved in the process, at the background
of their representatives, and for indications of the positions they took
during the drafting and adoption processes.

As regards the states that participated in those processes in the initial
stages after the establishment of the UN in 1945, the vast majority of
the peoples of Africa and Asia were still suffering external domination
by the colonial Western powers. Thus of the fifty-one original members
of the UN there were only three from Africa and eight from Asia, with

---

33. Gidon Gottlieb, "Global Bargaining: The Legal and Diplomatic Framework," in
Falk, Kratochwil, and Mendlovitz, eds., *International Law,* pp. 210–35.

seven more Asian states joining over the next ten years.[34] Of the sixteen states that joined the organization in 1955, only one was from Africa, and five from Asia. However, with the rapid decolonization of the late 1950s and early 1960s, thirty-four African states joined the UN between 1956 and 1967. In terms of our inquiry, it is clear that few African and Asian states participated in the drafting of the Universal Declaration of Human Rights and the formative early stages of the two covenants. Moreover, two related considerations need to be noted in regard to the quality of representation accorded to the few states that did participate.

The more obvious consideration has to do with the nature of the government that was accorded UN recognition. Thus, for example, that China was represented at the UN by the national government established in Taiwan in effect disenfranchised and excluded from all UN procedures the People's Republic of China, where the vast majority of Chinese people lived. Less obvious, but equally true, some governments of the time purported to represent their native populations yet barely allowed them participation in making decisions over their national and international policies. The imperial government of Ethiopia, one of only three African states at the UN before 1955 (the others being Egypt and Liberia), is an example of a government that was in effective control of the country but did not allow most of its population to participate in making policy decisions.

State Representation of Non-Western Countries at International Forums

The orientation and cultural identification of the elites who ruled African and Asian states and represented them at international forums determined their participation in the drafting and adoption of the International Bill of Human Rights. Some insights into the cultural perspectives and philosophical orientation of those African and Asian "representatives" who were most influential in the early stages can be gained through an examination of their educational background and careers. The significance of this factor has been underscored at a human rights conference:

> The previous speaker said that different nations accepted the human rights conventions. This is a surrealistic statement that could only be made by a lawyer. These laws were not adopted by nations but by a

34. On the stages of the expansion of the membership of the United Nations, see C. Wilfred Jenks, *The World beyond the Charter in Historical Perspective: A Tentative Synthesis of Four Stages of World Organization* (London: Allen and Unwin, 1969), pp. 92–93.

small clique of lawyers, bureaucrats and intellectuals who are highly westernized and most of whom have absolutely nothing to do with the cultures in which most of their fellow nationals live. . . . The most interesting problem to me is how notions of human rights, which are clearly of Western provenance and which are now institutionalized are related to the values by which human beings live in most of the world.[35]

Although it is a slight exaggeration to describe the small clique who represented African and Asian countries as having "absolutely nothing to do" with their native cultures, there is obvious validity in the point. The drafting committee of the Universal Declaration of Human Rights consisted of representatives of the governments of Australia, Chile, China, France, Lebanon, the United Kingdom, the United States, and the Soviet Union. The only representatives of non-Western countries in that committee were Chang Peng-Chung of China and Charles Habib Malik of Lebanon.[36] Both had been educated in American universities, and both reflected their "westernization" in the positions they took during the debates. For example, Chang and Malik emphasized individual rights over collective or peoples' rights, and the need for the protection of the individual from the state.[37] Regardless of one's agreement or disagreement with their position, it clearly reflects more the Western than the Chinese and Middle Eastern perspectives.

It is true that the Universal Declaration went through many stages of debate and drafting at the levels of the Human Rights Commission, the Third Committee of the General Assembly, and the General Assembly itself. But African and Asian countries were probably represented at all those levels by people of similar orientation to Chang and Malik.[38] For example, General Carlos Romulos was ambassador extraordinary and

35. Peter Berger of Boston College, as quoted in Theodor Meron, ed., "A Report on the N.Y.U. Conference on Teaching International Protection of Human Rights," *New York University Journal of International Law and Politics*, vol. 13, no. 4 (1981), p. 901.

36. As far as non-Western cultural perspectives are concerned, the Soviet Union is a Western country, though not a liberal one.

37. Peter Meyer, "The International Bill: A Brief History," in Paul Williams, ed., *The International Bill of Human Rights* (Entwhistle Books, 1981).

38. Malik represented Lebanon in twelve out of the first thirteen sessions of the United Nations. Karem Azkoul, another prominent representative of Lebanon, was educated at St. Joseph's University, Beirut, at the Sorbonne, and at Munich and Berlin universities. He was acting representative of the drafting committee of Human Rights, and acting representative of the Commission of Human Rights. "United Nations General Assembly, Official Records," Third Session, First Part, Plenary Meeting 98 (1948–49), p. 113.

plenipotentiary of the Philippines to the UN. Besides his master's degree from Columbia University, he had several honorary degrees from American universities. During the war Romulos was a high-ranking officer in the U.S. Army and served as aide-de-camp to General Douglas MacArthur on Bataan and Corregidor.

Moreover, as noted by delegates from the developing countries, certain Western delegates were particularly influential in drafting the Universal Declaration. For example, at the beginning of the Third Committee debate on the draft declaration, Chang of China "paid a particular tribute to the contribution to the work of preparing the draft declaration made by Professor Cassin, the representative of France, who had so ably exposed French doctrines of the eighteenth century."[39] Chang also found France to be a particularly appropriate place for discussion of rights because it was "the birth-place of modern ideas of freedom." At the General Assembly level, many delegates made favorable comparisons between the Universal Declaration they were about to adopt (in 1948) and the eighteenth-century declarations, especially the French Declaration of the Rights of Man and of the Citizen of 1789.[40]

In its formulation of civil and political rights, however, the final version of the Universal Declaration departed in important ways from eighteenth-century Western conceptions of natural rights. For example, it included economic, social, and cultural rights unknown to eighteenth-century European conceptions.[41] These aspects of the declaration were included because of the support of Latin American and socialist countries. As for the peoples of Africa and Asia, the format and process for adopting the declaration did not permit the effective participation of their indigenous cultures.

Although initially undertaken at the same time as the declaration, the Covenant on Economic, Social and Cultural Rights and the Covenant on Civil and Political Rights had a much longer and more complex history. By the time they were finally adopted by the UN General Assembly in 1966, most African and Asian countries had gained independence and joined in the last stages of the drafting and adoption. From a formal point of view, African and Asian cultural perspectives had a bet-

39. "United Nations General Assembly Official Records," Third Session, First Part, Plenary Meeting 98, p. 114.

40. "United Nations General Assembly Official Records," Third Session, First Part, Plenary Meeting 181 (1948–49), pp. 875–934.

41. Johannes Morsink, "The Philosophy of the Universal Declaration," *Human Rights Quarterly*, vol. 6 (1984), pp. 309–34.

ter chance of being represented in the drafting and adoption of the covenants. At a more substantive level, I submit that the elites who represented African and Asian countries at that stage did not have a clear conception of their respective cultural positions on most of the principles covered by the covenants. This deficiency may be somewhat obscured by the fact that representatives of African and Asian countries took strong positions on certain draft provisions of the covenants and managed to change some of them. Given the lack of popular input and debate on these issues at the national domestic level in most African countries at the time, it is difficult to see how those elites could have genuinely represented their respective cultural traditions.

However, neither the integrity and caliber of the representatives of African and Asian countries nor agreement or disagreement with their orientation is at issue here. Rather, the issue is the degree to which those representatives could reasonably have identified with, and genuinely represented, their indigenous cultural traditions at the time of the drafting and adoption of the Universal Declaration and covenants. Western higher education does not necessarily preclude a person from a developing country from being committed to her or his own cultural tradition. In fact, such an education may enable one to act as a bridge between the two cultural traditions. But this does not seem to have been true for those representatives who participated in the drafting and adoption of the Universal Declaration.

Furthermore, to criticize the degree and quality of concern with cultural legitimacy during the formulation of the declaration and covenants does not mean that these instruments are untenable within non-Western cultural traditions. As I hope to show in the next section, there may be significant cultural support for the philosophical foundations and moral values underlying the current human rights standards. Moreover, insofar as there is inconsistency between the two, I believe further reconciliation and resolution of conflicts and tensions is possible. The point here is simply that there was little initial concern with cultural legitimacy, and this may have diminished the validity of international human rights standards as seen from non-Western cultural perspectives.

Finally, despite their differences, the essence of cultural traditions reflects the continuity and interdependence of the total human experience. Eighteenth-century Western formulations of rights are as much a reflection of pre-eighteenth-century non-Western experiences as they are a result of the experiences of Western peoples. Seen in this light, and presented as the outcome of shared insights rather than as the model developed by a "superior" people, the diffusion of this conception of rights is more likely to be accepted as legitimate by non-Western cultures and less likely to be rejected as manifestations of cultural imperialism.

Subsequent Concern with Cultural Legitimacy

The initial deficiency in establishing universal cultural support for the declaration and covenants (the International Bill of Human Rights) has been partly addressed in subsequent educational and scholarly efforts. For example, the United Nations Educational, Scientific, and Cultural Organization (UNESCO) has sponsored many international conferences, seminars, and publications on human rights in different cultural and religious traditions.[42] Other institutions, such as the International Commission of Jurists, and individual scholars have also published volumes on human rights and cultural perspectives.[43] In my view, most of these efforts suffer from two main weaknesses: inadequacy of their treatment of cultural legitimacy within specific traditions and the lack of an integrated cross-cultural approach.

I find that most of the published works tend to treat cultural traditions from a static and ahistorical point of view, with little regard for the

---

42. See, for example, *Birthright of Man: A Selection of Texts Prepared under the Direction of Jeanne Hersch* (New York: UNESCO, UNIPUB, 1969); Karel Vasak, ed., *The International Dimensions of Human Rights*, 2 vols. (Westport, Conn.: Greenwood Press, 1982); and *Philosophical Foundations of Human Rights* (Paris: UNESCO, 1986).

43. See, for example, International Commission of Jurists (ICJ), *Human Rights in a One-Party State*, International Seminar on Human Rights, Their Protection and the Rule of Law in a One-Party State (London: Search Press in conjunction with the ICJ, Geneva, 1978); *Development, Human Rights and the Rule of Law* (Elmsford, N.Y.: Pergamon Press, 1981); and *Human Rights in Islam*, Report of a seminar held in Kuwait, December 1980 (ICJ, University of Kuwait and Union of Arab Lawyers, 1982). See also Wm. Theodore de Bary and others, eds., *Sources of Indian Tradition* (Columbia University Press, 1958); Evan Luard, ed., *The International Protection of Human Rights* (London: Thames and Hudson, 1967); Asbjörn Eide and August Schou, eds., *International Protection of Human Rights*, Proceedings of the Seventh Nobel Symposium, Oslo, September 25–27, 1967 (John Wiley, 1968); Adamantia Pollis and Peter Schwab, eds., *Human Rights: Cultural and Ideological Perspectives* (Praeger, 1979); Kenneth W. Thompson, ed., *The Moral Imperatives of Human Rights: A World Survey* (Washington, D.C.: University Press of America, 1980); Jack L. Nelson and Vera M. Green, eds., *International Human Rights: Contemporary Issues* (Standfordville, N.Y.: Human Rights Publishing Group, 1980); Ved P. Nanda, James R. Scarritt, and George W. Shepherd, Jr., and others, eds., *Global Human Rights: Public Policies, Comparative Measures and NGO Strategies* (Boulder, Colo.: Westview Press, 1981); and Alfred Hennelly, S.J., and John Langan, S.J., eds., *Human Rights in the Americas: The Struggle for Consensus* (Georgetown University Press, 1982).

constant evolution and change of cultural norms and institutions. If the point of the exercise is to support human rights standards within the given cultural tradition in order to encourage greater respect for and protection of these rights in *current* practice, cultural norms and institutions must be analyzed and discussed in terms of their manifestations and significance in the present life of the community. Even as historical accounts of the culture in question, some of the relevant works tend to be selective and misleading because they emphasize points of agreement between historical cultural norms and current human rights standards without identifying and addressing points of conflict and tension.

This criticism can be illustrated with reference to the available literature on human rights in the Islamic tradition.[44] Not only is this literature ahistorical in that it tends to deal with formal scriptural tenets of Islam in isolation from their current social reality, but it is also selective and misleading even in terms of those formal tenets. By quoting and citing selected general scriptural statements that are presented as supportive of human rights in Islam, while omitting others that cannot be so represented, and by failing to show the ways in which the allegedly supportive statements have been qualified in juridical interpretations, this literature presents a completely misleading view of its subject.

Fortunately, some authors have recently sought to expose the misleading effect of selective citation of scriptural sources out of juridical context, and others have tried to discuss those tenets in relation to current social reality.[45] However, much more needs to be done to clarify the internal situation within the Islamic and other cultural traditions and to relate it to current social reality. This work is a necessary prerequisite for addressing the second main criticism cited earlier—namely, the lack of a cross-cultural approach. Such an approach is necessary for developing universal cultural legitimacy for human rights beyond the least common denominator of cultural legitimacy within various traditions. The least common denominator will not suffice to protect the human rights of women, for example.

Efforts to identify existing cultural support for human rights, and to resolve conflicts and tensions between human rights standards and cul-

44. This criticism is particularly true of works such as Ali Abdel Wahid Wafi, "Human Rights in Islam," *Islamic Quarterly,* vol. 2 (1967), pp. 64–75; Khalid M. Ishaque, "Human Rights in Islamic Law," *International Commission of Jurists Review,* vol. 12 (1974), pp. 30–39; *Human Rights in Islam,* Report of a seminar; and Isma'il R. Al Faruqi, "Islam and Human Rights," *Islamic Quarterly,* vol. 27 (1983), pp. 12–30.

45. See the chapters by Ann Mayer and Bassam Tibi in this volume.

tural norms and values, assume some agreement on what universal human rights are. Initially, and for the sake of expediency, the current international standards must be accepted as identifying universal human rights. But since a genuinely universal approach was not used in the initial formulation of the current standards, which came primarily from the liberal and to some extent the Marxist perspectives, a truly universal substantive set of human rights standards is still needed.

Take, for example, the question of cruel, inhuman, or degrading treatment or punishment. Starting from the existing instruments, one finds that protection against such treatment or punishment is recognized as a human right. When looking into specific cultural traditions, one may well find that a culture supports this concept as a human right, in the sense of a right to which each person is entitled by virtue of being human. Nevertheless, this "consensus" on the right as a matter of principle does not extend to the precise content of the right or provide criteria for determining whether a particular form of treatment or punishment violates the right. Only through the development of a universal consensus on the content of this right, established, for example, by the systematic analysis of the underlying rationale of punishment in cross-cultural perspectives, can human rights discourse avoid being trapped in a situation of competing claims over what constitutes cruel, inhuman, or degrading treatment or punishment.

Toward a Model for Enhancing the Cultural Legitimacy of Human Rights

Despite the inadequate concern with cultural legitimacy in formulating the current international standards of human rights, it is advisable to work with these standards rather than to seek to repudiate and replace them. To discard the achievements of the last forty years by dismantling the International Bill of Human Rights (the declaration and two covenants) is to risk never being able to replace it with better instruments. I would therefore make the existing bill the foundation of future efforts to establish cultural legitimacy for human rights by interpreting the current provisions and developing an appropriate literature sensitive to the need for cultural legitimacy. For example, it would be useful to contrast the values and institutions of various cultural traditions with the values underlying the International Bill of Human Rights and the specific implications of those values. Processes of internal cultural dynamics and change may then be used to reconcile and resolve any conflicts and tensions that exist between the values and institutions of a given cultural tradition and those envisaged by the current standards of human rights.

Fundamental Values of the International Bill of Human Rights

I am not concerned here with the historical source of these values, whether as perceived by the delegates who formulated the International Bill of Human Rights or discovered through some other analysis.[46] Instead, I propose to state the underlying values of the bill as discovered through an interpretative reading of the final text of the instruments. This seems possible regardless of whether the delegates who drafted and adopted the instruments shared a common view of the philosophy of the bill, and whether they succeeded in implementing their philosophy in the final texts of the instruments. In other words, for the following discussion, I take the texts of the International Bill of Human Rights as the source of the underlying values of the bill.

An interpretative reading of the provisions of the bill reveals several fundamental values that are accepted as valid and worthy of implementation through the specific principles of these documents. As expected, however, these values have their own internal tensions, which can be resolved only through detailed discussion and balancing between their specific implications in given situations. Although it is not possible to do that in the following brief survey of these values, the point should be borne in mind. In other words, the survey does not assume that these values were adopted by the International Bill of Human Rights in an unqualified form. It assumes that the flexibility of the interpretation of these values and the possibilities of their mutual limitation offer good prospects for reconciling them with values and institutions of a variety of cultural traditions.

The fundamental value underlying the Universal Declaration and covenants is the notion of the inherent dignity and integrity of every human being. All the civil and political rights as well as the economic, social, and cultural rights recognized by the Universal Declaration and elaborated on in the covenants are the necessary implications or practical manifestations of the inherent dignity and integrity of the human

46. For the view that analysis of the debates at the Third Committee of the UN in the Fall of 1948 reveal that the philosophy of the Universal Declaration was perceived by many delegates to be emanating from eighteenth-century philosophy of natural rights, with some significant modifications, see Morsink, "Philosophy of the Universal Declaration."

person. For example, human dignity and integrity require not only that individuals satisfy their needs for food, shelter, and health care but also that they be guaranteed freedom of belief, expression, and association and afforded opportunities for education and communication with others to develop fully their personalities and achieve their human potential.

Equality is another implication of the inherent dignity and integrity of the human being, which, in turn, requires nondiscrimination on grounds such as race, sex, religion, and national or social origin. Both notions are explicitly affirmed in the Universal Declaration and the two covenants. The essence of human rights is that they are the entitlement of every human being by virtue of being human. For example, this essence will be defeated if a woman is denied her human rights because of her sex, race, or beliefs.

It is sufficient here to focus on these values and their implications because they can be taken as the foundation of all human rights and because they are likely to encounter problems or difficulties of legitimacy in the context of traditional African cultures. Although I propose to focus on issues of cultural legitimacy in relation to Islamic African societies, this does not imply that other cultural traditions are fully consistent with all the underlying values and implications of the International Bill of Human Rights. On the contrary, the assumption is that every cultural tradition raises some problems in this regard. However, it is the thesis of this chapter that alternative sources and interpretations within any given tradition may prove useful in overcoming the problems raised by a particular tradition.

An often cited example of the inconsistency between some human rights and the liberal tradition is the latter's presumed rejection of the notion of imposing positive duties on the state to provide housing, health care, and so forth for those citizens who are unable to secure these essential needs for themselves. Jack Donnelly convincingly argues in this volume, however, that it may not be true of all lines of thinking within the liberal tradition. The limited success of social democracy in some Western European countries, for example, clearly shows that the liberal tradition can sustain social services based on a positive obligation of the state to provide for the physical needs of its population. Nevertheless, the dominant theme in both the theory and practice of Western liberalism remains that of restricting human rights to the negative duty of the state not to interfere with the liberty of the individual rather than linking human rights to a positive obligation to provide for basic needs.

From the point of view of the proposed approach, however, the question is how to enhance the view of human rights as requiring both positive and negative duties from the state within the liberal tradition through internally legitimate arguments.

Cultural Legitimacy of Human Rights in Islamic Societies

Traditional African cultural perspectives on human rights are too diverse and volatile to permit neat generalizations about their position on the underlying values of the International Bill. Even when focusing on a specific cultural tradition, one must allow for significant changes in norms and attitudes over time, while taking into account the inevitable discrepancy between the theory and practice of those norms and attitudes. Provided one keeps these limitations in mind, one can gain some understanding of the relationship between the values underlying the current standards of human rights and the corresponding values of specific African cultural traditions. In this section I discuss my own Islamic tradition in order to demonstrate both the difficulties it has with some aspects or implications of human rights values and the prospects of resolving those difficulties.

Religion, in general, is central to the cultures of many African societies, though not the sole formative force behind the prevailing values and attitudes. Other local factors and external influences also contribute to the continuing processes of social and political change. In Islamic African societies, however, the religion of Islam seems to be a particularly important source of cultural legitimacy because of the comprehensive and forceful nature of its precepts. In contrast to most traditional African religions, Islam has a highly specific ethical code and well-developed and articulated views on almost every aspect of private and public life.

Islam is an extremely complex and multifaceted phenomenon that has been the subject of numerous, often violent, disagreements among its adherents for the last fifteen centuries. Many sociological factors and philosophical considerations influence and inform the understanding and practice of Islam at any given time and place.[47] However, any meaningful discussion of an issue from an Islamic point of view must be based on the fundamental sources of Islam, namely, the Qur'an, which

47. There are many good books on Islam available in English; for example, Fazlur Rahman, *Islam* (University of Chicago Press, 1979); and Marshall G. S. Hodgson, *The Venture of Islam: Conscience and History in a World Civilization*, 3 vols. (University of Chicago Press, 1974).

Muslims firmly believe to be the literal and final word of God, and the *sunna*, the traditions of the Prophet.

Although the text of the Qur'an, known in Arabic as *al-muṣḥaf*, was recorded within a few decades after the Prophet's death in 632 and is accepted as accurate by the vast majority of Muslims, the texts of the *sunna* were, and continue to be, much more controversial because they remained an oral tradition until they were recorded about two centuries after the Prophet's death.[48] Besides the controversies about the accuracy of many reported *sunna* texts, both the Qur'an and *sunna* have been the subject of extensive scholarly and popular interpretation and counter-interpretation for many centuries. This process has led to the evolution of *shari'a*, the comprehensive and complex codes ranging in subject from religious dogma and ritual practices to ethical norms, principles and detailed rules of private and public law, and matters of etiquette and personal hygiene.

Internal controversy and differences within the corpus of *shari'a* were encouraged for two reasons. First, some verses of the Qur'an and texts of *sunna* appear to contradict each other. Whenever Islamic scholars and jurists encountered this contradiction, they deemed one set of texts to have abrogated or repealed, for the purposes of *shari'a*, any other inconsistent text. This process of reconciliation through abrogation is known in Islamic jurisprudence as *naskh*.[49] Second, since both sources used the Arabic language to communicate their teachings, the understanding of those teachings has been influenced by the many shades of meaning of Arabic expressions as comprehended by different Islamic jurists and scholars.

As a result, today the official and formal *shari'a* position on many issues is based on decisions made by Muslim scholars and jurists either to adopt one set of texts rather than another, or to adopt one possible interpretation of the applicable texts rather than another. In other words, though the Qur'an and *sunna* as sources of *shari'a* are believed by Muslims to be divine, the interpretation and implementation of those sources have been the product of human comprehension and action in a particular historical context. Once this basic fact about the evolution of *shari'a* is appreciated, the door should be open for developing alter-

48. See generally, John Burton, *The Collection of the Qur'an* (Cambridge University Press, 1977); and Joseph Schacht, *The Origins of Muhammadan Jurisprudence* (Oxford University Press, 1950).

49. Abdullahi Ahmed An-Na'im, *Toward an Islamic Reformation: Civil Liberties, Human Rights and International Law* (Syracuse University Press, 1990), pp. 57–60.

native concepts and principles from within the Islamic tradition itself. So long as such efforts are consistent with the fundamental precepts of Islam and sensitive to concerns for Islamic authenticity, there is no reason to prevent the adopting or adapting of norms and ideas from other cultural traditions. Early Muslim scholars and jurists did just that in developing their understanding of shariʿa.

Looking at the totality of the Qur'an and sunna in relation to the values underlying current international standards of human rights produces a mixed picture. On the one hand, many general texts seem to emphasize the inherent dignity and integrity of the human person, and stress the equality of all human beings in the sight of God.[50] On the other hand, many other specific texts establish strict limitations on who is a human being entitled to full dignity and integrity and complete equality within the context of the Islamic society and state. In particular, certain texts of the Qur'an and sunna support a hierarchy of status according to sex and belief, with Muslim men being the only group entitled to the full implications of human dignity, integrity, and equality, followed by Muslim women, certain non-Muslim believers (mainly Christians and Jews), and finally other believers and unbelievers. Given the historical context within which shariʿa was developed, it was probably unavoidable that the early Muslim scholars and jurists should adopt that view of the source texts. In other words, the historical context of the eighth- and ninth-century Middle East determined the choices and interpretations Muslim scholars and community leaders made among the range of texts. By the same token, the present historical context that upholds universal human rights regardless of sex and belief should determine the choices and interpretations modern Muslim scholars and community leaders have to make among the range of texts and interpretations.

I have elsewhere documented human rights problems with shariʿa, and elaborated on the modernist approach to Islamic reform advocated by the late Muslim reformer, Ustadh Mahmoud Mohamed Taha.[51] This

50. See, for example, Riffat Hassan, "On Human Rights and the Qur'anic Perspective," Journal of Ecumenical Studies, vol. 19, no. 3 (1982), pp. 51–65.

51. See generally, Mahmoud Mohamed Taha, The Second Message of Islam, translated with an introduction by Abdullahi A. An-Naʿim (Syracuse University Press, 1987). See also, for example, the following works by Abdullahi Ahmed An-Naʿim: "Religious Freedom in Egypt: Under the Shadow of the Islamic Dhimma System," in Leonard Swidler, ed., Religious Liberty and Human Rights in Nations and in Religions (Philadelphia: Ecumenical Press, 1986), p. 43; "The Islamic Law of Apostasy and Its Modern Applicability: A Case from the Sudan," Religion, vol. 16 (1986), pp. 197–224; "Islamic Law, International

approach not only is feasible in the Islamic context but may provide a useful model for working within other cultural traditions to identify tensions and conflicts with values underlying the current human rights standards. The approach may also help to develop ways of resolving authentic and legitimate conflicts within the particular cultural perspective. The essential premise of this model is the recognition that cultural norms evolve in response to specific historical circumstances. Therefore, norms may vary or be modified with the change of circumstances. The sources of norms and values, and the techniques by which they evolve and change, may be specific to the particular culture. Nevertheless, there are certain principles that regulate the processes of cultural dynamics and change in general, and that may therefore be used in conscious efforts to enhance the legitimacy of human rights within any given cultural tradition.

Cultural Dynamics and Change

As mentioned earlier, this chapter takes a very broad view of culture as the totality of the experience of a given society. It also assumes that every cultural tradition contains some norms and institutions that are supportive of some human rights as well as norms and institutions that are antithetical or problematic in relation to other human rights. The constructive approach suggested here would seek enhancing the supportive elements and redressing the antithetical or problematic elements in ways that are consistent with the integrity of the cultural tradition in question. It is self-defeating and counterproductive to try to enhance the legitimacy of human rights within any culture in ways that are unlikely to be accepted as legitimate by that culture.

Against this background, this section investigates present knowledge of the processes of cultural dynamics and change and how it may help the endeavor to promote the cultural legitimacy of human rights. Is it possible to develop some guidelines for human rights advocates who may wish to undertake this task? A cross-cultural approach provides the appropriate balance between the relativism and universalism of human rights, but what does this approach entail and how can it be used to enhance the cultural legitimacy of human rights?

Relations and Human Rights: Challenge and Response," *Cornell International Law Journal,* vol. 20, no. 2 (1987), p. 317–35; and "Mahmud Muhammad Taha and the Crisis in Islamic Law Reform: Implications for Interreligious Relations," *Journal of Ecumenical Studies,* vol. 25, no. 1 (1988), pp. 1–21.

It is helpful to begin by emphasizing the major assumptions under-lying cross-cultural studies, such as the pioneering cross-cultural survey of the Institute of Human Relations of Yale University in 1937.[52] Ac-cording to the organizers and editors of the Yale survey, cross-cultural studies are founded on the conviction that despite their diversity, all human cultures have fundamentally a great deal in common, and that these common aspects are susceptible to scientific analysis. Further-more, such studies are said to be based on seven assumptions shared by most social scientists in the field. These assumptions may be summa-rized as follows:[53]

—Culture is not instinctive, or innate, or transmitted biologically, but is composed of habits, such as learned tendencies to react, acquired by each individual through life experience.

—Culture is repeatedly inculcated by transmission from parent to child over successive generations. Such inculcation involves not only the imparting of techniques and knowledge but also the disciplining of the child's animal impulses to adjust the child to social life.

—As such, the habits of the cultural order are social in that they are shared by human beings living in organized aggregates or societies and kept relatively uniform by social pressure. Since many cultures provide for the societal survival of their respective societies, they tend to reflect certain universals, such as sentiments of group cohesion, mechanisms of social control, organization for defense against hostile neighbors, and provision for the perpetuation of the population.

—To a considerable extent, the group habits of which culture consists are conceptualized (or verbalized) as ideal norms or patterns of behav-ior. Actual behavior, however, may not always conform with the cul-tural ideal because that ideal is only one of the determinants of behav-ior. Since individuals behave in response to the state of their organism and drives at the moment, and in response to their perception of the total situation in which they find themselves, such behavior may de-viate from the ideal norms.

52. On the conception and organization of the Yale survey, see George Peter Murdock, "The Cross-Cultural Survey," in Frank W. Moore, ed., *Readings in Cross-Cultural Methodol-ogy* (New Haven: Hraf Press, 1961), pp. 45–54.

53. The seven assumptions I list closely follow Murdock, "Cross-Cultural Survey," pp. 48–52. The basic premise and some of its consequent assumptions are further explained and supported in other essays in Moore, ed., *Readings in Cross-Cultural Methodology*, such as Clyde Kluckhohn, "Universal Categories of Culture," pp. 89–105. The assumptions in the text are also eloquently explained and emphasized by Ruth Benedict in *Patterns of Culture*.

—Since habits persist only so long as they bring satisfaction, elements of culture can continue to exist only when they yield to the people in a society a margin of satisfaction, a favorable balance of pleasure over pain.

—Culture changes through an adaptive process that is comparable to but different from that of evolution in the organic realm. In this way cultures adjust and adapt to the surrounding physical and geographic as well as social environments. To subscribe to this assumption of cultural adaptability is not to maintain a rigidly deterministic view of the process—that any culture would necessarily have to adjust in any given way—since different cultural forms may represent adjustments to similar problems and similar cultural forms may represent adjustments to different problems. Some similarities in different cultures may represent independent adjustments to comparable conditions. Thus while cultures always adjust to physical events and historical contacts with peoples of differing cultures, both kinds of stimuli exert only a conditioning rather than a determining influence on the course of a given culture. In other words, there is always an element of selection and choice of reaction to the particular event or historical context.

—In this adaptive process, cultures *tend* to form a consistent and integrated whole, but total integration is never achieved because historical events are constantly exerting a disturbing influence. Integration takes time, and long before one process is completed, many others will have been initiated.

These assumptions are useful for my present purposes provided they are seen in the context of a broad definition of culture and are perceived as being applicable to *all* the cultural traditions of the world, including those of materially developed societies. When seen in this light, these assumptions offer prospects for influencing the direction of cultural change toward enhancing the legitimacy of human rights. Given the radical transformation of the technology of communication of information and ideas in an increasingly globalized world, it is possible to manipulate the assumptions in favor of specific goals. Such manipulation is already taking place somewhat haphazardly to serve the narrow ends of commercial interests. Powerful symbols and images are constantly used to promote consumerism in fashion, entertainment, and so forth. Can appropriate techniques be used to promote universal legitimacy for human rights? And what is the content of the human rights message to be conveyed through those techniques?

Although limited by its subjects—normally small individual societies—and by its retrospective approach to understanding past processes of societal change, the available anthropological literature on cultural dynamics and change may nevertheless provide some guidance to effecting change in a particular direction. This literature can inform us about the factors facilitating change and about those opposing or resisting it within any given society. For example, Edward Shils's discussion of endogenous and exogenous factors affecting the inevitable process of change within a wide variety of traditions, and of patterns of change and stability in traditions,[54] may be useful in undertaking the *prospective* process of change in favor of the specific goal of enhancing the cultural legitimacy of human rights. The work of other scholars may provide useful insights into the psychological and sociological processes of interaction and change within a given culture.[55] Studies of the receptivity and resistance of specific societies to change may also provide some guidance.[56]

Examples of planned social engineering undertaken by totalitarian states may be particularly instructive on the negative side of this approach; for instance, the attempt by the Soviet Union to transform human relations in traditional Islamic societies of Central Asia in the 1920s.[57] While heeding the warning raised by such efforts, I view them as examples of what should not be done, not as reasons for abandoning my approach. The success of human rights–oriented cultural engineering depends as much on the sensitivity of its methods as on the validity of its goals. As to sensitivity of methods, I reemphasize the need to work from within the culture and to preserve its integrity. Since the Soviet experiment ignored both imperatives, it is not a strong argument against what I am proposing. But what about the goals of my proposal, the content of the human rights message I hope to realize through the manipulation of the processes of cultural dynamics and change?

As observed by Renteln, the work of anthropologists who have ar-

54. Edward Shils, *Tradition* (University of Chicago Press, 1981), chaps. 5–7.

55. See, for example, Melville J. Herskovits, *Cultural Dynamics* (Knopf, 1964); and Marvin K. Opler, "Cultural Evolution and the Psychology of Peoples," in Dole and Carneiro, eds., *Essays in the Science of Culture*, pp. 354–79.

56. See, for example, Simon Ottenberg, "Ibo Receptivity to Change," and Harold K. Schneider, "Pakot Resistance to Change," both in William R. Bascom and Melville J. Herskovits, eds., *Continuity and Change in African Cultures* (University of Chicago Press, 1959), pp. 130 and 144, respectively.

57. On that "experiment," see Gregory J. Massell, "Law as an Instrument of Revolutionary Change in a Traditional Milieu: The Case of Soviet Central Asia," *Law and Society Review,* 1968, pp. 179–228.

gued on behalf of universals may be criticized for basing them on concepts such as human needs, rationality, and human nature that may well be culturally determined. Nevertheless, Renteln seems to favor undertaking comparative analysis of cultural ideals ("oughts") to discover cross-cultural universals for which she adopts the definition of "those least common denominators to be extracted from the range of variation that all phenomena of the natural or cultural world manifest."[58] She then admits the possibility of the following problem of cross-cultural universals, in the sense of least common denominators:

> The objection might be raised that some cross-cultural universals might be discovered that Westerners would call "inhumane." . . . I view this as an unlikely possibility. Since the values in question are cultural *ideals*, it would seem most improbable that any "inhumane" ideal would be universal. Even if a universal ideal is found which some would regard as "inhumane," this is a part of morality. It is better to be honest and to admit that it exists than to pretend that it does not. The possibility for change means that concerted effort might lead the international community to reject it [p. 66].

Although Renteln's use of the designation "Western" is understandable because she is addressing a primarily Western readership, this usage unfortunately gives the impression that it is the Western value judgment that counts. The use of a neutral or broader designation would be preferable to express the same optimistic view that it is improbable that universal cultural ideals are inhumane. Realistically speaking, however, one has to face the possibility of a broadly held ideal being inhumane. Moreover, as mentioned before, a strictly relativist position may insist on maintaining a cultural ideal that is regarded by outsiders as inhumane. I now elaborate on my earlier response to these situations.

A dual approach to this problem would allow a human rights advocate to work within the cultural tradition while drawing on an enlightened universal conception of human rights. Cross-cultural studies can develop a universal conception of the inherent dignity and integrity of the human being. Insofar as any cultural tradition fails to uphold and

58. Renteln, "Relativism and the Search for Human Rights," pp. 65, 66. She adopts this definition from the distinction made by Herskovits between universals and absolutes, which he defines as fixed and not admitted to have variation, to differ from culture to culture, from epoch to epoch.

implement the full implications of the inherent dignity and integrity of human beings within the particular community, human rights advocates within that community should use the resources of their cultural tradition to redress that fault internally in ways that are perceived to be legitimate by the members of that culture. In so doing, human rights advocates can be supported by colleagues from other cultural traditions and by the international community at large. Here the technology of communication can be used to good effect. The golden rule for outside help and support, however, is the same as that for internal action; namely, respect for the integrity of the cultural tradition and sensitivity to its criteria for legitimacy.

In this endeavor the universal principle of reciprocity is particularly useful: the principle that one should concede to the other person whatever one claims for oneself. Otherwise, one would not be entitled to claim against the other person what one demands for oneself. According to this principle, *human rights are those that a person would claim for herself or himself and must therefore be conceded to all other human beings*. This principle can be used to inform and guide the cross-cultural search for the content and necessary implications of the inherent dignity and integrity of human beings. Whatever the members of a culture would demand for themselves in accordance with their inherent human dignity and integrity they would have to concede to members of other cultures. This is, in my view, the basis of universal cultural legitimacy for human rights.

Conclusion

The basic premise of this chapter views culture, broadly defined, as the context within which human rights have to be specified and realized. Despite the initial lack or inadequacy of concern with universal cultural legitimacy during the formulation and adoption of international standards of human rights, and despite the inadequacy of subsequent efforts to supplement that initial deficiency, those standards remain to be improved rather than abandoned.

It is not too late to correct the situation by undertaking cross-cultural work to provide the necessary internal legitimacy for human rights standards. The golden rule for both levels of action is the need for relativist sensitivity in developing universal standards. Each culture has its share of problems with human rights as well as the potential to resolve those problems. In working within the culture, and receiving guidance and support from without, external standards should not be imposed to enhance cultural legitimacy. The inherent dignity and integrity of the human person, taken as the fundamental underlying value of all human rights, can be extended beyond barriers of sex, race, religion, and so on, through the principle of reciprocity—namely, that one should concede to others what one claims for oneself. Thus the full range of human rights can gain cultural legitimacy everywhere in the world.

One important set of questions that I deliberately avoided here concerns the nature and scope of human rights in the abstract philosophical sense. It is premature to embark on such an inquiry before establishing its proper cultural frame of reference. Despite the abundance of literature on the subject from within a specific cultural tradition, usually the Western liberal tradition, and of literature comparing competing perspectives on the issues, I have not been able to discover an integrated cross-cultural examination of this question. I would therefore rather wait until a satisfactory methodology for cross-cultural analysis is devised before embarking on an inquiry into the abstract philosophical nature and scope of "human rights." The definition proposed here is a useful working model for the development of universal cultural legitimacy for human rights.

CHAPTER FOURTEEN

Human Rights in an Evolving World Culture

Richard D. Schwartz

THE CONFERENCE on which this book is based dealt with human rights, one of the crucial problems of postmodern society. In the enlightening papers on human rights in Africa that make up the contents of this volume, one finds extensive evidence of the efforts now under way to provide a comprehensive basis for human rights. Those efforts are not limited to Africa; human rights are a subject of interest everywhere in the world.[1]

We seem to have entered an era in which people in every country, on every continent, are searching for a universally valid concept of human rights. How fully this goal can be attained is of course problematic. Before events have occurred, there are no certainties in human history. Peering into the future, we can only speculate on the routes to follow in order to achieve the outcome we desire.

It is especially appropriate now that we try to understand how to move toward universal human rights. We are living at one of those junctures of history when a unique new culture, a world culture, is in the making.[2] To maintain its stability and humanity, world society must in-

---

1. Significant signs of an emerging world culture oriented toward human rights are to be found not only in the basic documents issued by the United Nations (see Paul Williams, ed., *The International Bill of Human Rights* [Glen Ellen, Calif.: Entwhistle Books, 1981]) and the Helsinki conference (see Mary Frances Dominick, ed., *Human Rights and the Helsinki Accord: A Five Year Road to Madrid* [Nashville: William S. Hein, 1981], pp. 335–402), but also in the subsequent activity they have generated. For a thoughtful analysis of the diverse ideological streams that converge to support human rights, see Jerome Shestack's "The Jurisprudence of Human Rights," in Theodor Meron, ed., *Human Rights in International Law: Legal and Policy Issues* (Oxford: Clarendon Press, 1984).

2. Among the signs of an emerging world culture are the convergent characteristics of "individual modernism" described by Alex Inkeles in an extensive set of studies. For a summary see Alex Inkeles, *Exploring Individual Modernity* (Columbia University Press, 1983), pp. 31–51. He has also addressed, more briefly, the relation between individual trends and social system effects. Alex Inkeles, "Continuity and Change in the Interaction

corporate in its intrinsic cultural foundations the fundamental principles of human rights. If it does not, future generations may be forced to choose between chaos and authoritarian control.

Formal declarations, though important, will not suffice to establish universal human rights. Legal systems cannot regulate societies unless the laws are supported by cultural norms. We must therefore address the question: how can the peoples of the contemporary world, so diverse in their cultures, arrive at a normative consensus that favors universal human rights in an emerging world order?

If human rights are to play a central role in the new world culture, those of us who favor that development should try to determine what paths will take us in that direction. I believe the following orientations should guide our efforts.

First, we should recognize that this is a crucial time in the evolution of world society, and that the worldwide culture patterns now in formation can be expected to persist for a very long time. Awareness of that prospect should lead us into intensive, shared efforts to understand the nature and quality of the emergent culture and, in light of that understanding, to take steps to ensure that it embodies as fully as possible the basic concepts of human rights.

Second, we should work to refine a theory and strategy to facilitate the acceptance and implementation of human rights everywhere in the world. Looking toward such a theory, I set out in this chapter a few ideas that might provide a basis for discussion. The gist of what I have to propose is as follows. Worldwide support for human rights, which is necessary if they are to become and remain central to the evolving world society, is most likely to develop and persist if the concept of human rights (a) draws on elements from all the great cultural traditions and is compatible with each of them; (b) serves as a way to obtain and maintain self-determination for all nations; and (c) integrates in full measure the political, economic, and civic components stated in the United Nations' Universal Declaration of Human Rights and in the two international human rights covenants.

These two orientations are intertwined in my chapter. My purpose is to be suggestive rather than systematic in presentation; the developments to which I refer are matters more of conviction than logic, more of intuition than deduction, more of participation than authoritative pronouncement.

---

of the Personal and the Sociocultural Systems," in Bernard Barber and Alex Inkeles, eds., *Stability and Social Change* (Little, Brown, 1971), pp. 265–81.

When Cultures Form

From history I infer that when conditions are favorable, a culture can emerge quickly, spread its influence widely,[3] and last a long time. If one takes major culture regions as illustration, the great cultures of China and India formed rapidly, diffused broadly, and retained their basic features for centuries. As they emerged in the middle of the first millennium B.C., each had distinctive characteristics. The technical conditions that made uniform culture possible over a wide area were similar: agriculture generated an economic surplus to support cities; transportation permitted the transfer and use of that surplus to support an elaborate division of labor; taxation and trade provided the mechanisms for collecting the surplus; and weaponry and military organization facilitated the protection and control that made empire possible.[4]

Within that general framework, one culture developed and spread throughout China and another throughout India. Both expressed and consolidated a particular form of society. But the content of each culture was remarkably different, and the social organizations these cultures maintained were worlds apart. In their basic form, each of these distinctive patterns survived for more than two millennia, even—it is fair to say—into the current era.

In China, the consolidation occurred at the time of the founder of the Ch'in dynasty, Shih Huang Ti. He rebuilt the Great Wall, developed the transportation system, and took many steps to consolidate the imperial power. Three of these steps were of prime importance. The emperor exiled hundreds of thousands of feudal nobles from their lands to a province close enough to his capital for him to keep an eye on them. He

3. A. L. Kroeber did the classic work on diffusion of cultures. See the chapters on "Culture Growth," "Spreads," and "Distributions," in A. L. Kroeber, *Anthropology: Race, Language, Culture, Psychology, Prehistory* (Harcourt, Brace, 1948), pp. 473–508, 538–71. See also A. L. Kroeber, *Configurations of Culture Growth* (University of California Press, 1944), particularly p. 845, and more generally pp. 761–846, in which he declines to claim findings that lead to comprehensive generalizations. His reference to a "first hearth" provides a possibly helpful clue that seems to apply to the Chinese and Western traditions. Geographically, a radiating spread of culture growth can usually be traced from a first hearth to the larger area finally occupied. That is in accord with what anthropologists have again and again noted in regard to specific diffusions.

4. See Ralph E. Turner, *The Great Cultural Traditions: The Foundations of Civilization*, 2 vols. (McGraw-Hill, 1941), for the classic comparative study of the ancient empires. S. N. Eisenstadt and A. Shachar provide additional information and a useful analysis of Chinese and Indian cultures, among others, in *Society, Culture, and Urbanization* (Beverly Hills, Calif.: Sage Publications, 1987).

consolidated an administrative examination system that selected talented young men from throughout his expanding domain to become career civil servants in the governmental hierarchy. And by suppressing the early version of Confucianism, he paved the way for a revised version of the master's teaching that included due respect for the new imperium.[5]

In India even earlier, an equally distinctive cultural system came into being. Under the Laws of Manu, hereditary strata, or varnas, formed the basis of organized society. Individual opportunity depended on the accident of birth rather than on the possession of talent. In each region, caste counterparts of the varnas took on a distinctively local significance that seems to have impeded the unification of the country.[6] Although Hinduism culturally dominated the entire subcontinent, it did not promote an effective central government. Indeed, the subcontinent was unified only when the rulers accepted an equalitarian non-Hindu ideology, whether the Buddhism of Asoka, the Islamic doctrine of Akbar and Aurangzeb, or the Christian faith of the British Raj.[7]

Although these examples cannot be discussed in detail here, they are intended to emphasize three points. First, great cultures develop when conditions are favorable; second, the basic norms of the culture are laid down at the outset and tend to persist for millennia; third, the nature of those norms helps to determine the political unity or diversity of the culture area.[8]

Applying these assumptions to the contemporary world, one can ask what kind of a world culture might be emerging at this time. Perhaps the new culture will be based on human rights. Those of us who seek a humane world strongly favor human rights as a basis for the emerging world order. The Universal Declaration of Human Rights of 1948 and the two covenants of 1966, on economic rights and political rights, might well become the equivalent of the Confucian texts or of the Laws of Manu in laying the foundation for a coming world order.[9] Before that

5. A concise account has been provided by C. P. Fitzgerald, China: A Short Cultural History (Praeger, 1950), pp. 137–229.

6. Romila Thapar, A History of India, vol. 1 (Penguin, 1966), pp. 37–40.

7. Thapar, A History of India, vol. 1, pp. 71–91; and Percival Spear, A History of India, vol. 2 (Penguin, 1966), pp. 40–60, 129–57.

8. For an elaboration of this theme, see Richard D. Schwartz, "The Limits and Possibilities of Governments," in James F. Short, Jr., ed., The Social Fabric: Dimensions and Issues (Beverly Hills, Calif.: Sage Publications, 1986).

9. The full text of the Universal Declaration is given in Williams, International Bill of Human Rights, pp. 3–12; the International Covenant on Economic, Social and Cultural

can happen, our social organization and culture must necessarily evolve to express and support these principles.

The concept of human rights has a powerful appeal to virtually all peoples. Consequently, laws could emerge that would be widely supported by culturally based norms. The congruence of laws and norms seems to be required everywhere if the formal legal system is to gain the support needed for enduring governance. As Montesquieu pointed out, a government that depends on repression ultimately falls because it is forced to use increasingly harsh, and therefore alienating, sanctions.[10]

If that is true, we must ask what politically relevant norms appear to have widespread support. It will not do merely to point to the Universal Declaration and the covenants. They are fine documents, subscribed to by many governments. But their implementation has been partial and slow, faced at every turn with domestic political impediments.

Some norms seem to have achieved general support from governments and grass-roots communities. For instance, using race as a basis for discrimination has been condemned by governments everywhere, and by large majorities of public opinion almost everywhere. Close behind in acceptance is the principle, advanced most clearly and objectively by Amnesty International, that torture for political reasons is unacceptable.

Although these developments encourage belief that a human rights–based culture will evolve, one cannot assume that such an evolution will be swift and automatic. Too many diversities exist in contemporary cultures for one to think that a normative convergence will necessarily occur. Rather, one ought to expect that some differences will persist. Distinctive cultural traditions and current conditions make it improbable that a single philosophy of rights will come to be widely accepted. Jack Donnelly is welcome to explore that possibility, of course,[11] but in

---

Rights, in ibid., pp. 13–29; and the International Covenant on Civil and Political Rights, in ibid., pp. 31–64. The Confucian texts appear to have been reconstructed during the Han period by several historians, of whom the foremost was Ssu-ma Ch'ien, author of the Shih-Ching. Fitzgerald, *China*, pp. 154–57, 209–17. Unlike the Confucian text, which is historically attributable to a particular historical figure and subsequent editors, the originals and the authorship of the *Laws of Manu* and other sacred Indian texts are more difficult to locate with certainty. For the text, see F. Max Muller, ed., *Laws of Manu* (Oxford: Clarendon Press, 1886).

10. This penetrating observation by Montesquieu, dating from the early eighteenth century, suggests a remarkably modern theory of governance. See, in particular, "The Troglodytes," in Montesquieu, *Persian Letters* (Penguin Books, 1973).

11. I refer to Jack Donnelly's chapter in this volume, and the same theme spelled out in detail in his book, *The Concept of Human Rights* (St. Martin's Press, 1985).

my view no single philosopher—not even John Stuart Mill—has found the keystone with which to build an evolving world culture.

Nor would it be helpful to a normative-legal consensus if the fundamental ideas all came from any single one of the world's great cultures. Unlike ancient empires, a world culture will probably not emerge through conquest or the authoritative imposition of an ideology. Our best chance for a stable world order, I suggest, is to rely on basic principles of human dignity, a respect for differences, and a growing capacity to reconcile those differences in mutually enhancing ways.

In that light, it would be promising to assume that each of the great culture areas has something important to offer in the evolution of world culture. The West has contributed a valuable conception of individual human rights, but it has overemphasized individualism and has assumed that its morality was justification enough for conquest, hegemony, and dominance. It is time for this ethnocentric parochialism to give way to a broader conception of the interrelationship of peoples.

The idea that social order must be based on wide adherence to a single uniform moral code threatens to impede the emergence of a stable world order. It is an assumption that must be identified, analyzed, and recognized as problematic. Although it exists to some extent in all societies, it has become a distinctive feature of the Western tradition. It is certainly present in the Judaic, Christian, and Islamic worldviews,[12] though each of these religions contains themes that, as discussed by twentieth-century theologians, limit and temper a dominantly ethnocentric religious ideology.[13] The persistence of ethnocentrism in modern thought, both secular and religious, is evident in every part of the world influenced by these religions, where nations prepare themselves for war by calling one another the evil empire or the great Satan.

In the emergence of a world order, ethnocentrism must take on a more modest role. Some degree of it, to be sure, is valuable in providing

12. For a sweeping attack on the ethnocentric theme in Western culture, see Jacques Derrida, *Of Grammatology* (Johns Hopkins University Press, 1976).

13. See, for example, the work of twentieth-century theologians who seek to counter religion-based ethnocentrism. In Islam, Mahmoud Ayoub, *Redemptive Suffering in Islam: A Study of the Devotional Aspects of Ashura in Twelve Shiism* (The Hague: Mouton, 1978), and Mahmoud M. Taha, *The Second Message of Islam* (Syracuse University Press, 1987); in Christianity, Paul Tillich, in particular, *The Courage to Be* (Yale University Press, 1952), and Reinhold Niebuhr, *The Nature and Destiny of Man: A Christian Interpretation* (Scribner's, 1964), especially vol. 2, pp. 213–43; in Judaism, Franz Rosenzweig, *The Star of Redemption* (Holt, Rinehart, and Winston, 1971), and Martin Buber, *The Prophetic Faith* (Macmillan, 1949), especially pp. 202–30 on Deuter-o-Isaiah.

group members with a sense of identity. The concept of citizenship in a nation carries with it some potentially valuable connotations. It limits the antagonism with which tribal units seek to dominate one another. It implies a certain standard of protection for the rights of all citizens, an idea that can help to restrain the unbridled concentration of power and privilege. But carried too far, the concept of the nation can become a threat to world order rather than a salutary contribution to it. If nations permit the principle of citizenship to become the moral justification for the oppression of minorities within their borders or aggression against countries beyond their borders, they detract from the prospect of a stable world order.

To deal with these problems, our common culture-to-be must be enriched by lessons from history. In seeking to temper ethnocentrism, the West can learn from Chinese history the great promise of building a social order on the principle of religious and ideological toleration. Unlike Europe, which over the centuries devoted itself to crusades and holy wars, the Chinese empire—having learned the futility of book burning from Shih Huang Ti's failure to suppress Confucian thought, and the value of intellectual synthesis as practiced during the dynasties that followed—eschewed belief-based inquisitions.[14] Instead, it promoted an easily learned set of behavioral principles that encouraged people to fulfill their moral obligations. On that Confucian base, revised during the Han dynasty to include loyalty to the emperor, many different beliefs were tolerated.

Authority that rests on a widespread normative consensus can benefit from diversity of belief. Even in contemporary times, the Chinese have tried to recover the principle of toleration after a period in which Marxism-Leninism manifested itself in the thought control, brainwashing, and harassment of the postrevolutionary period.[15] This effort received a serious setback in the events at Tiananmen Square in the spring of 1989. Whether a traditional culture of ideological toleration will reassert itself in China remains to be seen. If it can, the rest of the world stands to benefit from the ancient Chinese tradition of open-mindedness.

14. Although the attitude of toleration was particularly noteworthy in certain dynastic periods (for example, the Sung), even periods of militancy seem to have omitted any use of the concept of "holy war" or its equivalent. See Fitzgerald, *China*, passim.

15. Fox Butterfield's account of the Great Cultural Revolution in *China: Alive in the Bitter Sea* (Times Books, 1982) describes the mood of that period well.

Besides ideological toleration and the restraint of ethnocentrism, the emerging world order must find affirmative methods to limit conflict.[16] Reconciling differences without violence has become of vital importance. This century is the first ever—at least since the mythic time of Noah—in which all of humanity can be destroyed. I risk no embarrassment in predicting that the annihilation of humanity will not occur, being secure in the knowledge that if it does, there will be no one left to blame optimists like me for having made a faulty prediction. More seriously, I believe that "suigenocidal" tendencies—that is, the inclination toward self-destruction of all mankind—are not strongly present in the human race, since they would have been selected out in catastrophic events in which such tendencies succeeded. Humans are endowed with the ability to sense danger and to avoid it, the more so when it threatens the destruction of their way of life, their culture, and their society.

In a dangerous world, our best protection is to be found in the elaboration of means for reconciliation. Uniformity cannot be imposed without endangering us all—the dominators as well as the dominated. Rather, we should affirmatively cultivate experiences through which people can learn to live peacefully with one another. To do so, we must find ways of performing the praxis of reconciliation, so that it can develop into a norm of world culture.

Some of the best examples of reconciliatory norms are found in studies of African societies. Francis Deng has described the pattern among the Dinka in which the closest relative or best friend of a disputant assumes responsibility for advocating the position of the adversary.[17] How different an approach to conflict than the adversarial relations of the West!

Many non-African anthropologists have also described reconciliatory patterns in African cultures. Perhaps their attention has been drawn to these patterns because of the contrast with Western tendencies. In any

16. Among the pioneers in this effort have been John Burton, whose contributions are discussed in Michael Banks, ed., *Conflict in World Society: A New Perspective on International Relations* (St. Martin's Press, 1984); and Leonard W. Doob, *Patterning of Time* (Yale University Press, 1971). The recent remarkable efforts of President Oscar Arias Sanchez of Costa Rica illustrates the ability of political leaders to take the initiative toward reconciliation between nations.

17. In his extensive discussion of Dinka culture, Francis M. Deng has given much evidence of reconciliatory themes. See, in particular, his books *The Dinka of the Sudan* (Holt, Rinehart, and Winston, 1972); and *Tradition and Modernization* (Yale University Press, 1971; 2d ed., 1987), p. 108.

case, some of the best instances of reconciliatory praxis are to be found in African ethnography. A few examples will illustrate this characteristic:

—Max Gluckman's essay on "The Peace in the Feud," which describes the ways in which a feud is regularly brought to an end after it has established the rights of the parties, but before it becomes disruptive of social order or destructive of human values.[18]

—Paul Bohannan's description of the process of double institutionalization, derived from his observations of the Tiv, in which the formal process of adjudication conducted by a council examines the breakdown in relations between disputants that occurred within the original institution so that the relationship can be restored and future breaches of reciprocity can be avoided.[19]

—Stanley Diamond's description of the restraint imposed by the original culture on the measures used by the Asante-Heni or paramount ruler of the Ashanti Empire.[20] Though Diamond, drawing on Rattray,[21] sets out to chronicle the changes in power relations resulting from the consolidation of power, his account ultimately emphasizes the durability of the original culture and the effectiveness of the villagers' culture carriers in shaping the imperium.[22]

Many such examples come to mind. Perhaps the African culture area can provide a distinctive theme for an evolving world culture: that human rights achieve vitality through reconciliatory praxis.[23] The value

18. This essay of Max Gluckman's, in *Custom and Conflict in Africa* (Oxford: Basil Blackwell, 1955), a more popular presentation than most of his work, vividly describes a broad theme that has characterized many African societies.

19. Paul Bohannan's generalizations about law, particularly influenced by his intensive studies of the Tiv, may reflect a tendency for law-norm integration that is found among many African peoples. *Justice and Judgment among the Tiv* (Oxford University Press, 1957). For a presentation of his important concept of "double institutionalization," see Bohannan, "The Differing Realms of the Law," in *American Anthropologist*, vol. 67, pt. 2 (Supplement, December 1965).

20. Stanley Diamond, "The Rule of Law versus the Order of Custom," *Social Research*, vol. 38, no. 1 (1971), pp. 42–72.

21. The Ashanti have become particularly well known among primitive empires because of Robert S. Rattray's remarkable account in *Ashanti* (New York: Negro University Press, 1969).

22. See also Stanley Diamond's full-length study, *Dahomey: A Proto-state in West Africa* (Ann Arbor: University Microfilms, 1951).

23. In advancing the idea that African societies tend toward reconciliatory culture patterns, I draw primarily on impressions from ethnographic literature. In addition to the four authors already mentioned, the following writers provide some basis for thinking so: Edward E. Evans-Pritchard, *The Nuer: A Description of the Modes of Livelihood and Political*

and duration of these practices depend on their regular use throughout a society, from bottom to top, as well as between societies. Formal rights may set the stage and establish the boundaries, but people living together in mutual respect make them a reality.

When each of several nations has learned through experience the value of human rights, they may join together in common adherence to a universal, comprehensive concept of human rights. I turn now to the exploration of that prospect.

Human Rights and Self-Determination

Respect for human rights may be fostered by reason as well as by experience. In this section I suggest that human rights be viewed as a way to obtain and maintain a common goal: self-determination. Self-determination has been declared to be a human right, and a very prominent one in the formal covenants of the United Nations. Although not mentioned in the Universal Declaration, it appears in the first article of both covenants.

All people have the right of self-determination. By virtue of that right they freely determine their political status and freely pursue their economic, social and cultural development.

This language, adopted by the United Nations, expresses an aspiration that appears to be widely and deeply held everywhere in the world. Its most obvious manifestation has been found in the rejection of colonial rule, but it also describes domestic aspirations.

Institutions of a Nilotic People (Oxford University Press, 1940), pp. 171–76, on the Nuer leopard skin chief; Philip H. Gulliver, *Disputes of Negotiations: A Cross-Cultural Perspective* (Academic Press, 1979), pp. 131–41, 233–52, on dispute settling among the Ndendeuli and Arusha of Tanzania; John Middleton, "Ritual and Ambiguity in Lugbara Society," in Sally F. Moore and Barbara G. Myerhoff, eds., *Secular Ritual* (Amsterdam: Van Corcum, 1977), on the secular-ritual mechanisms of coping with conflict among the Lugbara of Uganda; and K. Oberg, "The Kingdom of Ankole in Uganda," in E. E. Evans-Pritchard and M. Fortes, eds., *African Political Systems* (Oxford University Press, 1940), especially pp. 121–38, on the symbiosis between the Bahima and the Bairu (even though they were respectively conquerors and conquered) among the Ankole of Uganda. This is not to say that reconciliation always works, or works more frequently, in the African cultural area. The intrusion of colonial powers bearing other traditions may have weakened initially reconciliatory tendencies in many parts of Africa. Even so, I am impressed by the pervasiveness and resiliency of the reconciliatory theme and would like to see the question studied further.

Clearly, throughout the world there is a strong undercurrent in favor of self-determination. This feeling is found at the level of individuals and small social units, at the level of nationalities, and at the political level of nation states. A people denied the right of self-determination tends today to grow discontented under the continued dominance of others. As that domination is maintained, those who are denied self-determination find ways of expressing their resentment.

Self-determination usually takes a long time to achieve and may be won only after great resistance. Occasionally those who seek self-determination become so discouraged that they give up the fight. But in general the means of resistance are sufficiently available to put those who dominate in an awkward position. They may decide to exercise sanctions against the people who assert the right of self-determination, but sanctions exercised against a united and determined nation always face difficulties. Rules seen as fair need little sanction; rules seen as unfair need heavier sanction.[24] As the unwelcome sovereign exercises ever greater force, his actions are ever less accepted. Finally the prohibited acts increase because they serve as expressions of defiance against the sovereign, and they are supported by the populace, who treat the "wrongdoers" (as officially defined) as heroes.

Before the established regime becomes discredited, the authority can sometimes draw back. Compromise that balances the demand for self-determination with the maintenance of hegemony sometimes succeeds. But timing is of vital importance. If the authority becomes hated by a broad enough spectrum of the subject population, it can easily find itself unable to repair the damage by reform measures.

This sequence has been repeated so frequently in this century that it begins to look like an accurate empirical generalization for our time. The decline of empires after World War I could have been explained as a measure imposed by the victors—largely to expand their own empires, or at least to diminish the domain of their vanquished adversaries. But World War II revealed a different dynamic: the victors as well as the vanquished saw the end of imperial control, with few exceptions. The principal exception was the Soviet Union, which expanded its territory—and its military control of the Eastern European countries.

Now, however, even these exceptions to national self-determination have slipped away. Forty-five years after the Soviet Union established its hegemony over the nations of Eastern Europe, that control has sud-

24. Montesquieu's formulation is the classic one. See note 10.

denly been rejected. Whatever compromise might earlier have been possible to legitimate the continuation of foreign authority, the chances for any such agreement seem to have vanished.

Not only have foreign regimes imposed on a national population been vigorously and widely resisted, but also intensive authority imposed from within the nation has been resisted if it impinges on self-determination for the majority. Those who feared or hoped that authoritarian states were inevitable have not so far had their expectations confirmed. Instead, such regimes have proved unstable in Africa, Latin America, and Asia. The tide now seems to be running toward self-determination of national populations, for freedom both from foreign domination and in domestic affairs. Independent nations such as Haiti or Chile seem to abhor authoritarian regimes even when no issue of foreign rule is involved.

But the aspiration for self-determination, though destabilizing to authoritarian regimes, does not inevitably produce stable self-determinant social systems. Much remains to be learned about how self-determination can be sustained. We would like to believe that a rule of law can mechanically achieve this goal. It was in that spirit that Jeremy Bentham made his famous offer: to draft a constitution for any nation that wanted one. We know now that a formal document, no matter how carefully drafted, cannot by itself ensure full self-determination. Far closer to the truth was Benjamin Franklin's reserved optimism. When he was asked after the U.S. Constitutional Convention what had been achieved, Franklin is said to have replied, "A republic—if you can keep it."

To maintain self-determination requires that the principles of the French Revolution be lived at all levels of a society. The stability of a democratic society can be secured only if liberty, equality, and cooperation are maintained to a considerable degree throughout the society. If that is to occur, the very fabric of society must embody those principles. It may be easier to enunciate them than to sustain them, even in a society that adopts them from the start.

The UN documents have given new nations a basis for moving toward human rights principles. In the struggle for self-determination, some have made use of these aspirations to measure the deficiency of the regime they seek to overthrow. Other nations have used these principles as a standard by which to measure and criticize existing regimes, to pressure them to change, and to oust them when they do not respond.

The use of human rights as a rallying cry can be powerfully effective. Not only does it put the authoritarian regime under pressure, but it unifies the population by mobilizing their sympathies for those most flagrantly deprived. And it may also invoke assistance from other nations for those who struggle to achieve a greater measure of self-determination.

The American Revolution provides one of the clearest and earliest examples of this process. When the English king sought to impose his officials, his laws, and his taxes on the colonies, he succeeded in uniting them in a conflict that ended his control over them. The colonists' struggle was particularly effective because the Americans drew on the emerging philosophy of human rights that had developed in England itself during the preceding century, embodied in the English Bill of Rights of 1689 that was incorporated in the Law to Regulate Succession to the English Throne. It was the struggle to obtain these rights that mobilized the colonists and set a lasting mark on the character of American society.

Do human rights serve the same function for all nations struggling to establish self-determination? One might have thought so. In the contemporary world human rights have been supported more widely in principle than they were two centuries ago. Yet in practice, international support for human rights has often been half-hearted or negative—that is, authoritarian, totalitarian, and neocolonial regimes have been accepted into the community of nations. Even when external support for human rights has put some pressure on a regime that deprived a nation of self-determination, such efforts could not succeed without a force from within to give them meaning.

It is within the nation that the demand for human rights must be voiced if a regime based on those principles is to be achieved and sustained. Nations that struggle for self-determination can and sometimes do make good use of human rights principles to unify themselves against a regime that denies them. I suggest that the use of human rights can be effective not only in rallying support for self-determination but also in forming and sustaining a society that maintains human rights after the initial struggle has been won.

To do so, however, the full range of human rights—political and economic—should be joined together. If either set is neglected, the other set becomes vulnerable. Balance between the two has been difficult to sustain.

Some emergent nations have placed economic rights above political and civil rights. This outlook has generally characterized the struggle for self-determination based on Marxist ideology. And though economic deprivation provides one legitimate basis for opposing a regime, it does not necessarily point toward full human rights. Because totalitarian government was practiced by the Soviet Union, the principal proponent of Marxism before and after World War II, the struggle for economic rights often led nations seeking self-determination to accept regimes that did not provide political and civil rights.

A corresponding limitation developed among nations that freed themselves in an earlier era from colonial rule under the banner of liberal democracy. Those nations often used the formal language of political and civil rights to justify their struggle for self-determination. But the ability of the population to make use of formal rights was limited— as in Latin America—by the poverty and ignorance of the majority. Efforts to implement economic rights in such nations proved difficult because of the dominance of elites that used the military at will to maintain a monopoly of wealth and power.

These experiences lead toward the conclusion that economic and political-civil rights complement each other; each may indeed be indispensable for the other. This interdependence can be seen to some extent in the struggle for self-determination, but it can be easily overlooked in the spirit of unity that binds a people together against a hated regime. Depending on history and current circumstances, a revolutionary nation can easily neglect one set of rights while pursuing the other.

Thus the revolution that brought unity to Italy left the economic inequality of southern Italy and Sicily largely intact. The poverty and ignorance of the population in those regions were, if anything, exacerbated by the national regime that emerged. As a result, the dominance exercised by a combination of large landowners, the Catholic Church, and the Mafia grew stronger after the unification of Italy. In these circumstances, the populace was ready to support a fascist party that promised economic relief through authoritarian rule. It was an exchange that in effect asked the people to surrender political and civil rights that had not proved useful in alleviating their economic distress.

Comparably, a regime may be overthrown because it deprives the population of political and civil rights. The revolution that ousted Ferdinand Marcos from power in the Philippines offers an illustration. Marcos' overthrow reflected a mass movement (but one the Marxists generally opposed) based primarily on his flouting of civil and political rights. As a result, the administration of Corazon Aquino rests on a mandate to enhance one set of rights, the political and civil, but not the other set, the economic. Having come to power with a consensus on the first set, it seems incapable of moving toward effective redistribution of land, an apparent prerequisite for the implementation of economic rights.

In developing a strategy for self-determination, then, putting equal emphasis on economic and political-civil rights may prove to be the most effective measure. In the struggle for self-determination, it may help to unify the population by addressing the felt deprivations of each segment. Just as important, it may provide—after self-determination is won—a cultural foundation that supports a full range of human rights each of which can support the others.

Conclusion

Every culture will have its distinctive ways of formulating and supporting human rights. Every society can learn from other societies more effective ways to implement human rights. While honoring the diversity of cultures, we can also build toward common principles that all can support. As agreement is reached on the substance, we may begin to trust international law to provide a salutary and acceptable safeguard to ensure that all people can count on a minimum standard of human rights.

Contributors

Abdullahi Ahmed An-Na'im
Professor, College of Law
University of Saskatchewan

Francis M. Deng
Senior Fellow
Brookings Institution

Jack Donnelly
Professor, Department of
Political Science
University of North Carolina

Rhoda E. Howard
Professor, Department of Sociology
McMaster University

Virginia A. Leary
Professor, Faculty of Law and
Jurisprudence
State University of New York at
Buffalo

David Little
Senior Scholar,
U.S. Institute of Peace

Ann Elizabeth Mayer
Professor, Department of Legal
Studies
Wharton School, University of
Pennsylvania

James C. N. Paul
Professor, School of Law
Rutgers, State University
of New Jersey

Richard D. Schwartz
Ernest I. White Professor,
College of Law
Syracuse University

James Silk
Attorney in private practice
Washington, D.C.

Bassam Tibi
Professor, Department of
Political Science
Georg-August-Universität Göttingen

Claude E. Welch, Jr.
Professor, Department of
Political Science
State University of New York
at Buffalo

Kwasi Wiredu
Professor, Department of Philosophy
University of South Florida

Subject Index

Addis Ababa Agreement, 284–85
African Charter on Human and Peoples'
Rights, 23, 166; participatory democracy and, 306. *See also* Banjul Charter
African society, 109; acceleration of
change and, 179; cultural values and, 3,
7; expansionism and, 164; and group
membership, 205–06; moral ideals in,
5; poor rights-record rationalization,
291; postcolonial rights record, 290,
315; rights strategy for, 186–87; urban-industrial change and, 170. *See also*
Akan society; Dinka of the Sudan;
Francophone Africa
African-Western rights debate, 160–61,
309; African perspective in, 178–79; international rights law and, 216; social
change and, 178; unique African concept of, 308; universal rights concept
and, 291
Agreements of the People, 98. *See also* Levellers
Akan society, 166–67; communalism and,
246–47; conception of person, 244–48;
cultural ties, 243–44; justice system,
252–53; kinship relations and, 248;
land in, 245–46, 253–55; matrilineal
nature of, 245; self-government, 251–
52; system of rights, 245–46, 257
American Revolution, 380
Amnesty International, 155, 372; CMRN
and, 199; Conté regime and, 184, 197–
98; effect on rights conditions, 207
Anomie, 174–75, 179; individualism and,
176
Apostate (*murtad*), 104, 110

Arab Organization of Human Rights, 117,
145, 150
Ashanti chiefs, 163, 376
Atheism, 71–72
Authoritarianism, 297; Burkina Faso, 194;
coexistence with rights, 301; colonialism and, 293–94; in francophone Africa, 190–91; Guinea, 198; in SSA, 221;
rights abuse and, 292; self-determination and, 379–80

Banjul Charter, 207, 215–16; ambivalence
of political leaders and, 216; Ivorian
nonratification, 196. *See also* African
Charter on Human and Peoples' Rights
Basic human needs, 218–19
Bill of Human Rights, International, 215;
African rights concepts and, 181; African rights scholars and, 160; authoritarian regimes and, 301; cultural legitimacy and, 357; foundation for rights
legitimacy, 355–56; francophone Africa
and, 204; fundamental values of, 356–
58; Iranian rejection of, 140–41; Muslims and, 135; normative standards and,
147; *shariʿa* and, 134; source of rights
norms, 291–92; Western values and, 8,
148, 290. *See also* Covenant on Civil and
Political Rights, International; Covenant
on Economic, Social and Cultural
Rights, International; Universal Declaration of Human Rights
Bill of Rights, U.S., 21
Buddhism, 109, 111; India and, 371
Burkina Faso, 184; civil justice system in,
194; civil-political rights in, 191; Comp-

385

aore's junta, 193–94; economic constraints in, 185; military intervention cycle, 191–93

Calvinism, 6; Conciliar tradition and, 85; human reason and, 83–84; human rights formulation and, 61; and Lockean theory, 76–77; natural rights and, 85–86; on property, 87; resistance theory in, 89–90, 94–95; in sixteenth century, 91–97

Catholic religion, 146; Calvin and, 85; Lockean theory on, 71; post-revolutionary Italy and, 381; rights theory and, 61; theologians, 60

China, 370; Ch'in dynasty, 370–71; ideological toleration and, 374

Christianity, 6, 175; in Akan society, 255–56, 258; Dinka society and, 279; fundamentalism and, 171; human rights and, 60, 61–62; international law and, 152

Christians: human rights and, 59; Islamic recognition and, 104; missionaries, 152, 172, 255, 279, 284; Orientals and, 153

Civil authority, 81; agreement of the people and, 100–01; enforcement of human rights and, 115; and enforcement of natural law, 85; Levellers and, 101; religious practice and, 91. See also Governmental power

Clan, 245; Akan political organization and, 248; Dinka immortality and, 265–66; indigenous political systems and, 310–11; traditional African culture and, 307

CMRN. See Military Committee for National Redress (CMRN)

Colonialism, 130; British imperial policy, 187; destruction of traditional institutions, 293–94; Dinka society and, 281–82; effect on non-Western cultures, 16; exporting revolution and, 108; francophone Africa and, 185–86, 187–90; French Fifth Republic and, 188–89; French Fourth Republic and, 188; SSA states and, 222–23

Committees for the Defense of the Revolution (CDRs), 192, 194

Communalism, 18; African rights concepts and, 160–161, 166, 167–68; in Akan

society, 246–47; basic rights and, 319; Dinka and, 263, 269; entitlements and, 110; individualism and, 35; religious duties, 118; rights declaration and, 24; status divisions in, 313

Conciliar movement, 80, 81, 92; Calvinism and, 85

Confucianism, 371; Han dynasty and, 374

Conscience: free, 95; natural right of, 91, 101–02; Reformed faith and, 94; spiritual-earthly separation, 88, 90, 101

Constitutionalism, 77; civil authority and, 81; Conciliar movement and, 80

Consultation (shura), 112, 120; democracy and, 123; Islamic constitution and, 129; modern interpretations and, 127–28; political participation and, 121–22; Qur'an and, 127–28

Côte d'Ivoire, 184; civil-political rights in, 195–96; human rights ambivalence, 196; social fragmentation and, 185

Covenant on Civil and Political Rights, International, 24, 25, 205; cultural legitimacy of, 351–52; francophone Africa and, 203; Optional Protocol to, 26; rights of participation and, 218

Covenant on Economic, Social and Cultural Rights, International, 25; basic human needs and, 218; cultural legitimacy of, 351–52; cultural protection and, 234; property rights and, 27–28

Cross-cultural perspectives, 1; consensus and human rights, 111, 355; eclecticism and, 8; ethnocentrism and, 340–41; evaluating cultures and, 343–44; human dignity and integrity in, 365–66; human rights instruments and, 353–54; model for scientific analysis, 362–63; on human rights, 8, 147, 344–45; Sudan and, 288–89; universal common denominators, 365

Cultural change, 172; rural populations, 223–24

Cultural norms, 337–38; reconciliatory praxis and, 375–77; societal evolution and, 371; world society and, 369

Culture, 332–33, 361; definition of, 232, 334, 363; evolutions of, 370; levels of, 335; normative convergence and, 372

Czarist Russia, 169

Declaration of Independence, U.S., 20
Declaration of the Rights and Duties of Man, American, 22
Declaration on the Right to Development, UN, 28, 215
Democracy, 98, 165; Arabic language and, 123; Arabic scholars and, 122; feudal inception of, 115; Islamic revivalists and, 127–29; modernization and, 301; Qur'an and, 127–28; rights of participation and, 217; in Senegal, 202
Development, economic, 29, 110; African societies and, 161; dimensions of rural development, 225–26; Dinka society and, 278; human rights violations and, 114; programs and basic needs, 218; Reagan administration and, 29; right of people and, 219–21; rights abuse and, 295–96, 320; rural poor and, 224; SSA and, 213; state's role in, 223
Dinka of the Sudan, 111, 166, 182, 375; birth control and, 325; Christianity's effect on, 285; concept of immortality, 264–66; cultural exclusiveness, 279–80; cultural values, 262–64; custom of levitate, 265, 275–76; ethnocentrism of, 325; human relations and, 266; human rights and, 262, 271–72, 280, 288; individual-collective dignity and, 267–68; moral code and, 9–10, 271; Muslims and, 284–88; nation-state and, 280–82, 287–88; political-legal principles, 269–71; resistance to change, 277–78; slavery and, 7; spiritual principles, 268–69; system inequities, 273–77; traditional African society model, 264; value system, 272–73, 280, 288
Discrimination: conventions on eliminating, 215; Islamic secularism and, 104–05; Japanese in U.S., 19; racial bias and, 372; shari'a and, 126
Due process, 220; and state security, 298; in traditional African values, 307

Economic and Social Council, UN, 26
Economic Community of West African States (ECOWAS), 207
Economic-social rights, 49–52, 114; African societies and, 161–62, 168
Elimination of All Forms of Discrimination against Women, Convention on the (CEDAW), 215; SSA ratification of, 219
Elimination of All Forms of Racial Discrimination, Convention on the, 215
Elite, empowered, 186; drafting of rights instruments and, 352; economic development and, 213; francophone Africa and, 189–90; implementation of rights and, 331–32; political ends and, 1; rights deprivation and, 179, 381
Enstoolment, 251, 257; land redistribution and, 254
Entitlements, human, 107; Akan society and, 247; essence of human rights, 357; Islam and, 110
Equality, 219; dignity and, 357; for women, 345
Ethiopia, 349; enforced resettlement in, 177
Ethnocentrism: cross-cultural criticism and, 340–41, 344; Dinka society and, 345; interrelationship of people and, 373; role in world order, 373–74; Western culture and, 159
Eurocentrism, 108; cultural relativism and, 339; international law and, 151, 153

Fascism, 24; populist socialism and, 179
Forums, international, 349–50
Francophone Africa: civil-political rights in, 190–91; common factors in states of, 185–86; economic development emphasis, 191; incumbent power elite and, 207–08; independence from France, 188–89; rights ratification record of, 203–04. See also Burkina Faso; Côte d'Ivoire; Guinea; Senegal
Freedom House, 204–05
French Declaration of Rights of Man, 21, 351
French Huguenots, 95
French Revolution, 113, 115, 131; self-determination and, 379

General Assembly, UN, 19; Third Committee of, 20, 24
Glorious Revolution, 52
God, will of: Calvin on, 88–89; resistance theory and, 90; ultimate authority, 95

Governmental power: French centralization of, 187–88; law of nature and, 68; life, liberty, and, 51; one-party control and, 190; *shura* and, 128; span of control, 70. *See also* Civil authority; Elite, empowered

Guinea, 184–85; authoritarian rule, 198; economic constraints, 185; justice system, 199; poor infrastructure, 198; social fragmentation and, 185

Horizon FM, 193–94

Human dignity, 3; African rights and, 165–66, 169; Akan value system and, 244; Dinka and, 266–68; and human rights, 4, 29–30, 109, 307, 344; human rights documents and, 356–57; world cultural emergence and, 373

Human needs. *See* Basic human needs

Human rights, 120–21; African collectivism and, 163; African concept of, 2, 169, 171; basic, 319–21; Christianity and, 6; contextual legitimacy of, 10; cross-cultural perspective on, 1, 111; cultural distinctions and, 106; and development rights, 28–29, 220, 225; international standards of, 4–5, 136–37, 159; Islamic culture and, 105, 117, 131–32, 138; legal enforcement system and, 107, 115, 121; liberal theory and, 31, 34; liberation theologians and, 59–60; social fabric and, 172–73; universal consensus on, 110; Western Europe and, 54, 357. *See also* Bill of Human Rights, International; Rights abuses and violations; Rights theory; Universal human rights

Human rights, African: defining, 318; effect of colonialism, 293–94; generalization trap, 323; nation building and, 294–95; nonuniversality concept and, 317; poor record rationalizing, 291; postcolonialism and, 290, 292; uniqueness of, 308, 316, 317

Human Rights Commission, UN, 20; Drafting Committee of, 21

Imperialism, cultural, 113, 151; human rights debate and, 161, 291; human rights movement and, 309; international law and, 153

Individualism: African rights concept and, 159–60; African societies and, 162; criticism of, 35–36; endemic conflict and, 173; human rights and, 31–32, 182; Islam and, 114–15; Muslim societies and, 149; North American society and, 175; place in society and, 35; primacy of, 18; property-based, 39; self-preservation and, 36–38

Institutionalizing rights protection, 113, 116, 145; constitutional framework and, 126; Muslim thinking and, 120

International Commission of Jurists, 207

International Labour Organization (ILO), 18, 215; francophone Africa and, 204; participation rights and, 237; security of land and, 219, 234

International Monetary Fund (IMF), 198, 200

Iran, 149; human rights denial and, 140–41; Islamic law and, 136; Islamic revolution in, 141, 155

Iranian Bar Association, 142, 155

Islam: contextual understanding and, 106–07; cultural exclusiveness and, 111; human rights and, 104, 108, 148, 154; human rights cultural legitimacy, 358–61; individual freedom and, 114–15; international law and, 137; legitimizing oppression and, 149; modernity and, 133; Pakistani Muslims and, 150; societal-state separation and, 116; tradition and, 2, 147; unity of outlook and, 130–31. *See also* Consultation (*shura*); Law, Islamic (*shariʿa*); Muslims; Qurʾan

Islamic Declaration of Human Rights (1981), 112, 117; ambiguity of, 139; European cultural concepts and, 118; Iranian government and, 154–55; Islamic scripture and, 131; Islamocentric view and, 118, 138; normative commitment and, 115–16

Islamic governmental system (*niẓam islami*), 104, 112

Ivory Coast. *See* Côte d'Ivoire

Judaism, 104
Judeo-Christian: tradition, 7, 133; values, 6
Justice, African, 166; concept of dignity and, 169, 181; natural justice, 173; Western-African contrast of, 171
Justice, social, 110, 173; human rights and, 180

Labor: property accumulation and, 40; self-proprietorship of, 50
Land, right to, 218–19; Akan society and, 245–46, 253–55
Law, international: international relations and, 347–48; treaties and, 348
Law, Islamic international (siyar), 136–37
Law, Islamic (shariʿa), 104; denial of freedoms and, 150; discrimination and, 126–27; evolving process of, 126; and general law, 121; governmental system and, 129, 135; human rights and, 107, 136; Islamic scriptures and, 124; limitations of scope, 144; modern-premodern reconciliation, 139; oppressive regimes and, 123; premodern form of, 134; Qur'an and, 125–26, 359, 359–60; reciprocity principle and, 345; Sudan and, 285
Law of nature, 34; governmental power and, 68; preservation of society and, 37; religious underpinnings, 63–64. See also Natural law
Laws of Manu, 371
League of Nations, 18
Legitimacy, cultural, 332; cultural levels and, 335–36; current rights formulation and, 333, 346–47, 366; international law and, 347–48; public policy and action, 336–39; reciprocity principle and, 366
Levellers, 97–98; civil authority and, 101; political defeat of, 99; theological foundations of, 99–100
Levitate, institution of, 265, 275–76
Liberalism: bourgeoisie revolution and, 53; human rights concept and, 31, 34, 173–74, 357; reality of the individual and, 36; roots of, 33–34; tradition of, 32–33

Liberation theologians, 59
Lineage: Akan land rights and, 167, 245–46, 253–55; Akan political system and, 248; Dinka immortality and, 265
Lockean theory: Calvinism and, 76–77; liberalism's roots and, 33–34, 52; natural rights and, 6; property and, 44–45, 74; and restrictions on liberalism, 51–52; role of religion in, 62–63, 70; unlimited accumulation and, 41–44; wages and, 73
Lome agreements, 207

Marxism, 60, 108, 335, 355; New Testament and, 60; self-determination and, 381
Military Committee for National Redress (CMRN), 198; Amnesty International and, 199
Missiriya Arabs, 182
Money, 40–41; distribution system and, 75; implicit value and, 42
Money economy, 74; SSA states and, 222
Muhammad, 111, 127
Muslims, 2; autonomy of citizens and, 143; Dinka of Sudan and, 284–88; European genesis of human rights and, 2; international human rights and, 134, 137–38, 143, 145; and Islamic tie, 104; and Khomeini's Islamization, 142; Lockean theory on, 71; political-religious separation and, 143–44; private Muslim ideas, 149; Qur'an and, 134–35; resistance theory and, 115–16; revivalists and, 131–32, 133; rights-religious synergism, 140; superiority and, 110–11; traditionalism versus historicism, 132; Zia's Islamization policy, 150–51. See also Islam
Myth of Merrie Africa, 164–65

National Union of Secondary School Teachers (SYNESCI), 196–97
Nation building, 294–96; curtailment of rights and, 299; national unity and, 298–99; rights abuse and, 302; traditional culture and, 303
Nation-state, 288; Dinka value system

and, 280–81; rights limitations and, 299–300; self-determination and, 216

Natural law: human reason and, 66, 84; modern theory and, 113; money and, 41; Muslims and, 105; preservation of mankind and, 49–50; property accumulation and, 40; right of conscience and, 91; rights theory and, 77, 322; unlimited accumulation and, 41–44

Natural right, 17, 61; Aquinas and, 78; Calvin's twin set of, 87–88; and conventional right, 81; equality and autonomy, 107, 108; later Calvinists and, 91–93; liberty of conscience, 70, 95; nonharm principle, 67; objective right and, 77; philosophy of, 6; religious groundings of, 63; subjective theory of, 96, 100

Nazism, 24

New Testament, 60

Ninth International Conference of American States, 22

Non-Western cultures, 2; colonialism and, 16; human rights application to, 15; human rights perspectives, 29; rights-dignity confusion, 109

North American culture: family in, 176; individualism and, 175

One-party systems: Akan society and, 259–60; francophone Africa and, 189; Ivorians and, 196–97; postcolonial period and, 301–02; SSA and, 221

Organization of African Unity (OAU), 215; Ivorian disdain for, 196

Oriental countries: international law and, 151; Western imperialistic mentality and, 152–53

Ottoman Empire, 151–52

Pakistan, 149; democratization of, 156; Islamization of, 142; *shari'a* and, 143

Participation rights, 217–18; activists and, 238–39; grass-roots activity and, 236; group interests and, 233; legal resources and, 236–37; mitigating state power and, 234; political, 342; strategies for developing, 235–39

Pluralism, cultural, 114–15; cultural relativism and, 109, 131; Dinka value system and, 280–82, 287; Islam and, 110; SSA states and, 232, 234; universality of human rights and, 117; worldwide, 10, 109

Political empowerment: Akan kinship and, 248; food security and, 229; Islamic (*shari'a*) and, 112

Political human rights, 135, 184; minority representation, 249–50; third-world authors and, 114

Political organization: African consensual form, 163, 250; Akan society and, 248; Dinka society and, 269–71

Popular Front (Burkina Faso), 193–94

Property accumulation, 39; African society and, 163; natural law and, 40; spoilage limit and, 40

Property rights, 21; Akan lineage and, 167, 245–46, 253–55; Aquinas on, 78–80; Calvinism and, 87, 93; concept of use and, 42, 74; covenants on rights and, 27; exclusive rights and, 74–75, 87; human rights concept and, 31; legislative power and, 45–46; liberal tradition and, 32–33, 50; nonnationals and, 27–28; Qur'anic revelation and, 120; the state and, 96–97. *See also* Land, rights to

Protected minorities (*dhimmis*), 104, 119; Islamic divisions of humanity and, 110

Qur'an, 111; basis for legal system, 125–26; consultation (*shura*) and, 112; democracy from, 127–28; human dignity and integrity in, 360; human rights and, 118–20, 121; Muslims and, 111; Western precepts and, 130–31

Reagan administration, 29

Reason, human, 66; Calvin on, 83–84

Reciprocity principle, 345; cultural legitimacy and, 366–67

Reconciliatory praxis, 375–77

Relativism, cultural, 1; criticisms of, 340–41; danger of excesses in, 341–42; human rights violations and, 151; international rights standards and, 135, 316–17; Islamic rights concepts and, 147–

49; pluralism and, 109; rights legitimacy and, 339; tests for assessing claims of, 342–43; Western versus African and, 171–72
Religious freedom, 255–57
Revivalism, Islamic, 122; derivation of democracy and, 127–29; governmental system and, 124–25; human rights and, 128–29; institutional framework and, 131; Islamization of modernism and, 133
Revolutionary committees, 185
Rights abuses and violations, 331; cultural relativism and, 151; development justification, 295–96; Islamic society and, 135, 139–40; Muslims and, 149; nation-building rationale for, 294–96, 302–03; non-Western values and, 109–10; preservation of the state and, 298; shari'a, 285–86; state power and, 180; women's rights and, 177–78, 180
Rights theory: bottom-up strategy for, 186–87, 206; Calvinism and, 77; concern for human dignity and, 321–22; and discrepancy with practice, 331, 331–32; economic-social conditions in, 300–01, 306; individual empowerment and, 304–05; natural law and, 77, 322; notion of humanity and, 261; right of resistance, 88; top-down strategy, 187, 206–07; Western influence on, 17, 30, 321–23
Right to die, 253
Roosevelt's Four Freedoms, 26
Rural development: bureaucratic pathologies and, 229; dimensions of, 225–26; food shortages and, 226; infrastructure and environmental deterioration and, 227–28; needed policy changes, 228–30; smallholder households and, 226–27; strategies for, 230–32
Rural populations, 213; economic deterioration of, 214; human rights and, 213, 232–33; social-cultural change and, 223–24; social gap with government, 224

San Francisco Conference (UN Charter), 19

Saudi Arabia: abstinence vote, 24; Islamic law and, 136
Secularism, 170; democracy and, 122; global movement and, 106; Islam and, 104–05; Muslim societies and, 143; natural law and, 105
Self-determination, 28, 216; cross-cultural studies and, 344–45; developing strategy for, 382; French Revolution and, 379; human rights and, 377, 380–81; world society and, 369, 378–79
Self-government, 251–52; British colonialism and, 187
Self-preservation, 36–38, 72; natural dominion and, 80–81; nonharm principle and, 67
Senegal, 184–85; human rights commitment and, 200; parlous economic situation, 201–02; political party organizing and, 200–01; post-election uprisings (1983), 201; semidemocracy and, 202
Shari'a. See Islamic law (shari'a)
Shura. See Consultation (shura)
Siyar. See Law, Islamic international (siyar)
Slavery, 7, 163, 286, 340
Social action litigation (SAL), 237
Social change, 182–83; African societies and, 165; rural populations and, 223–24; rural to urbanization, 176–77
Social contract, 69–71
Social fragmentation: Côte d'Ivoire, 185; global shrinking and, 130
Socialism, 43; populist theory, 179
Social stratification, 164, 169–70
Society: changes and, 337; cultural norms and, 337–38; interdependency with individuals, 336–37; nonconformity and, 338; protection-promotion of rights and, 338–39
South Africa, 180
Soviet Union: anomie and, 174–75; economic development and, 381; objection to rights declaration, 24; self-determination and, 378–79
SSA. See Sub-Saharan Africa (SSA)
State, U.S. Department of, 196
Sub-Saharan Africa (SSA), 213; cultural-ethnic minorities in, 217; cultural pluralism and, 234; economic change and,

233–34; ethnic conflicts, 234; exogenous historical process and, 222; human rights law and, 233; modern states in, 214; one-party systems and, 221; rural development and, 225–26
Sudan, 149; civil war in, 262–63; cross-cultural approach for, 288–89
Sudanese Muslim Brothers, 124
Sudan People's Liberation Movement (SPLM), 262; September laws and, 285
Syndicats, 185

Theological voluntarism, 82–83
Third world: alternative human rights language, 59–60; authors on liberal theory, 113–14; Eurocentrism and, 108; human rights cultural legitimacy and, 105–06
Traditional culture, African: ascribed status and, 311–12; communal values and, 310, 321; compatibility with Western concepts, 311; cultural legitimacy and, 357; Dinka cultural model of, 264, 324–28; distributive justice in, 314; generalization trap, 323, 358; and human rights, 303–04, 315, 322–23; inconsistencies in rights norms, 313–15; kinship with modern rights concept, 305; limited government power in, 305–06; role of dignity, 306–07, 314; unique concept of rights, 308, 316
Treaties, human rights, 348; cultural legitimacy of, 348–49, 352–53; static cultural viewpoint and, 353–54
Treaty of Paris (*1856*), 151–52

Unions, labor, 185; in Burkina Faso, 194–95; Ivorian teachers, 196–97; national austerity policies and, 184. *See also* International Labour Organization (ILO)
United Nations Charter, 19, 25–26
Universal Declaration of Human Rights, 17, 54, 129, 306, 342, 371; cultural legitimacy of, 348–49; development and, 295–96; francophone Africa and, 191,
203; Iranian rejection of, 153–54; Islamic rights formulation and, 138; Islamic states and, 105; nation building and, 294; non-Western cultures and, 23, 350–51; participation rights and, 220; subsequent elaboration on, 25; UN General Assembly and, 20; Western influence, 22, 350–51; world society and, 369
Universal human rights: consensus on, 110; economic development and, 320; necessity for common standard, 316–17; participatory development rights and, 214; standards for, 9, 15; Western concepts and, 16, 319; world culture and, 368–69

Value system: Akan society and, 244; Dinka and, 271–72; Judeo-Christian, 6

War: rationale for, 98; Sudan and, 284–85
Welfare state, 43; evolution from Locke, 54–55
Western culture: cultural ethnocentrism, 159, 373; definition of, 15–16; rights principles and, 148, 322; as universal normative model, 147
Women's rights, 164; abuses to, 177–78, 180; African women and, 175–76, 206; in Akan society, 249; convention on discrimination against, 215; cultural roles of, 234–35; Dinka value system and, 272, 273–75; in Pakistan, 143; participation rights and, 230–31; reciprocity principle and, 345; in rural populations, 229; and *shari'a*, 126; SSA and, 219
World culture: human dignity and, 373; universal human rights and, 368–69
World society, 368; ideological tolerance and, 375; reconciliatory norms and, 375–76; self-determination and, 378–79; strategy for rights implementation in, 369

Name Index

Abraham, W. E., 243n, 248n, 251n
Achour, Yadh Ben, 144n
Adegbite, Latif O., 205n, 312
Ahmed, M., 262n
Ake, Claude, 173, 174, 179n, 180, 181, 182
Aleu, Ayeny, 282n
Algar, Hamid, 141n
Almain, Jacques, 82n
Alston, Philip, 23, 24, 25n, 29, 217n, 293n
Anderson, James, 87n
An-Naʿim, Abdullahi Ahmed, 126n, 135n, 139, 140n, 147n, 168, 343n, 359n, 360n
Aquinas, Thomas, 78–80, 87, 90–92, 101
Aquino, Corazon, 381
Arblaster, Anthony, 32n, 113n
Arias Sanchez, Oscar, 375n
Arkoun, Mohammed, 144n
Asante, S. K. B., 293n, 296–99, 301, 306–07, 311, 313n, 316n, 318, 320, 321n
Ashcraft, Richard, 82n, 97, 98n, 99
Ashmawi, Muhammad Saʿid al-, 126n
ʿAshur, Muhammad Ahmad, 116n
Assmann, Hugo, 59n
Atiyeh, George N., 106n
ʿAwwa, Muhammad Salim al-, 111n, 112n, 119n, 121n, 122n, 126n
Axtell, James L., 74n
Ayoub, Mahmoud, 373n
Azkoul, Karem, 350n

Bakhash, Shaul, 155n
Bakr, Abu, 127
Baldo, Suleyman Ali, 286n

Banks, Michael, 375n
Banna, Muhammad Ibrahim al-, 116n
Barber, Bernard, 369n
Barker, Ernest, 96n
Barker, Judith, 221n
Barnes, Barry, 340n
Bascom, William R., 364n
Bates, Robert H., 221n
Battles, Ford Lewis, 82n
Baum, Guilielmus, 86n
Baumer, Franklin L., 62n
Bay, Christian, 32n
Bay, Edna G., 168n
Bazargan, Mehdi, 140
Bedjaoui, Mohammed, 114n
Beehler, Rodger, 340n
Beer, Lawrence W., 177n
Beitz, Charles R., 347n
Bellah, Robert N., 175n
Benedict, Ruth, 336, 337n, 362n
Bentham, Jeremy, 51, 379
Berg, Robert J., 228n
Berger, Carol, 182n
Berger, Peter L., 172, 317, 350n
Berlin, Isaiah, 32n
Bernhardt, Rudolf, 31n, 105n, 107n
Bhutto, Benazir, 150
Bidney, David, 340n
Biéler, André, 87n
Bilkuei, Makuei, 288
Bloor, David, 340n
Bohannan, Paul, 376
Bohatec, Josef, 86, 87n
Boisard, Marcel A., 137n
Bourguiba, Habib, 156
Bozeman, Adda B., 343–344
Brecher, Irving, 217n

Breslow, Marvin A., 92n
Brokensha, David W., 224n, 227n
Brown, Peter G., 48n
Brzesinski, Zbigniew, 130
Buber, Martin, 373n
Buergenthal, Thomas, 18n, 19n
Bulabek-Malith, 286, 328
Bull, Hedley, 130n
Burton, John, 359n, 375n
Busia, K. A., 243n, 248n, 252n
Butt, Audrey, 279, 280n
Butterfield, Fox, 374n

Cafagna, Albert Carl, 334n
Cahill, Lisa Sowle, 60
Calvin, John, 76–77, 82–95, 97, 99–103
Carneiro, Robert L., 334n, 364n
Carter, Jimmy, 27
Cassin, René, 20, 21
Cernea, Michael, 231n, 235n
Chang, Peng-Chung, 20, 350
Christaller, J. G., 243n
Clay, Jason W., 177n
Cobbah, Josiah A. M., 31n, 36n, 159n,
    160n, 175, 177n, 179
Coleman, James S., 189, 190, 191n
Colman, John, 64n, 65n, 82n
Compaore, Blaise, 192–95
Conté, Lansana, 184, 198
Cook, John, 340n
Coulon, Christian, 200, 202
Coulson, N. J., 107n, 124n
Cranston, Maurice, 26n, 32n, 318
Cromwell, Oliver, 98–99
Crump, Lucy, 97n
Cugoano, Ottobah, 303
Cunitz, Eduardus, 86n

D'Ailly, Pierre, 80
D'Andrade, Roy G., 334n
Danopoulos, Constantine P., 192n
Danquah, J. B., 243n
D'Arcy, Eric, 78
Davidow, Robert P., 72n
Dawson, J. G., 79n
De Bary, William Theodore, 353n
De Gaulle, Charles, 188
Dehousse, Fernand, 20
Deng, Francis Mading, 7, 8, 109, 166,
    167, 182, 264n, 269n, 272n, 278n,

282n, 284n, 287n, 288n, 289n, 323,
    324n, 325n, 326n, 327n, 375
D'Entrèves, A. P., 79n
Derrida, Jacques, 373n
Diamond, Larry, 200n, 221n
Diamond, Stanley, 376
Dias, Clarence J., 213n, 217n
Diouf, Abdou, 191, 200, 201, 204
Djaït, Hisham, 144n
Dole, Gertrude E., 334n, 364n
Dominick, Mary Frances, 368n
Donelan, M., 347n
Donnelly, Jack, 6, 16n, 34n, 35n, 49n,
    50n, 54n, 62n, 105n, 107n, 109n,
    114n, 147n, 159n, 165n, 176n, 177n,
    180n, 200n, 314, 317, 321–22, 322n,
    326n, 342, 343n, 357, 372
Doob, Leonard W., 375n
Downing, Theodore E., 232n
Downs, R. E., 224n, 227n
Drengson, Alan R., 340n
Dunn, John, 73n, 74n, 129n
Duri, Abdulaziz al-, 122n
Durkheim, Emile, 170, 174
Dworkin, Ronald, 32n, 43

Ebiasah, John K., 301–02
Eide, Asbjörn, 205n, 353n
Eire, Carlos M. N., 89, 90n
Eisenstadt, S. N., 370n
Elias, Norbert, 108n, 113n
Eliot, T. S., 333n
Emecheta, Buchi, 176n
Engels, Frederick, 36n
Erwin, R. E., 38n
Esposito, John L., 123n
Evans-Pritchard, Edward E., 376n, 377n
Eze, Osita C., 305n, 313

Fahmi, Mustafa Abu-Zaid, 127n, 128n,
    129n
Falk, Richard, 110, 129n, 335n, 347n,
    348n
Farer, Tom J., 31n
Farley, Benjamin W., 86n
Faruqi, Isma'il R. Al, 354n
Fatton, Robert, Jr., 202n
Feinberg, Harvey M., 207, 208n
Field, David Dudley, 152n
Filmer, Robert, 48

Fitzgerald, C. P., 371n, 372n, 374n
Flatham, Richard E., 48n
Forsythe, David P., 161n
Fortes, M., 377n
Frank, Joseph, 100n
Franklin, Benjamin, 379
Fraser, Aleander Campbell, 63n

Gallie, W. B., 52n
Garforth, Francis W., 63n
Gastil, Raymond D., 130n, 198, 204–05
Geertz, Clifford, 105n, 113n, 334n
Gellner, Ernest, 144n
Gerson, Jean, 80–81, 97
Gerwirth, Alan, 32n
Ghaffar, Abdel, 262n
Gittleman, Richard, 181n, 207n
Gluckman, Max, 313n, 376
Goldenweiser, Alexander, 336n
Goldstein, Robert Justin, 176n
Goodman, Christopher, 92–95
Gottlieb, Gidon, 348n
Green, Vera M., 159n, 205n, 293n, 353n
Grotius, Hugo, 98n
Gulliver, Philip H., 377n
Gully, Lois, 29n
Gyekye, Kwame, 243n

Haarscher, Guy, 182n
Hafkin, Nancy J., 168n
Haile, Minasse, 293, 294n, 300–301, 306,
    318–319, 320n
Hanafi, Hasan, 122n
Hanna, William John, 159n
Hannum, Hurst, 307
Hardy, Thomas, 169n
Hartung, Frank E., 340n
Hassan, Riffat, 360n
Hatch, Elvin, 340n
Hauerwas, Stanley, 59
Hay, Margaret Jean, 175n
Hayek, F. A., 32n
Hayford, Casely, 243n
Henkin, L., 105n, 106n
Hennelly, Alfred, 60n, 353n
Herskovits, Melville J., 340n, 364n, 365n
Hesselink, I. John, 82n, 83n
Higgins, Rosalyn, 347n
Hinsley, F. H., 108n, 129n
Hobbes, Thomas, 47, 48, 86n

Hobsbawm, Eric, 164n
Hodgkin, Thomas L., 303n
Hodgson, Marshall G. S., 112n, 358n
Hoffman, Stanley, 347n
Holcomb, Bonnie K., 177n
Hollenbach, David, 60, 61n, 106n
Hollis, Martin, 340n
Horkheimer, Max, 116n
Horowitz, Asher, 36n
Horowitz, Gad, 36n
Houphouët-Boigny, Félix, 190, 195
Howard, Rhoda E., 2, 3, 7, 8, 16n, 31n,
    50n, 54n, 104n, 109n, 114n, 159n,
    160n, 161n, 163n, 165n, 168n, 173n,
    176n, 177n, 178n, 179n, 180n, 200n,
    206, 216n, 232n, 291n, 299, 300n, 301,
    308n, 311n, 313, 315n, 317n, 326n
Hudson, Michael, 123n
Humphrey, John P., 20, 21
Huntington, Samuel P., 199n
Hyden, Goran, 229n

Iliffe, John, 164
Inkeles, Alex, 368n, 369n
Irfani, Suroosh, 142n
Ishaque, Khalid M., 354n

Jackson, Robert H., 195, 196n, 198n,
    221n
Jenks, C. Wilfred, 349n
Jesus, 66–67, 94–95
Jinnah, Fatimah, 150n
Jolowicz, John Anthony, 31n, 105n, 107n

Katz, Alan N., 208n
Kenyatta, Jomo, 172
Kenyatta, Margaret W., 175n
Khadduri, Majid, 136n
Khomeini, Ayatollah, 118, 131, 140, 142,
    155
Khoury, Adel Théodor, 104n
Khushalani, Yougindra, 16n, 308n, 309n,
    310, 319, 321n
King, Martin Luther, Jr., 139
Ki-Zerbo, Joseph, 159n, 163, 168n, 172n
Klein, A. Norman, 167n
Klein, Martin A., 200
Kluckhohn, Clyde, 334n, 362n
Knox, John, 92, 94
Kratochwil, Friedrich, 335n, 347n, 348n

Kroeber, A. L., 334n, 340n, 370n
Kushner, Gilbert, 232n

Lamizana, Sangoulé, 191–93, 205
Langan, John, S.J., 60, 353n
Laoust, Henri, 116n
Laqueur, Walter, 26n
Laroui, Abdallah, 132n
Laski, Harold J., 95n
Laslett, Peter, 33n, 65n, 169n
Leary, Virginia A., 1, 5
Lee, Laurie, 169n
Lefebvre, Archbishop, 146
Legesse, Asmarom, 36n, 159n, 162, 163,
    172n, 179n, 182, 308, 309, 316n, 320

Lemos, Ramon M., 32n
Leonard, Steve, 31n, 41n
LeVine, Robert A., 334n, 337n
Lewis, Barbara, 175n
Lienhardt, Godfrey, 265n, 268, 269n, 270,
    271n, 278, 284n
Lilburne, John, 98–99
Linz, Juan J., 200n
Lipset, Seymour Martin, 200n
Little, David, 6, 85n, 87n, 144n
Little, Peter D., 224n, 227n
Locke, John, 6, 33, 36, 37–54, 40n, 41,
    42n, 43–79, 82–85, 87, 90–91, 95,
    96n, 97, 99–103
Lomasky, Loren E., 32n
Lovejoy, Paul E., 167n
Luard, Evan, 353n
Lukes, Steven, 340n

MacArthur, Douglas, 351
MacCallum, Gerald C., Jr., 48n
McDougal, Myres S., 321n
McIlwain, Charles Howard, 77n, 78n
MacIntyre, Alasdair, 32n
Mackenzie, Ross, 90n
MacLean, Douglas, 48n
McNeill, John T., 82n, 94n
Macpherson, C. B., 31, 36n, 39, 40n, 43,
    45, 46, 47, 72n, 113n
Mahdi, Sadiq al-, 262n
Mahmassani, Sobhi, 137n
Mahmoud, Ushari Ahmed, 286n
Maine, Henry, 170

Mair, John, 81, 97n
Makino, Baron, 19
Malik, Charles Habib, 20, 22, 350
Malinowski, Bronislaw, 334n
Mansfield, Harvey C., Jr., 32n
Marasinghe, Lakshman, 304, 316
Marcos, Ferdinand, 381
Marie, John-Bernard, 203
Marks, Stephen P., 335n
Marx, Karl, 36n, 43, 55, 167
Massell, Gregory J., 364n
Mayer, Ann Elizabeth, 2, 5, 104n, 117n,
    118n, 124n, 125n, 136n, 354n
Mayerowitz, E. L., 243n
M'Baye, Kéba, 205n, 293n, 294–96, 305,
    311n, 313
Mehta, Mrs., 22
Melden, A. I., 32n
Meltzer, Ronald I., 139n, 166n, 181n,
    187n, 191n, 207n, 216n, 290n, 293n
Mendlovitz, Saul H., 335n, 347n, 348n
Menkiti, Ifeanyi A., 311n, 312
Meron, Theodor, 105n, 107n, 350n, 368n
Meyer, Peter, 350n
Middleton, John, 271n, 377n
Mijak, Biong, 286–88
Mill, John Stuart, 51, 373
Mojekwu, Chris C., 159n, 160, 164n,
    179n, 205, 293n, 311, 312n
Montesquieu, 372, 378n
Moore, Barrington, Jr., 115n, 178n
Moore, Frank W., 362n
Moore, Sally F., 377n
Mornay, Philippe du Plessis, 92n, 95–97,
    102
Morsink, Johannes, 351n, 356n
Moshoeshoe I, 324
Mughaizel, Joseph, 104n
Muhammad, 111, 127
Muller, F. Max, 372n
Murdock, George Peter, 362n
Murphy, Cornelius F., Jr., 16n
Mutawalli, Abdulhamid, 125n
Myerhoff, Barbara G., 377n

Nafziger, Wayne E., 227n
Nahum, Fasil, 159n, 162n, 176n
Naiem, Abdullahi Ahmed El, 139n
Nanda, Ved P., 217n, 353n

Nelson, Jack L., 159n, 205n, 293n, 353n
Ngom, Benoit, 159n, 162, 163
Nguema, Francisco Macias, 55
Niebuhr, Reinhold, 373n
Nimeiri, Jaafer Mohammed, 123, 140n, 284–85
Norman, Ken, 331n
Northrop, F. S. C., 130n
Nozick, Robert, 32n

Oberg, K., 377n
Ojo, Olusola, 160n, 162, 168n, 179n, 181n
Okere, B. Obinna, 181n
Okonjo, Kamene, 168n
Olenja, Joyce, 166n
Olusanya, G. O., 168
Opler, Marvin K., 364n
Ottenberg, Simon, 364n
Ouedraogo, Jean-Baptiste, 192
Overton, Richard, 99n, 100–01
Oweiss, Ibrahim M., 106n
Owen, John, 82n

Paige-Evans, A., 231n
Paine, Thomas, 43
Panikkar, R., 16n
Parsons, Talcott, 172n
Pateman, Carole, 113n
Paul, James C. N., 7, 217n, 221n, 225n
Peardon, Barbara, 92n
Pennock, J. Roland, 303n
Peters, Rudolph, 137n
Pollis, Adamantia, 16n, 23n, 31, 159n, 225n, 292n, 353n
Ponet, John, 92
Preiswerk, Roy, 332n, 335
Press, Robert M., 182n

Rahman, Fazlur, 358n
Raico, Ralph, 32n
Ramsey, I. T., 64n
Ranger, Terence, 164n
Rattray, Robert S., 243n, 376
Rawls, John, 32n, 43
Redfield, Robert, 340n
Renteln, Alison Dundes, 339n, 340, 341n, 364–65

Reuss, Eduardus, 86n
Reyna, S. P., 224n, 227n
Richards, Paul, 224n
Rifaʿa Rafi al-Tahtawi, 123
Robinson, Pearl T., 231n
Rodinson, Maxime, 112n
Romulos, Carlos, 350
Roosevelt, Eleanor, 20
Roosevelt, Franklin D., 19
Rosberg, Carl G., Jr., 189, 190, 191n, 195, 196n, 198n, 221n
Rosenzweig, Franz, 373n
Rubin, Barry, 26n
Ryan, Alan, 48n

Sabine, George H., 62n, 77n
Sahlieh, Sami Aldeeb Abu, 135n
Sai, Fred T., 228n
Salmen, Lawrence F., 231n
Sandbrook, Richard, 221n
Sandel, Michael J., 36n
Sankara, Thomas, 192–94
Santa Cruz, Hernán, 20
Scarritt, James R., 353n
Schacht, Joseph, 124n, 125n, 359n
Schneider, Harold K., 364n
Schou, August, 205n, 353n
Schuler, Margaret, 235n
Schwab, Peter, 16n, 23n, 31n, 159n, 225n, 292n, 353n
Schwartz, Richard D., 10, 371n
Scoble, Harry M., 186, 187n
Seligman, Brenda, 264n
Seligman, Charles, 264n
Senghor, Leopold Sédar, 189–91, 200, 204
Sesay, Amadu, 160n, 179n, 181n
Shachar, A., 370n
Shakankiri, Muhammad El, 144n
Shapiro, Ian, 31, 32n, 129n
Sharif, M. M., 128n
Shepherd George W., Jr., 217n, 353n
Shestack, Jerome J., 105n, 107n, 368n
Shih Huang Ti, 370, 374
Shils, Edward, 364n
Shlapentokh, Vladimir, 174n
Short James F., Jr., 371n
Shue, Henry, 29, 32n, 47, 48n, 49n
Shultz, George P., 195

Shweder, Richard A., 334n, 337n
Silk, James, 8, 9
Skinner, Quentin, 76, 82n, 89n, 93n, 94n, 96, 97n
Sklar, Richard L., 221n
Skocpol, Theda, 169n
Skurnik, W. A. E., 192n
Smith, Adam, 50
Smith, Wilfred Cantwell, 124n
Sohn, Louis B., 18n, 19n
Somerville, John, 31n
Sorbo, Gunnar M., 262n
Spear, Percival, 371n
Spencer, Charmaine, 331n
Spindler, George, 339n
Spiro, Melford E., 337n, 339n
Ssu-ma Ch'ien, 372n
Stackhouse, Max, 60
Stalin, Joseph, 55
Staudt, Kathleen, 227n
Stettinius, Edward R., 19
Stichter, Sharon, 175n
Stivers, Robert L., 87n
Stocking, George W., Jr., 339n
Strauss, Leo, 31, 36n
Summenhart, Conrad, 81
Swidler, Leonard, 140n, 360n

Taha, Mahmoud Mohamed, 140n, 360n, 361n, 373n
Taimiyya, Ibn, 116n, 121n
Tait, David, 271n
Taylor, Charles, 48n
Tesón, Fernando R., 147n
Thapar, Romila, 371n
Thiik, Giir, 282n, 289n
Thompson, Kenneth W., 36n, 159n, 308–09n, 353n
Tibi, Bassam, 2, 3, 4, 105n, 106n, 112n, 116n, 123n, 130n, 138, 143n, 144, 145, 354n
Tillich, Paul, 373n
Timberlake, Lloyd, 228n
Tomasevski, Katarina, 215n, 217n
Torrance, David W., 90n
Torrance, Thomas F., 90n
Touré, Sékou, 189–90, 198, 204
Trimingham, J. Spencer, 279
Trubek, David, 107n

Tuck, Richard, 77n, 78n, 79n, 80n, 81n, 86n, 94n, 98n
Tucker, Robert C., 167n
Tucker, Robert W., 347n
Tully, James, 72n, 74n, 75n, 79, 80n
Turner, Ralph E., 370n

Umar, Caliph, 127

Vasak, Karel, 293n, 353n
Vatin, Jean-Claude, 144n
Verdoodt, Albert, 19n, 20n-22n, 24n
Vincent, R. J., 106n, 107n, 110n, 115n, 116n
Von Hoof, Fried, 29
Von Laue, Theodore H., 113n
Von Leyden, W., 63n, 65n, 82n
Von Mises, Ludwig, 32n

Wade, Abdoulaye, 200, 201
Wafi, Ali Abdel Wahid, 354n
Wai, Dunstan M., 159n, 163, 225n, 292, 302–03, 305
Wai, Thon, 269n, 328
Walwyn, William, 99n, 100n
Walzer, Michael, 89n
Watson, Alan, 123n, 148n
Weber, Max, 119, 121n, 170
Weeramantry, C. G., 111n
Weinstein, Warren, 314, 319n, 323n
Weisfelder, Richard F., 293n, 305n, 323–324
Welch, Claude E., Jr., 4, 139n, 166n, 181n, 187n, 191n, 192n, 207n, 216n, 290n, 293n, 311, 323n
Whitaker, Jennifer Seymour, 228n
Wildman, John, 100
Wilkins, John, 83n
Williams, Paul, 350n, 368n, 371n
Williams, Raymond, 333n
Williams, Roger, 144n
Wilson, Woodrow, 18
Winckelmann, J., 121n
Wiredu, Kwasi, 8, 166, 167, 323
Wiseberg, Laurie S., 316n, 317n, 319n
Wolin, Sheldon S., 32n
Wood, James E., Jr., 144n
Wood, Neal, 73n

Woodhouse, A. S. P., 98n, 99n, 100n,
   101n
Worsley, Peter, 108n
Wright, Richard A., 311n

Yamane, Hiroko, 31n, 107n
Yamani, Ahmad Zaki, 36n

Yameogo, Maurice, 190n
Young, Crawford, 179mn

Zabih, Sepehr, 142n
Zerbo, Sayé, 192
Zia al-Haq, Mohammed, 123, 142, 150
Zurayk, Constantine K., 106n